The Evolution of British Town Planning

The Evolution of British Town Planning

A history of town planning in the United Kingdom during the 20th century and of the Royal Town Planning Institute, 1914–74

GORDON E. CHERRY

A HALSTED PRESS BOOK

JOHN WILEY & SONS

New York—Toronto

First published by
Leonard Hill Books
a division of
International Textbook Company Limited
Kingswood House, Heath & Reach, nr Leighton Buzzard, Beds.

First published 1974

Published in the U.S.A. and Canada by Halsted Press, a Division
of John Wiley & Sons, Inc., New York

Library of Congress Cataloging in Publication Data

Cherry, Gordon Emanuel
The Evolution of British town planning.
"A Halsted Press Book."
1. Cities and towns—Planning—Great Britain.
2. Royal Town Planning Institute.— Title.

HT169.G7C459 309.2'62'0942 74–470

ISBN 0–470–15350–4

Printed in Great Britain

Acknowledgments

Many people have contributed to the making of this book and I am glad of the opportunity of thanking them most sincerely.

To my friend Paul S. Cadbury I am particularly indebted. He really made the project possible, and opened up an area of personal interest to me for which I shall ever be grateful. The Cadbury family has an important place in the history of town planning; Paul Cadbury himself has been a distinguished contributor to developments in the West Midlands and it was a happy gesture of the Royal Town Planning Institute when he was invited to become an Honorary Member in 1972.

During this study the RTPI has given wholehearted assistance, and without the help of the Institute's staff much of the work could not have been effectively tackled. In particular I wish to thank Philip Rathbone (Secretary) for his encouragement and support, Margaret Cox and Mark Pritchard (Editors of the Journal) for their technical advice, and Robert Williams and Charles Herd, of the Institute staff, and their Assistants for constant help whenever required.

Stephen Ward acted as my Research Assistant for 18 months from 1971 to 1973. He has been loyal and dedicated, proving a first class research worker. We have differed on how to interpret certain events, and I have only been able to use a fraction of his material in this work, but I acknowledge his skill and thank him for his contribution.

Leslie Lane, Past President of the Institute has taken a kindly interest in this work from the outset. He was good enough to read and comment at length on my first draft. I thank him for his support and hospitality.

I have had the rare opportunity to contact many Past Presidents. Some have been good enough to write to me; others have spent time with me in their homes, or offices or at RTPI Headquarters. Unfailingly these contacts were rewarding, giving me great help in avoiding pitfalls and establishing the right 'feel' for a particular period. I am grateful to all these people for the time they spent with me.

In the early stages of this work I approached Branch Secretaries of the Institute and Heads of Planning Schools for local information. Their response was always helpful, and in some cases replies went far beyond what I could reasonably have expected. I hope I have done full justice to the many notes I received.

Early drafts of this book were read by Professor Sir Colin Buchanan, Professor J. R. Harris, Leslie Lane, E. H. Doubleday, Philip Rathbone, Graham Ashworth and Stephen Ward. I am grateful to them for undertaking this task and for their helpful comments.

I have received considerable assistance over photographs and other historical reminiscences, in particular from Lady Elizabeth Pepler and Mrs Constance Adams. For making photographs available, I also thank Mrs Brigid Grafton-Green of the Hampstead Garden Suburb Trust, Mrs Dorothy M. H. Betts (granddaughter of T. C. Horsfall), Mrs E. M. Crosskey (daughter of J. S. Nettlefold), the Cadbury family, Cadbury Schweppes Ltd, the Bournville Village Trust, David Hall (Town and Country Planning Association), and Professor A. S. Travis. I am grateful to the Royal Town Planning Institute for permission to copy freely from many issues of the Journal. Many other courtesies I acknowledge in the captions of the illustrations.

I am grateful to Graham Ashworth, President of the Institute 1973–74, for writing a Foreword to this book. His personal support has been very encouraging.

Typing has been shared by a number of people and I thank them all: Gill King, Mary Grant, Gillian Penny, Ann Penhallurick, Joan Pace.

Finally, I thank my wife for her help with typing and preparation of the index.

Gordon E. Cherry

Contents

Foreword

Anniversary celebrations are not always meet and proper and are rarely productive. The Diamond Jubilee of the Royal Town Planning Institute need not be either. But it can be both.

For all its stumbling uncertainties the profession of town planning has survived and evolved during the past sixty years, despite much professional jealousy and political reservation. Its evolution has spawned in Britain a thorough planning system second to none it its comprehensive coverage. Just now it is experiencing a period of considerable change and is involved in a fundamental reassessment of the nature of planning and the education and conduct of those engaged in its practice. At such a time it is not easy to be objective in looking back nor constructive in looking forward. But I believe the Royal Town Planning Institute must try to do so.

It will be immensely helped by Gordon Cherry's book, published to mark the Institute's Diamond Jubilee. From the date when Mr Cherry suggested that such a book might be attempted the Institute has been anxious to give as much encouragement as possible. This is now amply justified. Mr Cherry has produced a balanced account of the growth of the profession, illuminating what could have been an arid story with insights of drama and personality. We sense anew the aspirations of the founding fathers and we warm to the zeal and enthusiasm of the late 'forties and early 'fifties. In the middle 'sixties we watch with fascination as the Institute is tormented by the question of widening its membership. Intertwined with all this is the developing philosophy of planning, from the 'civic design' era through to 'modelling' and 'systems'. It is a complex story and could so easily have been either exceedingly dreary or very complicated. Even worse, it might have been superficial.

Happily it is none of these. Instead we have a very readable history of the development of a philosophy and practice that is probably much more important to the well-being of the British people than the present generation would acknowledge.

If history has any value it must be in helping us to shape the future. Should we fail to interpret this planning history in the right way it will not be Gordon Cherry's fault. For he has sifted it for us and, at the end of the book, given us some hints of at least one line of interpretation.

As a more than interested party, the RTPI welcomes this excellent book and commends it to all those interested in the management of the country's affairs.

Graham Ashworth
President of the
Royal Town Planning Institute

'If 50 or 100 years hence someone comes along and says what was the beginning of the change in the organization and the conscious order and growth of towns and cities in the last 100 years, you gentlemen and you ladies will be credited with earning, as you will deserve, from posterity, the grateful thanks of those who follow you for the fine enthusiasm, the good temper, the patient advice, and disinterestedness with which you have thrown yourselves into a movement that has for its object the emancipation of all communities from the mark of the beast of ugliness. And when posterity awards to you what will be your due, when the time comes for apportioning the praise or blame in the development of the community, I venture to say that the Town Planning Institute will not be the least of the factors that will be gratefully remembered and the members of that Institute that inaugurate this association tonight will not be ungratefully remembered by those who come after us.'

Rt Hon John Burns, MP,
President of the Local Government Board,
at the Inaugural Dinner of the
Town Planning Institute, 1914.

1 Introduction

There is a growing interest in British urban history. This is borne out by the success which has attended the Urban History Group and its *Newsletter*; the increasing concern for, and appreciation of, the relict features in our townscapes (as witnessed by the support given to Victorian Societies, Civic Trusts and similar organizations); and the growing number both of popular and academic publications in this field. The place of town planning in urban history has already been the subject of a number of analyses. A popular theme has been to trace the historical sequence of town plans, of which this country affords many examples, from the 'bastide' town layouts of Edward I, to the grand manner design of 17th and 18th century estates, and later schemes. *Towns and Town Planning, Ancient and Modern* by T. H. Hughes and E. H. Lamborn (1923) was one of the first in this tradition. More recently there has been *City Fathers: the Early History of Town Planning in Britain* by Colin and Rose Bell (1969). Historical case studies have provided another literary stream. London particularly has received attention, as, for example, from John Summerson, *Georgian London* (1945); Donald Olsen, *Town Planning in London* (1964); Stein Eiler Rasmussen, *London: the Unique City* (1948); and Donald L. Foley, *Controlling London's Growth* (1963). Analysis has also extended to other towns, for example, A. J. Youngson, *The Making of Classical Edinburgh* (1966) and Lyall Wilkes and Gordon Dodds, *Tyneside Classical* (1964). The tradition is brilliantly continued by Anthony Sutcliffe in *The Autumn of Central Paris* (1970) and one hopes to see more British towns covered in this manner. Another contributory area has been from the point of view of social history. Asa Briggs in *Victorian Cities* (1963) gave a general backcloth, expanded in *The Victorian City: Images and Realities* by H. J. Dyos and M. Wolff (1973). Dyos in *Victorian Suburb* (1966) pieced together the parts of a development jigsaw on the local scale of Camberwell in South London. The various elements were put together in a general review of urban growth over the last 200 years by G. E. Cherry in *Urban Change and Planning* (1972).

Nonetheless the subject matter of town planning in the 20th century has not been adequately researched from a historical point of view. The major work remains that of W. Ashworth, *The Genesis of Modern British Town Planning* (1954), and scholarly and constantly rewarding though it is, it is mainly a 19th century analysis, and certainly ends at 1947. *The Evolution of British Town Planning* seeks to remedy this deficiency. Its subject area is 20th century planning and it covers three main aspects. It relates to the legislative framework and statutory planning from 1909 onwards; the development of town planning practice; and the growth of the town planning profession. It is written on the occasion of the Diamond Jubilee of the professional body, the Royal Town Planning Institute (1914–74), and records a detailed professional history of town planning for the first time (the *Journal of the Town Planning Institute* in its issue of December 1963 contained articles to celebrate a Golden Jubilee, 1914–64, but this was a relatively minor contribution). The comprehensive story is set against the backcloth of other related developments, social and economic, political and cultural, in modern Britain.

The structure of the book follows these multiple intentions. The origins of the planning idea are traced in chapter 2 where it is demonstrated that the growth of planning as a complex movement embracing civic design, housing improvement and social reform stemmed from a context of economic, political and social factors. The importance of rapid and sustained urban growth in Britain is noted, together with the significant problems this posed, both from the point of view of housing difficulties and social agitation for reform. The influence of continental developments in town planning is acknowledged, as well as the contribution of innovations relating to design and architecture.

This is followed in chapter 3 by an account of the factors involved in the passing of the first town planning legislation and the founding of the Town Planning Institute. In a very short period before the First World War planning appeared on the Statute Book, an emerging body of planning knowledge took shape in the overlapping boundary zones of land based professions (architecture, engineering and surveying), a coherent system of planning practice developed, planning education began, and a new professional body was born. We note the contributions made in this period of rapid change by the propagandist bodies, the professional groups, and of notable personalities.

The book unfolds chronologically from this point. The structure of each chapter is very similar: the first part concerns developments generally in planning—the social and political context, legislative changes, statutory planning and how successfully or otherwise it dealt with the problems it had to face—and the second part concerns developments within the Town Planning Institute. (It was granted its Royal prefix in 1971.) The two parts are interlocked at all relevant places.

Hence chapter 4 covers the period 1909–19, and deals with the first town planning legislation of 1909 and the planning developments that ensued; it introduces the new legislation of 1919. Against this background events in the new professional body are traced. Chapter 5 deals with the whole of the inter-war period. On balance, it was found necessary to treat the two decades as one because of their obvious unity, but the recognition of a watershed year, 1932, enables two distinct periods to be identified. For each period the dual structure is maintained: a review of developments in the statutory planning process and related fields, followed by an examination of Institute matters. Finally in the chapter there are some general observations about professional matters over the inter-war years as a whole.

Chapter 6 deals with wartime affairs. It covers a relatively short period of five years, but one worth identifying individually because of its great importance in marking a time of significant change. This was the occasion when a new machinery of government was established and far-reaching planning legislation provided the basis for a freshly devised planning system. A mood of post-war reconstruction charged planning with new responsibilities. The profession responded with a new-found self confidence.

In chapter 7 the period 1945–60 is covered. During these years the planning system conceived during the war was given form and expression, and the first part of the chapter deals with developments in legislation and the planning system in operation. Against this background we review the new influences on planners as professional people, and the changes which took place in Institute affairs: in particular the significance of the Schuster *Report on the Qualifications of Planners* is examined, and the quest for a Royal Charter is traced in some detail.

The final period, 1960–74, is reviewed in chapter 8. After the relative quiescence and professional frustrations of the late fifties, a number of circumstances combined to re-awaken planning as an activity. The inherited planning system largely continued but deficiences increasingly appeared. With many stresses and strains planning shed an old image and moved into new areas of involvement. Old definitions of planning proved inadequate; fresh tasks were taken on. Serious implications for the profession followed, and a decade of anguished debate about membership and education is not yet over.

With chapter 9 the pattern of the book changes. Two chapters deal with professional matters which could not adequately be covered in separate chapters on a chronological basis. These are education (chapter 9) and the question of Branches and professional organization (chapter 10). Both are themes which are coherent case studies in themselves, and add a good deal of light on the course of professional developments.

In the final chapter we draw together the many strands in the evolution of British town planning. This enables observations to be made on the nature of planning in this country and the development of the planning profession, as well as speculations on the future.

The different aspects of the book have their own source material. The broad setting of the origins of the planning movement and its subsequent institutionalization has been compiled from an extensive literature in the field of social, economic and political history, which puts into context the early writings of key figures such as Raymond Unwin, Patrick Geddes and T. C. Horsfall. Propagandist literature of the Garden Cities Association and National Housing Reform Council was also found to be very helpful. On the developments of statutory planning, great reliance has been placed on the annual reports of Government Departments concerned with planning: for England and Wales the Local Government Board, followed by the Ministry of Health, the Ministry of Town and Country Planning and the Ministry of Housing and Local Government; for Scotland, the Local Government Board for Scotland, followed by the Scottish Board of Health and the Scottish Development Department. For Northern Ireland a useful summary was given by J. M. Aitken, *Regional Planning and Northern Ireland*, for the Town and Country Planning Summer School, 1967, recently updated by Alan Murie (*Town Planning Review*, October 1973). In addition there has been reference to a considerable number of local authority and consultants' reports and Government papers, with a comprehensive coverage of all the important planning literature over the past 50 years. A useful standard text for the present day is J. B. Cullingworth's *Town and Country Planning in Britain* (1972). Peter Hall's masterly study of *The Containment of Urban England* (1973) is essential reading for the post-war period.

Entirely new source material has been explored as part of the history of the Institute. Council and Committee minutes form a continuous record of the deliberations of the professional body. They are usually written in an anonymous style and record decisions rather than the course of debate. By themselves they are not particularly rewarding, but when taken in conjunction with the Institute's Journal a more comprehensive picture can be built up. The first papers read to the TPI were those by E. R. Abbott and F. M. Elgood in respect of the Ruislip–Northwood Scheme, in December 1914. For nine years *Papers and Discussions* formed the regular publication of the Institute. In November 1923 Reginald Bruce became Editor and the title *Journal* was first used. Even before this time, but increasingly afterwards, Council affairs were reported; more importantly a valuable cross section of information about professional activities was included. A dynamic picture relating to planning can be built up from articles and papers (no longer descriptive of schemes but discursive about the nature of planning and its association with related matters), Branch news, letters, advertisements and book reviews. Of particular importance are the Presidential Addresses which frequently summarize the issues of the day and the matters which were most pressing on planning and the affairs of the Institute. I have made frequent reference to Journal sources; these can be followed up readily for further analysis if required. I have used Council and Committee minutes more as a check on other sources; accordingly I give only infrequent references to particular minutes, first because they are not readily available for further public scrutiny, and second because in themselves they do not necessarily provide quotable material. However, where an important remark or piece of information, necessary for the understanding of a particular event, can be quoted, this has been done.

Other source material relates to personal correspondence, particularly from Branch secretaries, and interviews with a number of Past Presidents (including Lady Elizabeth Pepler, widow of Sir George). I used these interviews as checks on my understanding of various events and developments generally. The interviews were not taped and no specific record of the Presidents' conversations enter this book.

Any anniversary is a time for stocktaking. In 1974 the Institute celebrates its 60th birthday; town planning has been on the Statute Book for 65 years; and town planning as a coherent objective and set of principles has been recognizable for longer than that. This book attempts to draw together and explain the course of events in this century relating to the development, first, of a statutory planning process and second, of a professional, qualifying association. It sets both these in the changing political, economic and social contexts of our time. As such, the aim is to provide a comprehensive account of the evolution of British town planning up to the present day. The amount of available material to support such a venture is vast. All one can hope to do in one volume covering 60–70 years of change over such an enormous field is to provide a readable framework. The hope is of course that it will help a wide readership, professional and others, to understand rather more clearly how and why changes have occurred, and to illustrate how any movement, statutory system or professional body is so much hostage to the past. With understanding might come sympathy for the planning cause or for the Institute's position; alternatively there might come disenchantment with either or both. That consequence does not concern me; this history is not written with any prior motive, certainly not to portray planning in either a favourable or unfavourable light. It is, however, not easy to make that disclaimer effective. It is well nigh impossible to avoid all bias and slanted judgements. This is particularly so in the writing of contemporary history. This came to me very acutely in writing up the Institute's difficulties in the 1960s with regard to education and membership; as a practising professional planner during these years, these were issues with which I was very much concerned, having very decided views on the issues involved. I have not taken any opportunity in this analysis to portray the emotional debates from one side or the other, and the record relies entirely on the evidence of published material.

I should also add at this point that I have had absolute freedom in writing just what I have wanted about the Institute. This work was in no way commissioned by the Institute. It has been a research exercise, privately funded and seen as an academic project related to a number of other ongoing studies concerned with planning in the University of Birmingham. The Institute was good enough to express interest in my proposals and to open its doors (as far as I can see with unqualified freedom) to any research that was required. In return I can only trust that the record I have prepared is felt to be accurate by all the parties concerned, and my interpretation of events not unreasonable.

The historical framework here provided will, I hope, stimulate further studies. Much more remains to be done, and in many cases the research material is readily available. The Universities of Strathclyde, Manchester and Nottingham have papers relating to Pepler, Unwin and Abercrombie. Manchester City Library has a collection on T. C. Horsfall. The Bournville Village Trust and the Joseph Rowntree Memorial Trust have supported planning ventures, perhaps not yet fully documented. Local authority and regional planning schemes have lengthy and often uncharted histories. The contributions of pressure groups and propagandist bodies have not yet been fully evaluated. Personal papers of great value must lie in many places, with no great difficulty of access. People who played important parts in the development of planning at various periods this century are happily still with us; biographical records of their work and influence would help to fill in gaps of knowledge and act as a stimulus to historical research. Long before planning celebrates any other major anniversary I hope that a good deal of this work will have been accomplished.

This book aims modestly to sketch the development of statutory planning in this country, the growth of the subject matter of town planning, and the expansion of the town planning profession. The links between them are traced, as well as their relationship to a contextual background. It has not been possible to go beyond this stage. The gaps now need to be filled in: the personal contributions of politicians and technocrats, the parts played by dedicated individuals (Chamberlain or Nettlefold at Birmingham or the Simons at Manchester, for example), or the contributions of certain ground swells in human affairs which carried society along a particular path (represented for instance by the social reformers, civic designers or futurists). The book does not claim to unlock great secrets in the history of planning but rather to present the basic material collected and organized for ease of understanding of the present position. The next stages of research will complement this first review.

2 Influences on the Demand for Planning

The 20th century development of British town planning has a background of many different dimensions and perspectives. It was essentially a political, social, cultural, professional and technical response to a blend of circumstances which marked the years at the turn of the century. But this response was preceded and conditioned by a universalism throughout history of the fundamental aspects of planning as an activity. We can see the rudiments of town planning as a repetitive feature of civilizations the world over, representing both artistic creativity and a way of community life. On the one hand, town planning may be interpreted as an expression of utopian idealism, the constant striving to achieve the perfect world, the ideal city of a harmonious society. In this way the achievements of the present century may be seen as incremental to recurring postulates ranging in tenor from Plato's *Republic* to More's *Utopia*, or from St Augustine's *De Civitate Dei* to Robert Owen's *New View of Society*. On the other hand, town planning may be considered in architectural terms as attempts to provide ordered settings of dignity and beauty for man's human world. 'Cities' and 'civilization' are terms of common origin, and urban life has always had an important place in social values. Cities have been the mainspring of cultural innovation and repositories of everything that is worth while, and therefore the proper assembly of fine buildings has always represented an important part of the cultural achievements of any particular age, Sumerian, Roman, Inca, Renaissance Rome or Georgian and Regency Britain.

This world-wide and long-term backcloth may provide the initial setting, but the substantial economic and social transformations of 19th century Britain had a more direct influence. During this time Britain became an urban country, and the massive housing and other problems of the larger towns and cities made for a new national experience. It was a developing situation, the outcome of which could not possibly be foreseen, but gradually a system of housing, health and community and labour regulations was devised as a framework of urban management. From about 1820 onwards the century was marked by an increasing intervention in, and regulation of, community affairs. This was a political phenomenon and should be seen as part of our developing democracy. Ultimately, this affected wider and wider areas of everyday life; the ordering of our working hours and

6

conditions of work, our houses, towns and streets, our water supply, sewage, fuel and light, our education and health and welfare.

In this way, British towns and cities were watered, drained and sewered, lit and paved, and houses and buildings were regulated to provide the basis of an efficient, healthy and convenient way of life in the new rapidly growing industrial cities. It was in this context that 'planning', as a widely applicable term to these and other aspects of urban government, developed as an important feature of the 19th century. There were many facets to this, each with rather different emphases, but overall the result was a marked trend towards a comprehensive form of community regulation. With regard to public health, municipal concern was not an innovation of the 19th century—magistrates of medieval boroughs had responsibilities for the sanitary rules necessary for communal life—but following the cholera outbreaks of the 1830s national and local supervision intensified. Again, with water supply, medieval towns commonly had elaborate systems of conduits, but considerable 19th century improvements were necessary. Control over burial procedures increased. By mid-century town churchyards were often offensive and dangerous; closure and prohibition of new grounds that were a danger to health was followed by general supervision by Burial Boards. Growing intervention in housing matters was a feature of the 19th century, and later in this chapter we trace a number of the steps taken. Powers to provide a whole range of social amenities were granted to local authorities: public wash houses, libraries, museums, allotments and parks. Compulsory education opened up another vast field of muncipal enterprise.

As the century went on there were other areas of local authority involvement: municipal trading undertakings and traffic for example. Only Manchester and a small number of other towns had a municipal supply of gas early in the century, but with electrical generation in the last quarter of the century a rather different pattern emerged. The Electric Lighting Act of 1882 placed local authorities in a favourable position by discouraging private schemes. With transport, horsedrawn and electric tramways encouraged the idea of municipal control because the local authorities were responsible for the streets and therefore constructional work in the roadway required their approval.

This is a brief and admittedly selective review, but sufficient to make the point that the idea of municipal control and public direction in urban and community affairs was widely established by the turn of the century. The degree of state enterprise should not be over exaggerated, however, for an individualist type of thought persisted strongly. Samuel Smiles' *Self Help*, first published in 1859, was one of the most widely read books of the century, and faithfully reflected the spirit of the age; and we should note the importance of anti-socialist societies such as The Liberty and Property Defence League and The Personal Rights and Self Help Association. But the point remains: an apposite context for the growth of a town planning movement existed, and when the first town planning powers were provided in 1909, their general provisions followed logically on the approaches of past Public Health legislation.

Modern planning is, therefore, very much a child of our recent economic, political and social history. World history might be the parent, but the midwife belongs to the last century and the problems it threw up. Town planning was essentially a reactive development; while it aimed at the future, its immediate concern was a response to the past and present. There are a number of factors in this situation which played a particular part, and in this chapter we examine them in some detail.

In the first place there was the fact of unparalleled urban growth in Britain, Western Europe, North America and increasingly over much of the rest of the world. Cities of very large size had not been unknown in past civilizations but they had been exceptional; now they were becoming the rule. The problems posed by the big city—moral, social and technological—commanded the intellectual energies of the Victorians, and town planning, which embraced solutions for urban growth, owes much to this setting. Of the many difficulties, those relating to the housing question and social problems were probably the most acute and distressing. The latter years of the century ended in a welter of social agitation and advocacy for reform, and it is no idle claim that the town planning movement grew in substantial measure out of the activities of housing reformers and social philanthropists. But there were other immediate forces too. For example, there was the influence of contributions particularly from the Continent and also from America. Here, town planning movements were also taking root, nourished from rather different sources. In many ways a number of countries were making rather more rapid strides than Britain, and invidious comparison of practical achievement was to prove a stimulus in this country. There was also the international influence of new movements relating to design and architecture. The years at the turn of the century were marked by considerable intellectual activity in the arts, science and the humanities; there was an eagerness to strive for new things, and the possibilities offered by a new urban form as a setting for the new culture had its own bearing on the development of town planning.

The Spectre of Urban Growth

There was no shortage of evidence of, and comment on, the rise of cities in the 19th century. The rural fringe became building land in successive waves as housing spread outwards: the loss of the countryside and old frequented haunts provided repeated popular complaints. An urban population, growing rapidly through natural increase of births over deaths, was swollen by migration from rural areas and overseas, both Ireland and the Continent. Novelists and commentators described the urban scene; social scientists and reformers revealed the appalling conditions for many. Statistics from decennial censuses provided the facts of growth.

Between 1801 and 1901 the population of England and Wales almost quadrupled, increasing by nearly 24 millions from 8.9 to 32.5 millions. Since the middle of the century, England and Wales had been an urban country in that the majority of its population was classed as urban; it was the 1851 Census which recorded for the first time more than 50% of the population resident in urban districts, and after that date the proportion continued to increase. At the end of the century England and Wales had 75 towns of more than 50 000 people and 74 of these had an aggregate total of 10 millions; London accounted for another 4.5 millions. There were eight cities of more than 250 000 (Liverpool, Manchester, Birmingham, Leeds, Sheffield, Bristol, Bradford and West Ham in declining order) and a further 24 in the range of 100 000–250 000. This impressive number of medium and large-sized towns gave an indisputed urban character to the whole country.

8

Moreover, these towns were continuing to grow. In the 75 towns, the aggregate population increase during the 1891–1901 decade was 14%, compared with just over 12% nationally. Every town except Huddersfield showed some increase.

The centres with the most rapid growth at the end of the century were the suburbs of the large cities. For example, during the last decade East Ham, in East London, recorded a threefold increase of population and the neighbouring towns of Walthamstow, Leyton and West Ham showed rates of increase of 105%, 57% and 31% respectively. In West London, Willesden increased by 87%, Hornsey and Tottenham in North London by 62% and 44%; and Croydon in the south by 30%. Around Birmingham, King's Norton and Northfield, and Handsworth increased by 102% and 62% respectively. Wallasey, adjacent to Liverpool, grew by 62%.

This suburban expansion pointed to a transfer of population from inner to outer areas, which in the case of London had been the subject of official comment for more than 20 years. The population of the central area boroughs of London had reached a peak in 1861. A virtually identical population was recorded in 1871, but subsequently each decade had shown slight decreases: 1.4%, 4.1% and 3.4% for the last three decades of the century. On the other hand, the rest of London was continuing to grow, though at a markedly reducing rate: 33.9%, 19.7% and 12.8% for the last three decades of the century. These figures were for the Administrative County where the population totalled 4.5 millions, but beyond this area the Census identified an 'outer ring' where dramatic rates of increase were being sustained: the last three decennia recorded increases of 50.0%, 50.1% and 45.5%. The population of Greater London exceeded 6.5 million and almost 1 million people had been added to this total since 1891. It was now seen that the population was spreading even beyond Greater London, and the enormity of this expansion was strongly impressed on the observers of this situation. There were sanitary and building controls over this vast housing development, but the way in which the land was laid out was subject to no regulations. Growth was haphazard and unco-ordinated and land was used wastefully with little thought for future requirements.

In Scotland four cities had populations of more than 150 000 in 1901. Glasgow was the largest with 761 000 which meant that with one in every six Scots being a Glaswegian the city had rather a more dominant position than London had to England and Wales. Parts of Lanarkshire and Clydeside were filling in as continuous areas of urban growth, in ways typical of English centres. Edinburgh had been overtaken in size early in the 19th century and now recorded 317 000. Dundee had a population of 161 000 and Aberdeen 153 000. In Ireland, Dublin and Belfast were established as the major centres with no serious rivals.

The facts of urban growth on the world scene were shown by the analysis of Adna Ferrin Weber, who became Chief Statistician of the New York State Department of Labor. In a remarkably comprehensive book published in 1898, he reviewed urban development country by country: at the top of the league was England with 62% of its population city dwellers. He noted the obvious relationship with the pace and character of industrial development and forecast a continuation of the trends of urbanization, particularly of a centralizing kind. 'The prospect is', he declared, 'that the larger cities, including of course their suburbs, will continue to absorb the superfluous population of the rural districts and villages; Greater London, New York, Paris, Berlin and Chicago show no signs of falling behind the smaller cities in rate of growth.'[1] Sober assessment confirmed the impressions of most observers.

There is good reason to suppose that at the turn of the century the urban situation was uppermost in the minds of many. The fact of increased city size was an issue itself. On the one hand, there was pride in Victorian achievement and urban growth was seen as 'progress'; as England was pre-eminent in this respect it corresponded to her superiority amongst the countries of the world. But the continuing and seemingly unending growth in city size, particularly London, raised real spectres for the future. Local government had recently been reformed, but the prospect of unmanageability had not diminished and was likely to get worse. Technical problems of dealing with transport, housing and sanitation might be solved, but there was still the old fear of the mob, and urban riots and large concentrations of population constituted a political dilemma. Housing reform was embraced eagerly by those whose concern was industrial stability and peace.

However, the urban situation caught the popular imagination, not so much in statistical terms relating to population size, but through perceptions of particular problems. It was the moral and social conditions of cities which attracted most attention. The physical characteristics of urban population were anxiously observed; it was widely believed that health and vigour had declined, and if the statistics and arguments used by the believers in town degeneracy were dubious, nonetheless they helped to promote provision for open-air exercise, cleanliness and a pure food supply. Military performance by town dwellers and country people was compared: in Germany, Prussian conscripts had superior bodily fitness to those from Berlin, but Weber was pleased to compare how 'American city lads marched to victory on Cuban soil, side by side with the rough cowboys of the western plains'[2]. With regard to urban morality, the facts of vice and crime were recorded in statistics of illegitimacy, drunkenness, prostitution and criminal activity. These were variously interpreted, but nearly always showed the cities in poor light as compared with the rural areas.

In addition to this comparison, urban concentrations were known to have a range of economic, political and social implications, the importance of which were just becoming apparent. There was the threat to agriculture, the question of the organization of labour in towns, and the distribution of wealth and employment. There was the problem of municipal government, and national power and stability. Soaring land values in the centres of large cities caused great problems and were held to be responsible for housing shortages. On the community side, an urban way of life was thought to promote individualism and anonymity to an extent that prejudiced the stability and cohesiveness of rural society.

For all these reasons, it was common to consider remedies for urban growth, largely conceived in terms of arresting inward migration from the rural areas and, as a counterbalance, of making rural life more attractive. For the biggest cities, there were propositions to stabilize or reduce their size by providing new settlements in the rural areas. Land nationalization was advocated by some. By the end of the 19th century it was already clear that cities were not only symbols of achievement but sources of concern, and that the size and growth of London, in particular, was a matter that demanded close attention.

10

Sustained urban growth was one canvas against which the rise of the planning movement might be sketched, but probably the most important immediate factor rested with housing and social reform. The question of poor housing conditions can be separately identified, but the very close association in the public mind with the wider aspects of social conditions makes it necessary to consider the two issues together.

Housing was one of the many problems which faced the growing urban populations of the 19th century. Some of them had already been tackled relatively effectively, others remained for the next century. By 1900 the town dweller in Britain had been given safe water to drink, an efficient sewage disposal system and, therefore, relative freedom from water-borne disease. He had paved streets which were clean by prevailing standards, and they were lit. A public transport system had developed and there were public amenities ranging from parks to libraries and swimming baths. But there were still many obstacles to satisfactory living. Low real wages failed to provide a margin for sickness or unemployment for many. Poverty was widespread and endemic. The idea of a comprehensive health service had been conceived, but remained to be developed; there were as yet no adequate medical services generally available for the sick. In the field of public health, preventive medicine extended little beyond the reduction of the toll of pestilence; health education for mothers and school medical inspection were developments for the future. With regard to housing, legislation over the past 50 years had failed to tackle adequately the problems of unfit dwellings, poverty of living conditions for many, and, in particular, the question of providing accommodation for the working classes. But housing was the field where most progress could, perhaps, be anticipated at that time—other developments were clearly for the future, others were not of pressing need. Housing represented a failure of past efforts which troubled the national conscience; it was an immediate challenge which new legislation and political will could perhaps put right, and was consequently a principal focus for attention.

There were three separate, but related factors: overcrowding, density and insanitary conditions[3].

The 1891 Census was the first to make an investigation into the extent of overcrowding. The official definition was fixed at more than two persons per room (it is now 1.5 persons per room) and the 1901 Census revealed the extent of severe overcrowding in urban areas. In the Administrative County of London, 16% of the population were living in over-crowded conditions, and within the authority some of the constituent boroughs recorded very high, above-average, figures:

	Per cent population living in overcrowded conditions		Per cent population living in overcrowded conditions
Finsbury	35.2	Southwark	22.4
Stepney	33.2	St Marylebone	21.1
Shoreditch	30.0	Bermondsey	20.0
Bethnal Green	29.6	Islington	17.0
Holborn	25.0	Poplar	16.4
St Pancras	24.0		

Elsewhere in England and Wales, the North East recorded high proportions; other towns were mainly in the Midlands and the North. Moreover, individual districts within these towns and within the London boroughs had concentrations in excess of the average for the authority. In order of intensity of overcrowding the towns were ranked as follows:

Gateshead	34.5	Huddersfield	12.9
South Shields	32.4	Merthyr Tydfil	12.2
Tynemouth	30.7	Willesden	11.6
Newcastle	30.5	West Hartlepool	11.6
Sunderland	30.1	Middlesbrough	10.9
Plymouth	20.2	St Helens	
Dudley	17.5	Birmingham	10.3
Devonport	17.4	West Bromwich	10.2
Bradford	14.6	Barrow in Furness	10.1
Halifax	14.5	Leeds	
Wigan	13.4	Stockton	

The figures indicate the proportion of the total population living in overcrowded conditions in 1901. Scottish cities were even more notorious for overcrowding, resulting from a common building style of one- and two-room houses, a characteristic which in England was only shared by the North East.

Overcrowding was related to a number of medical and social conditions, not the least of which was infant mortality. Figures for London for the years 1891–1900 showed the relationship clearly. The death rate per thousand infants under one year was 142 in districts with less than 10% of the total population living in overcrowded conditions, but 223 in districts where overcrowding was more than 35%. In between these two extremes, the progression was as follows:

Death rate (per thousand infants)	Overcrowding (per cent)
142	less than 10
180	10–15
196	15–20
193	20–25
210	25–30
222	30–35
223	more than 35

Medical opinion was also concerned at the density question. It was widely considered that no town could be healthy when its total population exceeded 25 persons to the acre, but the 1901 Census showed many towns in excess of this figure. Several of the London boroughs exceed a density of 100 persons per acre: Southwark 182, Shoreditch 180, Finsbury 172, Bethnal Green 171, Stepney 169, Holborn 147, Chelsea 112, Islington 108 and Paddington 106. These figures cover, of course, averages over the whole borough; within the authority there were individual districts with yet higher figures, particularly within Stepney. Overall, the Administrative County of London recorded 60.6 persons per acre.

Elsewhere in England and Wales there were a further 26 towns with average densities above 25 to the acre. These were:

West Ham	57.1	Gateshead	35.0
Liverpool	51.7	Hanley	34.8
Brighton	48.8	Middlesbrough	32.3
South Shields	47.6	Derby	30.7
Plymouth	45.6	Oldham	29.0
Sunderland	43.6	Birkenhead	28.8
Salford	42.5	Preston	28.2
Manchester	42.1	Bristol	28.1
Birmingham	41.4	Wigan	27.8
Newcastle	40.0	Hull	26.8
Portsmouth	37.8	Wolverhampton	26.7
Bootle	37.2	Cardiff	25.7
Stockport	35.9	Northampton	25.1

The figures are persons per acre, 1901.

Individual differences between towns were not particularly significant because the overall figures were greatly affected by the existence of old-established areas of open space within towns or the constraint of tightly drawn local government boundaries. What mattered more was that such a large number of towns recorded these high figures at all: it clearly reflected the existence of crowded concentrations of people throughout the country and suggested an indelible feature of the national urban situation. The Scottish position was similar though the important concentrations were localized to the four major cities. While high densities as a general characteristic prevailed, excessive densities within certain cities were recorded. The London black spots have been indicated, but elsewhere there were others. In Liverpool the district of North Everton contained 54 000 people at a density of 178 per acre; in St Martin 53 000 lived at a density of 102 per acre. In Newcastle, Westgate contained 30 000 inhabitants crowded at a density of 133 per acre. In Manchester the district of St George had 58 000 people at 117 per acre, and Ancoats had 44 000 at 110 per acre.

The 1901 Census did not necessarily record the worst rates of overcrowding and high density. There was, in fact, already a general trend towards falling overcrowding rates. In 1891 there had been nearly 600 000 persons more than in 1901 living in overcrowded tenements in England and Wales. But the decline continued slowly, and in 1911 more than a third of the population still lived at a density of more than two persons per room in certain districts of London—Finsbury, Shoreditch, Stepney and Bethnal Green. Conditions were still bad in the North East and the West Riding.

The third issue was that of insanitary housing. The Royal Commission on the Housing of the Working Classes, 1885, the ensuing Housing of the Working Classes Act of that year, and the consolidating Act of 1890, all strengthened the hand of the local authorities in securing the proper sanitary conditions of their dwelling-stock. Unhealthy areas could be represented to the local authority by the medical officer on grounds of unfitness for human habitation, or that bad arrangement and want of light were injurious to health, and that the best method of dealing with the problem was an improvement scheme. But these schemes, which had to be confirmed by the Local Government Board, were expensive because of the compensation payable, and progress on their implementation was slow. Additionally, although individual dwellings could be demolished by the local authority, this action was subject to the owner's right of appeal to a court of quarter sessions, and therefore could be retarded.

In 1903 a writer on the housing situation observed that 'Fifty years ago, the "Housing of the Poor" was a burning question. Today it is the Housing of the Working Classes, and it threatens to be the Housing of the People.'[4] This perceptive remark highlights the developing situation with regard to intervention in housing matters. The last decade of the century witnessed a marked extension of housing powers. In 1890, the Public Health Acts Amendment Act amended the 1875 Act. In the same year, the Housing of the Working Classes Act consolidated and amended the Shaftsbury, Torrens and Cross Acts of 1851, 1868 and 1879. In 1891 the Public Health Act consolidated the sanitary law relating to London. In 1894 the Housing of the Working Classes Act extended the borrowing powers exercised under Part II of the 1890 Act. In 1899 the Small Dwellings Acquisition Act enabled local authorities to advance monies for the purchase of small dwellings by their occupiers. In 1900 a further Housing of the Working Classes Act amended Part III of the 1890 Act, enabling land to be acquired outside the area of jurisdiction of the local authority. Further amendments of the 1890 Act followed in 1903. Great hopes had been pinned on the breakthrough of the 1890 Act. In fact, progress was to be desperately slow. The contribution of the private and philanthropic sectors were found to be inadequate for the task in hand and legislation which put the obligation of rehousing the working classes on the local authorities was still a generation away.

In the meantime the continued existence of inadequate housing inclined the debate to a wider front—the social and physical conditions of our towns as a whole. As an illustration of the very great influence that this had on the emergent planning movement we might refer to the *Report on Housing Conditions in Manchester and Salford*, published in 1904. The general situation was stated thus: 'We see in our towns today many evils. Poor physique, impaired health and premature senility; drunkenness, sexual immorality and other vice; betting and thriftlessness; decay of family life and lack of civic spirit; these are all too common. We find, too, poverty, houses unwholesome from many causes, lack of provision of open spaces and other means for healthy recreation, narrow and gloomy streets, an excessive amount of coal smoke and a superabundance of public houses.'[5] This was the situation as the writer's Citizens' Association saw it. This was indeed the urban problem as identified and perceived by many observers at the turn of the century, and the author went on to draw particular attention to poverty, and unwholesome houses and their surroundings.

It is in his set of proposals for dealing with this situation that the link between housing, urban environment and social conditions becomes clear, and where we should see the embryo comprehensive planning movement taking shape. For example, he urged a comprehensive housing policy for Manchester–Salford which provided 'not only for the demolition of unwholesome dwellings and the statutory obligation to rehouse the occupants, but would also definitely provide for the growth of the towns, planning roads, streets and open spaces for the new districts long before they are actually required for building' (op. cit.). He proposed to extend the work of the sanitary departments and use more fully the powers of the 1890 Act. He would stimulate self-help with voluntary organizations, determine the needs of the locality, and emulate conditions at Bournville and Port

Sunlight. He would extend the powers of the town council, enabling them to acquire land; he would levy a rate on unoccupied land.

This sort of prognosis and prescription built on many years of agitation about urban social conditions, and a relationship with poor housing was always seen as a central fact. Although the language and underlying assumptions of late 19th century observers were very different from our own, the situation was in many ways similar. There was, for example, the same concentration of people economically underprivileged and disadvantaged from the point of view of their housing environment, and the problem was to devise satisfactory ways of alleviating their position. A book called *Town Swamps and Social Bridges* by George Godwin, published in 1859, may be beyond our period of concern, but a recent commentator has suggested that what was described then would appear today as *Urban Poverty and the Role of Voluntary Action*. 'Instead of the emotion-charged journalism typical of mid-nineteenth century England there would be an appropriate theoretical framework, empirical research and an action-oriented programme for planned change'.[6] Godwin's swamps were the breakdowns of social organization—crime, poverty, disease, sickness, unemployment, economic distress, ignorance, superstition, overcrowding, bad drainage, drink and lack of recreational and educational provision. His bridges were the voluntary organization of an institutional infrastructure required by urban society—schools, hospitals, homes and playgrounds. The situation was not very different even at the end of the century, but increasingly individual concern gave way to public action, as realization dawned of the links between poverty, housing and social deprivation. Godwin's maximum was 'as the homes, so the people', and this physical determinism continued to characterize much of the remainder of the century and beyond.

The immediate growth of the planning movement owed much to the protest literature of the last two decades of the century[7]. The tradition had been well laid. As early as the 1840s a public indictment of urban squalor was built up by the Reports of the Poor Law Commissioners and the various Select Committees and Royal Commissions of the time. But the next 30 or 40 years failed to maintain a systematic analysis of the slum situation. The revelations of Henry Mayhew as 'letters' to *The Morning Chronicle* during 1849 and 1850 were journalistic in flavour. An exception was the study of slum housing in Central and South London, *The Rookeries of London,* by the Reverend Thomas Beames in 1851. It was not until the 1880s that the monthlies and quarterlies as well as the weekly and daily presses were again publishing articles on aspects of slum life. A 21-page penny pamphlet, *The Bitter City of Outcast London,* commonly attributed to the Secretary of the London Congregational Union, the Reverend Andrew Mearns, published in 1883, revealed the horrors of urban living for countless thousands in a portrait of squalor, destitution and vice. In 1885 *The Pall Mall Gazette* serialized the findings of a survey undertaken by the Social Democratic Foundation in working-class districts of London; one in four persons was stated to be living in abject poverty.

A clinical analysis of London conditions came with Charles Booth's seventeen volumes of *Life and Labour of the People in London,* the first appearing in 1889, based on data he had begun to collect three years earlier. His initial concern was poverty in East London, which then contained a population of 900 000. He divided the people into eight classes, and he found the first three to comprise 35% of the total. These were the poor and the very poor, his definition of 'poor' being those with a regular though bare income of 18s to 21s per week for a moderate family; the very poor were on casual earnings, and beyond these there were the occasional labourers. To complete his survey of poverty, he later turned his attention to Central, South and outlying London, where with an overall population of three millions he again found that approximately one-third (30.7%) lived on or below his definition of poverty. Booth painstakingly described families and streets, where poverty was based on lack of work, low pay, family size and ill-health, and gave complementary descriptions of decrepit housing and on overriding urban squalor.

With regard to housing matters, he classified undesirable conditions as follows: old property in bad condition; new houses badly built; property neglected by the owner; property abused by the occupier; houses built on insufficient space; those erected on damp or rubbish-filled ground; houses occupied by families of a class for which they were not designed or suited; insanitary houses; badly arranged block dwellings; badly managed blocks; excessive rents; and crowded homes. All these, of course, overlapped and were mutually reinforcing. Booth summarized the position: 'low buildings and wider streets are the things needed, and instead the people are offered depressing streets, dark and narrow, or tall, prison-like dwellings'[8].

Booth noted the direct methods of dealing with these housing difficulties, namely the statutory powers then available, but he concluded that, 'It is not too much to say that the action taken so far in London in any of these directions has been very half hearted. Confidence is lacking; public opinion unconvinced. It is felt to be impossible to press regulations against overcrowding when other house room is not available, and very difficult to reform sanitary conditions when landlord and tenant are in league to "let well alone" (as they regard it). Thus it is just where things are worst that it is most difficult to amend them by direct attack. Schemes for demolition and reconstruction, great and small, have proved, as we have seen, in many ways unsatisfactory. A nuisance is indeed removed, but at a very great cost, largely owing to the terms of compensation for compulsory purchase, and to the obligation to re-house. Good houses are built only to be occupied by a superior class; the evicted poor crowd in elsewhere. Though formulated with the best intentions, the rehousing clauses attached to Parliamentary powers of purchase have proved of doubtful benefit, or rather in some respects certainly injurious' (op. cit.). Many years later with his final volume, Booth noted improvements in the situation, but writing when he did, this indictment of the state of affairs undoubtedly fuelled the activities of the housing reformers.

The social analysis of General William Booth of the Salvation Army was of a different kind, but no less arresting. The Army published his *In Darkest England and the Way Out* in 1890, and sales of more than 200 000 in the first year testified to its popular appeal. He described the conditions of the 'submerged tenth' of the population, three million people, including the homeless, the out-of-work, drunkards, criminals, prostitutes and demoralized children. He likened our own civilization to that of Darkest Africa, as revealed by Stanley's explorations: 'may we not find a parallel at our own doors, and discover within a stone's throw of our cathedrals and palaces similar horrors to those which Stanley had found existing in the great Equatorial forest?'[9] His proposal for a Social Lifeboat Institution, 'to snatch from the abyss those who, if left to themselves, will perish as miserably as the crew of a ship that founders in mid-ocean', was similar to others that saw merit in hiving off colonies of people in new settlements away from London.

Finally, there was the contribution of Seebohm Rowntree to the study of poverty in York. His book *Poverty, a Study of Town Life* was published in 1901. His investigations began in the Spring of 1899 and he found that in York over 15% of the working-class population and nearly 10% of the total population were in what he termed 'primary poverty'; a further 18% were in 'secondary poverty'. Using the same definition of poverty as that used by Charles Booth for London, Rowntree concluded that nearly 27.8% of York's population were living in poverty, compared with 30.7% for the capital.

The evidence from social and economic inquiry into housing, labour and environmental conditions underpinned the case for housing reform. The measures advocated were often fragmentary and failed to get to the hub of the problem, because the underlying reasons for slum formation were imperfectly understood. At the heart of the matter was the inequitable economic system of the time. As Dyos has remarked: 'One of the most general reasons for the slums of Victorian England simply was that the capital which might have wrought a change was being ploughed heavily back into the commercial machine instead of being distributed in higher wages, and its earnings benefitted particular social classes differentially...slums helped to under-pin Victorian prosperity.'[10]

In the vicious spiral of poor housing and deprivation, there was a close relationship with low and irregular incomes. Much unemployment remained on a casual basis, with available jobs fluctuating from day to day or even hour to hour; this applied not only for the unskilled but also for some skilled trades, and it was imperative for men to live within close walking distance of work. Additionally, perhaps in London, at any rate, the leasehold system was at the root of many personal difficulties. Under the London system the legal conditions for development of land and housing were ultimately the responsibility of the lessor, and a string of sub-leases often stretched between the landlord and the tenant, so dividing responsibilities and inflating rents.

As we have suggested, attempts to deal with the problem had been tentative and the results were disappointing. Housing improvements alone, involving slum clearance, proved to be disruptive and aggravated the situation because their effect was to reduce the supply of working-class housing. In any case, the slums had become a long-standing urban feature permanently inhabited by a particular class of people. In the capital they could no longer be regarded as settlement areas for provincial immigrants, as had frequently been thought, but 'settlement tanks for submerged Londoners'[11]. The general position was that there were two social gradients for a city population, one upwards to the suburbs, and the other leading downwards to the slums of the inner city. Slum conditions were self-reinforcing—those who could, left; those who could not, stayed. It was to this general position of inequality and social deprivation, and to the facts of poor housing and environmental conditions that various reform movements were directed.

INDUSTRIAL PHILANTHROPISTS

The building of villages by wealthy manufacturers for their workers, often in rural surroundings, with good housing and the provision of a range of community facilities as the keynote, had been a repetitive feature of the 19th century. As contributions to solving the problem of providing good housing in attractive settings for the working classes, they proved important stimuli to the planning movement. The best known estates were exemplary in that they were 'well planned', spacious and they embodied all the social idealism of the time[12].

Robert Owen's experiment at New Lanark at the very beginning of the century set the scene. Here, a cotton mill built at the Falls of Clyde in 1784 provided the setting for a manufacturing village to be governed according to the social reform ideas of Owen during the first three decades of the century. He made his name as the archetype of the benevolent entrepreneur. For some time 2 000 visitors went annually to New Lanark, many of them eminent people, the Tsar of Russia included. His educational and social reform measures, including his emphasis on 'the formation of character', encouraged many idealists for the rest of the century. The actual design of a town to accommodate communities of a larger size was suggested in mid-century by James Silk Buckingham in a book published in 1849, *National Evils and Practical Remedies*, in which he advocated a Model Town Association and described the layout of an ideal settlement, Victoria, for 10 000 people. This example was also a stimulus to later reformers: the aim was a community from which ignorance, vice and disease would be banished, and a settlement which provided good houses and a range of social facilities.

The century provided plenty of similar illustrations. Some were small and barely kept the idea alive. But we should mention the village of Bessbrook near Newry, Northern Ireland, built in 1846 by John Grubb Richardson; the company cottages built by the Strutt family at Belper, Derby; and the many other workers' colonies of this type both in this country and on the Continent. More impressive as innovations were those built consequent upon industrial relocation. A prime example was the creation of Saltaire near Bradford, by Sir Titus Salt from the 1850s onwards. The scale of this Model Town was scarcely matched by the development by Price's Patent Candle Company, also from the 1850s onwards at Bromborough Pool, Cheshire, but the principle was the same. In America the Company Town of Pullman near Chicago was a development of the 1880s and there were other industrialists' ventures on the Continent. The founding of the Society for Promoting Industrial Villages in 1883 with the support of a number of distinguished Victorians suggested the national interest in this sort of activity. The century closed with three experiments, Port Sunlight, Bournville and Earswick, the first two of which in particular contributed markedly to the growth of the planning movement.

By 1887 the Warrington soap works of Lever Brothers had become cramped for space and a 56-acre site was chosen further down the Mersey on the banks of the Bromborough Pool for a new development. During the next 20 years the site was increased to 221 acres; a new works was built, and between what was then the London and N.W. and G.W. Joint Railway Line and the New Chester Road 130 acres were devoted to the village of Port Sunlight. 720 houses were built at a low density. Adequate open space was provided, and the street blocks had open interiors used for allotments. There was a good variety of house types. The dwellings were almost solely occupied by Lever employees and the Company provided a range of controlled Institutions, for example, the Auditorium, the Collegium, the Bridge Inn, Library and Museum, and the Hospital. There were other facilities including Church and Sunday Schools, shops, and athletic, literary, scientific, provident and philanthropic societies. The paternalism with which this development was managed will be appreciated from a remark of an observer, W. L. George, in 1909. Every house was fronted by a garden, which was maintained communally: 'At one time these front gardens were given up to the tenants, but their aesthetic possibilities were not appreciated; they were used as fowl-runs, and even as dustbins, while the family washing was unblushingly exposed on the palings.'[13]

Port Sunlight was regarded as an important experiment in showing the place of good housing in social reform. George, a prolific writer on this topic, expressed a commonly held view: 'We know or should realize that at the root of all forms of vice, particularly drunkenness, lies the problem of housing; evil conditions mean depression, and, for the slag of our social system, the only resource, fleeting but efficacious, is the public house and its costly hospitality.' (op. cit.) The proof of the pudding was in the eating: Port Sunlight amply expressed good results. There was no record of drunkenness, wife beating, immorality, assaults and deserted wives and children. Cleanliness, temperance and open spaces were seen to be causally related to both general well-being and to physique. Infant mortality was half that of an immediate neighbour, Liverpool, and physical fitness of both children and adults was held to be superior to that of town dwellers.

George Cadbury's Bournville stemmed from similar convictions about social progress. He is said to have remarked that, 'The best way to improve a man's circumstances is to raise his ideals; but it is not enough to *talk* to him about ideals. How can he cultivate ideals when his home is a slum and his only place of recreation the public house?'[14] His Quaker philosophy, a practical social idealism, his long-standing knowledge of slum life in Birmingham and contact with the working classes through the Adult School in which he taught, promoted his new estate development. Once again it was factory relocation which provided the opportunity. In 1879 George and Richard Cadbury moved their cramped factory in central Birmingham to a new site on the outskirts to which they gave the name Bournville. A small number of semi-detached houses was built close to the Works for key workers and this proved to be a valuable pilot scheme for later years.

In spite of their similarities, there were important differences between Port Sunlight and Bournville. Lever's experiment was an attempt to establish a new understanding between Capital and Labour. It was an 'attempt to Socialize and Christianize business relations and get back again in the office, factory and workshop to that close family brotherhood that existed in the good old days of hand labour'[15]. Cadbury, on the other hand, was a housing reformer, showing through experiment how working-class housing could be better provided.

In 1893 George Cadbury bought 120 acres next to the factory and began building the estate the next year. By 1900, 313 houses had been built and the estate had grown to 330 acres. In that year he founded the Bournville Village Trust as an instrument of promoting social betterment through housing reform. The preamble to the Trust Deed summarizes the objectives: 'The founder is desirous of alleviating the evils which arise from the insanitary and insufficient accommodation supplied to large numbers of the working classes, and of securing to the workers in factories some of the advantages of outdoor village life, with opportunities for the natural and healthful occupation of cultivating

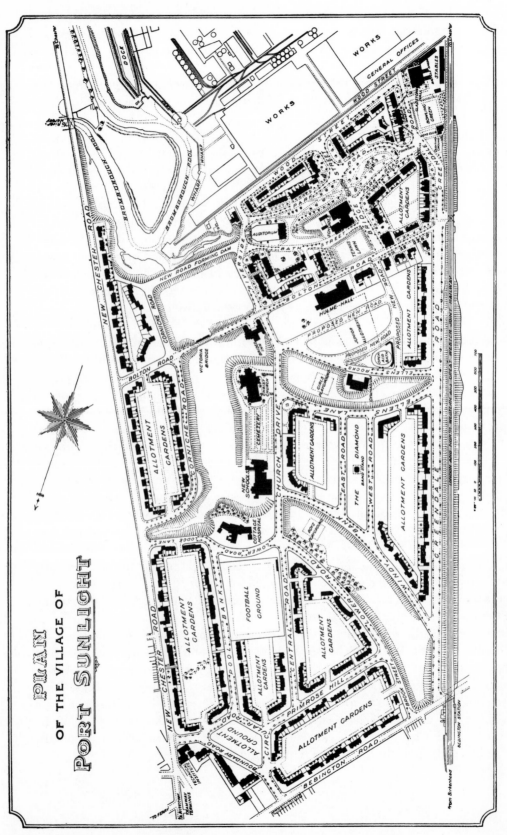

Port Sunlight, developed as a self-contained community on low density lines between the New Chester Road and the Birkenhead–Chester railway. Note the priority accorded to open space, allotments and community buildings.

George Cadbury, 1839–1922, founder of Bournville, photographed at the age of 78. An early biography was *Life of George Cadbury*, A.G. Gardiner, Cassell, 1923. A recent illustrated biography is by Walter Stranz (Shire Publications, 1973).

Bournville at the turn of the century. This is what the housing and social reformers were striving for: well-built dwellings, open space, fresh air and sunlight, and gardens. Happy, healthy children would be the outcome. (*Courtesy of* Cadbury Schweppes' archives)

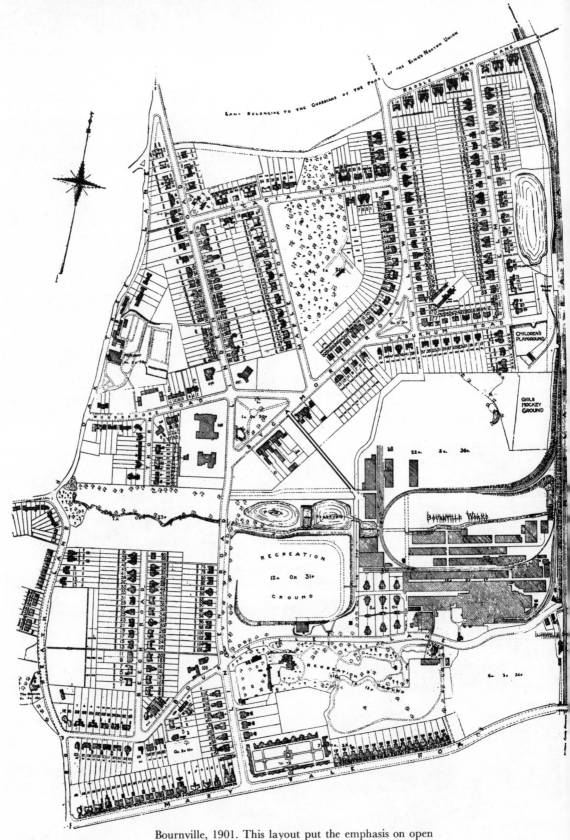

Bournville, 1901. This layout put the emphasis on open space in the form of gardens attached to every house. A new suburban architecture emerged. Public open space, landscaped around the setting of the stream integrated the industrial and residential uses of the village.

the soil. The object is declared to be the amelioration of the condition of the working-class and labouring population in and around Birmingham, and elsewhere in Great Britain, by the provision of improved dwellings, with gardens and open spaces to be enjoyed therewith.'

In the actual development of the estate the principle of a mixed community was followed and from the very start only about 40% of the dwellings were occupied by workers at the factory. The importance of a community spirit was recognized, and a Village Council was founded. Estate management with human, personal sensitivity was aimed at. Community facilities were soon provided: village schools administered by the local education authority, Ruskin Hall (an institute for teaching arts and crafts), shops, a Friends' Meeting House and (later) an Anglican parish church. Estate design put the emphasis on generous space standards, gardens and tree-lined roads; the individual houses were well built and airy. Bournville Tenants Limited was launched in 1906 as a co-operative housing society and after 1911 much of the development was carried out by this and four other societies formed under the Village Trust.

The Bournville experiment attracted considerable attention and Cadbury himself became very much involved in aspects of the growing planning movement. The newly formed Garden City Association held a conference at Bournville in 1901 and Cadbury was prominent among those agitating for new legislation some years later. As we shall see in other chapters, Birmingham was to be one of the cities which regarded town planning as important. The influence of the Cadbury family in general and the Bournville experiment in particular was very marked.

The Earswick experiment at York by the Rowntree firm was on a smaller scale. Joseph Rowntree founded the Joseph Rowntree Village Trust in 1904, the object being 'the improvement of the condition of the working classes...by the provision of improved dwellings with open spaces, and, where possible, gardens to be enjoyed therewith, and the organization of village communities, with such facilities for the enjoyment of full and healthy lives as the Trustees shall consider desirable...'[16]. An estate was built at New Earswick, York, and the name Garden Village was applied. Tree-planted and grass-verged roads were incorporated in Raymon Unwin's layout. The Trust's publication in 1954, *One Man's Vision*, traces the development of the estate.

There were a number of other small schemes promoted by or on behalf of industrialists. Hull Garden Village, covering nearly 100 acres in the northeast of the city adjoining Reckitt's works, is probably the best known, dating from 1907. Woodlands Mining Village north of Doncaster was started in the same year to house the workers of the nearby Brodsworth Main Colliery, and the scheme when finished provided 650 houses. Percy Houfton was the architect, having earlier designed Cresswell Model Village in Derbyshire (1898). By this time, the Garden City Movement was vigorous and its contribution is reviewed in chapter 3.

THE SITUATION IN OTHER COUNTRIES

The British town planning movement developed in an international context, as well as in a purely national setting. In many countries of continental Europe there had been

23

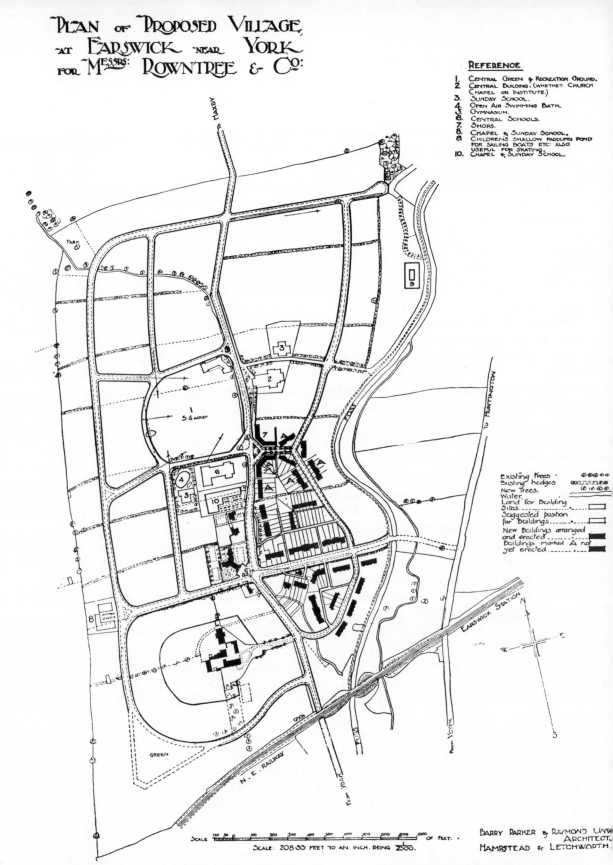

Earswick, a plan prepared by Barry Parker and Raymond Unwin, from which many departures were made when the development was carried out. Note the new form of layout which introduced a rural irregularity as a reaction to the symmetrical bye-law streets of the late Victorian city.

progress in planning for some years and the lack of British steps in their directions was a point of criticism. In America too there was a developing planning tradition, although the actual influence on Britain was less marked than was that of Germany and France.

For some years many European cities had undergone transformations in the field of public works, and in some cases planning legislation had been introduced to control town extensions[17]. In Austria the example of Vienna was well known. In 1858, when it had been decided to dismantle the fortifications of the inner city, a public competition was announced for the planning of the area of the old bulwarks. This led to the building of the Ring Street (Ringstrasse) where new public buildings were built to high architectural standards. A second planning competition led to a proposal for a large metropolitan green belt for the city, an idea which worked into schemes for many European cities, following similar plans for Greater Boston in America.

An even larger enterprise was seen in France. Napoleon III resumed the street opening operations in Paris which had been interrupted by Waterloo; street fighting in 1848 had shown how troops could be beleagured without possibility of relief because of the lack of convenient streets of access. Under Baron Haussmann's direction an extensive programme took place of new street engineering, the construction of new monumental buildings, and others with harmonious façades and uniform cornice lines, a new sewer system, gas lighting scheme, tree planting and a new road system. Anthony Sutcliffe has described this phase and subsequent developments in Paris in great detail[18].

In Belgium, city centre developments in Brussels between 1860 and 1880 created new avenues and boulevards. In Germany, plans were prepared for many large towns including Dusseldorf, Nuremberg and Frankfurt in the later years of the century. In Prussia, a Street and Building Lines Act in 1875 provided a basis for the planning of new areas.

In Spain, a general law regarding the preparation and execution of city plans dated from 1870, and it was under this legislation that the extensions to Madrid and Barcelona were carried out. An 'extension' was the incorporation by a city of surrounding districts required by the probable increase of the city's population as estimated by the Government; in the case of these two cities the extension took place planned on a gridiron layout. The legislation was modified in 1892 to make it applicable to other cities and in 1895 legislation was extended to give permissive regulations for sanitation, replanning and city extension for authorities with a population of more than 30 000 people.

Advances in Sweden came in 1866 when plans were prepared for the regulation and extension of Gothenburg. It was soon followed by a programme of public works in Stockholm between 1875 and 1881. National legislation took the form of a Building Law for the Towns of the Realm in 1874 which decreed that all towns must have a plan sanctioned by government; detailed regulations were provided so that the requirements of spaciousness, aesthetics, comfort, variety, neatness and hygiene were met.

In Holland an Act of 1901 obliged municipalities of more than 10 000 people, or the population of which had increased by more than one-fifth within the last five years, to make an extension plan. This was to be revised at least once in every ten years.

This progress in public works and municipal control over town expansion bore little comparison with the British situation. It was not that our urban improvements had been absent: in London there had been a programme of road improvements (for example, the cutting of Charing Cross Road and the construction of the Embankment) and drainage works. Elsewhere a few minor city centre improvements had taken place involving slum clearance and the construction of new thoroughfares, as in central Birmingham. But essentially the emphasis had been quite different: housing and attention to related social problems had provided the focus for action. In fact, the British tradition was to prove the great influence, because it erupted into the Garden City Movement, and it was from this line of activity that a comprehensive town planning movement emerged. Nonetheless the European movement at the turn of the century contained elements which Britain lacked and which were needed.

Technical literature dealing with town planning was scarce, and even so, almost entirely confined to Germany and France[19]. Dr J. Stübben, city architect of Cologne, wrote about city construction, and Camillo Sitte, an architect of Vienna, wrote on town planning from a design standpoint—his particular contribution is noted later in this chapter. In 1876 Professor R. Baumeister of Karlsruhe published a standard work on the planning of suburbs, *Stadt Erweiterungen*. (In Germany most large towns prepared plans to regulate the development of their suburbs.) In 1904 a monthly publication *Der Stadtebau* was founded by Theordor Goecke and Sitte. By comparison, in Britain the emergence of planning literature was delayed until well into the first decade of the century.

In France there was more of the British concern for public health and social matters to accompany a pre-occupation with municipal reform. In Paris, a single institution became the focal point of these interests: the Musée Social, founded in 1894, dedicated to improving the 'situation materielle et morale des travailleurs'[20]. Eugéne Hènard became the director of a new section formed within the Musée in 1908, the 'section d'hygiene urbaine et rurale'; it had the objective of translating desirable hygienic and social reform principles into legislation and urban plans. An architect, Hènard became internationally known among planners.

At the turn of the century Britain exhibited very little of this intellectual activity about urban affairs; it had its pressure groups for housing and social reform, and, as we shall see later, for civic art, but these and other contributions were not yet brought together in any comprehensive way. Meanwhile, the real advances made by Germany in municipal planning were stressed by T. C. Horsfall, active in Manchester in late Victorian and Edwardian years in fields of housing and social reform. He visited Germany in 1897 for some weeks when he met many of the leading men who were concerned in social questions. Afterwards he steeped himself in German periodicals dealing with planning matters to such an extent that he became known to his friends as 'German Horsfall'. He was certainly very strongly influenced by German thought and practice in town planning, noting particularly the importance of municipal control over land and housing development.

Horsfall's principal contribution was his publication in 1904, *The Improvement of the Dwellings and Surroundings of the People: the Example of Germany*. The following passage illustrates what he regarded as fundamentally lacking in British urban affairs at that time: 'Experience has proved that it is only private enterprise which can cope with the vast work of supplying the greater part of the immense number of new houses which must be built in and near a town, the population of which is increasing rapidly; but experience has also shown that, without control and guidance and assistance of many kinds from Town

T.C. Horsfall, a photograph taken appropriately in Berlin in 1896 when he was collecting information on German planning schemes. A social reformer with wide interests, he did much to pave the way for British town planning legislation by pointing out the advances made earlier on the continent. (*Courtesy of* Mrs D.M.H. Betts)

Vienna, diagrammatic town plan at the turn of the century. Observers of the continental scene were keen to recommend comprehensive town plans, not simply piecemeal schemes. Vienna was a good example with six distinct zones: 1. The Inner Town where six-storey buildings were permitted. 2. The districts within the girdle line (five-storey buildings). 3. The four-storey dwelling house zone, chiefly immediately to the west of the girdle line. 4. The three-storey dwelling house zone between the girdle line and the meadow girdle. 5. The industrial zone to the south east (sectors 10 and 11). 6. The open spaces. British planning was not yet so advanced. (See *Town Planning Review*, **1**, No. 3, 1910)

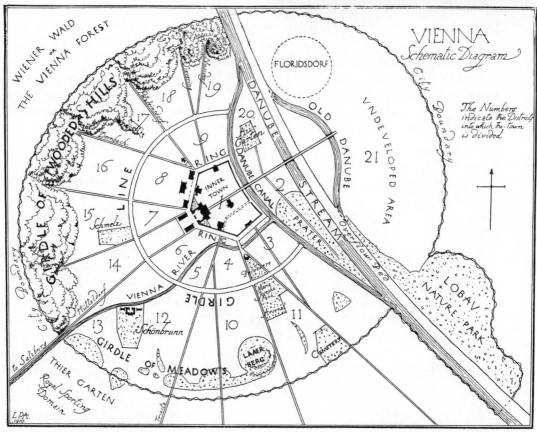

Note: The area of the Inner Town is exaggerated in comparison with that of the whole City.

Councils, private enterprise does not, and cannot, provide enough new houses; does not place what houses it does supply in right relation to other buildings; and does not supply the kind of house which the community needs; and, further, does not keep the houses which it supplies in good order'[21]. If one is looking for watersheds in the direction of planning thought at this time, Horsfall's plea for recognizing the importance of the public sector in guiding and shaping urban growth on behalf of the community is as fundamental as any. Many European countries had advanced a long way along the line of plan preparation obligatory through national legislation; Britain so far had not. Horsfall pointed out with great clarity the difference in approach and attitude between the British and German authorities.

In Britain the approach to the solution of the housing problem had been to ensure the supply of an adequate number of fit houses, well built, well drained and sewered and surrounded by a minimum of open space for air and light. The German approach was to secure a satisfactory environment through street and building plans for large areas of land approved by Municipal Governments over periods of 10, 20 and up to 30 years. The role played by the local councils was significantly different from that in Britain. In Germany they gave loans to Co-operative and other Building Societies at low rates of interest to build houses of a kind most needed by the community, and in their plan making the claim, at least, was that the interests of land owners took second place to the needs of the whole town. The German system had its defects (it had failed to reduce overcrowding and densities for example) but the interventionist role of the local authority in land assembly was much in advance of Britain: Horsfall remarked on the inability of the British system to enable a town to obtain land, and gave as an example the failure of the Manchester Town Council to purchase Trafford Park in the 1890s. In fact, when planning powers were first provided in this country (1909) these aspects of scheme preparation and local authority control over the use of land were essential features.

Compared with the Continent the influence of America on British planning was relatively slight. But many similar issues were being considered, and it is right to recall the internationalism of the incipient planning movement. Landscape planning had made particular advances from as early as the middle of the century, led by people such as Frederick Law Olmsted, the designer of Central Park, New York, his disciples Calvert Vaux and A. J. Downing, and others. Thus it was that the public works side of urban improvement embraced popular features such as tree-lined boulevards with a broad strip down the centre; Boston had the most ambitious project on these lines, but Detroit and many other cities won fame for their new city designs. At the turn of the century the 'city beautiful' movement emphasized the preparation of city plans for metropolitan centres and capitals. New York and Boston attempted comprehensive street and park planning under municipal or metropolitan boards, but Hartford advanced a step further when it secured permission in 1907 to create the first city planning commission. Chicago followed two years later, Baltimore and Detroit the next year and others subsequently[22].

The other side to American planning concerned housing. A growing protest movement developed against the congested tenements of the day; in particular the notorious 'dumb bell' tenements had spread over New York City. A vivid description by Jacob A. Riis in *How The Other Half Lives*, published in 1890, was akin to British exposures of London slumland. Organizations were formed for the purpose of building better housing for low income workers; in Chicago the Settlement House Movement of Jane Addams was a focal point for social reform; and legislative measures offered some improvement, for example the Tenement House Act of 1901. From this point of view at least the planning movement was operating on a similar front to Britain.

DESIGN AND ARCHITECTURE

A new generation of continental architects with fresh approaches to the questions of public art and urban form were also influences on the planning movement. A Viennese architect, Camillo Sitte was particularly prominent in this connection[23], occupying a pivotal position in the architectural and city building tradition. Sitte, whose father had also been an architect and artist, had a wide background of art and travel; in 1883 he was called to Vienna, the city of his birth, to organize the new State School of Applied Arts. In 1889 a small volume of his essays was published under the title *City Planning According To Artistic Principles (der Stadtbau nach seinen künstlerischen Grundsätzen)*, in which he analysed the civic and artistic character of old European towns. He abstracted from their layout a series of clear principles on which city planning might be restored to an artistic basis.

Engineers had so far played the leading role in city planning in Germany. Reinhard Baumeister, for example, helped to orient the tradition of city building round the needs of vehicular traffic; his book in 1876, *Städterweiterung*, was influential in this way. Joseph Stübben maintained the same approach, and in his *Handbuch des Städtebaues* (1890) he evolved a hierarchy of street types, classified according to their function. Against this tradition, Sitte saw the building of cities as simply one aspect of a greater totality of all the arts and promoted a concept of city environments from the point of view of man as a social and aesthetically sensitive being. He argued that planning should not be regarded as a matter of traffic flow, or drainage (in which the German engineers also specialized), but rather it was a question of how to shape a city so that it would be psychologically and physiologically adequate for the needs of city dwellers. Sitte's image of the city was architectonic, and his great contribution was a subjective set of design principles. His publication of 1889 summarized his views, and with the case study of the Ringstrasse in Vienna before him he showed how this development illustrated a clumsy handling of space around the major buildings and placing of public monuments.

Another important figure concerned with the architectural side of planning was Burgomaster Charles Buls of Brussels. Although apparently not influenced by Sitte's writing, he was personally involved in the preservation of the old parts of the Belgian capital. His small book published in 1893, *Esthetique des Villes*, stimulated the world-wide movement towards public art; Brussels in fact accommodated the Congress of Public Art in 1898. In 1903 the Cities Exhibition was held in Dresden, reflecting the internationalism of the interest.

Britain also had a 'city beautiful' phase of artistically oriented planning. Indeed, Britain's first town planning journal, the *Town Planning Review*, was launched in 1910 on this very note with reports on various world capitals and civic art. There was a reaction to the visual chaos of Victorian cities and the architectural poverty of mass housing; additionally, the traffic congestion, smell and bustle of city centres, particularly London, called for new approaches. The Arts and Crafts movement provided a source of inspirations, and W. R. Lethaby, the architect, was an important influence, writing and lecturing widely. His *Architecture, Mysticism and Myth* (1891–2), was an early example of his approach. Better known is his chapter 'Beautiful Cities' in an Arts and Crafts Exhibition Society publication of 1897[24]. This reproduced his lecture delivered to the fifth Exhibition of that Society in London in 1896 under the general title of 'Art and Life', in which he compared the enormity of the London of his day and its poverty of art form with the richness of the past supported by craftsmen and the guild system. This sense of reaction against the philistinism of the Industrial Revolution bit deep into artistic circles at this time. The emergent planning movement owed much to developments in civic art and new forms of residential architecture. It was significant that one of the first important planning textbooks of this country, Unwin's *Town Planning in Practice* (1909), had as its subtitle *The Art of Designing Cities and Suburbs*. It was the architect who gave form and identity to many of the principles which planning embraced.

One example of concern over visual matters was the matter of display of advertisements in British cities at that time. George Gissing described the typical urban scene: 'High and low on every available yard of wall, advertisements clamoured to the eye: theatres, journals, soaps, medicines, concerts, furniture, wines, prayer meetings—all the produce and refuse of civilization.'[25] The National Society for Checking the Abuse of Public Advertising was formed in 1893 with a view to preventing the disfigurement of countryside and towns; also in that year a Bill to prohibit advertisements in public places in rural districts was introduced into the Commons but failed to obtain a second reading. It took until 1907 to secure a public Act, the Advertisements Regulation Act, which contained a provision expressly directed against or regulating advertisement hoardings or poster advertisements; low public sensitivity, combined with vested commercial interests which the 'public art' movement had to combat, ensured slow progress.

A variation on the design influence on planning was the Futurism movement launched in the Manifesto of F. T. Marinetti in 1909. He gathered round him a formidable group of painters, writers, thinkers, poets, musicians and architects who, in a desire to break with the past, sought to create new and dynamic art forms. The New City in architecture was one of the ingredients, and there developed a technological mania about future cities. New transit systems were devised, for example, in futuristic schemes that bore little resemblance to the street networks of the city of that time. Antonio Sant' Elia, a young Italian architect, exhibited a visionary project in Milan in 1914 called 'La Citta Nuova', which showed impressionistic sketches of a multi-level city of towering buildings and elevated roads. Planning was seen to be a matter for dramatic new invention or speculation. H. G. Wells' *When the Sleeper Wakes* (1899) was printed with illustrations of a science-fiction type. Visionaries dreamed of the ideal future; William Morris' *News From Nowhere* (1890) showed how London of the next century might be. Architects conceived new utopian schemes; for example Tony Garnier, a French architectural student, designed his 'Cité Industrielle' as a project between 1904 and 1917[26].

Summary

The town planning movement took shape as a result of the coming together of a number of influences. Of primary importance was the intellectual response to the industrial urban scene of 19th century Britain. The association in men's minds between ugliness, squalor and poverty, compared with the possibility of attractive new futures, stimulated new attitudes. On the one hand there were those who rejected the machine age and its urban products; on the other there were those who would reform and adapt it. In this setting, what ultimately emerged as a town planning movement began with a number of different strands of thought and action concerned with the problems of modern industrialization and the city. Within that context matters came to a head towards the end of the century from a number of influences which were more specific in character. In Britain the question of housing reform was now more urgent than ever; a Royal Commission in 1885, a wave of protest literature and the spectacle of new legislation still failing to get to the heart of the matter, could be set against real though limited achievements in the experiments of the industrial benefactors. On the Continent the new design movement gathered momentum and built on the traditions of city planning already laid, particularly in Germany.

To ascribe dates to developments as fluid and inconclusive as broad movements like these is very difficult; it can indeed be even misleading to attempt it. But we can usually say that before a certain date and after another situations were essentially different, and between those dates we might recognize formative years. Perhaps the decade 1895–1905 represents such a period. Certainly it is remarkable that during this period internationalism in planning made distinct advances, for the previous impression of separate and autochthonous movements became one of international co-ordination around some clearly defined principles. The term 'town planning' itself was born in 1906.

We have seen in earlier pages how there were already similarities in approaches to urban questions among different countries, although each one made its contribution. The public works approach in continental cities had some echo in Britain; the emphasis on housing reform and social matters in Britain was also being taken up in France; the recognition of new approaches to public art and urban form, stimulated in Vienna, was not without reflection in London; the German emphasis on municipal control and scheme preparation backed up by legislation was recommended in Britain as something that this country should embrace; workers' housing projects which came to brilliant fruition at Bournville were also taken up in continental centres such as in Krupp's colonies in Germany.

This was a period of considerable intellectual activity about city problems. In Britain the idea of new settlements held out great promise and indeed it was this contribution, popularized by Ebenezer Howard, that did so much to bring together the various threads. It is to this and related influences and their consequences that we should now turn.

References

1. Weber, Adna Ferrin, *The Growth of Cities in the Nineteenth Century*. Macmillan, New York, 1899.
2. Weber, Adna Ferrin, *The Growth of Cities in the Nineteenth Century*. Macmillan, New York, 1899.

31

3. This section is based on Dewsnup, Ernest Ritson, *The Housing Problem in England: its Statistics, Legislation and Policy*. Manchester University Press, 1907.

4. Thompson, W., *The Housing Handbook*. National Housing Reform Council, Leicester, 1903.

5. Marr, T. R., *Housing Conditions in Manchester and Salford*. Sherratt and Hughes, Manchester and London, 1904.

6. King, Anthony D., Introduction to *Town Swamps and Social Bridges* by George Godwin, London, 1859; Leicester University Press, 1972.

7. Dyos, H. J., The Slums of Victorian London. *Victorian Studies*, **XI**, No. 1, 1967.

8. Fried, Albert and Elman, Richard (Eds.), *Charles Booth's London*. Hutchinson, London, 1969.

9. Booth, General William, *In Darkest England and the Way Out*. Salvation Army, 1890.

10. Dyos, H. J., The Slums of Victorian London. *Victorian Studies*, **XI**, No. 1, 1967.

11. Dyos, H. J., The Slums of Victorian London. *Victorian Studies*, **XI**, No. 1, 1967.

12. For further reading see: Cherry, Gordon E., *Town Planning in Its Social Context*. Leonard Hill Books, London, 1970. Cherry, Gordon, E., *Urban Change and Planning*. G. T. Foulis, Henley-on-Thames, 1972.

13. George, W. L., *Labour and Housing at Port Sunlight*. Alston Rivers, 1909.

14. *The Bournville Village Trust, 1900–1955*. Bournville Village Trust, Birmingham, 1955.

15. George, W. L., *Labour and Housing at Port Sunlight*. Alston Rivers, 1909.

16. Culpin, Edward G., *Garden City Movement Up to Date*. Garden Cities and Town Planning Association, 1913.

17. A useful review is given in *International Cities and Town Planning Exhibition Catalogue*. Gothenburg International Federation for Housing and Town Planning, 1923.

18. Sutcliffe, Anthony, *The Autumn of Central Paris: the Defeat of Town Planning 1850–1970*. Edward Arnold, London, 1970.

19. Triggs, H. Inigo, *Town Planning: Past, Present and Future*. Methuen, London, 1909.

20. Wolf, Peter M., *Eugène Hénard and the Beginning of Urbanism in Paris, 1900–14*. International Federation for Housing and Planning, 1968.

21. Horsfall, T. C., *The Improvement of the Dwellings and Surroundings of the People: the Example of Germany*. Manchester University Press, 1904.

22. McKelvey, Blake, *The Urbanization of America, 1860–1915*. Rutgers University Press, 1963.

23. Collins, G. R. and C. C., *Camillo Sitte and the Birth of Modern City Planning*. Phaidon Press, London, 1965.

24. Lethaby, W. R., *Of Beautiful Cities*. Arts and Crafts Exhibition Society, 1897.

25. Briggs, Asa, The Victorian City: Quantity and Quality. *Victorian Studies*, **XI**, No. 4, 1968.

26. Webenson, Dora, Utopian Aspects of Tony Garnier's Cité Industrielle. *Journal of the Society of Architectural Historians*, **19**, 1960.

3 The Founding of the Institute

In this chapter we look at the early years of the 20th century, before the outbreak of the First World War, during which period the planning movement developed rapidly and assumed an increasingly recognizable identity. By 1914, we can say that town planning had arrived, the product of a decade or so of interlinked events. The outcome was the first planning legislation in 1909, the emergence and partial development of a coherent body of knowledge and practice, the beginnings of planning education in Universities and the establishment of a new professional body, the Town Planning Institute. The steps by which these were achieved were interlinked, and it is difficult to give a precise identity to the separate influences that shaped the course of events.

The immediate background was formed by the social and political context of Edwardian Britain[1]. The 19th century trends which we have noted in chapter 2 continued and certain features were thrown into prominence. Important demographic changes could now be recognized. The birth rate had begun to fall in the 1870s, and from 36.3 per thousand for England and Wales in 1876 the figure fell to 28.5 in 1901 and 24.1 in 1913. This meant that in 1881, for example, for every million persons in England and Wales there had been 135 000 children aged under five years; in 1901 there were 114 000 and in 1911 there were 106 000 children of this age group. Britain was no longer a 'young' country. Improvements in health were recorded: a sharply falling death rate brought the figure from 16.9 per thousand in 1901 to 13.8 in 1913. Infant mortality rates fell more sharply, from 151 per thousand live births in 1901 to 108 in 1913.

These improvements represented advances in medical health rather than in urban conditions. The urban problem first seen by the Victorians as a stimulating challenge, was now a perplexing burden. New evidence of ill-health and bad conditions among the working classes, and of overcrowding and smoke pollution was collected by the Inter-Departmental Committee on Physical Deterioration, set up by the Balfour Government in 1903. A generation of young people was now growing up which had been born in towns and urban ill-health was widespread. The underlying causes associated with housing problems were well known, but there were other factors involved. For example, a study of West Ham in 1907 blamed casual and irregular labour for the worst social and industrial evils[2]. Beveridge's pioneering survey, *Unemployment, a Problem of Industry* appeared in 1909.

Other problems for urban management were emerging. A. R. Sennet put it quaintly in 1896: 'The days of long-distance road travelling by horse-drawn vehicles are over, but the days for the production by our engineers and carriage-builders of self-propelling equipages worthy of our position among nations are with us.'[3] Within a very short space of time this new development was not only adding to congestion problems but helping to give a further spatial spread to cities. The word 'suburbia' had been coined in the 1890s and the social phenomenon of the suburbs was reviewed in C. F. G. Masterman's widely read book *The Condition of England* (1909). The movement of the suburbanites was noted. *The Birmingham Mail* in 1903 expressed it vividly: 'Like the Arab, they are folding their tents and stealing silently away in the direction of Knowle or Solihull...a little revolution is in progress.'[4]

In contrast, the rural problem was perhaps checked. The downward trend in rural depopulation slackened. At least, labourers left on the land enjoyed protection against accidents (1900) and insurance against sickness (1911). But rural housing conditions were poor, and wages stayed below the poverty line. Agriculture was depressed.

The other important feature in this background context was the political scene. Significant developments took place. At the beginning of the century municipal freedom and enterprise was at a peak. A network of *ad hoc* authorities was superceded by a full coverage of popularly elected, multi-purpose authorities: County Councils in 1888 and County Boroughs, Municipal Boroughs and District Councils in 1894. But municipal 'socialism' lost ground when central government developed its own intervention, so much so that by 1914 important political issues were centred round, not municipal activities, but state policies. The Liberals were in power from 1905 to 1915, and before 1914 at least this was a period of social reform. Only slowly did the Liberals become a party of reform (the issue was not prominent in the 1906 election), but important measures were passed. In 1906 local authorities were permitted to arrange school meals; school medical inspection was authorized in 1907; pensions were provided in 1908, and health and unemployment insurance followed in 1911. It is significant that the first town planning legislation in 1909 fell in this period.

Within this context the development of town planning was influenced from a number of different directions. First there were the activities of a number of propagandist bodies; second, there were the results of inter-professional relationships, particularly after the 1909 Act; and third, there were contributions made by particular people whose range of interest often defy categorization. To these matters we can now turn.

THE PROPAGANDIST SOCIETIES

The Garden City Movement had roots well into the 19th century, and in the last chapter we noted the context in which it came to the fore at the turn of the century. The Continent pointed to a number of precedents. A number of cities in Germany and Austria were expanding in the form of garden suburbs; the idea of a ring of greenery round a metropolis had been under consideration in Vienna for some time, and certain aspects of the satellite idea had been incorporated in a book of 1896 by Theordor Fritsch, *Die Stadt der Zunkunft*. In America, planned suburban development on low density lines was favoured.

Weber concluded his statistical work on world cities with the remark that: 'The "rise of the suburbs" it is, which furnishes the solid basis of a hope that the evils of city life, so far as they result from overcrowding, may be in large part removed. If concentration of population seems destined to continue, it will be a modified concentration which offers the advantage of both city and country life.'[5]

In Britain, the idea of combatting urban growth and dealing with the housing problem by providing new settlements elsewhere was a popular one. General William Booth, for example, proposed 'self-helping and self-sustaining communities, each being a kind of co-operative society, or patriarchal society' as three types of colonies: the City Colony, the Farm Colony and the Over-Sea Colony[6]. The anarchist movement, through Peter Kropotkin and his *Fields, Factories and Workshops* published in 1898, encouraged the formation of small colonies supported by factory workshops and agriculture. A variation of the back-to-the land movement came from the Nationalization of Labour Society and the Land Nationalization Society. The American economist Henry George had a strong influence in Britain as city centre land values were held to be an important cause of the housing problem.

Ebenezer Howard's book *Tomorrow—a Peaceful Path to Real Reform*, published in 1898, was concerned with the satellite type of solution. He acknowledged the universal agreement that, 'it is deeply to be deplored that the people should continue to stream into the already over-crowded cities, and should thus further deplete the country districts'. Howard's solution was the Garden City, and when his book was republished in 1902 it was titled *Garden Cities of Tomorrow*. His promise was that in his new settlement it would be shown how 'equal, nay better, opportunities of social intercourse may be enjoyed than are enjoyed in any crowded city, while yet the beauties of nature may encompass and enfold each dweller therein; how higher wages are compatible with reduced rates and rents; how abundant opportunities for employment and bright prospects of advancement may be secured for all; how capital may be attracted and wealth created; how the most admirable sanitary conditions may be ensured; how beautiful homes and gardens may be seen on every land; how the bounds of freedom may be widened, and yet all the best results of concert and co-operation gathered in by a happy people'[7]. To achieve this he conceived the idea of a satellite town of 30 000 people, built at a distance from the parent city, and self-supporting by its own industry. Between the two there should be a permanent belt of open land used for agriculture. The ownership of the satellite town would be in the hands of the municipality and the unearned increment from the growth of the town would be reserved for the community as a whole.

A number of identical schemes were developed, and some similarity is shown by the plan for Adelaide, South Australia, prepared by Colonel Light of The Royal Engineers. Certainly, Howard's were not novel suggestions but his book had immediate practical results in the formation first of a Garden City Association and then of a Pioneer Company actually to build a Garden City. The Garden City Association was formed in June 1899, with the simple objectives 'to promote the discussion of the project suggested by Mr Ebenezer Howard in "Tomorrow" and ultimately to formulate a practical scheme on the lines of that project, with such modifications as may appear desirable'[8]. The aims were gradually expanded and it is interesting to recall the objects as approved in July 1903:

'To promote the relief of overcrowded and congested areas to secure a wider distribution of the population over the land, and to advance the moral, intellectual and physical development of the people by—

(a) Taking initial steps to establish Garden Cities in which the inhabitants shall become in a corporate capacity the owners of sites, subject to the fullest recognition of individual as well as public interest;

(b) Encouraging the tendency of manufacturers and others to move from crowded centres to rural districts, co-operating with such manufacturers and with public bodies in securing healthy housing accommodation for the work people in proximity to the places of employment;

(c) Co-operating with other organizations in promoting legislation to enlarge the powers of public authorities with a view to securing a solution of the housing problem and improved systems of communication;

(d) Stimulating interest in and promoting the scientific development of towns so that the evils arising from the haphazard growth may in future be avoided;

(e) Promoting the erection of sanitary and beautiful dwellings with adequate space for gardens and reception.'

The words 'town planning' had not yet appeared in these rules but this was the first coherent pronouncement of any society or body in Britain in its favour. The set of objectives indicated the rapid changes that were taking place in both formalizing and making operational a body of thought about the new subject matter.

The name of the Association was changed in 1907 to the Garden Cities and Town Planning Association. In 1908 its monthly journal which had been started in 1904 was changed from *The Garden City* to *Garden Cities and Town Planning*. The Aims of the Association were amended, and in July 1909 the following objects were adopted:

(a) To promote Town Planning

(b) To advise on, draw up schemes for, and establish Garden Cities, Garden Suburbs and Garden Villages

(c) Housing and the improvement of its sanitation

(d) The collection and publication of information as to the above

(e) The education of public opinion by lantern lectures, cheap literature, conferences, for example

(f) The influencing and promotion of legislation

(g) The improvement of local by-laws.

As a propagandist body it had taken coherent shape and from the start had very great influence on the planning movement. Compared with other societies, which are outlined below, it was not so much a political body, concerned with influencing political opinion directly, but one which relied on attracting attention to its 'higher' social purpose as enshrined in the utopian Garden City and the ideals of its founder. Its influence in the formative years of the first decade of the century was essentially threefold. It was first and foremost a practical body; it had an enormous impact on planning thought elsewhere in Europe and America; and on the home scene it provided a forum for a number of people many of whom were to become leading members of the first generation of town planners.

A prominent lawyer, Ralph Neville became Chairman of the Association in 1901 and

Ebenezer Howard, 1850–1928, founder of the Garden City movement. Entirely devoted to his creations, he lived at Letchworth from 1905 and at Welwyn from 1921. He was President of the International Housing and Town Planning Federation, and knighted in 1927. (*Courtesy of Town and Country Planning Association*)

Garden City Strategy, Ebenezer Howard, *Tomorrow: A Peaceful Path to Real Reform*, 1898. This is a diagram that sums up much of the garden city concept: medium-sized, self-contained satellites in a functional relationship to a parent city, making the most of an agricultural hinterland and a rural setting.

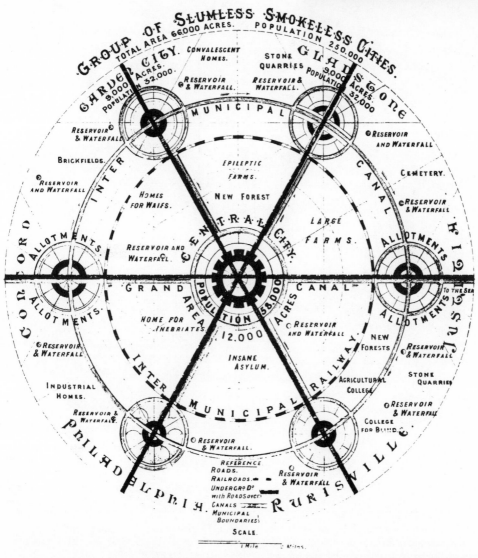

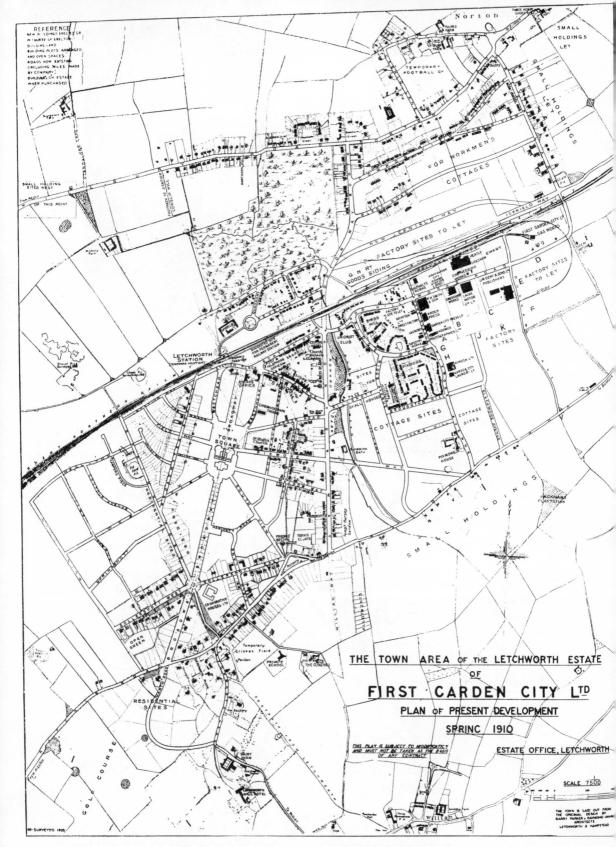

Letchworth, plan by Barry Parker and Raymond Unwin. This was the first attempt in Britain at building a complete, self-contained town of 30 000 people, according to Howard's principles. The plan differed greatly from Howard's ideal scheme and was an adaptation to the peculiarities of the site.

when the Cadburys, W. H. Lever and Alfred Harmsworth all gave their support to Howard's ideas, a Pioneer Company was formed in 1902. In the following year the Letchworth estate was purchased, a company was formed to develop the land and the first Garden City was laid out during the next few years. Raymond Unwin and his partner Barry Parker won a design competition and architectural form was given to Howard's strategic principles. By 1914, 9 000 people were living there where only 400 had lived before. Howard showed that better living and working conditions could be provided by the co-ordination of private enterprise on a profitable basis. The subsequent development is traced by C. B. Purdom in *The Letchworth Achievement* (1963). By the outbreak of war there were many developments on Garden City lines throughout the country. Letchworth remained the only Garden City until Welwyn was begun in 1920. Howard wanted a second experiment, and when King Edward VII died in 1910 he had tried to get support for another garden city, as an international memorial, called King Edward's Town.

Meanwhile Garden Suburbs and Garden Villages continued to provide new opportunities for planned residential development at low densities. Hampstead Garden Suburb was laid out from 1907 onwards, also to the designs of Unwin, and soon became one of the best known examples of this type of development. In Manchester, Alkrington Hall Estate was laid out from 1911 onwards on low density lines although a Garden City Company was not formed. In Bristol, a Bristol Garden Suburb Limited was formed in 1909. A Cardiff Workers' Garden Village Society was established for a small suburban development there. Coventry had a Garden Suburb, Hertfordshire had its Cuffley Garden Village, Wolverhampton its Fallings Park Garden Suburb, and Romford its Garden Suburb at Gidea Park. Ilford had a scheme, Merthyr had a Co-operative Garden Village, Oldham a Garden Suburb, and so too did Southampton and Warrington. These are just a few examples to show how the ideal of the Garden City was harnessed to the technical skills and specialized knowledge of enlightened estate development throughout the country.

The Garden City idea spread rapidly. G. Montagu Harris wrote a small tract in 1906, *The Garden City Movement*, complete with a foreword by Howard; it was adopted as the official Handbook of the Association. The practical achievements of suburban estate layout went hand in hand with a rediscovered idealism. A. R. Sennett's two volumes *Garden Cities in Theory and Practice*, published in 1905, captured the 19th century utopian ring. Volume One begins, '"A Garden City"! To the summer toilers in our smoke-beshrouded towns, half suffocated in their narrow, stagnant streets, half grilled by the reverberated heat of imprisoning buildings, overwrought and oppressed—how refreshing the name! To them, what a vista of freedom, of light, of air, of sky!'[9] This social fervour found form in the contribution of Unwin and others to suburban architecture, a unique British offering around which town planning was centred in its early days.

On the Continent, the Garden City was also favourably received. Similar experiments had begun to pave the way, and Sitte's challenge to the engineering supremacy in city layout allowed for an enthusiastic response. In Germany, Fritsch's *Die Stadt der Zunkunft*, a standard text of 1896, had *Gartenstadt* added to the title in the second edition of 1912. *Gartenstadt* was also the title of a monthly magazine popularizing this form of development. A number of Garden Suburb schemes were started as at Hellerau, near Dresden, Altona near Hamburg, Stockfeld near Strassburg, and another near Berlin. Margaretenhohe near Essen was built by the Krupp family on Bournville lines, and there were many instances of co-partnership housing schemes. In France a Garden City Association was founded in 1904 under the guidance of George Benoit-Levy, and this example was followed by other countries later. An International Garden Cities and Town Planning Association was formed in August, 1913; 18 countries were represented on the Committee.

As a forum of thought and action the Association in Britain was a considerable influence. Thomas Adams, the first permanent secretary of the Association, and first manager of Letchworth, ultimately became the first President of the Town Planning Institute, and the Association had other members who became prominent figures in the new professional body when it was formed: Raymond Unwin, for example, and G. Montagu Harris, W. R. Davidge, George L. Pepler, Patrick Geedes and S. D. Adshead. From the start, the Association was able to secure important patronage for joint meetings. A conference in October 1907, for example, held in Guildhall, London, had the Presidency of the Lord Mayor of London. Over a hundred local authorities were represented together with an interesting and impressive range of complementary bodies: the First Garden City Limited, Hampstead Suburb Trust, Association of Municipal Corporations, Co-partnership Tenants Limited, Royal Institution of British Architects, Society of Architects, Institute of Sanitary Engineers, Metropolitan Public Gardens Association, Mansion House Council on the Dwellings of the Poor, Housing Reform Council, Incorporated Institute of Hygiene, Surveyors Institution, Land Nationalization Society, Co-partnership Tenants Housing Council, Institute of Builders, League of Physical Education and the Sociological Society. The function of the Association in bringing together such a disparate collection for the first time in Britain (international conferences had been held on the Continent for some years) was important at this stage.

It went further than any other single organization in advocating a course of action to which a range of individual bodies could subscribe. At this conference, Councillor J. S. Nettleford, Chairman of Birmingham Housing Committee, moved this resolution: 'That this meeting...affirms its belief that the present planless and haphazard extension of towns is detrimental to the best interests of the nation, in as much as, by the creation of new slums and overcrowding, it produces mental, moral, and physical degeneration, and is also burdensome to the ratepayers; it, therefore, calls upon all parties to welcome the Government's promise of legislation upon the matter'. From pressure of this type, widely supported, came developments in town planning which ultimately paved the way for the rise of a professional association.

Another propagandist society was the National Housing Reform Council. Its aims were 'To educate and stimulate public opinion and local authorities so that the fullest possible use may be made of existing Housing and Sanitary legislation. To urge that Parliament shall remove from municipalities and societies of public utility those shackles which cripple or make difficult the execution of housing schemes and to promote experiments and organizations tending to secure better and cheaper methods of town planning, local development and house building'. It was founded at the turn of the century through the initiative of Henry R. Aldridge of Leicester, who was connected with the Land Nationalization movement[10]. During the course of his lectures in the North of England, throughout the 1890s, meetings with miners' leaders were held and the idea of the Council

S. Nettlefold, Birmingham Councillor, Chairman of the
ousing Committee and propagandist for town planning.
e was instrumental in the development of the Harborne
enants Scheme in Birmingham. (*Courtesy of* Mrs Evelyn
osskey)

arch 1912, complimentary dinner to Ebenezer Howard,
ven by the Garden Cities and Town Planning Associa-
n, Holborn Restaurant, London. Howard is the short
gure on the left of the three standing at the head table.
homas Adams is on the extreme right at the end of the
ng table in the foreground. (*Courtesy of* Mrs Constance
dams)

arose. This enabled the campaign for housing reform to be carried on even more energetically through lectures, tours and conferences, and cottage exhibitions.

The immediate importance of the Council stemmed from one of these very conferences. At one held in conjunction with the Workmen's National Housing Council during the Trades Union Congress at Leeds in 1904, a resolution was moved for the adoption of town planning (although it was not yet referred to by those words) in Britain. The mover of the resolution was T. C. Horsfall, Chairman of the Manchester Citizens' Association and advocate of German advances in planning. The resolution was passed unanimously and this marked the beginnings of the campaign for town planning legislation.

In November 1906, the Council organized a deputation to the Prime Minister, Sir Henry Campbell-Bannerman, and John Burns, the President of the Local Government Board, submitting a suggested programme of housing and town planning legislation. The Prime Minister pledged that legislation would be introduced as soon as circumstances permitted. The deputation advocated a number of reforms covering housing and public health, the creation of model suburbs, a simplified procedure for compulsory purchase of land, a proposed Town and Village Development Commission, town extension planning and availability of cheaper money. The deputation was led by Alderman William Thompson, the Chairman of the Council, an author of a number of books on housing matters, a London schoolmaster and member of Richmond (Surrey) Town Council; his party consisted of 16 others including George Cadbury, the Bishop of Wakefield, T. C. Horsfall and others[11].

The delegation were not to be disappointed at least in the fact of legislation, although Cadbury was very disillusioned with the content (see p. 64). A Bill was introduced in 1908. It passed through the Second Reading Stage without opposition, but only left the Standing Committee in December that year, a few days before the end of the parliamentary session. The Government decided to place the Bill aside until the following session. It was reintroduced in 1909 and by general consent the procedure was shortened by considering it in a Committee of the whole House. The Housing, Town Planning etc Act, 1909 is referred to in more detail in chapter 4.

The Council, which changed its name to the National Housing and Town Planning Council in 1909 clearly played an important part in the movement for housing reform and town planning. Its annual income at this time shows it to be larger than that of the Garden Cities and Town Planning Association (£1 275 as against £600 in the year 1911–12). Henry Aldridge as secretary was certainly indefatigable in popularizing the idea of town planning and housing reform as a function of local government. He concentrated on educating elected representatives and influencing public opinion; in 1911–12, for example, the Council organized three national conferences and 12 district conferences while Aldridge himself delivered 52 lectures in 23 towns that winter. Although the Council was not so much concerned with the technical aspects of planning, many of the early TPI members, notably Raymond Unwin, were associated with its work.

A third propagandist society advocating town planning was the Co-partnership Tenants Housing Council, the chief proponent of which was Henry Vivian. This advocated and assisted the foundation of Public Utility companies to develop garden suburbs on co-partnership lines. Though the ideas of low density development were embraced in association with co-partnership organizations, they were not crucial to the Council and the first such suburb at Ealing (1888) was initially developed at densities higher than then prevailing. A large number of these suburbs were built or projected. Apart from Ealing, two extensions of Hampstead Garden Suburb were accomplished by these means, as was the Harborne Garden Suburb at Birmingham. No schemes were to be more than about 500 houses, this being regarded as the comfortable maximum for co-partnership development. It seems likely that the interests of the Council increasingly merged with those of the Garden Cities and Town Planning Association, and by 1913–14 Henry Vivian was a member of the Council of that body.

Other associations should be mentioned, which, incidental to their main concern— often housing—were interested in town planning. The Workmen's National Housing Council was one such body. Other important bodies joined the campaign for the passing of the 1909 Act, though town planning was not by any means their primary concern. Of these, we should note the Association of Municipal Corporations, which prepared its own draft of a Town Planning Bill. Birmingham City Council was also influential; J. S. Nettlefold, Neville Chamberlain and George Cadbury Jnr were Councillors who took an early interest. Other bodies which lent support and shared a growing interest in town planning were the professional bodies and it is to these that we should now turn.

THE PROFESSIONAL BODIES

Marian Bowley, in her study of the building industry, has described the position of the different design professions before 1914, and their attitudes to each other, as follows: 'The architects were members of a profession concerned with a major art, they were the confidants of gentlemen, and to a considerable extent, arbiters of taste. Successful architects at least were members of the upper middle class elite. They were gentlemen, or regarded as such. Engineers on the other hand were closely associated with trade and industry; their training had no cultural significance; they were not artists; they might be industrialists. In the nineteenth century social stratification they were not regarded quite as gentlemen, although some aristocrats had made notable contributions to engineering. Certainly, they seem to have been regarded by architects as their social inferiors... Surveyors of all sorts were even more inferior.'[12] This was the sociological context in which the planning profession was, itself, created.

The Royal Institute of British Architects had been founded, after a number of false starts, in 1834, and secured a Royal Charter almost immediately in 1837. During the 19th century it grew increasingly separate from the other design professions, although in the early days there had been considerable overlap with engineers and surveyors, or rather the groups from which these professions grew. The divorce of interests from the engineers was the most complete, the Institution of Civil Engineers having been formed in 1818, receiving a Charter in 1828.

The ICE was the parent professional body of all the engineering bodies. During the 19th century, however, there was a proliferation of engineering institutions dealing with particular aspects of the subject, in response to development of new applications of engineering knowledge. One of these—the one most intimately concerned with town

43

planning—was the Incorporated Association of Municipal and County Engineers founded in 1873 (and known after 1909 as the Institution of Municipal and County Engineers). Its objects were defined as: 'The promotion of the science and practice of engineering applied to the health and improvement of counties and towns and rural districts.' The relationship between the IMCE and the ICE by 1914 was rather complicated. It appears that any member of the latter who was engaged on work that fell within that defined by the Municipal and County Engineers was likely to be a member of both Institutions. However, they were usually styled only as members of the Institution of Civil Engineers. It seems that the junior Institution was the first engineering Institution to introduce qualification by examination, so that increasing numbers of its membership were qualifying solely as municipal and county engineers, and were styled as such. Most members, whether so styled or not, were, as their name suggests, employed as local government technical officers; they were the borough engineers and surveyors, and it was in this capacity they come into contact with town planning.

The Surveyors' Institution tended to be composed of surveyors in private practice, acting on behalf of landowners. The Institution had been founded in 1868, and received a Royal Charter in 1881. Thus, though it was fairly well established by comparison with the Municipal and County Engineers, it was rather less so than the Architects and Civil Engineers. In view of this, it is perhaps necessary to modify Bowley's description when applying it to the formal associations of professions. The established professions were architecture and civil engineering, while surveying was still a slightly upstart profession, though increasingly respectable. On the other hand, the Municipal and County Engineers were still a young body and anxious to gain recognition and approval.

The last of the parent professions, law, was an old and respected body. The Law Society had been formed in 1739, though the legal profession went back to the Middle Ages. There seemed to be no dispute that law had a place in town planning, and it seems that the legal profession took considerable interest in the 1909 Act, together with associated legislation, which had many novel features.

Each of the land-based professions felt they had a claim in planning and each was mutually jealous or suspicious of the other. The passing of the 1909 Act gave a new attention to town planning beyond the activities of propagandist bodies and their projects, and there was competition for supremacy in handling the statutory powers in preparing schemes.

The architects were the first professional body to consider town planning. A memorandum, addressed in December 1904 to local authorities regarding muncipal buildings of architectural importance, pointed out 'that when the official is an engineer or surveyor, the artistic aspect of buildings designed by him is apt to be overlooked or misunderstood by reason of his not having received the artistic training of the architect'[13]. Instead, the work should be done by a RIBA member as a municipal official or in the case of large works, as an independent practitioner. The Institute took the view that the problems of town extension and suburban growth were not solely matters for the engineer and borough surveyor. This initiative was followed in November 1907, when a Development of Towns and Suburbs Committee (later to be called the Town Planning Committee) of the RIBA was formed with reference to the Town Planning Bill, and they sent a deputation to John Burns, President of the Local Government Board, urging the case of architects' advisory committees.

In October 1910, the RIBA accomplished its major work, the Town Planning Conference, a massive affair which represented a major triumph for the architectural view of planning. For his services in organization, Raymond Unwin was elevated to a Fellow of the Institute. Reporting the conference in the *Town Planning Review*, Adshead, by training an architect, noted that 'The passing of the Act seems to have roused the interest of the whole profession, who, feeling that Town Planning was essentially and firstly a matter with which the architect was concerned, thought fit to give public expression to their views.'[14] By any standards the conference was a superlative affair. The Plans, Drawings and Models which were shown at the Royal Academy made for a fine exhibition. Under the patronage of the King, the list of 64 Honorary Vice-Presidents including the Archbishop of Canterbury, the Maharaja of Baroda, a string of Bishops, Dukes and Earls, Kitchener of Khartoum and a range of well-known names from Thomas Hardy to Ebenezer Howard. More than 1 300 representatives including those from over 200 different Corporations, Councils and Societies attended. The Transactions of the Conference were published in a massive volume of more than 800 pages; 43 separate papers were delivered, and discussions recorded[15]. Site visits were made to places including Letchworth, Bournville and Hampstead Garden Suburb. The whole affair was an impressive indication of the position reached by the new activity, town planning.

The conference focussed the attention of the whole profession, and helped bring about a change in attitudes both within the RIBA and outside it. One thing became clear: it was no longer adequate to regard town planning as the prerogative of the architect, being the fountain head of good taste; town planning was something more and demanded practical solutions on a wide front. The August 1911 Report of the Town Planning Committee, 'Suggestions to Promoters of Town Planning Schemes', indicates this change. Though promulgated by a group who were to the fore in advocating town planning (including Unwin, Adshead, Beresford Pite, Lanchester and Aston Webb), nevertheless it was adopted as official RIBA policy. Basically, while it did not move from the position that the problem of town planning in its final form was essentially an architectural problem, it was admitted that 'The preparation of all the data upon which the design must be based hardly falls within the province of the architect, and it would seem that this formulation of the city's requirements, and of the limits within which the designer must work is the proper sphere of the surveyor (aided, of course, by the engineer, the valuer, the economist, the sociologist and the antiquarian).'[16] The emphasis placed here on the surveyor is interesting: the differences of view between architects and surveyors were less than that with the engineers. John Burns praised this report and called upon engineers and surveyors to prepare similar reports from their points of view.

From this 1911 position, the spirit of inter-professional co-operation advanced further, and in July 1912, a conference of members of the Royal Academy, the Institution of Civil Engineers, the Surveyors' Institution, and the Institution of Municipal and County Engineers met at the RIBA, and addressed a letter to the Prime Minister on the problems of unco-ordinated town planning schemes in Greater London, and their effect on arterial roads. In July 1913, a joint deputation met Asquith and Burns and a joint conference was arranged, with Burns presiding (see also p. 69).

Within the architectural profession over this period, a fairly introspective professionalism was replaced by increasing willingness to co-operate with other institutions. However, it should not be forgotten, for it is crucial to an understanding of the subsequent formation of the Town Planning Institute, that this progressiveness depended on a small group of architects, many of whom were on the Town Planning Committee, who were more advanced in their understanding of the situation than the rest of the profession.

The Municipal and County Engineers began taking an interest in town planning about 1906. In that year, for example, Horsfall addressed them on the 'Planning and Control of Town Extension in Germany'. By June 1907, a special committee was discussing problems associated with planning with the National Housing Reform Council, and in his Presidential Address of that month, John A. Brodie, Chief Engineer of Liverpool, discussed 'the two subjects which are now occupying so prominent a place in municipal and public opinion—viz the laying out of towns and the requirements of improved access by means of roads'[17]. Clearly it was felt that municipal engineers and surveyors would play a leading part in this, though they recognized that co-operation with the other professions was necessary. The introduction of the Housing, Town Planning etc Bill increased interest, when it became evident that the preparation of schemes would be chiefly the duty of the borough or city engineer.

During the 1909–10 session, a Town Planning Committee was set up and the engineers began, in more detail, to consider the problems of statutory town planning from a practical point of view. Though the principle of co-operation was recognized, some engineers actually engaged in statutory scheme preparation had no delusion about their own position. Consider, for example, the following remark by Henry Stilgoe, City Engineer of Birmingham, in a reply during the discussion on his paper 'Town Planning in the Light of the Housing, Town Planning etc Act, 1909' in June 1910: 'I think the people who administer it [the 1909 Act] will be the borough engineers and surveyors of this country. It is their right. They are the officials, the statutory officials, appointed under the Public Health Act, and without their co-operation, and, in fact, without their intimate knowledge of their districts, this Act cannot be put into proper and efficient working order…what we want is men who will come forward and with a bold scheme, leaving the little matters, good as they are, the small garden suburbs, to develop of themselves. We must drive forward the great engineering works. The others will follow. Those people who talk so much about town planning do not know what they want; would not know what to do with it if given the opportunity'[18].

The engineers were very sensitive to professional claims in this new area of town planning. Many years later, T. H. Mawson recalled the 1910 RIBA Conference, particularly Beresford Pite's address, 'The Architect and Town Planning', when he remarked that 'The town is too precious a possibility if not already a possession of beauty, to be entrusted to the consideration only of its expert surveyors and engineers. The problems are architectural and will ultimately be judged as such.' Mawson recollected: 'Just as this statement was offered, a borough engineer sitting next to me exclaimed with evident opposition and deep resentment, "I'm sure they won't!". To him all town planning problems came within the sphere of his direction and he was not prepared to hand them over to the architect or anyone else without a struggle'[19].

The Institution organized conferences on Housing and Town Planning in West Bromwich, Great Yarmouth and Cheltenham. They were not the grand occasions that the RIBA Conference had proved, but their Proceedings offer a useful insight into the engineer's developing approach to town planning.

At West Bromwich in July 1911, for example, the generally accepted position was stated by Albert D. Greatorex, the Borough Surveyor of West Bromwich. With regard to the carrying out of the Act, 'Who, after all, is better able and qualified than the local surveyor, by reason of his knowledge of not only the internal working of the Act, but by his general knowledge as to what is necessary as regards the development of the district, and the lines which it should take?' The point was pressed home by John A. Brodie: 'Specialists may be of use in certain cases, other professions may give useful help and advice, but the real planning of the main outlines of the town in the first instance, and to some extent also the filling in, must be the work of the municipal engineer'. Professor Adshead, although an architect, thought that 'the problem of town planning rests in the first place with the municipal engineer', and Thomas Adams, then of the Local Government Board, acknowledged that only in one or two of the larger cities were professional men, other than the municipal surveyor, engaged in planning work. But he added: 'no doubt it is desirable that there should be other experts engaged; there is room, not only for the municipal engineer, and not only for the architect, but for men who have studied the question from other points of view, the doctor, the economist, the housing reformer'[20].

As time went on, the engineers' conferences and meetings became more open, in that they were addressed and attended by architects, lawyers, surveyors and landscape architects. Basically, however, the engineers tended to be introspective and since they were in possession of statutory authority under the Act, it put them in the position of first being eyed with envy and suspicion, and later courted by the other professions. Certainly the instigation of a professional examination—the first—in Town Planning by the Institution of Municipal and County Engineers in about 1914, tends to reinforce this impression of a self-centred profession, though since the Institution was still a relatively new body, it might also be interpreted as an attempt to win further adherence as the professional body for municipal technical officers.

A modification of this general impression, as with the architects, is that there was a small group (perhaps four or five) who were prepared to take the initiative and look beyond the single professional viewpoint. These four or five occupied important positions in their profession and considerable prestige outside. Though they retained their engineering outlook, they were prepared to talk with others and join in the development of a more balanced town planning organization.

Despite their related work in private estate development, the Surveyors' Institution, as a body, only really began to consider town planning as such when the Town Planning Bill was before Parliament. In 1908 a memorandum concerning the Bill was drawn up and submitted, in which they expressed 'cordial support' with the objects of the Bill but made suggestions to effect its smoother operation[21]. In his Presidential Address in 1909, Alexander Stenning, stressed that while town planning was a step away from the older system, it was not socialism—a point of importance to the surveyors who largely represented landowners rather than local authorities. He called for the nationwide adoption of Garden Cities and Town Planning, stressing the development of planning by enlightened employers.

In November 1909, W. R. Davidge presented a paper to the Institution on 'Town Planning Systems', which considered types of planned layouts. It affords useful evidence as to the place of the surveyor in planning. He was modest, compared to the forthrightness of architects and engineers: 'The best advice obtainable must be secured and thus will, no doubt, be readily and cheerfully given by surveyors, architects, valuers and all concerned with the material development of the town'. With regard to the operation of the Act, he thought that 'it is not too much to hope that our profession will be privileged to perform its share of the great work'[22].

However, there was one aspect of town planning which affected surveyors, and set them acting on behalf of their clients, potentially at odds with the borough engineers. This was the question of landowners initiating schemes, and it was hoped that good working arrangements would develop between landowners and local authorities. Leslie Vigers examined this question of the private surveyor in town planning in his Presidential Address; while it was impossible to tell immediately what the impact of the Act would be, there was definite unease about the potentialities of collective land use control. The question of development tax on land was an associated aspect of this concern.

Thus the Surveyors' Institute did not stake a total claim to town planning, as the two other professions had done, but it wanted a say in the process and was suspicious of planning purely by municipal authorities. Nevertheless, as we have noted in the other professions, there was a small number of surveyors who were interesting themselves in town planning and the broader issues. Several of them were associated with the Garden City Association. They were to form part of the inter-professional nucleus that made up the TPI.

OTHER FACTORS IN THE DEVELOPMENT OF PLANNING

The ten years preceding the outbreak of war were a period of intense activity when reinforcing strands of thought and action pushed along the ideas and the practice of planning. At best it is a confused scene and only with hindsight can we separate out the various components for individual analysis. We have already considered the influence of the propagandist bodies and the sparring between professions. The planning movement also owed much to developments in other fields and these we review now: first the contribution of the 'new architecture', second the contribution of civics as applied sociology, third the influence of those who wore the reformist mantle, fourth the contributions to literature and the build-up of a core of knowledge, and last developments in the Universities.

New developments in residential architecture formed an important source of inspiration to town planning. Raymond Unwin and Barry Parker, related through marriage, were outstanding in their contribution to the development of site-planning both in theory and practice[23]. They have a particular place in the history of planning, standing astride the old order and the new; they formed a practical link between the Victorian social and housing reformers and central government housing programmes of the 1920s and later. Their work linked the Arts and Crafts movement to town planning.

Unwin began working in Manchester in 1885 at the age of 22 as a draughtsman-fitter attached to a cotton mill. He became a member of the Manchester Socialist Society, much influenced by Edward Carpenter, the socialist poet, and William Morris. When Morris founded the Manchester Branch of his Socialist League in 1886, Unwin was its first secretary. Between 1887 and 1896 he was head draughtsman and subsequently engineer and architect for the Staveley Coal and Iron Co in Derbyshire. In the 1890s he was engaged on cottage design and in 1896 he joined Parker in architectural partnership at Buxton. They began to publish their ideas on architecture in a series of articles which culminated in a book of 1901, *The Art of Building a Home*. The breakthrough came when they were appointed joint architects for Earswick. The idea of lining roads with trees and grass verges first appeared here, to be developed further at Letchworth; cottages were designed with generous space standards, internal toilets and bathrooms, and their own gardens; a density of ten dwellings to the acre was averaged over the estate. The 150 acres originally purchased by Rowntree were bounded on the east by the River Foss and on the west by farmland in other ownerships; through the centre ran the main Haxby Road, and in contrast to Bournville, for example, there were no natural features for the designers to exploit. Unwin and Parker used this experiment as a prototype for later ideas.

At Letchworth, their plans incorporated culs-de-sac for the first time, the principle of zoning was established, and a proper pedestrian and vehicular circulation pattern was organized. The desirability of low density was maintained, with no more than 12 dwellings to the acre. At Hampstead, the cul-de-sac form of development was advocated, but it was found not to be permissable under local bye-laws. Consequently the Hampstead Garden Suburb Act was promoted by the Trustees, the Bill being introduced by Henry Vivian. The Act, passed in August 1906, might well be regarded as a model for later planning legislation; it conferred powers on the Trust 'to develop and layout lands as garden suburbs,' and some of the provisions were incorporated into the 1909 Act. The contributions of Unwin and Parker continued for another 30 years or more, and frequent mention of their subsequent activities is made in later chapters. Their early importance at least was that they gave new architectural shape to ideas of housing reform and provided in suburban layouts a recognizable focus for the new subject of town planning. Unwin in particular was an advocate of the new concept, using the term freely in a paper to an International Congress of Architects in London in 1906 and at the Garden Cities Association Conference at Letchworth the same year (although Nettlefold claimed to have been the first to use the expression[24]). He proved an important catalyst in the translation of Victorian sanitary reform into Edwardian town planning. His theme was that 'endless rows of brick boxes, looking out upon dreary streets and squalid backyards, are not really homes for people, and can never become such, however complete may be the drainage system, however pure the water supply, or however detailed the bye-laws under which they are built. There is needed the vivifying touch of art which would give completeness.'[25]

Turning to the question of civics, *Cities in Evolution*, published in 1915, is a landmark in the history of town planning. In it Patrick Geddes displayed his comprehensive grasp of

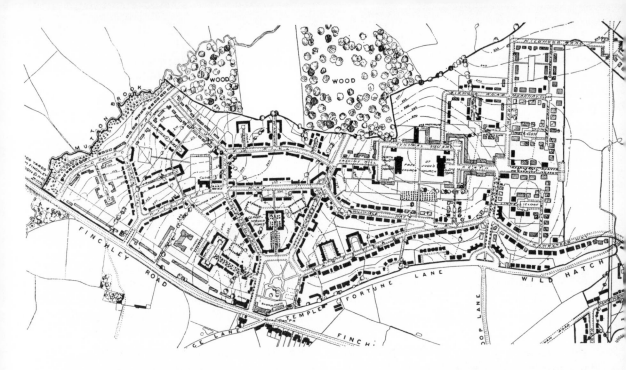

Hampstead Garden Suburb, an early plan by Barry Parker and Raymond Unwin published in 1909 which translated the philanthropic zeal of Henrietta Barnett into suburban architecture of high renown.

Hampstead Garden Suburb, Asmun's Place, a close of working-class houses, built by one of the co-partnership companies on the north west of the estate. This early photograph shows the importance attached to landscaping and garden layout in a comprehensive scheme designed to promote mixing between social classes.
(*Courtesy of* Mrs Brigid Grafton Green)

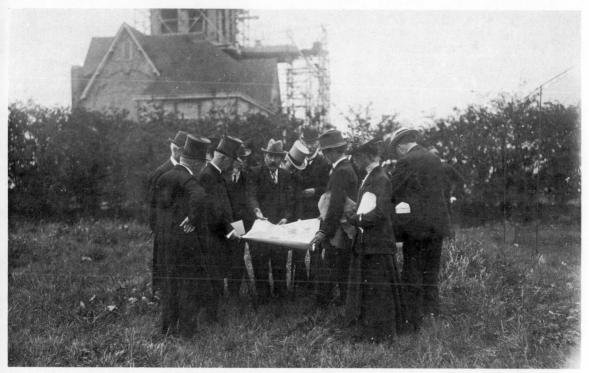

Raymond Unwin (centre), explaining his plans for Hampstead Garden Suburb to a visiting group of MPs in 1911. Unfinished in the background is St Jude's Church. Perhaps one of the earliest planning site meetings on photographic record. (*Courtesy of* Mrs Brigid Grafton Green)

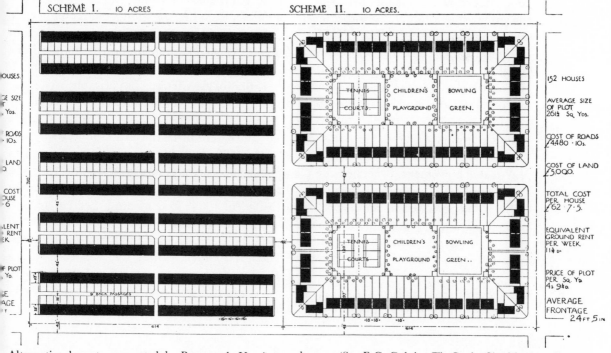

Alternative layouts, suggested by Raymond Unwin to show the actual financial results of development on garden city lines as compared with the more usual disposition of houses. (See E.G. Culpin, *The Garden City Movement Up to Date*, GC and TPA, 1913)

the urban scene and showed how town planning might be seen as something more than technological or aesthetic expertise. Geddes established a tradition in planning which has repeatedly come to the fore over the last 60 years: that of the synthesis in the age of the specialist, bringing harmony and understanding to a physical, economic and social complex which is the city. Trained as a biologist, but assuming other technical skills such as that of landscape designer, he had the remarkable ability to see a situation through different eyes and to ascribe new significances which, perhaps, were lost to others. In this way he was an essential contributor to the development of town planning as something above and beyond any subject matter covered by the then disciplines or fields of practice. Making an intellectual contribution to town planning, he complemented and enriched the work of others. The trouble was that even among the intellectuals of his day he was an extreme and often incomprehensible man. Perhaps he left ordinary mortals a little unsure. A wry sideline came from J. W. Cockrill (Borough Engineer of Great Yarmouth and a President of TPI); commenting favourably on *Cities in Evolution*, he thought it added 'possibly a page to the next English dictionary'[26].

He coined the word 'conurbation' for our new urban phenomena and so encouraged a regional scale of thinking. He saw cities not in physical terms but in human ones, and harnessed the social science approach to understanding urban change. His ability to think globally assisted in the internationalization of town planning. His historical grasp enabled him to understand the processes of city evolution; his use of the words 'paleo-technic' and 'neotechnic' was taken up by others. As a thinker he offered principles of planning practice ranging from the environment and conservation of nature to site planning at local scale. He was interested in planning education, and social and housing reform. Above all he offered a social philsophy which gave form to the utopian idealism which most planners naturally inherited: 'Town planning is not something which can be done from above, on general principles easily laid down, which can be learned in one place and imitated in another...it is the development of a local life, a regional character, a civic spirit, a unique individuality, capable of course of growth and expansion, of improvement and development in many ways, of profiting too by the example and criticism of others, yet always in its own way and upon its own foundations. Thus the renewed art of town planning has to develop into an art yet higher, that of city design—a veritable orchestra-tion of all the arts, and correspondingly needing, even for its preliminary surveys, all the social sciences.'[27]

This was very different thinking from the contributions of the practitioners we have recorded earlier. If planning was to take a place of academic respectability as well as practical achievement, it needed the Geddesian influence; it came at the right time. His major publication was in 1915 but the force of his contribution was in evidence much earlier. The Sociological Society was constituted in 1904; four meetings were held that year when papers were read, and in one of 'Civics: as Applied Sociology' Geddes outlined his early thinking. He made a plea for a systematic study of cities and a gradual develop-ment towards an orderly regional survey. His standpoint was that 'a city is more than a place in space, it is a drama in time'[28], and advocated sociological, as well as historical and geographical, method in inquiry. He gave a new dimension to the term 'civics', think-ing of it as a branch of sociology dealing with city surveys and guidance of city growth.

52

As we have seen, the civic movement in the United States at this time was manifest in most of the big cities, but it never achieved the comprehensive bridge between technology and design that Geddes advocated. However, this is not to say that his influence was limited; his ideas spilled out to affect other contemporaries. One writer who embraced his views was C. R. Ashbee, an architect who also preached the idea of an integrated approach to city life, praising art against the dullness of 19th century mechanization. *Where the Great City Stands: a Study in the New Civics* was published in 1917 but reflects his thinking of earlier years. It is an astonishing collection of utopian ideas for post-war re-generation, harnessing art, religious purpose and community strength to the potential of the city. He wrote that his generation 'no longer believe with Karl Marx in the Class War, nor with Morris in rebellion to overturn Society on behalf of the Arts. We aim at a gradual ordering; we demand intelligent co-ordination.'[29] This sense of unity in city life was an important contribution to town planning.

All the contributions to planning cannot neatly be categorized as propagandist bodies, professional groups or intellectuals. Some indeed almost defy categorization, bridging as they did many societies or fields of interest, but nonetheless played an important part in identifying issues and popularizing solutions. There were many of these and space permits only brief treatment, but the influence of T. C. Horsfall cannot go unmentioned[30]. As an Honorary Secretary of an association of working men's clubs from 1878, he was active in promoting cultural and artistic schemes in Manchester: museums, concerts, reading circles, handicrafts in schools, and so on. His better known causes were housing and smoke abatement and his advocacy of German approaches to municipal development. He was concerned with the establishment of Letchworth. He lectured widely, wrote many papers and is well known for *The Example of Germany* published in 1904. He popularized certain statistics in support of his causes; for example, in Manchester, in 1899, of rather more than 11 000 men who wished to enlist some 8 000 were at once rejected and of the remaining 3 000 only 1 000 were sent into the army, the rest into the Militia: 'although coal smoke, drinking and licentiousness are amongst the factors which produce this physical deterioration, bad housing is the chief factor.'[31] Against this could be set out his ideal city in which social and cultural opportunity, healthy surroundings and physical attractiveness of our towns went hand in hand. It was this complete philosophy of life that was so important in giving to town planning a characteristic which people then saw as a 'higher quality', with a special kind of support which stood it in good stead.

During the years preceding the First World War a growing literary contribution enhanced the town planning reputation. Probably the most significant was that of Raymond Unwin; *Town Planning in Practice: an Introduction to the Art of Designing Cities and Suburbs* was published in 1909. He was already establishing a formidable reputation and his book became a standard text; even as a design manual it was of a high standard, but his early chapters on civic matters, the history of town design and city surveys were also masterly. By comparison A. R. Sennett's *Garden Cities in Theory and Practice* (1905) and H. Inigo Trigg's *Town Planning: Past, Present and Future* (1909) were of much less significance. *Nothing Gained by Overcrowding!* was a further well-known paper by Unwin in 1912. The *Town Planning Review* from Liverpool University was the first planning journal and quickly established a reputation as a forum for advanced thinking about the new activity. Additionally, there were a number of laymen's contributions in which the planning idea was articulated as a popular concept based on personal experience. As an example, J. S. Nettlefold's *Practical Town Planning* (1914) was an interesting product from the Birmingham point of view, as was George Cadbury's (Jnr) *Town Planning*, published in 1915, which described town planning with particular reference to the Birmingham schemes.

The increasingly widespread attention devoted to town planning in popular, intellectual, technical, literary, reformist and government fields, was finally matched by its acceptance in university circles. The Department of Town Planning and Civic Design was established in the University of Liverpool in 1909, following a grant from W. H. Lever. The circumstances of this venture were recounted by Thomas H. Mawson in his autobiography, *The Life and Work of an English Landscape Architect* (1927). In 1908, a group of newspapers attacked Lever for attempts to amalgamate a number of competing firms of soap manufacturers. His purpose was to reduce the cost of production to compensate for the soaring cost of raw materials. The newspapers thought they saw the introduction of the American trust in its most pernicious form, but in their attack went beyond the bounds of reasonable criticism. The result was an action in which Lever received damages amounting to over £100 000, and this sum was subsequently presented to the University for the further development of the School of Tropical Medicine and to establish a new Department of Civic Design. Lever's donation resulted from contact with C. H. Reilly, the Liverpool architect. His own autobiography, *Scaffolding in the Sky* (1938), tells the story. He was disappointed in John Burns' apparent neglect of architecture in the first Town Planning Bill of 1908, and contacted Lever, 'a short fiery little man with opalescent eyes changing from green to red if you dared to disagree with him, and fair hair standing up on end.'[32] Reilly recommended Adshead for the Chair, whom he had met previously at a London practice, and provided his own assistant, Patrick Abercrombie, for the Department. T. H. Mawson, the landscape architect also joined the staff, and they were accompanied by John A. Brodie, the Liverpool City Engineer, Dowdall, a barrister and Lord Mayor of Liverpool, and Hope, the City's Medical Officer of Health. A journal, the *Town Planning Review* referred to above, was commenced. Professor S. D. Adshead stated the new disciplinary position in the introduction to the Departmental prospectus: 'Town Planning, although intimately connected with Architecture and Engineering, is a distinct and separate study in itself, and the primary object of the school is to equip Architects, Engineers and others with a knowledge of the supplementary subjects that Town Planning connotes.' The first examinations for the Diploma in Civic Design were held in March 1910.

The Department went from strength to strength and an Exhibition of Town Planning and Housing was held in the School in March 1914. This was well patronized and the Transactions of the Conference[33] brought together a number of good papers. The Exhibition was opened by the Marquis of Salisbury who 'expressed his sense of the greatness of the Town Planning and Housing movement, which he compared in importance and power to the Renaissance of the 15th and 16th centuries'. The Secretaries were Professor Adshead and Patrick Abercrombie and the speakers included many of the familiar names of the day: J. A. Brodie and H. E. Stilgoe, Raymond Unwin, Percy Runton, architect of Hull Garden Suburb, E. G. Culpin, and Henry Vivian.

Patrick Geddes, incomprehensible to some, but an important intellectual prop to the early planning movement. Biologist, sociologist, landscape designer and planner: a generalist in an age of specialists, he provided an integrative framework for the new discipline. (*Courtesy of Professor A.S. Travis*)

William Hesketh Lever, Lord Leverhulme, 1851–1925, industrial philanthropist, founder of Port Sunlight, propagandist for garden cities and benefactor of town planning at Liverpool University. (*Courtesy of* Town and Country Planning Association)

Other university developments at Birmingham and London are reviewed in chapter 9. Demand for town planning 'knowledge' was growing—Thompson, the historian of the Chartered Surveyors, notes that local practicing surveyors attended Unwin's lectures at Birmingham[34]. The same feature can be noted in the Summer Schools of Planning held under the auspices of the University of London during 1912, 1913 and 1914. Certificates issued by the Extension Board of the University proved of great advantage to architects and engineers.

FORMATION OF THE TOWN PLANNING INSTITUTE

These academic developments, the effect of the 1909 Act on planning practice, and the inability of the separate institutes to provide the training or knowledge that was required, do much to explain how the need for a new professional institute arose. A new nucleus was required where planning could be discussed separately from the other professions. An early approach led by Thomas Mawson and Patrick Abercrombie called for the formation of a Society of Landscape Architects, and Mawson discussed this matter in two articles in the *Town Planning Review* in 1911–12[35]. It should be noted that the terms 'landscape architecture' and 'town planning' were almost interchangeable, though with an emphasis on civic art, and what Mawson was proposing was a generalist co-ordinating body. The practical weakness of the idea was the unlikelihood of any new body of this nature exerting supervision over the work of the existing professions.

The *Town Planning Review* was an important forum for discussing planning matters beyond the narrow professional outlooks, which as we have seen tended to rely on some-what assertive viewpoints. For example, Adshead in discussing the West Bromwich Conference wrote in 1911: 'The town planner of today may emerge from almost any profession engaged in one way or another in the construction of towns and in the development of suburbs. All that is required in order that he may be justified in calling himself a town planner is that in addition to such primary qualification he must possess sufficient knowledge of the technicalities of other professions to be able to co-ordinate these with his own.'[36] This reveals a 'generalist' approach as opposed to a specialist viewpoint. The existing professional bodies never really advanced beyond recognizing the need for co-operation with other professions, and perhaps admitting that some extra knowledge of their own profession was necessary in its application to the new activity. They were loathe to consider that town planning could be done equally well by other professions. Adshead seemed to represent the contrary view that the town planner of the future would be firstly a member of the existing technical professions, although, through a co-ordination of many technical skills and understandings he would be something more. Comparing these early pages of the *Town Planning Review* with those of the professional journals, one is certainly struck by the comparative absence of a narrow 'single-minded' professional outlook.

The necessity of working together was actively canvassed and, indeed, practiced by virtually all the members of the nucleus that later formed the Town Planning Institute. Adshead, Unwin, Mawson and Adams took part in meetings of the Municipal and County Engineers, Unwin and Adams exhorted the Surveyors to co-operate, and members of the introspective engineering profession began attending conferences of other professions. In

56

this matter of bringing people together, Thomas Adams deserves special mention. His technical ability is reflected in the posts he occupied: first Permanent Secretary of the Garden City Association, first Manager of Letchworth (1903), a surveyor and planning consultant with G. L. Pepler (1906) and first Town Planning Inspector of the Local Government Board. Additionally, this work involved him in settling opposed interests and gave him a great opportunity of meeting people. He seems to have played a leading part in the informal discussions which lead to the formation of the Institute: as the *Town Planning Review* observed in 1914, 'the spirit of co-operation, the first essential of town planning...could not have had a better encourager than Mr Adams.'[37]

Adams was a young dairy farmer living south of Edinburgh in the 1890s. He became interested in land ownership and went to London to earn his living as a freelance journalist writing mainly on land problems. Many references point to his dynamic personality and the important role he played in the formation of the Institute. The most specific came from Adshead who recalled[38] that in or about 1910 Adams went to Liverpool and mentioned his thoughts on the formation of a Society. A small group of twelve resulted and for three years they met regularly with the intention of founding an Institute. Another recollection came from T. Alwyn Lloyd after Adams had died in 1939; he remembered 'a long railway journey back from a Town Planning tour in Germany when he talked to some of us about his ideas for forming a professional Institute.'[39]

In January 1913, the *Town Planning Review* noted that a group of town planners, all practically engaged on the subject and representing every aspect of it, including architects, engineers, and surveyors, had organized themselves into a body and held several meetings in London. 'A combination of experts such as this should do much to advance the interest of Town Planning in the country. We regard this group as the nucleus of a society to which all Town Planners may, in time, belong.'[40] This is the first mention of what we might call a 'proto-Institute'.

The first meeting of a Provisional Committee of this body was held at the Westminster Palace Hotel on 11th July 1913. Present were five architects: Lucas, Soutar, Lanchester, Adshead and Unwin, and three surveyors: Adams, Davidge and Pepler. Business was concerned with the nominations or suggestions for membership. Basically, the list was dominated by professional architects, engineers and surveyors in that order, but there was also a general category of Associated Member, which included propagandists and a solicitors' category.

This issue of the qualifications and classes for membership predominated in the early work of the Provisional Committee (and, indeed, later the Council). A letter dated 11th November 1913[41], was sent out to those nominated at the first meeting. The names of all twenty of the provisional committee appeared in the letter. All were experts: eleven architects, four surveyors, four engineers and Patrick Geddes, the pioneer sociologist. They were: T. Adams (surveyor), S. D. Adshead (architect), J. A. Brodie (engineer), J. W. Cockrill (engineer), W. R. Davidge (surveyor), P. Geddes (sociologist), P. B. Houfton (architect), Brook Kitchen (architect), W. T. Lancashire (engineer), H. V. Lanchester (architect), G. Lucas (architect), E. L. Lutyens (architect), T. H. Mawson (architect), G. L. Pepler (surveyor), P. T. Runton (architect), A. S. Soutar (architect), A. R. Sterling (surveyor), H. E. Stilgoe (engineer), R. Unwin (architect), Aston Webb (architect). However, the letter spoke of widening membership to embrace those interested 'professionally or otherise'. They were invited to join together and form 'a Town Planning Institute in order to advance the study of Town Planning and Civic Design to promote the artistic and scientific development of towns and cities and to secure the association of those engaged on or interested in the practice of town planning'. The letter was ambiguous within itself and the actual classes of membership had been altered. By adhering strictly to the letter, not only were propagandists and those interested otherwise than professionally excluded from membership, but also apparently so was Patrick Geddes, one of the people who signed the letter. The first general meeting rectified this with regard to propagandists, in that they were enabled to become associated members. This meeting, held at the Westminster Palace Hotel, on November 21st 1913 (and preceded by dinner at 3/6d per head) represents the transition from the Provisional Committee to the Institute. Thomas Adams presided at the meeting, and the first Council was elected. Thirty-five Members, twelve Associate Members and seventeen Honorary Members were elected although there were difficulties in defining precise classes of membership.

At the Council meeting on December 12th, 1913, Thomas Adams was elected first President, and Cockrill and Unwin, Vice-Presidents. Geddes was elected Honorary Librarian (though there is no record of a Library) and Pepler, Honorary Secretary and Treasurer. More new members were elected, but at this stage this was 'subject to their consent', in order to establish the Institute as a body or association for those interested in Town Planning. At the next meeting the details of an inaugural dinner were finalized for January 30th 1914. John Burns (President of the Local Government Board) was to be guest of honour, and the invited guests were to be the Presidents of ICE, RIBA, SI, IMCE, and the Law Society. Others included H. G. Wells, C. Harmsworth, the Prime Minister, George Bernard Shaw, various Lord Mayors and Bishops and the editors of *The Times*, *The Daily Chronicle* and *Westminster*. This dinner, which also happened to be a farewell dinner for John Burns, who left the Local Government Board soon afterwards, did not quite secure this distinguished company but was a gathering representative of town planning, including highway specialists, government officials, housing reformers, town clerks, surveyors, architects and borough engineers. Sir Aston Webb, the chairman, referred to John Burns as the 'father of Town Planning', and said that the Institute owed its foundation to him and his work. In reply John Burns stressed that the organization was loose and informal, including as well as experts, 'artists and idealists', and he felt that in retrospect the idealists would be seen as the only practical men.

This dinner marked the public launching of the Town Planning Institute, but the formal completion of the details was still incomplete. Membership policy was still not finalized, though the broad lines were drawn. The IMCE Engineers had been excluded from the initial membership qualifications, but this was rectified upon a request from the Institution. The final membership classes were adopted as the final constitution at a general meeting in April 1914, following a report of a Sub-committee to Council in February. As adopted, the system consisted of four classes of technical membership: *Members* who could be specifically members of RIBA, ICE, SI and IMCE, who had had practical experience in town planning, or members of professions who had attained a special eminence in connection with the practice of town planning; *Associate Members* who were members of professions who had achieved an approved standard of proficiency in town planning; *Legal Members* who had legal experience in preparing town planning schemes or had reached an approved standard of proficiency respectively. As well as these were the *Associates* and *Honorary Members* who were those associated with town planning in their capacities as medical officers of health, councillors, or actively identified as members of propagandist societies aiming to further the pursuits and objectives of town planning; and distinguished persons associated with planning respectively. The first membership list, as at May 1914, is given below. There were 52 Members, 18 Associate Members, 6 Legal Members, 28 Honorary Members and 11 Associates. Seventeen held qualifications as surveyors, 18 as engineers and 28 as architects.

The Council was to be composed of 24 members: 14 Members, four Legal Members, three Associate Members, one Legal Associate Member, one Associate and one Honorary Member. It had earlier been established that no one profession should be allowed to dominate the proceedings by numerical superiority on Council. Later, in practice, it was established that: 'Membership of no Institution *ipso facto* gave the right of membership to this Institute; that the Council do not intend to mention specifically any other Institution; that membership is not limited to persons belonging to those Institutions particularly mentioned.' The Institute, therefore, almost from the outset, set down definitively that something demonstrably 'extra' was required of professionals wishing to join. It was proposed that membership would be by direct election initially, but that examinations would be introduced from 1916 onwards.

Town Planning Institute: first membership, May 1914

Hon Vice-Presidents

The Rt Hon John Burns, MP

Sir Alexander R. Stenning, PPSI

Sir Aston Webb, RA, FRIBA

Members

Abercrombie, Patrick	Hayward, F. G., FSI	Parker, Barry, FRIBA
Adams, Thomas, FSI	Houfton, Percy B.	Pepler, George L., FSI
Adshead, S. D., FRIBA	Humphreys, G. A., FRIBA	Pite, Beresford, FRIBA
Brodie, John A., MInstCE	Jenkin, Charles J., MInstCE	Platt, S. Sydney, MInstCE
Bullmore, A. W. E., AMInstCE	Kelley, Sydney A., FSI	Richards, E. F., AMInstCE
Campbell, A. H., MInstCE	Kitchin, Brook, FRIBA	Runton, Percy T., ARIBA
Carr, W. Louis, MInstM & CyE	Lancashire, W. T., MInstCE	Soutar, A. S., LicRIBA
Cockrill, J. W., MInstCE	Lanchester, H. V., FRIBA	Soutar, J. C. S., LicRIBA
Crickmer, C. M., FRIBA	Little, John W., FRIBA	Stenning, Sir Alexander, PPSI, FRIBA
Crow, Arthur, FRIBA	Lloyd, T. Alwyn, LicRIBA	Stilgoe, Henry E., MInstCE
Davidge, W. R., FSI, AMInstCE, ARIBA	Lucas, Geoffrey, FRIBA	Sutcliffe, G. L., FRIBA
Elgood, Frank M., FSI FRIBA	Lutyens, E. L., ARA, FRIBA	Thomson, James, MInstM & CyE
Garrard, Norman, FSI	Martin, Howard, PPSI	Unwin, Raymond, FRIBA
Geddes, Professor Patrick	Mawson, Thomas H., Hon, ARIBA	Waterhouse, Gilbert
Hall, W. Carby, FRIBA	Meade, T. de Courcy, MInstCE, FSI	Waterhouse, Paul, FRIBA
Harpur, W., MInstCE	Mears, F. C.	Webb, Sir Aston, RA, FRIBA
Harvey, W. A.	Monson, E. C. P., FRIBA, FSI	Wike, C. F., MInstCE
		Williamson, J. A.

The formal recognition of the Institute was completed with the signing of the Articles of Association under the Company Acts on 4th September 1914. The Institute was thereby formed into a company, limited by guarantee. This procedure had, during the 19th century, become an alternative to a Royal Charter as a means of securing professional association, though the latter remained the status symbol of official recognition and approval. The procedure enabled the initial articles to be framed in such a way that transfer to a Chartered body could be relatively straightforward, and the word 'Limited' need not appear at the end of the Institute's name.

Thus, the Town Planning Institute was founded. The onset of war and the departure of the first President, Thomas Adams, to take up an appointment in Canada, undoubtedly put strains on the new body, which was also without meeting premises, but it survived and grew. Its foundation was an intriguing situation capable of different interpretations. Many years later Alfred Potter considered that the Institute was established consciously as a new professional body to further the profession of town planning[42]. The Surveyors' historian Thompson has commented that 'town planning was regarded as a new and distinct profession, whose practitioners required to be something more than surveyors'[43]. It may well have been that the idea of quite a different professional body was in fact in the minds of the nucleus of members, and indeed the intention of regulating entry by examination soon after formation seems to indicate this. But against this one has to admit that the formation of the Institute led to very little reaction on the part of the other professional bodies. The RIBA Journal was the first to mention the TPI (in November 1914) when it published without comment the programme of lectures to be held under the auspices of the Institute. On balance, it seems likely that far from consciously creating a new profession, separate and distinct from the other professions, the TPI in effect began as a meeting of different professions. Perhaps its inception was as much a piece of political astuteness as anything else whereby on one Council the technical professions, neatly balanced, were mixed with a variety of propagandists and famous people. Birth in relative obscurity, with outlook promising but uncertain, is perhaps a fair assessment.

The predominance of three founder professions was significant. The relative absence of medical officers of health and sociologists scarcely reflected their importance to the subject matter, but they seem to have pressed no claim and the town planning field was divided up by the land based professions. An important implication of this was that because they were technique- and practice-oriented, planning itself was soon vested with skills and expertise. The propagandists and the social idealists soon became a minority as the Institute took form.

The people who founded the Institute were, by and large, professionals who saw town planning as extra to the contribution of any one parent profession. They saw that it was necessary to create a separate organization for the full flowering of the new activity. In coming to this view it is impossible for us now to say how they were individually motivated: clarity of rational thought with sharp insight for the future, or a disappointment with the conservativism of the existing bodies? aggressive 'empire-building' or fortuitous eventuality? real creativity by restless energies, or opportunism? We shall never know, but at least we can suggest a few of the common features of the men who were at the heart of the matter. Liberals and Quakers were strongly represented. Radical leanings were much in evidence. A marked social conscience was expressed in a concern for a range of issues: better working-class housing, temperance, reform, and an improvement in living conditions and environmental surroundings. Openness to new developments, as in residential architecture, was a feature. But town planning was by no means the preserve of radicals. Chamberlain believed in compromising with social change and Nettlefold appreciated planning as a means of enhancing worker productivity. Perhaps the most important common characteristic of those who were responsible for the founding of the Institute was that they were professional men. From now on the course of town planning was to be very considerably affected by professionalism and the liberal, humanitarian and social reform element was partly squeezed into a professional frame. This 'inner drive' both gained through technical expertise and lost through institutionalization.

REFERENCES

1. A useful review is given in Donald Read's *Edwardian England*, Harrap, 1972.
2. Howarth, Edward G. and Wilson, Mona, *West Ham: A Study in Social and Industrial Problems*. Dent, London, 1907.

3. Sennett, A. R., *Carriages Without Horses Shall Go*. Whittaker, 1896.

4. Briggs, Asa, *History of Birmingham*, 1952, quoted in Read, Donald, reference 1.

5. Weber, Adna Ferrin, *The Growth of Cities in the Nineteenth Century*. Macmillan, New York, 1899.

6. Booth, General William, *In Darkest England and the Way Out*. The Salvation Army, 1890.

7. Howard, Ebenezer (F. J. Osborn, Ed.), *Garden Cities of Tomorrow*, 1902. Faber and Faber, 1946.

8. Culpin, Ewart G., *Garden City Movement Up to Date*. Garden Cities and Town Planning Association, 1913.

9. Sennet, A. R., *Garden Cities in Theory and Practice*, vols. 1 and 2. Bemrose and Sons, 1905.

10. Baker, G. A., Housing Reform—The Early Years. *Housing and Planning Review*, **27**, No. 2, 1971.

11. Aldridge, Henry R., *The Case for Town Planning*. National Housing and Town Planning Council, 1915.

12. Bowley, M., *The British Building Industry*. Cambridge University Press, 1966.

13. *Journal of the Royal Institute of British Architects*, **XIL**, 3rd series, 113, 1905.

14. *Town Planning Review*, **1**, 178, 1910–11.

15. *Transactions of the Town Planning Conference*, Royal Institute of British Architects, 1910.

16. *Journal of the Royal Institute of British Architects*, **XVIII**, 3rd series, 662–8, 1911.

17. *Proceedings of the Incorporated Association of Municipal and County Engineers*, **XXXIII**, 59–70, 1906–07.

18. *Proceedings of the Institution of Municipal and County Engineers*, **XXXVII**, 44, 1910–11.

19. Thomas H. Mawson, The Art and Craft of Landscape Architecture and its Relation to Town Planning. *Journal of the Town Planning Institute*, **X**, December 1923.

20. *Proceedings of the Housing and Town Planning Conference*. Institution of Municipal and County Engineers, West Bromwich 1911, E. and F. Spon, 1911.

21. Surveyors' Institute, *Professional Notes*, **XV**, 109, 1908–9.

22. Surveyors' Institute, *Transactions*, **XLII**, 62–3, 1909–10.

23. Day, M. G., *Sir Raymond Unwin (1863–1940) and R. Barry Parker (1867–1947): a Study and Evaluation of their Contribution to the Development of Site Planning Theory and Practice*. M.A. Thesis, University of Manchester, 1973.

24. Adams, T., *Journal of the Town Planning Institute*, **XV**, 310, 1928–29.

25. Unwin, R., *Town Planning in Practice*. Ernest Benn, 1909.

26. *Journal of the Town Planning Institute*, **II**, No. 4, 87, 1916.

27. Geddes, P., *Cities in Evolution*. Ernest Benn, 1915.

28. Geddes, P., Civics: as Applied Sociology. *Sociological Papers*. Macmillan, 1905.

29. Ashbee, C. R., *Where the Great City Stands*. Essex House Press, 1917.

30. Reynolds J. P., Thomas Coghlan Horsfall and the Town Planning Movement in England. *Town Planning Review*, **XXII**, 1952.

31. Horsfall, T. C., *Housing of the Labouring Classes*. Conference paper, 1900.

32. Reilly, C. H., *Scaffolding in The Sky*. Routledge, 1938.

33. *Transactions of Conference*, Town Planning and Housing Exhibition 1914, Liverpool University Press, 1914.

34. Thompson, F. M. L., *Chartered Surveyors*. Routledge, 1968.

35. Mawson, T. H., The Position and Prospects of Landscape Architecture in England. *Town Planning Review*, **II**, No. 3, 1911, and No. 4, 1912.

36. *Town Planning Review*, **II**, 175–6, 1911–12.

37. *Town Planning Review*, **V**, 249, 1914.

38. *Journal of the Town Planning Institute*, **XVII**, No. 3, 69, January 1931.

39. *Journal of the Town Planning Institute*, **XXVI**, No. 3, 115, March–April 1940.

40. *Town Planning Review*, **III**, 220, 1913.

41. The Council Minute Book provides the details of the founding of the Institute.

42. Potter, Alfred R., The History of the Institute. *Journal of the Town Planning Institute*, **49**, No. 10, December 1963.

43. Thompson, F. M. L., *Chartered Surveyors*, Routledge, 1968.

4 The Beginnings of Statutory Planning

We consider in this chapter a number of developments that took place, first prior to the outbreak of the First World War, during the war period itself, and then in the immediate aftermath. These concerned the first town planning legislation of 1909; the growing importance of the traffic problem; plans for reconstruction; and the legislation of 1919. Against this background we consider professional developments in the Town Planning Institute.

THE 1909 ACT

The Bill, the passage of which had been thwarted in 1908, was reintroduced in 1909 with the assurance of widespread support. As we read in chapter 3, the Bill had resulted from the pressure of the housing reform lobby but the Liberal Government perhaps needed little encouragement to incorporate this piece of social legislation in its programme. The President of the Local Government Board, John Burns, explained the need for the Act as follows: 'Whereas in the past, without any scheme, roads had been badly laid, of insufficient width, and without any relationship to other roads, the Government, by this Bill, gave the responsible local authority power to initiate a town planning scheme, so that private owners would improve their own properties instead of acting to their individual or collective betterment.'[1] In the event, the Act which received the Royal Assent on 3 December, 1909, had the object 'to ensure, by means of schemes which may be prepared either by local authorities or landowners, that, in future, land in the vicinity of towns shall be developed in such a way as to secure proper sanitary conditions, amenity and convenience in connection with the laying out of the land itself and of any neighbouring land'.

The Act was the Housing, Town Planning, etc Act, 1909, the second part of which, in sections 54–67, dealt with town planning. The essence of this part of the Act was that it provided permissive powers for the preparation of schemes for controlling the development of new housing areas. What town planning actually constituted was uncertain but the Fourth Schedule listed the most important elements of a scheme as: streets, roads and other ways, and stopping up, or diversion of existing highways; buildings, structures and erections; open spaces; the preservation of objects of historical interest or natural beauty; sewerage, drainage and sewage disposal; lighting; water supply; and ancillary works. The powers were logical extensions of existing ones concerned with housing and public health, whereby local authorities over the last 20 years had assumed wider powers of public control over physical development. One step forward was the compensation and betterment provisions, although in practice they proved virtually unworkable. Perhaps the remarkable aspect of the legislation was that it turned out to be as successful as it did. Hedged about with cautious safeguards of administrative detail, ranging from the need for consultation at the local level with everyone who was affected by the scheme, to laying the general provisions of each scheme before Parliament, nonetheless, a number of local authorities worked the legislation enthusiastically and the furtherance of town planning was positively enhanced.

But the mild, almost timid provisions must have been a disappointment to many. George Cadbury, for example, wrote to John Burns expressing his disappointment in the Housing Bill: 'I believe that town planning is infinitely more important than anything else in the Bill, and on that practically nothing definite will be done... Suburb planning is of the greatest importance to towns of 50 000 inhabitants and over. Every town, and the District Councils within a radius of ten to fifteen miles, should form a Housing Board. No new streets should be allowed to be made in their neighbourhood without a plan being submitted or prepared by this Board as to how the unused land in the neighbourhood is to be laid out ... I wish you could have left everything else out and tackled this problem alone, because I believe it would have been a practical non-contentious measure and yet would have done more for the United Kingdom than anything else you will ever accomplish.'[2]

Cadbury and others had urged mandatory powers, but the Government relied on permissive legislation followed by exhortation through various means at its disposal. As a letter from the Secretary of the Local Government Board to Borough and District Councils on 31 December 1909 explained, 'The Board trust that Councils in whose districts signs of development are visible will give every full consideration to the opportunities which the Act offers of guiding and controlling that development for the benefit of the community, and that, in doing so, they will bear the heavy burden which has fallen on the rate payers of many districts in the past in remedying defects of the kind which it is now within their power to prevent.'[3]

The Act had the advantage of being timely. As we saw in chapter 3, significant developments were taking place in the field of town planning and Government action was a useful new initiative. In June 1910 a major town planning exhibition was held in Berlin, and the Board's architect and town planning assistant both went; similarly, there was representation at the RIBA Conference in October. Meanwhile, Raymond Unwin's *Town Planning in Practice* had been published (1909), the Garden City movement was advancing, the professional bodies were taking increasing note and the Liverpool School had been established. The principles of site planning were beginning to be understood and a number of new housing developments showed real advances. Under W. H. Riley, who had become the second architect to the London County Council in 1899, the Council began to establish an architectural reputation by abandoning the idea of the utilitarian tenement established by the artisans' dwellings trusts, and developing an architectural style in the spirit of the arts and crafts movement. Between 1903 and 1912 the first cottage developments were built in Tooting, Tottenham and Hammersmith. Local authorities were now asked to respond to the new legislation, and the Local Government Board had 'good reason for supposing that the subject is arousing widespread interest, and that, in the near future, considerable advantage will be taken of the Act'.[4]

The first application received by the Board for authority to prepare a town planning scheme was from Birmingham, in respect of 2 320 acres comprising the whole of the parish of Quinton and parts of the Parishes of Harborne, Edgbaston and Northfield. Authority to prepare the scheme was given in February 1911 and formal application for approval submitted in June 1912. The area was situated between two populated areas, to the north at Smethwick and Oldbury and to the south at Selly Oak and Northfield. The scheme aimed to provide communication between these two centres, and two main arterial roads were proposed, starting from the north-east and the south-east and meeting near the western boundaries. The proposed land use was entirely residential, apart from four acres set aside for parks and open spaces. The average number of dwellings to the acre was to be twelve, with a maximum number of twenty on any one acre.

Authority to prepare two other prominent schemes was given in March 1911. One was the East Birmingham Scheme, which covered 1 442 acres in the Washwood Heath, Saltley, Small Heath and Sparkbrook wards of the city. Here again, the scheme provided for improved communications, controlled land use and lower densities. Primarily residential, there was also provision for playing fields and open spaces and 270 acres for factory sites; with regard to density, the area was divided into three zones with limitations of 18, 15 and 12 houses to the acre. The other was the Ruislip–Northwood scheme which covered 5 906 acres in that urban district and in the parish of Rickmansworth (rural) in the rural district of Watford. The existence of one major landowner, interested in development, was a major factor behind this scheme. New roads were provided, and building lines prescribed; land was set aside for allotments, public buildings and open spaces; special areas were reserved for shops and warehouses; the main area was divided into four zones for densities of 12, 8, 6 and 4 buildings to the acre.

The first scheme to be formally approved, having gone through the procedure of publication in the *London Gazette* and being laid before both Houses of Parliament for the statutory period of 40 days, was the Quinton, Harborne and Edgbaston Scheme, in May 1913, three and a half years after the Act was passed. This was a measure of the administrative incumbrances of the legislation, but the Local Government Board were reasonably satisfied with the progress being made. Their Annual Report for 1912–13, for example, stated that 'it is a matter of great satisfaction to us ... that there has been a forward movement of a decided character in favour of the ideas involved in what is commonly referred to as town planning'[5]. A number of schemes had been referred to them concerned with the laying out of main routes of communication, the provision of open spaces, density limitations, the prescription of building lines to secure open space and to enable road widenings, and the restriction of factories to particular areas. There was clearly a good deal of work to handle and when in 1914, Adams left the Board after $4\frac{1}{2}$ years. Pepler was

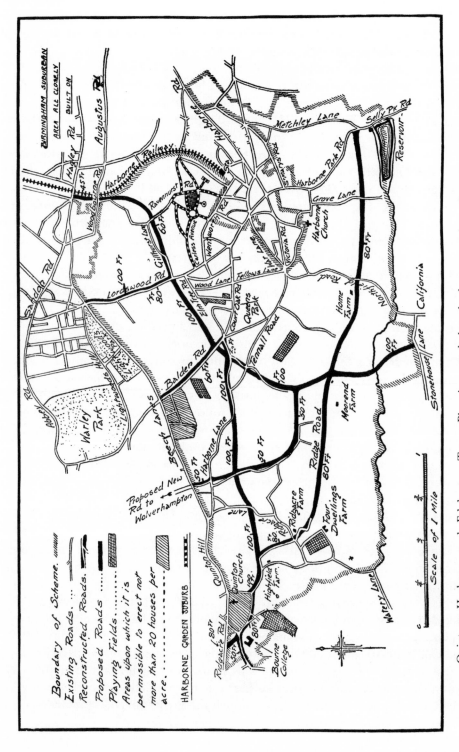

Quinton, Harborne and Edgbaston Town Planning
Scheme: a simplified map of this first Birmingham
scheme under the 1909 Act. It provided a framework for

orderly suburban expansion. (See Henry R. Aldridge,
The Case for Town Planning, National Housing and Town
Planning Council, 1915)

appointed with special responsibility for arterial roads and town planning conferences. Unwin became Chief Town Planning Inspector.

The rate of progress in England and Wales during the ten years after the passing of the Act is shown in the table below. The rapid fall off after 1915 and the pick-up in 1919 is particularly striking. During the war local authorities were compelled to curtail considering schemes owing to seriously depleted staffs. After ten interrupted years, 172 schemes had been authorized to be prepared or adopted by local authorities; over 300 000 acres were involved in these schemes. However, in only 13 of these cases were schemes actually submitted. Of these, five were prepared by Birmingham (including an amending scheme) and the other eight by Rochdale, Chesterfield and Leeds Corporations, Ruislip–Northwood, North Bromsgrove, Otley and Margam U.D. Councils and Hunslet R.D. Council. The acreage of these individual schemes varied substantially, some being quite small.

Town planning schemes authorized to be prepared or adopted by local authorities in England and Wales, 1911–1919

Year ended 31 March	UDs		RDs		Total	
	Number of schemes	Total acreage	Number of schemes	Total acreage	Number of schemes	Total acreage
1911	3	9 668	–	–	3	9 668
1912	11	4 174	–	–	11	4 174
1913	17	27 563	2	9 173	19	36 736
1914	17	23 060	6	16 731	23	39 791
1915	42	60 211	7	16 991	49	77 202
1916	16	33 249	2	7 335	18	40 584
1917	12	24 493	3	9 582	15	34 075
1918	1	306	–	–	1	306
1919	12	27 239	4	9 409	16	36 648
*1919	14	18 159	3	11 553	17	29 712
Total	145	228 122	27	80 774	172	308 896

* 1 April to 30 July 1919.

Source: Annual Reports, Local Government Board.

In Scotland progress was even slower, in spite of early interest being expressed in a number of towns. An extension of Dunfermline was projected with the creation of a town on garden city lines in connection with Admiralty development at Rosyth. Edinburgh and Dundee also proposed to use the new Act. The Local Government Board for Scotland reported progress in 1913 as 'substantial and promising, though not so rapid as we could desire'. During the war town planning operations fell into virtual abeyance, and Rosyth development was undertaken under the Housing (Rosyth Dockyard) Act, 1915, which permitted immediate progress with a large housing scheme. By the end of the war not one town planning scheme in Scotland had been approved, though 27 applications for authorities to prepare schemes had been granted[6].

Greater Birmingham Municipal Election,

1911.

WAST HILLS,

KINGS NORTON,

October 19th, 1911.

To the Electors of King's Norton Ward.

Ladies and Gentlemen,

I have been honoured with an invitation to stand as your representative in the Greater Birmingham Council, of which King's Norton Ward (including the Cotteridge, Stirchley, and part of Bournville) now forms a part.

TOWN PLANNING.—The Ward has a population of 22,000, and more than half the area is agricultural land. It is of vital importance that a wise and long-sighted Town Planning Committee should frame a policy to cover future schemes of building.

I advocate the provision of ample playgrounds and open spaces as the first consideration of such a policy.

TRAMS.—The tram service is slow and inadequate, and some means must be found of improving or supplementing the highway from Dogpool to King's Norton.

I will vote for ½d. tram fares and half rates for children.

EDUCATION.—I support the continuance of the progressive policy of the late District Council, and specially with regard to the training of every boy in some practical handicraft, and every girl in domestic economy.

I support the late Council's scheme for providing schools and large playgrounds on the north-west of the Cotteridge.

I heartily support the establishment of Dental Clinics for the benefit of every child in the district.

FAIR WAGES.—The municipality as an employer of labour should be impartial, generous and just. Contracts and sub-contracts should be subject to the fair wages clause.

If elected, I shall do all in my power to promote the best interests of the inhabitants of this Ward, and the welfare of Greater Birmingham.

Yours faithfully,

WILLIAM A. CADBURY

Election Address, William A. Cadbury, 1911. This is indication of the part played by town planning in mingham politics before 1914; and of the continu influence of the Cadbury family in promoting ge planning as part of social policy in local affairs. (*Cour of* the Cadbury family)

Arterial Roads, Birmingham. Plans for new roads we important features of the City's planning schemes. width of 120ft was regarded as a minimum for a suburb arterial road. The central tram track left 'nothing spare for anything but the barest form of ornamentatio (H.E. Stilgoe, 'Arterial Roads in the Birmingham Tov Planning Schemes', *TPI Papers and Discussions*, **IV**, No. 1918)

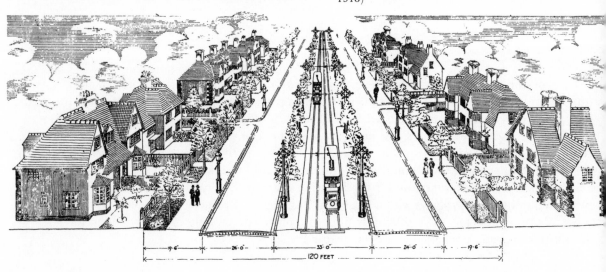

TRAFFIC

A Royal Commission on London Traffic had been set up in 1903, under the chairmanship of Sir David Miller Barbour, with terms of reference 'to inquire into the means of locomotion and transport in London'. The Commission examined an area of 693 square miles, and the rapidly changing situation was fully investigated. The population changes concerned with growth and suburban redistribution, referred to earlier (see p. 9), were common knowledge from the census returns, but transport statistics were, perhaps, less well known. The number of passengers carried annually by local railways and trams had risen dramatically from 269 million in 1881 to 847 million in 1901; moreover, substantial changes were taking place in means of communication as an underground railway system developed and petrol-driven vehicles replaced the horse-drawn carriage. The fabric of London's streets was increasingly challenged to accommodate the extra road users.

In 1904 there were just 8 400 private cars and vans, 5 300 public transport vehicles and 4 000 goods vehicles licensed in the country. By 1914 regular increases brought these figures to 132 000, 51 100, and 82 000 respectively, to which should be added 123 600 motor cycles. After a stabilization, and a decline in 1917–18, a rapid increase was again in evidence in 1919 and 1920. What began as an expensive toy rapidly became a major problem for an urban environment. In public transport the change from horse-drawn buses to motor buses was virtually complete in ten years, between 1903 and 1913, as big a revolution as electric traction was for the underground railway.

The Royal Commission recommended a Traffic Board to deal with London's problems in its eight-volume report published in 1905, but there was only a half-hearted response: in 1907 the London Traffic Branch was formed within the Board of Trade, but without any real powers. The next stage proved more significant. In 1909 the Road Board was established under the Development and Road Improvement Act to administer the receipts from vehicle and fuel taxation. Rees Jeffreys was secretary and Colonel R. E. Crompton consulting engineer. Jeffreys' name has been commemorated in Institute circles through the Trust Fund and the triennial lecture which bears his name; this symbolizes the very close link between transport problems and town planning from the early days of the century, a natural link to be thwarted as we shall see during much of our period.

In the meantime, Colonel Hellard was preparing arterial road plans at the Board of Trade, and it was in this field that progress was made. In July 1913, the Prime Minister received a deputation on behalf of local authorities in Greater London concerning the traffic planning problem and in November that year, the President of the Local Government Board presided at a conference of 115 local authorities, 12 societies and associations, the Board of Trade and the Road Board at Caxton Hall. The purpose was to consider arterial road communication in and around London; the need was recognized for local authorities in preparing town planning schemes to confer with one another to arrange for suitable through roads. This Arterial Roads Conference was, in fact, the first official attempt to prepare a regional plan (albeit on a selective topic basis) for Greater London. Burns himself defined the aim of the conference as 'to arrange some methods by which the Greater London Traffic can be better served by better roads and more spacious and dignified approaches'[7]. The link between transport and civic design was clearly illustrated. Subsequently, the transport component of town planning assumed an importance of its own and in 1919 the repeated request for a central authority was partially acknowledged by the formation of the Ministry of Transport; the Road Board was incorporated into that Ministry. For more than 50 years the function of traffic and planning was separated in the institutional framework of Government administration, and not until the formation of the Department of the Environment did the two come together again.

PLANS FOR RECONSTRUCTION

The onset of war disrupted the work of the various reform organizations with which the planning movement was associated. Typical was the response of the Garden Cities and Town Planning Association whose leader in August 1914 automatically assumed the worst and 'wrote to his cohorts that, of course, they must suspend work'[8]. But, as we have seen, the statutory process of town planning did not cease entirely. Moreover, during the war years, three successive governments sustained a continuous effort to plan for reconstruction and herald a new era of reform.

The phase of reconstruction began in 1916 with an informal group of powerful heads of departments, working with the Prime Minister, but with little staff; Asquith set up a Reconstruction Committee in March that year. This stage ended with Asquith's resignation in December 1916, and the second began when Lloyd George assembled his own Reconstruction Committee in February 1917. This was a group with only slender ties with the Cabinet and no links with departments; it consisted of 'brainy amateurs almost wilfully selected for their prideful pugnacity'[9]. (Mrs Sidney Webb, Dr Marion Phillips, Leslie Scott and B. Seebohm Rowntree were among those recruited.) In the housing panel, Lord Salisbury, past President of the Garden Cities and Town Planning Association, was a member. There developed strong support for the idea of a Ministry of Health and a huge housing programme for the working classes. The third stage was a full-fledged but small Ministry of Reconstruction with Christopher Addison, a member of Cabinet, at its head. Between July and December 1917, there was a continuing study of commercial and industrial policy, local government and housing. The final stage came in 1919 with a mixture of innovations: a Ministry of Health, a Ministry of Transport, a Housing and Town Planning Act and new legislation on assessment of land values.

The Housing Act was seen as the most important feature of post-war reconstruction. It was the culmination of three years' hard work and continual lobbying. During the war the scale of the housing problem was suggested by Aldridge, secretary of the National Housing and Town Planning Council: he estimated that 400 000 new urban and rural cottages were needed. But the problem was quality as well as quantity. One reminder of the backlog of bad conditions was the Report of the Royal Commission on the Housing of the Industrial Population of Scotland, set up in 1912 under the Chairmanship of Sir Henry Ballantyne, which reported in 1917, work having been temporarily suspended for a year in 1916. The instances of bad housing conditions that were described, not only in the Burghs (particularly Glasgow), but also in areas of miners' housing, in rural and crofter districts, in fishing communities and in respect of the accommodation for migratory and seasonal workers, all made disturbing reading. The main recommendations related to the need for the State to assume full responsibility for housing, to impose definite obligations and to provide, through the local authorities, a simple and effective organization. The message for the immediate post-war years was clear: 'We believe that the nation will never again tolerate the apathy which has obtained hitherto in regard to the conditions of life of a great part of the population of the British Islands. That those who have been called upon to defend the country should, on their return to their native land, have the opportunity for themselves and their dependants, of obtaining conditions of domestic comfort and opportunities of a happy and useful existence, is, we think, now the accepted creed of all.'[10]

During the war the Local Government Board had sponsored the Tudor Walters Committee to consider building construction and the provision of dwellings for the working classes. Their report was published in 1918[11]. Sir J. Tudor Walters was a Director of the Hampstead Garden Suburb Trust, and he had a faithful and energetic worker in Unwin as a member of his Committee. Indeed, Unwin's personal contribution shone through, because the Committee's sweeping recommendations all followed the work of Parker and himself, begun at Earswick and developed at Letchworth and Hampstead and elsewhere. The proposals covered density, site planning and house design, and specified a high standard of working-class housing. The density of dwellings in working-class development should not exceed 12 to the acre in urban areas and eight in rural areas. Sites for future development should be properly surveyed and selected from the points of view of amenity and industry. In the layout aesthetic and artistic considerations were essential; road needs and road widths had to be assessed; good access to the rear of houses was essential; the proper orientation of houses was vitally important; the cul-de-sac, courtyard and green were all necessary elements together with open spaces, allotments and playgrounds in a proper layout. With regard to the dwellings themselves, space standards must be generous; each house should have its own garden, large living rooms with a sunny aspect, a bath (on the first floor), a w.c. approached under cover, a larder and a coal store. These far reaching recommendations were adopted in the *Housing Manual* of 1919 and were not superceded for a quarter of a century, until the Dudley Report (see p. 131), and were not fundamentally altered until the Parker Morris Report of 1961.

During this time pressure came from a number of bodies on housing matters: the Health of Munitions Workers' Committee, the RIBA, the War Emergency Workers' National Committee, the Garden Cities and Town Planning Association and the National Housing and Town Planning Council. The TPI played no direct role, but individual members belonging to other organizations were involved, for example, Unwin. The NHTP Council, in particular, claimed enormous influence. Their Annual Report for 1918–1919 reported, 'The history of the housing and town planning development of this period is indissolubly bound up with the efforts of the Council and we can, therefore, regard the passing of the Act of 1919 as memorable in our history in a specially intimate sense.'[12] But the Government was well aware of the need for effective housing reform. When the Housing Bill was considered by the War Cabinet, the Prime Minister recognized the financial implications but counted the proposals cheap. 'He could foresee the possibility that this country might have to stand alone for social order and common sense against anarchy, as we had stood for freedom against despotism. So long as we could persuade the people that we were prepared to help them and to meet them in their aspirations ... the same and steady leaders amongst the workers would have an easy victory over the Bolsheviks among them.'[13] This idea of planning a new social order as a bulwark against totalitarianism was to be a familiar theme in the inter-war period.

The Housing, Town Planning, etc Act, 1919, received the Royal Assent on 31 July. It had four parts, the main two of which related to Housing of the Working Classes (sections 1–41) and Town Planning (sections 42–48). The new housing provisions were far reaching, introducing measures to make it obligatory for local authorities to prepare surveys of their housing needs and draw up plans for dealing with them; it became the duty of the local authority to carry out its schemes. The 1909 Housing Act had rendered obligatory the local authority adoption of the housing provisions of the 1890 Act, but the 1919 legislation was a considerable extension of State intervention in working-class housing provision. On the other hand, the initiative was not as dramatic as all that, because in view of the size of the housing shortage, some of the larger authorities had already begun to make surveys of the local situation. Section 1 of the Act read that 'It shall be the duty of every Local Authority ... to consider the needs of their area with respect to the provision of houses for the working classes, and within three months after the passing of this Act, and thereafter as often as occasion arises ... to prepare and submit to the Local Government Board a scheme for the exercise of their powers'. The scheme should specify the approximate number and nature of the houses to be provided, the extent and location of any land to be acquired, the average number of houses per acre, and the time scale of the proposed scheme. Up till now, only a few councils (notably London and Liverpool) had been active house builders; most regarded municipal action as a last resort. Birmingham, for example, may have pioneered town planning, but hesitated over municipal land ownership because of the uncertainty about interference with private property rights. Neville Chamberlain, Lord Mayor of Birmingham in 1915–16, admitted that the best choice of sites and streets and the ideal standards of housing density were 'often thwarted and checked in town planning, because we find that what would be best for the community would involve injustice or hardship to individuals.'[14]

The town planning part eased administrative obligations in scheme preparation and for the first time made scheme preparation compulsory for certain local authorities, although when the Bill was first introduced, Dr Addison, its sponsor, warned against compulsory town planning, and the relevant clauses were only introduced in Standing Committee. Section 42 provided that it was no longer necessary for a local authority to obtain the authority of the Local Government Board to prepare or adopt a town planning scheme. Section 46 required every borough or other district council containing, on 1st January 1923, a population of more than 20 000 according to the last census, to prepare within three years a planning scheme in respect of those areas for which a scheme may be made under the 1909 Act (i.e. land in course of development or likely to be developed). This was modest progress indeed, but the obligatory requirement for the preparation of schemes heralded a period of greater planning activity than the 1909 Act had engendered.

In the meantime, the war years had not dimmed the garden city ideal, although there was a real clash of opinion as to what the best tactics were to meet the housing needs of the country, now with a shortage of about 600 000 dwellings. Within the National Housing and Town Planning Council, for example, one group propagandized for garden cities but others insisted that mass housing must be the great aim. Speculation was rife. A tract of the National Garden Cities Committee advocated new towns and the development of existing small towns as a means of dealing with the post-war housing problem and as part of the process of industrial, agricultural and social reconstruction[15]. A group of largely Quaker reformers formed themselves into a New Town Council with a proposal to found a new 'Country-Town' in England. A Pioneer Trust was formed to prospect for a suitable site. It was proposed 'to purchase a portion of the surface of England, of about 300 acres, and to exemplify upon it a more rational method of arranging homes, workshops and factories, so that its inhabitants shall all be in some direct touch with Mother Earth, and yet so grouped that all kinds of healthy and varied social intercourse in made easy.' It was to be 'a social experiment in the provision of a fit environment for the minds and bodies of men and women; inwardly it is to be a call to the spirit of men and women to enter the joy of active service together for the glory of God.'[16] In actual fact, the proposal was still-born as Howard's scheme in 1920 for the development of Welwyn as the second Garden City was implemented, so siphoning off the energies of many of those involved. But the importance of this confused period of enterprise was that it revealed the underlying social idealism which continued to imbue the planning movement with so much of its character. F. J. Osborn published his *New Towns After the War* in 1918; it proved to be more than a passing justification for New Towns, because his book needed only slight revision for it to be reissued in 1942.

THE TOWN PLANNING INSTITUTE

In its early months of existence the TPI suffered two setbacks. Thomas Adams, its first President and guiding light, left in early October 1914 to take up an appointment in Canada as town planning adviser to the Dominion's Commission of Conservation. His departure was the occasion for an informal farewell dinner. The outbreak of war threatened an even greater disturbance but it was decided to continue meetings, and these contributed a comforting therapy. As Unwin observed in 1915, 'Our meetings and our discussions have afforded a useful interlude, taking us for a time out of the all pervading atmosphere of war, of its enthusiasms and its sorrows.'[17]

Certainly, the war imposed considerable difficulties on the new Institute. Potter, the first secretary, appointed in December 1914, went off on active service at the beginning of 1916, and Pepler, the Honorary Secretary, took over his functions for three years. The German members of the Institute were expelled (and were only reinstated in 1922). A national partisanship existed within the TPI, so that Pepler, at a general meeting, spoke of the 'dominant forceful arrogant culture and architecture', representing, 'the German outlook on life'[18]. However, on another occasion, Unwin was able to comment with 'much pleasure' on the good work of a German colleague, Werner Haggermann, in the USA during this 'sad period'[19]. Town planners were torn between the old sense of fellowship with those working for urban improvement, and the patriotic denunciation of Germany.

Nevertheless, despite difficulties, the TPI and its members were involved in some ventures of considerable importance during the war. In 1915 Unwin moved from the Local Government Board which he had joined in 1914 to the new Ministry of Munitions to take charge of the planning of munitions settlements; he prepared layouts for the new estates of the cordite factories at Gretna and Eastriggs, Dumfries and elsewhere. He found himself with no spare time to prepare a Presidential address in 1915. Later, his contribution to the Tudor Walters Committee was outstanding.

The fall of Belgium and the wholesale destruction of Belgian towns attracted the interest of the TPI (and British society generally when faced with the Belgian refugee problem). A considerable number of refugee Belgian architects and engineers came to this country, and an exhibition on Belgian towns was arranged by the TPI, with help from other bodies, at University College, London, in early 1915. To continue their work, and to enable co-operation to take place regarding reconstruction, the Council agreed to a Joint Committee being set up with other interested bodies, particularly the International Garden Cities and Town Planning Association.

During the war the first steps were taken on certain professional matters and the story can be pieced together from Council and Committee Minutes. An Examinations Committee was set up in July 1915, later being renamed the Education Committee. Initially, it had been intended to hold the first examinations in 1916, but in the abnormal conditions of wartime, this scheme fell through. Nevertheless, considerable progress was made, and, in December, Council approved the syllabus. The more detailed aspects of education are dealt with in chapter 9, but we should note that, despite exceptional circumstances, progress was made at a relatively early date towards making the Institute a qualifying profession. There was little delay either, particularly in view of the war situation, in other aspects of professional advancement. In the sphere of planning practice, a scale of fees and regulations for competitions were drawn up and approved, again in December 1916.

On the other hand, the Institute did nothing towards a wartime project aimed at facilitating planning after the war. This was the RIBA's Civic Survey which began soon after the outbreak of war, partly to provide useful work for unemployed professionals, and partly to provide a basis for sound planning. Certain TPI members were involved but the Institute, as a body, was not associated with it. The main project was concerned with London, but the idea was taken up elsewhere. The Schools of Civic Design and Geography at Liverpool University conducted surveys of Bolton, Liverpool, Manchester, Leeds and Bradford; a Sheffield Survey owed much to municipal initiative; and a South Wales Survey was sponsored by Government.

However, the TPI took a more direct interest in other aspects of reconstruction. The need to provide adequate, good housing after the war became of paramount importance and had considerable implications for the planning movement. The matter was considered at a general meeting in December 1916, when Harrison Barrow, a Birmingham Councillor, read a paper on the 'Housing and Town Planning Requirements at the End of the War'. Paying regard to the patriotic sacrifices of the community, he asked, 'Can we not retain some of that magnificent spirit and devotion and apply it to the good government of the cities in which we live?'[20] This topic dominated the TPI for several years. In January 1917, Council considered the question of town planning after the war was over, and in February, Adshead, Abbott and Willis were appointed to draft a memorandum on the subject. This was approved in March, and presented to Lord Rhondda, President of the Local Government Board, under the title 'Town Planning After the War'. The document, signed by the President, Cockrill, expressed serious concern as to: 'the prospects of important public works and improvements proceeding after the war in areas where Town Planning schemes are in operation, and the consequent creation of conditions adverse to national efficiency'. With regard to the general admission of the need for public works and housing, it went on: 'The Council feel that in the event of such schemes being carried on *without regard to the proper planning of the areas in which they may be undertaken*, the very objects for which the Housing, Town Planning etc Act of 1909 was passed may be defeated.'[21] To combat this the memorandum did not propose compulsory town planning, but rather a simplification of regulations; it suggested that the Local Government Board should pressurize recalcitrant authorities by refusing to sanction loans. This advice fell short of recommendations made by other bodies, but the Institute's assessment of possibilities was probably the more realistic in view of the inadequate staffs and limited expertise that existed throughout the country.

In his Presidential Address in October 1917, E. R. Abbott returned to the theme of speedier action in the planning process: 'We are told that 500 000 houses are required at once, immediately upon the declaration of peace. How are they to be built? Are we to have the same kind of house, a hundred all alike in a row, the same dreary monotony, the same lack of open space, the same miserable backyards? No, we must have something better than this for the men who have been willing to give all for their country. If Town Planning is not simplified and speeded up, how is this to be prevented? These men who have been willing to obey any order given to them, to face any danger on sea and land, in the air and under the seas, are they to be denied a comfortable house when they return because we must consider the so-called rights of owners of property that before we can say he shall not overcrowd his land with buildings we must issue eight separate advertisements, and serve him with notice four times over?'[22] Abbott, former Town Clerk of Ruislip–Northwood UDC, was the first Legal Member to be elected President. He was particularly interested in this aspect of revising town planning law, and when in December 1917, some months after Cockrill's memorandum, Council considered detailed modifications of the Act, it was resolved that local authorities should be able to plan without previously obtaining the permission of the Local Government Board, and to plan all land thought necessary, whether built upon or not. If local authorities were in default, it was resolved that a government department or some other body should have power to prepare schemes. The 1919 Act, as we have seen, took up these points.

A further resolution called for some national policy of transport and intercommunication because this question was not seen as suitable for administration under the town planning legislation. This was very significant. The question of roads and transport had brought many engineers into the sphere of town planning, and the decision by Council not to urge a co-ordination of transport and planning, must, with hindsight, be regarded as prejudicial to the subsequent development of planning. Rees Jeffreys of the Road Board, and an active Honorary MTPI, had read to the Institute in May 1917 a long paper on 'Road Construction and Improvement by Means of Town Planning Schemes'. Its subtitle described his theme: 'an examination revealing deficiencies in the machinery of local government which delay and render difficult the solution of the twin problems of housing and road transport'. As remedies he advocated the establishment of a central Town Planning Commission that would deal with all aspects of Town Planning— roads as well as housing. He wanted stronger local authorities, rather than complete central control. Council's decision did not follow his point of view, and in fact in government circles from this time on, the functions of highways, housing and town planning developed on separate lines.

Rees Jeffreys did have some success, however. In April 1918, he successfully proposed that a Committee of the TPI should be formed to prepare a scheme for a Traffic Development Board for London and the Home Counties. The Committee was given power to co-opt and co-operate with other bodies. This problem of London's roads and planning was particularly intractable, and, as we have seen, had attracted attention before the war, both in the Royal Commission of 1905 and a deputation by various interested bodies to the Prime Minister in 1913. Rees Jeffreys had advocated to the Royal Commission the setting up of a single authority exercising jurisdiction over all means of communication in Greater London. He chaired the TPI's Committee, as well as a similar London Society Committee. These two produced a joint report which proposed a single town planning traffic and housing authority for London and the Home Counties[23]. Despite another Royal Commission (this time on Local Government) to which TPI in January 1922 submitted evidence calling for a single authority to co-ordinate the communication and development of London and the Home Counties, nothing resulted and the same unsatisfactory state of affairs continued.

Regarding the 1919 Act, the TPI, through Abbott and others, had been consulted by the President of the Local Government Board on the drafting of the Bill, and Abbott commented that virtually all their demands had been met. Nevertheless, he expressed the fear that: 'In the midst of the demands for housing and the desire of the Local Authorities to fulfil their obligations in that direction, we, as members of the Institute, must hope that the enormous possibilities of Town Planning will not be overlooked… In fact, it is almost essential that, if housing schemes are to be a success, they must be accompanied by Town Planning Schemes.'[24]

In contrast, Aldridge and the NHTPC pressed for compulsory Town Planning as one way of ensuring that housing development would be on proper lines. Aldridge wanted the TPI to discuss this at a general meeting, and for a vote to be taken. In spite of the reluctance to follow this propagandist device, Aldridge was allowed to present his case, which he did in no uncertain terms: 'If our belief in the value of Town Planning is worth anything at all, it should mean that we shall end once and for all with the policy of pitiful and inexcusable neglect of government control of every area in which development is to take place.' He ended with a warning. 'Let me say quite frankly that I do not envy the man, whoever he may be, who, for lack of courage in action and clearness in views, advocates any policy other than that of thoroughness. I never think of the years before the war and the difficulties then raised when strenuous action was opposed, without feeling hot with anger at those who opposed it.'[25] In the discussion which followed, the argument was held that, while town planning was essential, quality was preferable to quantity, and Aldridge's views received little support. The NHTPC's campaign was successful, however, and, following the intervention of a number of MPs as the Bill went through the House, the Act finally embodied the element of compulsion that had been sought.

By the end of the war the TPI could look back on some years of solid progress with some satisfaction. Membership had grown spasmodically, early enthusiasms dwindling in the war years. But there was a pick-up, and after gaining only nine members in 1917–18, 29 joined in 1918–19, and 65 in 1919–20. Pepler, in his Presidential Address in October 1919, was able to remark that 'Our Institute is only five years old, conceived in one world but born and beginning life in a world entirely changed by the fearful upheaval, in which, while nursing this lusty infant, we have all been involved'. He spoke of their '... good fortune to be engaged in a profession that is so essentially constructive and which offers so many opportunities for helping to make our country a pleasant place to live in.'[26]

But this was no time for self congratulations, and in the following year Adshead bewailed the ignorance of public opinion in failing to distinguish between a town planning scheme and a housing scheme. To further the public acceptance of planning, he thought that 'propaganda is clearly what is needed, and propaganda, to be successful, must appeal to the public on simple and direct issues. It is not one of the objects of this Institution to become a propagandist Institution. There are other organizations better able to do this and I think that if some three or four very definite objects to be attained by Town Planning were outlined, and their realization pressed by our propagandist societies, both directly and also through the Press, it would do much to awaken a revived public interest in the completion of schemes commenced before 1914.'[27] The Institute's concern to conform with the traditional idea of professionalism limited the role it could take in advocating policy. Thus, when in late 1921–early 1922, the question was raised of co-operating with NHTPC, to urge a definite Housing and Town Planning Policy, it was resolved: 'that the Institute does not think it expedient to take part in propagandist work, but within the limits and scope of the Institute, will be pleased to give any assistance to the NHTPC in respect of any specific case.'[28] This conflict between cautious professionals and the advocates of propaganda continued for many years.

The Institute could enter the twenties in a mood of some optimism sustained by social purpose. Its material possessions were scanty: 'one deed box, plus several framed portraits of former Presidents' according to Pepler[29], but the demand for professional work was increasing. The next few years were to throw up new challenges in the form of economic and social developments, and the town planning movement and the professional body responded accordingly.

REFERENCES

1. *The Times*, 1 September 1909, quoted in Bright, Tom, *The Development of Building Estates*. B. T. Batsford, 1910.
2. *Bournville Village Trust, 1900–1955*, Bournville Village Trust, Bournville, 1955.
3. *Annual Report of the Local Government Board*, 1909–10, Cd.5275.
4. *Annual Report of the Local Government Board*, 1910–11, Cd.5978.
5. *Annual Report of the Local Government Board*, 1912–13, Cd.6981.
6. *Annual Report of the Local Government Board for Scotland*, 1918, Cmd.230.
7. Buchanan, C. M., *London Road Plans 1900–1970*. Greater London Research Report No. 11, GLC Intelligence Unit, 1970.

8. Johnson, Paul Barton, *Land Fit For Heroes: the Planning of British Reconstruction.* University of Chicago Press, 1968.
9. Johnson, Paul Barton, *Land Fit For Heroes: the Planning of British Reconstruction.* University of Chicago Press, 1968.
10. *Report of the Royal Commission on the Housing of the Industrial Population of Scotland,* 1917, Cd.8731.
11. *Report of Committee on Building Construction in Connection With the Provision of Dwellings for the Working Class in England and Wales and Scotland,* 1918, Cd.9191.
12. Johnson, Paul Barton, *Land Fit For Heroes: the Planning of British Reconstruction.* University of Chicago Press, 1968.
13. Johnson, Paul Barton, *Land Fit For Heroes: the Planning of British Reconstruction.* University of Chicago Press, 1968.
14. Read, Donald, *Edwardian England.* Harrap, 1972.
15. New Townsmen, *New Towns After War.* Dent, London, 1918.
16. Hughes, W. R. (Ed.), *New Town: a Proposal in Agricultural, Industrial, Educational, Civic and Social Reconstruction.* Dent, London, 1919.
17. Unwin, Raymond, The Work of the Town Planning Institute. *Town Planning Institute Papers and Discussions,* **I**, No. 9, 1915.
18. *Town Planning Institute Papers and Discussions,* **III**, No. 5, 86, 1917.
19. *Town Planning Institute Papers and Discussions,* **II**, No. 8, 166, 1916.
20. Barrow, Harrison, Housing and Town Planning Requirements at the end of the War. *Town Planning Institute Papers and Discussions,* **III**, No. 3, 1916.
21. *Town Planning Institute Council Minutes,* **I**, pp. 86–7.
22. E. R. Abbott, President's Address. *Town Planning Institute Papers and Discussions,* **IV**, No. 1, 1917.
23. *Town Planning Institute Papers and Discussions,* **V**, No. 4, 39–70, 1919.
24. *Town Planning Institute Papers and Discussions,* **V**, No. 6, 92, 1919.
25. *Town Planning Institute Papers and Discussions,* **V**, No. 6, 98, 1919.
26. Pepler, G. L., President's Address. *Town Planning Institute Papers and Discussions,* **VI**, No. 1, 1919.
27. Adshead, S. D., The Effect of the Act of 1919 on Uncompleted Schemes Commenced Before the War. *Town Planning Institute Papers and Discussions,* **VII**, No. 1, 1920.
28. *Town Planning Institute Council Minutes,* **I**, p. 177.
29. Pepler, G. L., President's Address. *Town Planning Institute Papers and Discussions,* **VI**, No. 1,1919.

5 The Inter-War Period

The twenty years between 1919 and 1939 have a certain unity imposed by the shadow of war—the consequences of one and the onset of another—and the fact that the period has a distinct beginning and an equally distinct end. New circumstances were presented at the commencement of the period, and the subsequent course of events during the two decades have a certain continuity. This chapter begins with a brief sketch of the main social and economic features of the period; these provided the problems and issues against which town planning developed. It continues with a review of developments, first in the statutory planning process and in related fields, and then in professional matters within the Institute. This part of the chapter is divided into two parts, the passing of the 1932 Town and Country Planning Act being an important intermediate point. This gives the advantage of considering the 1920s separately from the 1930s, for, in spite of the acknowledged unity of the whole period, nonetheless, there are real differences between the two decades. In conclusion, some general observations are made about the activities of the Institute over the inter-war years as a whole.

THE BACKGROUND[1]

Population growth slowed down markedly. The birth rate of 24.1 per thousand population for England and Wales in 1913 fell to 14.8 in 1939. The increase in population for England and Wales between 1921 and 1931 was 5.5%; between 1901 and 1911 it had been almost double at 10.9%. An urban concentration continued to be the chief characteristic. Two out of five of the population of Britain now lived in seven areas: London, Manchester, Birmingham, West Yorkshire, Glasgow, Merseyside and Tyneside. But the proportions in these largest aggregates were now about stationary and the other large and medium towns showed a great increase. Greater London, with a population of more than 8 millions had about one-fifth of the total population of England and Wales.

The tightly drawn urban boundaries masked the real dominance of the largest cities and conurbations. The process of dispersal carried population into the county authorities, beyond the boroughs; population densities declined in the urban centres, and sectors of peripheral growth ate substantially into the rural fringes. The new residential standards of around 12 houses to the acre contributed to a substantial spatial explosion. London, of course, was a prime example with development following lines of road and rail communication, as described by A. A. Jackson in *Semi-Detached London* (1973). 'Stake your claim in Edgware', proclaimed the Underground in 1926. 'Omar Khayyam's recipe for turning the wilderness into paradise hardly fits the English climate, but provision has been made at Edgware of an alternative recipe which at least will convert pleasant undulating fields into happy homes.'[2] Some exceptionally large local increases of population were recorded in major developments; in London, notable examples were at Dagenham and Hendon in the 1920s. Clough Williams Ellis' *England and the Octopus* (1928) was a title that described the threat of urban sprawl, and the seemingly insatiable spread of the big cities, London in particular, provoked a sense of frustration in failure to deal with the urban problems of the day. Later, Robert Sinclair's *Metropolitan Man* (1938) was a swingeing commentary for the layman on the planlessness of London in this period.

Population movements within regions, were overlain by movement between them. There were, in fact, substantial shifts in the regional distribution of population throughout the country, some areas recording marked increases, while others declined. London and the Home Counties showed the highest figures: between 1921 and 1937 there was a population increase of 18%. Other areas to show increases were the Midland Counties (by 11%), the West Riding, Nottinghamshire and Derbyshire (6%), the Lowlands of Scotland (4%) and Lancashire (marginally, less than 1%). On the other hand, South Wales recorded a decrease of 9% and Northumberland and Durham 1%. The association with fluctuating economic fortunes is indicated below.

The health of the country (and particularly the urban population) was still an important national issue. The flu epidemic of 1918–19, which killed more than 150 000 people in England and Wales, causing more deaths relative to the population than anything since the cholera epidemic of 1849, suggested a low level of general physical health. The same was reflected in the war years of 1917–18 when only 36% of the men examined for military service were passed Grade I. (We have noted the much lower fitness figures at the time of the Boer War; during the Second World War the Grade I figure was 70%.) Attention became focussed on a range of related policies including free milk in schools, provision of ante-natal clinics, campaigns against rickets, advocacy of the health-giving qualities of sunlight, demands for the reduction of overcrowding and improvement of housing conditions, and agitation for smoke control. The incidence of poverty was highlighted again with social surveys in York, Merseyside and elsewhere, and when linked to the questions of poor housing and widespread unemployment the state of British towns remained the serious national issue which it had been before the war.

A new national problem, though with a discriminating regional flavour, was posed with changes in Britain's industrial structure, associated with important expansions and contractions in a number of industries. The clothing and textile industries, agriculture and personal service showed decreases in their work force compared with before 1914; on the other hand, during the 1930s in particular, large employment gains were recorded in the manufacture of electrical apparatus, entertainment services, vehicle construction and building. Extractive industries, heavy engineering and shipbuilding were depressed trades. Unemployment in areas outside London was a relatively new phenomenon.

Before 1914 the highest unemployment rates in Britain were in London, when the national average fluctuated between 4% and 8%. During the 1920s and 30s when unemployment was never below 9% (after 1924), and reached more than 20% at its peak, London and the Home Counties were the relatively favoured areas, and the jobless areas of the North, Scotland and Wales became officially 'distressed'. A growing interest in economic planning, as reflected in the founding of PEP (Political and Economic Planning) in 1931, was matched by the beginnings of Government intervention in economic affairs. PEP thought that the appointment of the Barlow Commission might have been a statesmanlike move in 1927; in 1937 it was long overdue. Town planning was slow to become involved in aspects of economic planning, but by the end of the 1930s there were signs of a quickening interest.

The inter-war years saw a substantial expansion of housing with new changes in tenure structure. One in ten of the four million dwellings built between 1919 and 1939 were local authority houses. London and the big cities built large council estates with Government subsidies. Private ownership also increased, greatly assisted by the rapidly expanding Building Societies. Within the older housing areas a major housing evil of unfit dwellings remained, largely untackled until the slum clearance drive of the 1930s (and not adequately tackled then). Every major city, particularly in the North, had bad housing conditions with large numbers of dwellings classed unfit for human habitation. A modest local authority redevelopment programme began, frequently with development in the form of flats in emulation of central European architecture. Squalid accommodation exacerbated the problem of overcrowding. Improvements were taking place as the supply of dwellings outstripped the growth of population, but a national overcrowding survey in 1936 showed unacceptable conditions still obtaining, with Scotland, the North East and London still recording high overcrowding rates.

A phenomenal growth in road traffic provided another aspect of the inter-war period. The number of private cars licensed in Great Britain increased from 187 000 in 1920 to 2 034 000 in 1939; the total number of vehicles licensed rose from 650 000 to 3 149 000. There were a number of new features. The first roadside petrol station (with hand pump) was established by the AA at Aldermaston on the Great West Road in 1920. Roundabouts for traffic circulation made their appearance from the middle of 1920s, first of all in London. Wolverhampton became the first town to experiment with traffic lights in 1927. A programme of road improvements included tunnels, bridges, arterial roads and bypasses, but financial considerations kept these to a minimum. The traffic problem established itself as a national issue in the big towns and, of course, London, but very little progress was made in dealing with the problem on a comprehensive basis.

The countryside began the period beset with difficulties, and while agricultural employment fell sharply and many of the large estates were broken up for sale, nonetheless, some aspects of the situation were improving. The advent of the motor bus broke down rural isolation. Rural Community Councils started in 1921, as did Young Farmers' Clubs. Later, in 1930, there was the idea of Village Colleges in Cambridgeshire, a combination of secondary school and community centre for a group of villages. But the countryside was very much at risk from the point of view of despoilation by sporadic residential development. The need for rural protection was a recurrent theme in town planning. The development of farm tractors heralded a new era of mechanization on the land. Government support came with agricultural advice and assistance; Marketing Boards were set up and subsidies encouraged the growing of certain crops. The Rural Industries Bureau was founded in 1921.

This was the period of a renewed interest in the countryside, particularly for recreation. In 1927 the magazine *The Countryman* was launched and books on rural themes were popular. The Council for the Preservation of Rural England was formed in 1926. Hiking and cycling were popular activities; in the north, mass rambling led to conflict with land-owners and sporting interests in the grouse moors. The Youth Hostel Association was founded in 1930 and there were nearly 300 hostels and 83 000 members in England and Wales before the war. The attractions of outdoor pursuits in the countryside, and the new-found possibilities for family movement (car and motor bus supplemented excursion rail travel) presented a new situation, that of catering for mass recreation in a new way. However, town planning was slow to react with positive solutions, or even accept recreation as an issue with which it should be concerned.

The question of the use of leisure time was part of the social changes that were taking place in the inter-war years. Within the cities there was a great shortage of playing space, and the National Playing Fields Association did much to encourage higher standards of provision: its recommended six acres of open space per thousand population advocated in 1924 long remained a target. This was very much bound up with the urban health factor. New public measures secured attention: for example, George Lansbury, First Commissioner of Works in the Labour Government of 1929, created Lansbury Lido for mixed bathing in the Serpentine and sunbathing on the shore. The availability of leisure time increased considerably; in the early 1920s, holidays with pay were given to about $1\frac{1}{2}$ million employees, but with the Holidays with Pay Act, 1938, the figure reached 11 million. New features of the holiday industry were born. The first factory production of the trailer caravan took place in 1922; Butlin's Skegness Holiday Camp opened in 1936. Within the cities, there were new popular activities: the first dog track opened in Manchester in 1926, dirt-track motor cycling began at Loughton in 1928, a new cinema boom came in the 1930s, and the days of mass home radio entertainment arrived—by 1939 there was a receiver in three out of every four homes.

STATUTORY PLANNING 1919–1932

Under the Housing and Town Planning Act, 1919, the procedure for making town planning schemes was simplified. It was no longer necessary for a local Council to obtain the authority of the Minister of Health for the preparation of a scheme (the new Ministry having replaced the former Local Government Board). All that was required was the formal resolution of the local authority to prepare a scheme in respect of an area of land. With the recommencement of building operations after the war, the need for schemes was apparent; it will be recalled (see chapter 4), that after 1st January 1923, the preparation of schemes was compulsory on all borough and district Councils with a population of more than 20 000, and the schemes had to be prepared within three years of that date. Local authorities were urged to make their schemes simple and to concentrate on securing

82

'the essentials of town planning, viz the principal routes of communication and restrictions in regard to the character and density of buildings to be erected on the area.'[3]

The required procedure in the preparation of schemes was given in the Town Planning Regulations which came in to force on 2nd May, 1921. The first stage was the *resolution* to prepare a scheme. Then followed the *preliminary statement* of the proposed main outlines of development to be submitted to the Minister within six months of the resolution. This outline, to be accompanied by a map, was intended to show the principal new roads to be constructed, the open spaces to be reserved and the restrictions proposed in regard to character, density and height of buildings. The third stage was the *draft scheme*, adopted by the local authority within 12 months of the Minister's approval of the preliminary statement. Within a further six months it was to be finally adopted and submitted to the Minister. It should be noted that the schemes were in respect of undeveloped land, although some developed land could be included for 'round off'. Before final approval, interim development could be permitted if proposals fell within the general scheme of the preliminary statement.

The statutory provisions enabled the practice of town planning to develop. At a Planning Conference in Manchester in 1922, George Pepler, now Chief Town Planning Inspector at the Ministry of Health, stated the general premise: 'Unless the development of our towns is governed by a general plan, those whose duty it is to safeguard and improve the health of the community and those interested in its material progress, can have no solid basis to go upon, because there can be no guarantee that a good piece of work in one direction will not be vitiated by independent action in another, or because the surroundings are not under control, or will not show far less fruitful results than are warranted, because other efforts are not co-ordinated'[4]. He stressed the co-ordinating role of the town planner, whose aim was to avoid the waste that inevitably accompanied piecemeal development. This idea was also expressed by Frank M. Elgood (Ruislip–Northwood) at the same Conference: whereas the medical officer was concerned with sanitation and healthy houses, the engineer with roads and bridges, the policeman with the regulation of traffic, and others with open space and garden plots, town planning 'meant all these things and more, collected and welded into a whole which shall satisfy by intelligent anticipation, not only all practical requirements, but in doing so, create a work of art'[5].

With the preparation of an increasing number of town planning schemes advances were made in planning method. The Ministry, for example, explained in 1921 that one of the main objectives of a town plan was to fix those areas in which certain types of development should be allowed. 'This system has become known by the name of "zoning". It has received much attention in the United States of America, but it has, as yet, been but little studied in this country.'[6] Another technique which was recommended was the drawing up, 'in some form or other' of a civic survey. Certain information was quite vital 'to enable a town planner to arrive at a proper elucidation of the problems which face him'. Sheffield was praised as an outstanding example of the way in which some local authorities had begun to collect this sort of information on systematic lines.

The Ministry were confident of the growing appreciation of the value and importance of town planning. A large scheme covering 3 173 acres, approved in 1921, was a good example to be followed. This was the Birmingham City, North Yardley and Stechford

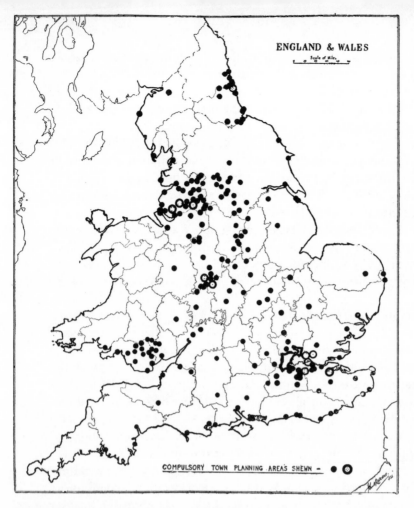

ENGLAND & WALES

Scale of Miles

COMPULSORY TOWN PLANNING AREAS SHEWN -

Compulsory Town Planning Areas. The 1919 Town Planning Act made the preparation of town planning schemes obligatory on only a certain number of local authorities. There were 1 798 local authorities in England and Wales who could voluntarily prepare and adopt town planning schemes, and 249 to whom the compulsory provisions applied. This map shows the vast areas 'sometimes whole counties, where town planning may be relegated to the limbo of forgotten things.' (J. A. Rosevear, 'Compulsory Town Planning: Should it be extended?' *Journal TPI*, **X**, No. 10, 1924)

Plan for Bexhill, 1931, showing zoning proposals and the road system. The plan put particular emphasis on proposals for the development of the sea front. (*Courtesy of* Churchill Livingstone. Taken from Thomas Adams, *Recent Advances in Town Planning*, J. & A. Churchill, 1932)

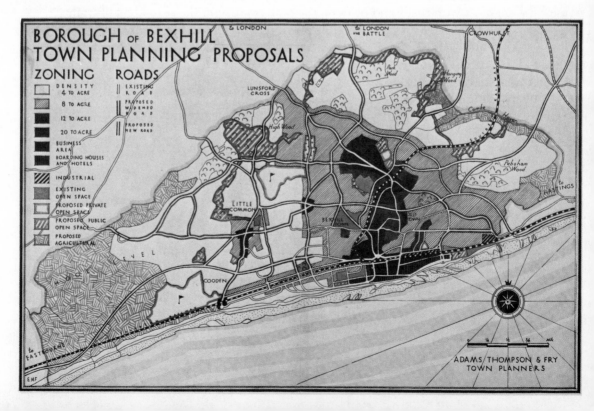

BOROUGH OF BEXHILL
TOWN PLANNING PROPOSALS

ZONING   ROADS

ADAMS, THOMPSON & FRY
TOWN PLANNERS

Town Planning Scheme, allowing for new roads, widening of existing ones, residential density restrictions, and the provision of recreation space. However, as the 1920s went by, the Ministry became more and more concerned that local authorities were not progressing more quickly with their proposals. By 1928, there were still 98 out of 262 urban authorities, with a population of more than 20 000, which had still not submitted any proposals in the form of either resolutions, preliminary statements or schemes, and many of those who had submitted proposals had done so only in respect of parts of their town planning areas. The date for submission of obligatory schemes had already been extended, and the Local Government Act of 1929 extended it further to 1st January 1934, with power to the Minister to extend the date again but not beyond 31st December 1938. By 1930 there were still 58 urban authorities which had submitted no proposals.

In 1931, 21 years of town planning legislation were celebrated, and to ascertain the results the Ministry conducted an inquiry among local authorities. The findings were that 'Local authorities and landowners alike are generally alive to the advantages of wise planning as a means of securing orderly and healthy housing conditions, and there can be little doubt that what is now being done at comparatively trifling expense under town planning schemes, to secure amenity and convenience in the laying out of land, will be a source of large ultimate saving to the community in many directions.'[7]

The measures of the 1919 Act had been consolidated in the Town Planning Act, 1925, (the first planning legislation not to be an appendage of Housing). The provisions were superceded by the Town and Country Planning Act, 1932. For some time, a combination of slow progress and the need for more effective legislation covering rural as well as urban areas, was necessitating a new Planning Act. None the less, the 1919 Act provisions had served their purpose. The upper table on p. 86 summarizes the position. More than 9 million acres in England and Wales were covered by Town Planning Schemes when the 1932 Act came into operation in April 1933. On the other hand, just 94 schemes had so far been approved, submitted by 50 local authorities. Much more progress was needed.

In Scotland progress was even slower; the Scottish Board of Health in 1928 confessed that 'town planning has been a plant of slow growth'[8]. The first scheme has been approved in 1920, in respect of land at Dunfermline, and the second in 1921, the Fountainbridge Scheme, Edinburgh. Local authority attention was more devoted to the preparation of housing schemes under the 1919 Act, although interest was being shown in regional planning. A Clyde Valley Joint Town Planning Advisory Committee was formed; in 1928 a Conference at Kirkcaldy organized by the Scottish National Housing and Town Planning Committee stimulated a regional planning approach in Fife; and a Joint Committee was also set up in Aberdeen. A considerable help to regional planning was the fact that the Local Government (Scotland) Act, 1929, transferred the town planning powers of district committees and small burghs to county councils; this was not the case in respect of legislation for England and Wales.

It was not until 1929 that the first two schemes were submitted for approval since the war. They related to two small areas in Edinburgh. One was quickly approved; this was the Charlotte Square Scheme made to preserve the area and to protect the special architectural, historic and artistic features. The situation regarding schemes is summarized in the lower table on p. 86.

85

Town planning schemes in England and Wales as at 31st March 1933

Position of scheme	No. of schemes	No. of L.A.s submitting schemes	Acreage covered by schemes
(1) Schemes finally approved	94	50	152 182
(2) Schemes sumitted and under consideration	34	17	56 464
(3) Draft schemes adopted for local deposit but not yet submitted	33	20	67 758
(4) Preliminary statements approved	236	152	948 557
(5) Preliminary statements submitted and under consideration	113	97	829 658
(6) Schemes authorized under Act of 1909 to be prepared, but schemes or preliminary statements not yet submitted	43	29	85 741
(7) Special schemes authorized to be prepared for already developed areas under Act of 1925, but schemes or preliminary statements not yet submitted	4	4	878
(8) Resolutions under Acts of 1919 and 1925, deciding to prepare schemes, but schemes or preliminary statements not yet submitted:			
(i) Resolutions not requiring approval	627	502	6 536 293
(ii) Resolutions requiring approval, and approved	63	48	706 285
	1 235*	742 (net)	9 383 816

* Excluding amending schemes.

Source: Ministry of Health Annual Reports.

Town planning schemes in Scotland as at 31st December 1932

Position of scheme	No. of schemes	No. of L.A.s concerned	Acreage covered by schemes
(1) Schemes finally approved	5	3	8 722
(2) Schemes submitted to Department but not yet approved	4	4	79 911
(3) Draft schemes prepared and adopted by L.A.s but not yet submitted to Department	1	1	796
(4) Schemes authorized under 1909 Act to be prepared	15	4	17 210
(5) Resolutions under Acts of 1919 and 1925 deciding to prepare schemes:			
(i) not requiring Department's approval	23	16	57 573
(ii) requiring Department's approval, and approved	4	4	
	52	27	177 294

In the period between 1919 and 1932, a number of legislative measures affected the statutory planning process. The Housing etc Act, 1923, referred to compensation and altered the date for submission of schemes. The provisions in section 21 enabled the Minister to authorize the preparation of a town planning scheme for land, whether developed or not, with the object of preserving the existing character and features of a locality with special architectural, historic or artistic interests. The first authority to use these new powers was Oxford, which, in 1925, was authorized to prepare a scheme for two areas including the University quarter. Canterbury, Exeter and Winchester followed suit. Elsewhere, town planning powers were also extended by Local Act to cover developed parts of cities; Newcastle was an example at this time.

The Allotments Act of 1925 made it obligatory on local authorities to give special attention to the matter of open spaces and allotments in preparing their schemes. The Minister urged more land to be reserved for these purposes.

County Councils began to display an increasing interest in town planning matters. This was because of their own road powers, and the interests they had in their own building development and other land uses. The Local Government Act, 1929, extended to County Councils in England and Wales the right to share in the preparation and administration of any joint town planning scheme, although it stopped short of giving them any direct power of initiating schemes themselves. Surrey and Buckinghamshire organized conferences of local authorities in their counties to review the planning position from a county standpoint, and some County Councils considered the appointments of County Directors of town planning.

The financial implications of reserving land for one use as against another began to pose practical difficulties, especially when the restriction of general building development was required in favour of open space and agricultural belts. The Town Planning Act, 1925, empowered local authorities to claim betterment from other owners whose land was increased in value owing to the reservation. Only half of the increase in value could be recovered, however, and local authorities were deterred from taking action, so that most reservations were worked out on the basis of voluntary co-operation.

REGIONAL PLANNING

A feature of the 1920s was the great interest shown in regional planning through the agency of Joint Committees. It had long been recognized that the planning problems of a local authority were not confined to its administrative boundaries. The development of the 'concealed' Yorkshire coalfield, for example, had been the subject of discussion during the war years, and shortly afterwards a Joint Committee was constituted consisting of various local authorities centred on Doncaster; Abercrombie and a local consultant, Johnson, were appointed to report on the area and prepare, in outline, a town planning scheme.

But the first major study was in respect of South Wales. In February 1920 the Minister appointed a Committee to inquire and report on the special circumstances affecting the distribution and location of houses to be erected with state aid in the region of the South Wales coalfield. The terms of reference implied a regional survey. The Survey Committee reported in 1921. It was recommended that the provision of houses for miners should be, for the most part, outside the valleys and off the coal measures; 15 localities were suggested as centres for grouped housing schemes to serve particular valleys, with two established as complete dormitory towns. For further work, four Joint Town Planning Committees were recommended to work under a Regional Town Planning Board to prepare a regional development plan. Abercrombie waxed eloquent on this geographical scale: 'so logically and all-compelling was the result of this study that among other remarkable phenomena county councils appeared ready to sign their own death-warrants in order to promote unity, and the only discordant notes came from some of the owners of delectable spots in the agricultural plains, who foresaw an avalanche descending from the Pennant Hills and human torrents issuing from the carboniferous valleys to settle like an alluvium on their sequestered acres.'[10]

The practical example of regional planning probably first came from America, where, in the Metropolitan District of Massachusetts, the park system of Greater Boston, covering 15 000 acres and 25 miles of parkways, was owned and maintained by 38 local authorities. This sort of joint action and financial responsibility was behind the strong British regional planning movement. Another aspect was the need to adopt common standards, such as common definitions for zoning regulations, number of dwellings per acre, and heights of buildings. The promotion of positive planning on a regional scale also came through the demand for co-ordinated road systems. Furthermore, regional action was seen to benefit municipal services such as water supply and sewage disposal.

With this background, there were some notable early developments in regional planning. A Joint Town Planning Advisory Committee was constituted for Manchester and District in 1920; in September of that year, Manchester Corporation had convened a conference of 76 local authorities covering an area about 15 miles radius from the city centre. In October 1920 a Dee-side Conference was called by the Minister at Chester at which representatives of English and Welsh Councils resolved to set up a Joint Town Planning Committee. In November 1920 a similar Conference was called at Thornaby; it was resolved to set up two Joint Committees, for North and South Teesside. The following year, Joint Advisory Committees were formed for North, and South Tyneside and West Middlesex. New Committees were established for Mansfield and District, the Wirral, Rotherham and District, North-East Surrey, the Thames Valley, South Essex and East Glamorgan. Thereafter, each year saw the formation of new Committees and many extensions to those already formed.

New problems arose which could best be tackled on a regional basis. One was the need to preserve considerable tracts of land against the spread of building development. The saving of quality landscape areas in the prevention of urban sprawl, was seen as a matter for regional town planning schemes. The question of rural planning and the preservation of the countryside was at an early stage. The usual practice of simply proposing low densities was a far from appropriate remedy, and comprehensive schemes for land reservations over the areas of many local authorities was the regional answer. Other factors promoting regional planning included the traffic problem, which necessitated regional co-ordination, and new interest shown in planning by County Councils. Another factor was a response to a new situation—air transport. The RIBA set up an Aerodromes Committee,

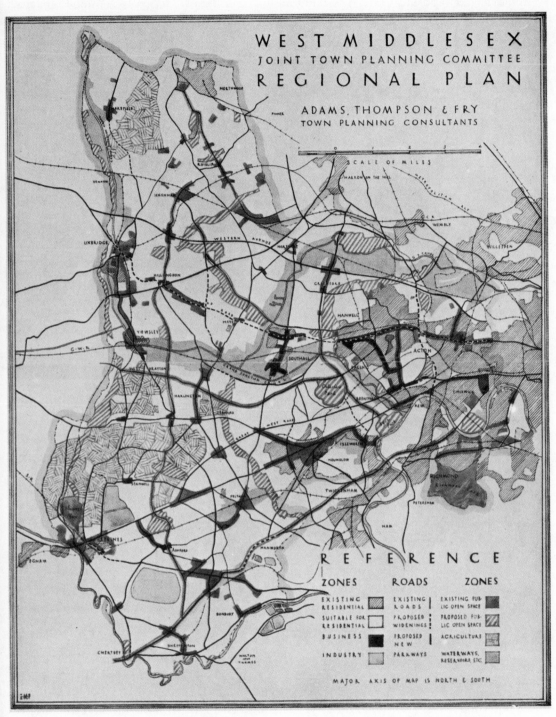

West Middlesex Regional Plan. The suburban areas of West Middlesex formed the first London subregion to be planned. The plan indicated suitable land use zones and an improvement of the road system. Published in colour.

(*Courtesy of* Churchill Livingstone. Taken from Thomas Adams, *Recent Advances in Town Planning*, J. & A. Churchill, 1932) and in its first report in 1931 ('Town Planning and Aviation') it drew attention to the need to provide further aerodromes in order to develop internal air transport: it suggested safe and properly equipped landing fields at intervals of not more than 20 miles. Some measure of regional co-ordination was necessary to achieve this.

An early successful regional plan was that prepared in 1926 by the Manchester and District Joint Committee of which the newly established North of England Division of the TPI was a member. The area covered 1 000 square miles within four counties, constituting seven County Boroughs and 89 other authorities. An outline was presented of regional and main roads, and a zoning for residential, commercial and industrial land and open spaces. Belts of land were to be kept free from development so that the main built-up areas could be defined, and there was some open country for agriculture and recreation. Remarkably quickly, the main spatial elements of regional planning had become established. An important administrative recommendation of this Report was for a number of regional committees to serve the constituent authorities, each to be served by a regional planning officer. This recommendation was taken up, and regional planning officers started to operate from 1928 onwards. Ernest Doubleday, a future President of TPI was appointed planning officer to one of these regional committees (Bolton and District) in 1935. The sheer geographical scale of collaborative regional enterprises was also noteworthy. The Midlands Joint Town Planning Council, which became the largest regional planning unit in the country, covered an area built round six centres—Birmingham, Coventry, Kidderminster, Walsall, Warwick and Wolverhampton. All seventy local authorities were represented on the Council except one Urban District and three Rural Districts.

One major advance in regional planning can be seen in the substantial contribution made in the most noteworthy regional exercise of all, that for Greater London. In December 1926, the Minister of Health called a conference of all the local authorities (including County Councils) and Joint Committees within the London Traffic Area. (We shall see later how this invitation came about, see p. 97.) It was decided to establish a Regional Committee for the whole area, and this first met in November 1927. Raymond Unwin was subsequently appointed Technical Adviser.

This initiative was overdue. A collection of essays, *London of the Future*, had been published by the London Society in 1921. Unwin had reviewed the problems then and written of decentralization and redistribution, but London's sprawl was scarcely checked. With no overall strategy to guide development, it rested with the individual units to prepare what policies they could. Hertfordshire had suggested a green belt running through the southern part of the County to form part of a continuous open area surrounding London. The North Middlesex Joint Committee advised a ring of satellite towns as part of a systematic distribution of population. In this situation, Unwin worked energetically and the First Report of the Greater London Committee was issued in 1929. This dealt particularly with the question of open spaces and a green belt, and with ribbon development on main roads. He estimated that at least 62 square miles of additional playing fields and 142 square miles of additional other or general open space were required. Two Interim Reports followed, one on open spaces in which Unwin pointed out the rate at which the existing spaces were being used up, and one on-decentralization. He recommended self-

90

contained satellite communities at distances of up to 12 miles, and still more complete industrial garden cities located between 12–25 miles from Charing Cross.

But this creative thinking was to be nipped in the bud and in 1931–32 questions of economy led to the expenses of the Committee being curtailed. The Ministry's Annual Report notes that 'but for the public spirit shown by their Technical Adviser, Dr Raymond Unwin, it might have been impossible for the Committee to continue their activities.'[11] The Second Report of the Committee, was published, however, in 1933, but the smallness of financial resources had effectively terminated the enterprise. Considerable developments in the field of regional planning had taken place during the last ten years. A large number of Joint Committees had been established, increasingly Executive Committees rather than Advisory in function. By 1926, thirty-three Advisory and one Executive Committee had been established; by 1932, the figures were sixty and forty-eight respectively. At least 30 regional planning schemes in England had been the subject of reports by Joint Committees or Consultants; there were at least three in Scotland. In January 1931 the Minister of Health, Arthur Greenwood, asked Lord Chelmsford to chair a Committee to consider these Reports and assess what was now required. Raymond Unwin, W. R. Davidge and T. Alwyn Lloyd were members. The Committee, in an Interim Report, found that many aspects of the schemes were already in hand and they did not see any case for the establishment of a new form of organization, national or local to carry out the work[12].

OTHER ASPECTS OF PLANNING 1919–32

High hopes were expressed of the Housing Act, 1919. Johnson, the historian of British reconstruction during the war, remarks that 'of all the measures passed in 1919, this was what men meant when they spoke of a new and better England'[13]. Housing became a social service and although the number of local authority dwellings approved was small in the early months, continued government action seemed assured. An Unhealthy Areas Committee, originally known as the Slum Areas Committee, was appointed by the Minister of Health in 1920 to advise on the principles to be followed in dealing with unhealthy areas. The Chairman was Neville Chamberlain. Pepler was a member and so too was R. C. Maxwell, President of TPI in 1931–2. It issued an Interim Report the same year, recommending an increase in the housing and town planning powers of London local authorities. A Final Report in 1921 concluded that the reconstruction of slum areas could only be dealt with satisfactorily by the simultaneous consideration of housing, transport and other land uses over a wide area. The beginnings of comprehensive planning were neatly illustrated: 'many of the factories now located in London might apparently have been placed elsewhere without any disadvantages to themselves, and we are strongly of the opinion that side by side with the restrictions upon factories in London, there should be encouraged the starting of new industries and the removal of existing factories to Garden Cities.'

But in a panic retrenchment in 1922 the Government's housing policy was reversed. Christopher Addision resigned in bitterness and later wrote that it was 'a matter for grave concern when it was decided in July 1922 ... to ignore the obligations which the State has assumed under the law passed in the year 1919, whereby assistance would be afforded in the replacement or improvement of insanitary dwellings for some years to come, and to substitute a grant in respect of all the unsatisfactory houses in Great Britain which ... will not suffice even to make good the amount of deterioration that is progressively occurring.'[14] But all was not lost, and under John Wheatley's Housing Act of 1924, Government subsidies for Council housing were provided for a number of years.

Unwin by this time was Chief Technical Officer for Building and Town Planning at the Ministry of Health, and until 1928 he was responsible for the evaluation of all the country's housing projects. Local authority estates became new urban features with low density, geometrically shaped layouts. Some were very large indeed, and Becontree became a by-word for extensive one-class housing areas of this kind. Garden city principles were adopted by Manchester in the estate development at Wythenshawe. However, council development was not welcome everywhere. A guide for estate developers in 1926 warned of the devaluing effects of the 'construction of sewage works, a dust destructor, the erection of a fever hospital, a "Government Housing Scheme" and land for industrial purposes.'[15]

Housing design and estate layout was indeed of mixed quality. In Scotland housing schemes were generally poor; barren and monotonous, and lacking in amenities. Only a few examples showed what could be done, as in some imaginative groups of housing in Dunbartonshire. In English cities the flats and houses controversy began. Birmingham, for example, was always against the building of flats. In London on the other hand, five-storey, neo-Georgian blocks were common place.

Wythenshawe deserves special mention. The development of the Tatton Estate, covering more than 2 500 acres was first mooted in 1918, but it was not begun until 1928. Barry Parker was appointed consultant. During the war he had spent three years working in Portugal and Brazil and his experience was now considerable. He adopted a zoning policy with ten residential neighbourhoods; American practice was followed in a road layout which included parkways; the whole was enclosed by an agricultural belt. It was a considerable undertaking, at that time one of the largest areas of comprehensively planned development carried out by a single agency in the world.

The garden city ideal was again popularized after the success at Letchworth by a second development at Welwyn in 1920. Ebenezer Howard had always wanted a second experiment but his project for King Edward's Town failed. Welwyn was very much his personal creation in that, at the age of 71, he bought the site at an auction (without even being able to afford the 10% deposit). The Garden City was laid out by the architect Louis de Soissons. C. B. Purdom became Finance Director, F. J. Osborn became estate manager and Howard, almost the first resident, lived there until his death in 1928. It became a centre of garden city propaganda and C. B. Purdom's *The Building of Satellite Towns* (1925) kept the idea of the garden city before an informed readership.

With regard to transport, we have seen the importance of road planning in the preparation of town planning schemes; also, that a forerunner of the Greater London Regional Planning Committee was the concern over effective transport planning in the metropolitan area. But most aspects of road planning were still divorced from town planning. The London Arterial Roads programme was drawn up in the absence of an overall plan for London, and highway improvements were seen in terms of road engineering and in no

Plan for Welwyn Garden City, prepared by Louis de Soissons. The informality of the new suburban architecture was now accompanied by traces of a geometric road layout; the essentially cellular structure of the residential areas was emphasized. (*Courtesy of* Town and Country Planning Association)

Residential layouts, inter-war variations. These and others formed models for local authority developments. (See Barry Parker, 'Economy in Estate Development', *Journal TPI*, **XIV**, No. 8, 1928)

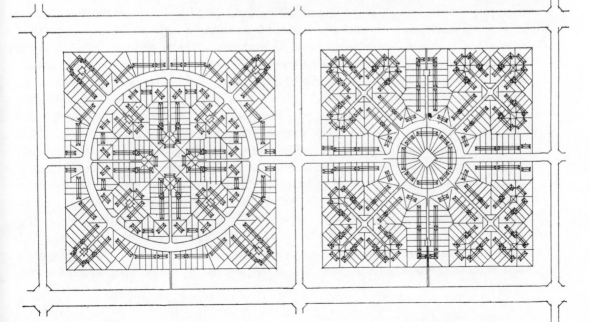

way as constituent parts of wider development. Unwin drew attention to the unsatis-factory nature of ribbon development along the arterial roads in his Greater London Regional Planning Reports. He favoured the parkway idea of a dual carriageway road for the exclusive use of cars, lined on either side by landscaped areas. One decision which had repercussions for the future, was that the Royal Commission on Transport, chaired by Sir Arthur Griffith Boscawen, which reported in 1930, came down against the develop-ment of motorways, although these had already been built in Italy.

Finally, we should note the advances made concerning the idea of National Parks, based on the examples in America and Canada. In September 1929, the Prime Minister (Ramsay MacDonald) appointed a Committee of Inquiry to examine the idea; the chair-man was Christopher Addison, at that time Minister of Agriculture and Fisheries. The Committee reported in 1931[16]; the TPI was one of a number of bodies giving evidence. The Committee envisaged National Parks as a component part of a nationwide scheme of parks, open spaces and playing fields. They found that National Parks in the North Ameri-can sense were not practicable in Britain, but that there was a need for adequate measures for preserving the countryside. The recommendations varied as to what financial assist-ance could be expected. In essence, the Committee found in favour of reserving areas which, on landscape grounds, constituted important national assets, and thought that a National Authority would be necessary to supplement the efforts of local authorities. No Government action was taken on this Addison Report, but an influential lobby was to promote the idea further during the 1930s.

THE TPI IN THE 1920s

The professional Institute developed slowly and cautiously. It was very much concerned with the new statutory planning process and, therefore, with advances in techniques and in the operation of town planning schemes. The Institute became practice-based, and its members made their contribution in a technical capacity concerned with land assembly and town design. Throughout the period the TPI was concerned very much with its professional image, being very resistant to association with propaganda. Advances were made on the questions of professional standards and education.

Planning mostly concerned the operation of town planning schemes and the activities of the Joint Regional Planning Committees; this form of practice gave the Institute its first distinctive professional recognition. Of the two, it was through regional work that the greater professional advances were made. Professor H. J. Fleure, the geographer, ad-dressed the Institute on 'The Regional Survey, Preparatory to Town Planning' in 1922; the Geddesian influence had not been lost and Abercrombie was an enthusiastic advocate of regional work. It was perhaps through regional understanding that the wider context of planning became apparent. Certainly it was Abercrombie who provided some early ideas. In his Presidential Address in November 1925, he recognized that: 'it is not likely that everyone would agree as to what is the actual extent over which broods today the spirit of Town Planning.' For some its boundaries were those delimited by the powers of existing Acts, and so what was wanted was the intensive cultivation of this field rather than an extension. Abercrombie, himself, went for a wider approach in regional planning, claiming that 'it is not a dissipation of energy that I am advocating, but a radiation of influence.'[17]

However, one thing uncomfortably in the minds of planners was how little of their work was understood, appreciated or even known about by the general public. Bernard Townroe, of the Ministry of Health and who wrote on planning matters for *The Times*, commented on 'not merely the apathy, but the almost complete ignorance of the man and woman in the street with regard to questions studied with so much enthusiasm, and practised with so much skill by members of the Town Planning Institute'. He praised the Regional Reports but noted of their authors that: 'The foolish majority seem to be so busy trimming their lamps of technical learning that they forget the oil that lubricates the way to publicity.'[18]

At the onset of the period, the governmental framework of planning was slender in the extreme. As Adshead noted in 1920, 'to find in that vast hive of industry at Whitehall, known as the Ministry of Health, one small room labelled "Town Planning" is a state of affairs which will have rapidly to be altered.'[19] But the situation could only change when planning was widely accepted and demanded. The question of the need for public education in planning was therefore repeatedly to the fore. The prevailing view was that the Institute, as a professional body, could not take part in propagandist activities. Thus, it was resolved that TPI should not appoint a representative on the committee of the International Garden Cities and Town Planning Association. On the other hand, the TPI did nominate two members to the Council for the Preservation of Rural England in 1926—though only after assurances that there would be no appeals to the public for funds. When there was a further postponement of compulsory town planning under the Local Government Bill, Council resolved to take no action, but said they would welcome any action the National Housing and Town Planning Council would take on the matter. It is true that there was some co-operation with propagandist bodies over the Town Planning Conference and Exhibition held at Wembley in 1924, but the contribution was for technical experts rather than the general public. The Institute, at this stage, was taking its professional role very seriously and cautiously, considering that an emphasis on its specialist expertise was the proper image to promote.

An aspect of the operation of town planning was still the remarkably piecemeal and fragmented approach to tackling what were, in fact, co-ordinated problems. It would be wrong to think that as a body the Institute was particularly far-sighted in recognizing a wider approach, but there were individual members who did. As Pepler wrote in January 1931, reviewing 21 years of town planning: 'In our good old English way, we prefer to reverse the order of logic and work up to the general from the particular. We began with the idea of planning the extension of towns ..., next we saw that even this required regional planning, and now we realize that any sound system of planning must give equal weight to and provide a proper balance between the national, urban and rural points of view.'[20]

Perhaps it was in respect of London's problems that the TPI had its greatest influence. The development of planning in London came largely as a result of intervention from outside bodies, rather than enthusiasm from within; the contrast with Birmingham is notable. The attitude of the LCC was cautious. Culpin described the LCC during the

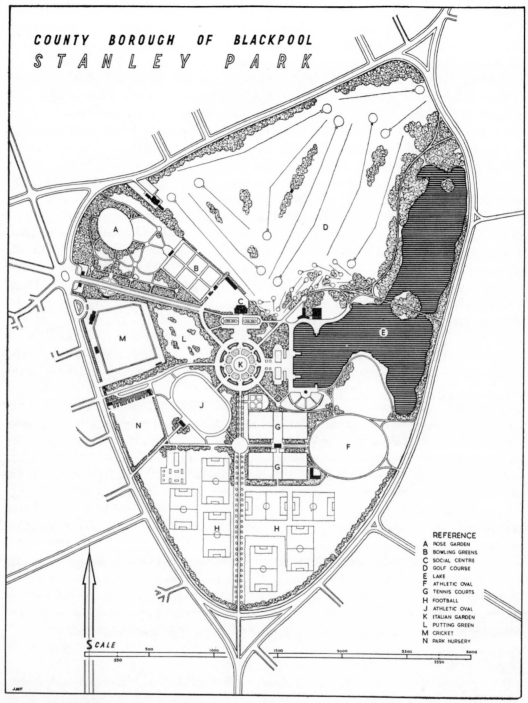

COUNTY BOROUGH OF BLACKPOOL
STANLEY PARK

REFERENCE
A ROSE GARDEN
B BOWLING GREENS
C SOCIAL CENTRE
D GOLF COURSE
E LAKE
F ATHLETIC OVAL
G TENNIS COURTS
H FOOTBALL
J ATHLETIC OVAL
K ITALIAN GARDEN
L PUTTING GREEN
M CRICKET
N PARK NURSERY

SCALE

Stanley Park, Blackpool. The site of 288 acres was acquired by the town in 1922, and the plan prepared by T. H. Mawson the same year. The formal design focused on the Italian Garden and a Social Centre. T. H. Mawson was followed by his two sons and his nephew Robert Mattocks (also a President TPI), their work representing the landscape design element in town planning. The Institute of Landscape Architects was founded in 1929.

early twenties, as 'an authority which regarded the conservativism of Birmingham as the uttermost Bolshevism' and 'was very much afraid of doing anything'[21]. The TPI took up the cause of Regional Planning for Greater London and submitted a petition to the Prime Minister in January 1926, to the effect that 'it is imperative that a regional policy with regard to development and zoning should be formulated forthwith for London and the Home Counties and outline plans prepared.'[22] It was signed by Abercrombie as President, and the Presidents of the London Society, RIBA, Commons and Footpaths Preservation Society, Garden Cities and Town Planning Association and IMCE; and the Chairmen of the National Playing Fields Association, National Housing and Town Planning Council, Roads Improvement Association and the Metropolitan Public Gardens Association. A deputation was received by the Minister of Health, Neville Chamberlain, in March, and following receipt of a further memorandum, which he had requested, he set up an advisory Committee on a budget of £3 000 p.a. Unwin was appointed technical adviser.

During the 1920s, however, many of the significant steps taken by the Institute were internal and concerned its role as a professional body. This must have been a confusing time. Certainly not everyone regarded town planning as a distinct technical skill. The parent professions kept a lively interest in planning, there was considerable overlapping of active membership between professions, and there was, as yet, no 'surrendering' of town planning to the TPI. The conscious steps taken to cement professional status by the TPI, and the emphasis on this aspect during the 1920s, should be seen in this context. The ultimate aims were clearly set out by Thomas Adams and Thomas Alwyn Lloyd in a paper in 1926, read by the latter, on 'Professional Practice': 'we should have the ambition to make town planning not merely an auxiliary branch of other professions, but, in the course of time, a distinct profession—to which the architect, engineer and surveyor will still have contributions of expert aid to make, but in which many will be engaged exclusively in the practice of regional and rural planning, of town designing and town building.'[23] Differing opinions were voiced however. Davidge, for example, felt that town planning was a matter of co-operation between experts and Adshead warned that it was 'dangerous to walk too fast'. F. Longstreth Thompson doubted whether town planning was a technical field in the sense that the parent professions were. But the fact was that the technical classes of membership grew faster than the non-technical classes. Their entry to and practice in town planning was increasingly governed by the standards and fees laid down by the TPI scales of fees that were provided by no other bodies. (Estate development scales of fees were provided by other bodies, but as planning grew away from housing and became increasingly distinct, so new criteria arose which were met by TPI and not the other bodies.)

Hence the foundation of the profession as a body of technical expertise was solidified. Certain developments in the educational field considerably helped this; the newly established Planning Schools were applying for recognition and the setting up of a Joint Board for Institute examinations in 1932 indicated a recognition of distinct skills (see chapter 9). Another significant development was in the Institute's publications. Up to 1923 Papers read at General Meetings formed the staple diet of monthly reporting. With the beginning of volume X in November that year, Reginald Bruce was appointed Honorary Editor and the Journal was begun.

An important turning point in the inter-war period as far as planning was concerned, was the Town and Country Planning Act, 1932. The origins of this legislation were particularly protracted. The Council for the Preservation of Rural England and other bodies, had been drawing attention to problems of rural land use and development during the late 1920s, and Sir Edward Hilton-Young, a Conservative Private Member, introduced a Rural Amenities Bill, designed to extend planning powers to rural land. This was superceded in 1931 by the Labour Government's Town and Country Planning Bill, introduced by Arthur Greenwood, Minister of Health. It met with the general approval of all parties, although the Conservatives spoke against the proposed right to recover 100% betterment, previous legislation having only acknowledged 50%. When the Government fell, the Bill had virtually completed its progress, substantially unaltered. It was re-introduced in 1932 following pressure from a number of bodies (and the role of the TPI in this, is recounted later, see p. 108). There was a good deal of criticism of the new Bill; betterment was to be recovered at 75%, planning procedure became more complicated, and many of the clauses were weakened by Ministerial interpretations and provisoes. In the event, it received the Royal Assent on 12 July 1932, and it came into operation on 1 April 1933.

Its importance was that it repealed and consolidated almost the whole of the general and local enactments relating to planning. It materially extended the powers of local authorities by enabling schemes to be made with respect to any land, whether urban or rural and whether containing buildings or not, provided that the Minister was satisfied that certain conditions were fulfilled. The likelihood of administrative delays was suggested by the fact that a scheme could not become operative until it was laid before each House of Parliament, and had passed through the Parliamentary procedure required by the Act, and opportunity had been given for questioning its legal validity.

Although the Act authorized the making of schemes for almost any land, the adoption of these schemes, previously obligatory on some local authorities, now became merely voluntary for all. This was strongly criticized as a retrograde step (in spite of the fact that the obligatory requirements had proved largely inoperative). During the time the scheme was under preparation, a developer was under no obligation to obtain planning permission for his development, but if he carried it out and it did not conform to the scheme, he was liable, when the scheme became operative, to demolish the buildings without compensation. In practice, therefore, development took place in agreement with the planning authority's own proposals, but this was a very unsure method of control. The machinery for bringing a scheme into operation was cumbersome. It began with the passing of a resolution by the planning authority, to be approved by the Minister of Health. In many cases a local authority did not progress further but relied on the phase of 'interim development', while a scheme was being drafted; this allowed them to have a measure of control over development—short term, regulatory powers which was as far as many local authorities aspired. There were many other criticisms that could be applied. There was, for example, the largely ineffective betterment provision which resulted in extravagant and unreal zoning allocations being made to avoid claims for compensation. Also we should note that the planning authorities were still the Councils of County

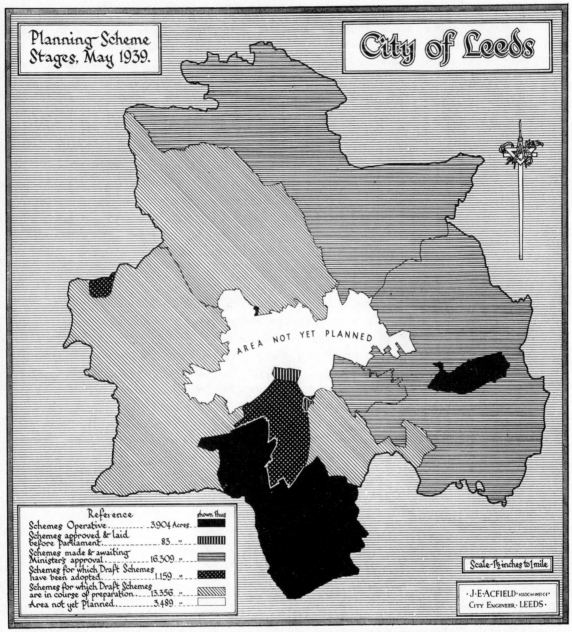

Planning Schemes, City of Leeds, 1939. The fragmented approach to urban planning through the piecemeal preparation of schemes during the inter-war period is well shown in this map. (See J.E. Acfield, 'Planning in Leeds', *Journal TPI*, **XXV**, No. 8, 1939)

Boroughs and County Districts, more than 1 400 in all; County Councils were only called upon to undertake planning if a County District Council felt unable to carry out the duties themselves. Accordingly, plans were often prepared in isolation.

Under the new Act, there was slow progress at first, but the pace quickened towards the end of the 1930s, so that most of the large towns were wholly or almost wholly under planning control. The original intention had been that local authorities should adopt draft schemes before the end of March 1935. This proved too optimistic an estimate because of delay over production of Model Clauses and because of the shortage of planning staff, but in due time local authorities made surprisingly good use of the Act. In England and Wales 402 local authorities were wholly or partly subject to planning by virtue of Resolutions prior to the 1932 Act; by March 1938, a further 530 local authorities had made Resolutions. By this date, 208 schemes had been submitted under the 1932 Act covering 2.8 million acres. Altogether, the area of land under planning control totalled 24 million acres. These figures are impressive but we should recognize with caution the world of difference between a Resolution, a 'draft scheme not yet submitted', and an 'approved scheme actually operative'. The fact remained that only 92 approved schemes in England and Wales were operative at March 1938, covering just 236 000 acres of the 24 million to which we have referred[24]. By 1942 only 5% of England and 1% of Wales was actually subject to operative schemes, although 73% of the land in England and 36% of the land in Wales had become subject to interim development control[25].

Statutory planning in Scotland developed rather more in the 1930s than in earlier years. In 1932 the first town planning scheme in Glasgow was approved. This was the Western Avenue Scheme, covering 3 786 acres; four-fifths of the land was reserved for housing and had a maximum density of 12 to the acre. Next year three other schemes were approved for Glasgow, the Southern, Northern and Eastern Area Schemes, totalling nearly 18 000 acres, and this meant that nearly all the undeveloped land in the city was covered by town planning schemes. Elsewhere progress was made sporadically. Full time planning officers were appointed by the County Councils of Fife and Roxburgh, and some large county Resolutions inflated the statistics of town planning schemes to unrealistic proportions. At the end of 1939 the area covered by schemes and resolutions was as follows[26]:

Schemes (10)	89 410 acres
Resolutions (59)	1 711 552 acres
	1 800 962 acres

The majority of the schemes followed the pattern set in the 1920s, appropriate to the control of suburban development. The main features were the allocation of land to residential zones at varying densities; the location of small shopping and business centres; industrial zones; reservation of open spaces and allotments; and provision for new roads and improvement of existing ones. New features, consequent upon the Act, were the preservation of trees and control of advertisements. The fact that the Act enabled land, both developed and undeveloped, to be included in planning schemes, meant that some of the Resolutions passed referred to very large areas indeed; areas of more than 100 000 acres submitted by Joint Committees became commonplace. This had the result of increasing the number of possible objections and the Minister's Inspectors had many more formal inquiries to deal with. The total number of appeals received reached more than 1 000 for the first time in 1936–37, and although about half were usually withdrawn or settled by agreement, this aspect of work began to be a feature of the central planning system.

Perhaps the most noticeable progress was in respect of London. We have already seen that in the 1920s planning in London was at a very low ebb. As Sinclair reminds us, after 25 years of town planning legislation, the total area in the County of London for which the authorities had finally approved schemes (apart from a measure preserving Hampstead Heath) was just 20 acres—'not twenty square miles out of the hundred and twenty square miles of the inner county, but twenty rustic acres.'[27] But the Greater London Regional Planning Committee was reconstituted under section 3 of the 1932 Act, and in 1935 the London County Council decided to contribute £2 million during the next three years to the formation of a green belt around Greater London. This followed Unwin's proposal for a narrow green girdle around London, made in the *Second Report of the Greater London Regional Plan Committee* (1933). A Green Belt (London and Home Counties) Act followed in 1938. The Regional Planning Committee was dissolved but a Regional Standing Conference took its place.

This planning progress in London was striking. During the twenties the London County Council had introduced a small number of schemes covering, as far as legislation permitted, the undeveloped areas of the County such as Eltham or places of high amenity such as Hampstead. A few individuals scattered through the Architects, Engineers and Valuers Departments were the dedicated planners who pioneered and administered them. (Leslie Lane, a future President, joined this small band as No. 13 in 1931.) A decision to prepare a plan for the whole of the County under the 1932 Act was momentous. It was hotly opposed at the first mammoth Public Inquiry on Planning in London by the major London landowners. But in May 1935 the proposal to subject all London to planning control was approved. It was during the following years, up to the outbreak of the Second World War, that the foundations of a planning system for the heart of the metropolis were laid. But it was a period of frustration for those engaged in this task. The procedures for finalizing a scheme were so tortuous that none had been approved by 1939. Under interim development control a great weight of applications descended upon County Hall necessitating a substantial increase in planning staff including the recruitment of those engaged in administering the London Building Acts. But whilst private development became subjected to regulatory planning control, Highway and Housing Departments resisted intervention by this new fangled upstart regime. Thus began, in real earnest, the war of attrition between emergent planning philosophy and entrenched departmental prerogative within the field of London Government.

Elsewhere regional planning continued with the impetus shown in the 1920s and by 1938 there were 138 executive Joint Committees in England and Wales. Together, they were responsible for the preparation of schemes over about two-thirds of the total acreage under planning. Additionally, there were a number of instances where District Council powers were relinquished to County Councils, thereby giving a regional flavour to planning in those areas. In Scotland the Clyde Valley Regional Advisory Committee

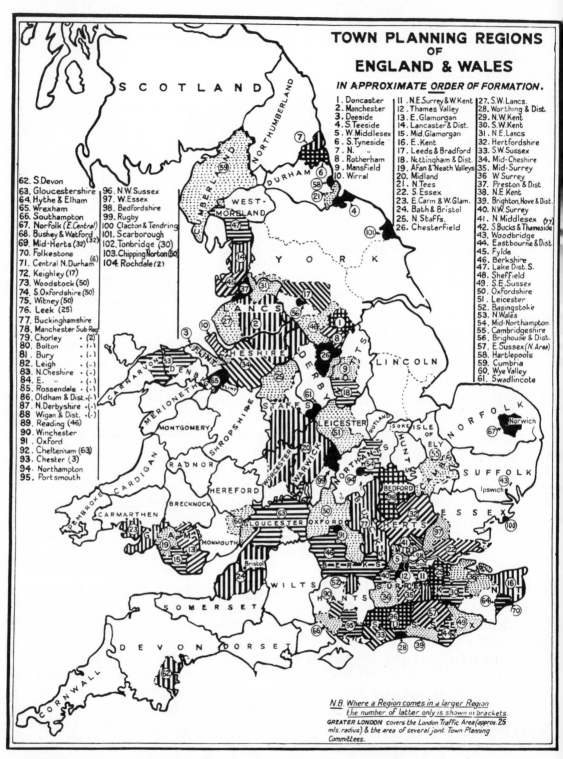

TOWN PLANNING REGIONS OF ENGLAND & WALES IN APPROXIMATE ORDER OF FORMATION.

1. Doncaster
2. Manchester
3. Deeside
4. S.Teeside
5. W.Middlesex
6. S.Tyneside
7. N. "
8. Rotherham
9. Mansfield
10. Wirral
11. N.E.Surrey & W.Kent
12. Thames Valley
13. E.Glamorgan
14. Lancaster & Dist.
15. Mid.Glamorgan
16. E.Kent
17. Leeds & Bradford
18. Nottingham & Dist.
19. Afan & Neath Valleys
20. Midland
21. N.Tees
22. S.Essex
23. E.Carm & W.Glam.
24. Bath & Bristol
25. N.Staffs.
26. Chesterfield
27. S.W.Lancs.
28. Worthing & Dist.
29. N.W.Kent
30. S.W.Kent
31. N.E.Lancs
32. Hertfordshire
33. S.W.Sussex
34. Mid-Cheshire
35. Mid-Surrey
36. W.Surrey
37. Preston & Dist
38. N.E.Kent
39. Brighton, Hove & Dist.
40. N.W.Surrey
41. N.Middlesex (77)
42. S.Bucks & Thameside
43. Woodbridge
44. Eastbourne & Dist.
45. Fylde
46. Berkshire
47. Lake Dist. S.
48. Sheffield
49. S.E.Sussex
50. Oxfordshire
51. Leicester
52. Basingstoke
53. N.Wales
54. Mid-Northampton
55. Cambridgeshire
56. Brighouse & Dist.
57. E.Sussex (N.Area)
58. Hartlepools
59. Cumbria
60. Wye Valley
61. Swadlincote
62. S.Devon
63. Gloucestershire
64. Hythe & Elham
65. Wrexham
66. Southampton
67. Norfolk (E.Central)
68. Bushey & Watford
69. Mid-Herts (32)
70. Folkestone
71. Central N.Durham (6)
72. Keighley (17)
73. Woodstock (50)
74. S.Oxfordshire (50)
75. Witney (50)
76. Leek (25)
77. Buckinghamshire
78. Manchester Sub-Reg
79. Chorley · (2)
80. Bolton · (·)
81. Bury · (·)
82. Leigh · (··)
83. N.Cheshire · (·)
84. E. · (·)
85. Rossendale ·(·)
86. Oldham & Dist.·(·)
87. N.Derbyshire ·(-)
88. Wigan & Dist. ·(-)
89. Reading (46)
90. Winchester
91. Oxford
92. Cheltenham (63)
93. Chester (3)
94. Northampton
95. Portsmouth
96. N.W.Sussex
97. W.Essex
98. Bedfordshire
99. Rugby
100. Clacton & Tendring
101. Scarborough
102. Tonbridge (30)
103. Chipping Norton (50)
104. Rochdale (2)

N.B. Where a Region comes in a larger Region the number of latter only is shown in brackets.
GREATER LONDON covers the London Traffic Area (approx. 25 mls. radius) & the area of several joint Town Planning Committees.

Regional Planning, England and Wales, 1931. The preparation of plans through Joint Town Planning Committees had made surprisingly good progress during the twenties. The first Joint Town Planning Conference had been held at Doncaster in 1920 and there were now over 100 Joint Committees of various kinds, covering about one-third of the country. (See, G. L. Pepler, 'Twenty-One Years of Town Planning in England and Wales', *Journal TPI*, **XVII**, No. 3, 1931) was the most active. Consultants' Reports were published in large numbers. Those by Davidge, Abercrombie (with partners such as S. A. Kelly), Adshead and Adams, Thompson and Fry and others, made a notable contribution to the planning literature of the thirties.

Other aspects of planning which developed in the 1930s reflected the widening spread of planning's concern. A symptom of this was the setting up, by the Minister in June 1934, as promised during the debate on the 1932 Bill, of an Advisory Committee on Town and Country Planning[28]. Its first task was to report on the new clauses drawn up in the Department for use in the preparation of town planning schemes by local authorities. Little work followed, but the Committee resumed importance in 1937 and 1938 when they were asked to consider a motion of the Commons with regard to the destruction of beauty through ill-planned development. At this time, members included Abercrombie, Culpin, Lloyd and Unwin, all past Presidents of TPI.

The preservation of the countryside was an increasingly important problem, and began to be a feature of planning schemes. The steps taken in respect of the Green Belt around London have been noted; elsewhere the need to reserve extensive tracts of land was apparent. The preservation of the South Downs, for example, particularly around Brighton, was a matter of concern. In many cases, where it was necessary to preserve a stretch of country and to prevent anything but agricultural development, the only practicable method was for a local authority to secure an agreement with the owner of the land to that effect. Owners of large estates frequently showed willingness to make restrictive agreements. An agreed scheme for the avoidance of death duties was an encouragement in this direction. Where agreement was not forthcoming, an authority could include in their schemes complete reservation of land from development, but as a general rule, they could not begin to consider to face claims for compensation from owners. Hence, the idea of rural zoning was taken up, and several rural schemes were proposed for controlling building in the undeveloped countryside, at densities ranging from one house to two acres to one house to 100 acres. Other alternatives were an agricultural zoning where nothing but agricultural buildings were allowed, or a zoning of 'general development' where the amount of building to be permitted was left to be determined when an Order releasing the land was made. There were obvious difficulties about all these procedures. The Town and County Planning Advisory Committee's Report in 1937 on the Preservation of the Countryside advocated an adaptation of the 'general development, temporary restriction' procedure.

One aspect of countryside protection, although not the main one, concerned the Restriction of Ribbon Development Act, 1935. In its passage through Parliament it had been subject to a large number of amendments, and emerged an emasculated measure. From the point of view of planning, the main provisions were that any highway authority could adopt a 'standard width' for any road in their area and that the consent of the highway authority was required for access or development within 220 feet of the middle of a classified road. In the practical application of this legislation, there were divergent interests. Highway authorities might be content to set ribbons back behind a service road, but planning authorities were urged to take the advantage of breaking up linear building development and secure grouping in depth.

103

An example of planning having a wider concern than hitherto was in respect of aerodromes. An Aerodromes Advisory Board was set up in 1934 comprising representatives of a number of professional bodies, including the TPI. The Secretary was John Dower. It was necessary to secure the right relation of aerodromes with planning schemes and to work towards a national system of air routes. In December 1936, the Report of Sir Henry Maybury's Committee on the Development of Civil Aviation recommended that the local authorities in all the larger towns and cities should take steps to secure a suitable site for a 'standard' aerodrome.

The broad question of planning and design and amenity was repeatedly to the fore in the operation of planning. A. Trystan Edwards, in a widely read book, *Good and Bad Manners in Architecture* (1924) had proclaimed the 'danger that one day in the not very distant future we shall be confronted with an obituary notice writ in large and monstrous letters across the whole breadth of England. "Here lies the art of Civic Design. It was killed by the science of Town Planning".'[29] Scheme preparation had its place; but zealous application of rigid zoning procedure was held in ridicule. Local authorities were reminded in a Ministerial circular in March 1933, that for new public buildings of importance the advice of the Royal Fine Art Commission, set up in 1924 was available, and they were urged to consult them on any important project involving public amenity. Additionally, the Council for the Preservation of Rural England in collaboration with the RIBA and the Institute of Builders, instituted a panel system for planning authorities for skilled advice on the external appearance of buildings. The first Preservation Orders for buildings of architectural or historic interest, made under section 17 of the 1932 Act, were submitted in 1936/37; the first approved was in respect of the Watergate at Bridgwater, and other Orders were approved in the next year. Surrey made a survey of all buildings of historic or archeological interest in the county.

There were two aspects of planning which did not, as yet, figure in the generally recognized scope of the subject matter, but we should mention them here because of their importance at a later stage. One concerned recreation and the provision of facilities in the countryside. The Commons, Open Spaces and Footpaths Preservation Society urged the desirability of including in schemes provision for new cross-country footpaths, and the Minister drew the attention of local authorities to this in 1938. The big question, however, was the number of difficulties experienced by ramblers particularly in the grouse moors of the North. Countryside problems were changing and public demand for rural facilities increased sharply. As an agricultural authority, Sir R. G. Stapledon, observed: 'No longer can the country be the prerogative of the few—that happy time for the favoured few has definitely ended; it is useless to resist.'[30] A Private Member's Access to Mountains Bill, introduced in 1938, sought a remedy. It had had a number of predecessors but these Bills had made no progress. In this case, however, a combination of circumstances secured its acceptance, although in the passage through the House, it was so altered that it failed to win the support of those it was intended to help. In the event, the Act of 1939 was entirely an abortive measure.

The other matter concerned the economic prosperity of the regions. In 1937 a Royal Commission was appointed under the Chairmanship of Sir Montague Barlow to consider the geographical distribution of the industrial population. This turned out to be one of

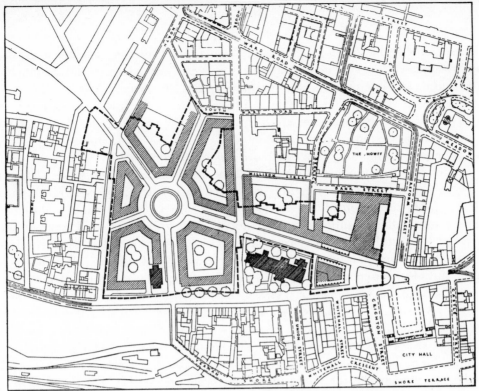

Overgate Redevelopment Scheme, Dundee, layout and perspective. The scheme by Thomas Adams provided for the enlargement of the civic, business and shopping centre of Dundee. A main street, up to 150ft wide, with shops only on the north side, together with a 289ft diameter roundabout, around which professional business interests were to be located, were the principal features. The area was ultimately redeveloped in the 1960s to a very different design. (See Thomas Adams, 'The Overgate Redevelopment Scheme, Dundee', *Journal TPI*, **XXIV**. No. 7, 1938)

the most influential Reports in the history of planning, and we consider it in the next chapter. Suffice for now to note that there was increasingly widespread support for decentralization of big cities as a national policy, and this extended to halting economic development in the prosperous regions in favour of the distressed areas. These were broadly the views of Sir Malcolm Stewart, who was Commissioner for the Special Areas before the Royal Commission was appointed.

By comparison, planning was still more obviously concerned with housing matters; the location and layout of new housing, and the eradication of unfit houses. In the early thirties, it was apparent that the time was ripe for a concerted effort to tackle the slum clearance problems within a limited period of time. The fall in the cost of building and in rates of interest allowed subsidies under the 1924 Act to be stopped. The main housing activity of local authorities had been the provision, with the aid of these subsidies, of working-class accommodation, but now the concentration was on slum clearance. In 1933 housing authorities were asked to speed up their action and to submit demolition programmes under the Housing Act, 1930. The building of replacement dwellings was assisted by subsidy. A 5-year programme of demolishing 280 000 houses and replacing them by 300 000 ensued.

The next attack was on overcrowding. The Housing Act, 1935, gave statutory force to new machinery for ascertaining and abating overcrowding. New forms of Exchequer subsidy were directed to the rehousing of overcrowded families. On the basis of local authority returns, it was estimated that 3.8% (341 000) of the dwellings inspected were overcrowded and that the worst areas in England and Wales were in the East End of London and in North East England. More than 70 000 families (about 7%) in the County of London (except the City) were living in overcrowded conditions. In the majority of cases an appointed day was fixed at 1st January 1937, after which overcrowding was taken to be an offence.

The Garden City movement was still supported by a vigorous propagandist lobby. F. J. Osborn was indefatigable in his denunciation of continuing urban growth. Turning his attention from London to Glasgow at the time of the Empire Exhibition there in 1938 he warned 'The greatness of a city is not measured by the number of its citizens. The time is coming when cities, like ladies, will boast of slimming and not of their middle-aged spread.'[31] A stream of literature from other sources analysed the problem and popularized the solution. S. Vere Pearson's *London's Overgrowth and the Causes of Swollen Towns* (1939) was a plea for government to direct, control and locate development in an ordered way, and an advocacy of decentralization. But the advocates of low density and urban decentralization were challenged by Thomas Sharp in his *Town and Countryside* (1932), which presented his concern for urban quality without a loosening of the physical structure. His was a savage indictment of open development: 'Already it is notorious that "amenity" and "urbanity" are incompatibles that have been divorced, with the whole body of the town planning profession cited as co-respondents.'[32] But his was a voice crying in the wilderness. More typical was the founding of the Hundred New Towns Society in 1934 with a ten-year programme for the migration of at least 5 million people to a hundred new urban centres. Of the hundred towns, 76 were suggested for England, 15 for Scotland and 9 for Wales; about 40 were to be located south of the Wash–Severn line.

106

Perhaps the most influential statement on this theme came from the Report of a Departmental Committee on Garden Cities and Satellite Towns, chaired by Lord Marley. Appointed in 1931, but first meeting in 1932, it reported in 1934. Unwin was a member of the Committee. Marley's recommendations were far reaching and paved the way for more authoritative statements in later years. The fullest adoption of Garden City development was advocated, with a planned guidance of the distribution of industry and population. The Committee believed that 'when a town reached a certain size (which must vary within wide limits), continuous growth around the fringe tends to create evils that outweigh any advantages; and we therefore advocate a definite policy of outward development taking the form of complete planned units with due provision for industry, residence, social services, and recreation, at some distance from the original nucleus.'[33] To achieve these objectives a Planning Board was recommended, composed of a Chairman and not more than four members appointed by the Minister of Health, who would speak for it in Parliament. There were dissenting notes in the Report against the idea of the Board, but this method of controlling the national development of land was echoed later in the Barlow Report (see p. 120).

With regard to the transport question, the situation was almost always out of control. In 1934, the Minister of Transport, Sir Leslie Hore-Belisha, set in hand a comprehensive survey of highway developments required in the London traffic area, in view of the expansion of traffic. The first Origin and Destination Census made in London was conducted in June 1936, at London Docks. (A much earlier example of this form of traffic survey had been in respect of Manchester Docks in 1924.) The Survey was published in 1939. Elsewhere it was the familiar scene of piecemeal efforts of small-scale road improvements and new road constructions. But new ideas were being generated. For example, traffic considerations formed an important aspect of the design proposed for London in 1939 by a Committee of the Modern Architectural Research (MARS) Group. The Chairman of the Committee was Arthur Korn and it included among others, Arthur Ling, a future President of TPI. The master plan was a conceptual solution rather than a detailed design; essentially, it considered London as a working organism and it showed how the layout might be rearranged in order that the many activities within it might be located more efficiently. A special subcommittee dealt with transport aspects of the plan.

This unusual readiness to see transport and land use in relationship was accompanied by an advance on another front. A Commissioner of Police, Alker Tripp, approached the question of traffic circulation on a systematic basis and devised a hierarchy of roads: arterial, subarterial and local, each one with its own traffic function. His *Road Traffic and Its Control* (1938) was followed by *Town Planning and Road Traffic* in 1942.

THE TOWN PLANNING INSTITUTE IN THE 1930s

In the words of Arnold Toynbee, 1931 was the *'annus terribilis'* when 'men and women all over the world were seriously contemplating and frankly discussing the possibility that the Western system of society might break down and cease to work.'[34] A frequent picture of the thirties is a decade in which progressives became totally disillusioned with the Parliamentary democratic process, dating from the demise of the Labour Government in 1931, and its replacement by a National government, powerful and Conservative. Yet, as Marwick has pointed out, there were progressives who were prepared to change government by reform, and national economic planning was a central part of their programme. He quotes Macmillan's proposition of the case in 1933: 'Planning is forced upon us . . . not for idealistic reasons but because the old mechanism which served us when markets were expanding naturally and spontaneously is no longer adequate when the tendency is in the opposite direction.'[35] The various progressive groups involved were from all-party political sympathies, and, indeed, what brought them together was the recognition that, in the face of militant fascism and communism, they must rally to the defence of democracy and show that it too was capable of vigorous attack on its social and economic problems.

In short the idea of planning took shape as the rational, eminently sensible and a political solution to many of democracy's problems. In this situation, the TPI and some other professionals found a new purpose for their activities, that of using their expertise and specialist knowledge on behalf of democracy, rather than the older role of technical expert and private client. This theme of planning and democracy is central to an understanding of the TPI during the thirties.

It was in the reactions to the changing fortunes of the Town and Country Planning Bill that the first overt indications of a more positive spirit can be found. It will be recalled that Sir Edward Hilton-Young introduced a Rural Amenities Bill to extend planning powers to rural land, with the help and support of the CPRE. The TPI intially refused to lend their support to the measure though this was later given in March 1930 after some reconsideration. When the Labour Government fell, its Bill had virtually completed its progress. The TPI joined the Presidents and Chairmen of other principal professional and propagandist bodies in a letter to the Prime Minister, deprecating the apparent death of the Bill. The Bill was reintroduced under the new Administration, but there was anxiety at the opposition expressed in Standing Committee, and Council in February 1932 unanimously approved circularizing members of the Standing Committee as to the merits of the Bill. In March a gathering of over 500 representatives of local authorities expressed grave concern and acute disappointment at the course of the Bill. Maxwell, then President of TPI, commented: 'The Institute has always refrained from taking part in any political controversy and is in no sense a propaganda body, but the gravity of the present situation demands that the general public should be informed as to what will be the effect if the opponents of this national measure have their way.'[36]

These interesting developments illustrate how the Institute's position changed, from initially declining to be involved in a public measure according to past tradition, finally, to active agitation, a posture for the future. Attitudes were changing for there were too many straws in the wind suggesting that planning was at risk: no action was taken on Addison's Report on National Parks, Unwin's London Regional Planning Committee virtually folded up, and within the Ministry Pepler was fighting hard to keep the idea of town planning alive. The realization must have been that planning was still a subject that had received little support or attention from the general public. The TPI had done little to rectify this and the difficulties over the Bill must have appeared as a backlash of ignorance. From this time onwards the Institute, having built its professional structure in the twenties, looked wider in the thirties.

One indication of the broadening base of planning was the relationship with geography. Dr L. Dudley Stamp's Land Utilization Survey, set up in 1931, capitalized on the previous experience of geographers and planners in regional surveys. Geddes was, for a long time, a member of the Council of the Geographical Association which fostered the Survey. The interests of geographers and planners coalesced. Stamp declared, in 1934, that 'the subject of town and regional planning has suddenly assumed a great importance for every teacher of geography'.[37] In 1937, Abercrombie, as President of the Geographical· Association, commented that geography 'provides the background upon which the plan is prepared, and the foundation upon which the realization of that plan must be placed.'[38]

We should not over-emphasize the extent to which statutory planning embraced this wider context. There was, for example, little professional comment on the social problems of unemployment and economic depression (apart, that is, from occasionally noting that some members in depressed areas had difficulty in paying their fees). So far, planning was a matter for providing for orderly urban development, and a question of town design. Certainly there were developing ideas about an industrial location policy, for example, but these stemmed from the problems of an oversized London, rather than an informed concern over the needs of depressed areas. Thus, even in February 1938, a request that the TPI take part in a Research Co-ordination Committee for South Wales met with the feeling of Council that 'the investigation of conditions in South Wales hardly came within the scope of the Institute'.[39]

On the other hand, there is evidence that, while planning was taking place on the small scale, there was a realization that problems were larger and wider. F. J. Osborn spoke on 'Industry and Planning' in July 1932, the first paper on this subject since W. H. Gaunt's in March 1920. A paper was given on 'Electricity in Town and Country Planning' in March 1934, and on 'Education Buildings and Town Planning' in July the same year. However, we shall see, in chapter 9, that these shifts of interest were scarcely reflected in changing education policies. Moreover, the rank and file of planning assistants in local authorities were not exposed to the wider issues.

On balance, it seems fair to say that in this period town planning underwent considerable self education. First it began to widen its boundaries of interest and contribute more directly as a body and through individual members to safeguarding the public interest. This was increasingly equated with serving democracy, itself the bulwark against totalitarianism. A different slant to professionalism and planning was taken up—the a-political, rational, common sense protection of the public interest. Second, planners began to be rather more sure of their contribution to society; moreover they knew what still needed to be done.

One can only pick up straws in this interpretation but there are some useful pointers to rely on. Consider the remarks of Sir Ernest Simon, Honorary Member of TPI and instigator of Wythenshawe in a perceptive paper to the 1937 Summer School: 'Town planning in this country can only come as part of a new spirit, a revivified democracy determined to build a new civilisation, determined that its people shall be housed in the most magnificent cities the world has seen. We all of us believe here, whatever political party we may belong

Sir Ernest Simon, Lord Mayor of Manchester, for long connected with the 'reform' element in planning circles and in promoting the idea of planning in Manchester. (*Courtesy of* Town and Country Planning Association)

Town and Country Planning Summer School, Welwyn, 1933 was the first annual venture of this kind. *Front row*: 7th from left, F. J. Osborn; 10th, Thomas Adams; 13th, Raymond Unwin; 14th, Leslie Scott; 15th, Barry Parker; 16th, J. W. R. Adams; 18th, Harding Thompson; 19th, Leslie Roseveare; 20th, Sir Ernest Simon. *Second row*: extreme left W. S. Cameron; 7th left, W. H. Gaunt; 8th left, T. F. Thomson. *Back row*: 11th left, Edward Mawson. (*Courtesy of* Mrs Constance Adams)

to, that democracy is the best form of government. But we are forced to admit, with regret, that in this matter of town planning it is falling, not only behind Russia … , but also other countries under dictatorships, and yet the building of fine cities, the preservation of the beauties of the countryside are surely fundamental factors in civilization. There are signs of a new spirit. Almost nothing was done in the way of planning up to the war; a good deal is being done now, but not nearly enough. I firmly believe that if British democracy makes up its mind, it can, within the next two generations, make the cities of England once more places of beauty in which it is good to be alive.'[40] A considerable shift in thinking was taking place. The original professionalism to which the TPI aspired, namely a distinct expertise used in the interests of individual clients, was being superceded by a new professionalism which was a safeguarding of the public interest through adherence to a-political objectives. Planning was expressed as a matter of finding a rational solution to which everyone could agree, supported by fact-finding research.

There also seemed to be a new maturity about planning, based on the pragmatism of a quarter of a century's experience. Abercrombie's prescription, for example, was that 'The plan should not be in the hands of the drill sergeant nor should the city be under the domination of the muddler who will talk about the Law of Supply and Demand and the Liberty of the Individual. Town and Country Planning seeks to proffer a guiding hand to the trend of natural evolution, as a result of careful study of the place itself and its external relationships. The result is to be more than a piece of skilful engineering, or satisfactory hygiene or successful economics: it should be a social organism and a work of art.'[41] These were not the words of persuasion as might have been written earlier; they were a personal testament of experience reflecting a sure professional position. But at the same time new methods of approach were required. Sir Ernest Simon could point to three very readily: 'We need economic reform; the whole question of town planning is crushed under the burden of compensation to private interests. We need political reform; both central authorities and local authorities are wrongly constituted and have inadequate powers. We need spiritual reform; we need a new enthusiasm and determination to build fine and beautiful cities.'[42]

From 1933 onwards a new venture contributed to a broadening of planning outlook. This was the Town and Country Planning Summer School, originally instigated and financed largely by Thomas Adams; its Proceedings were published by the Garden Cities and Town Planning Association though the TPI gave some financial support. The first School was held at Welwyn Garden City and it was resolved to continue and develop it as a permanent institution. This, in fact, proved to be the case and the TPI took on an increasing responsibility, publishing the Proceedings of the School from 1934 onwards. Financial difficulties meant that the Proceedings could only be presented in a restricted way, but it is clear that there was a wide variety of papers, speakers and discussion. The Journal commented (rather quaintly, it might seem now), in October 1934, that one of the most pleasing features of the School was 'the enthusiasm of the younger members of the profession, their knowledge of the subject and the clear and courageous manner in which they aired their opinions.'[43] In other ways, too, planning was strengthening its base of learning, and during the thirties an increasing output of literature appeared.

The developing professional role can also be seen in a more active influence in public affairs. The TPI nominated a member to the Minister's Town and Country Planning Advisory Committee. It was also prepared to offer more adventurous comment on public matters. An observation on London is an example. In 1934 the Labour Party was pledged to introduce planning for the whole LCC area if returned to power. They took immediate action and by May 1935 the whole of the London County was under interim control; just a short while earlier there were 16 piecemeal schemes in various stages of completion. The Journal described the new action as 'the greatest town planning movement that has occurred in this country' and thought it 'an example, not only to England, but to the world.'[44] The TPI Council was also active over the question of planning legislation. An example was the concern over the Restriction of Ribbon Development Act, 1935. Council had set up a Standing Parliamentary Committee in May 1935, and the 1935 Act was the first matter referred to it. The Committee was asked to review the anomolous situation in which the Joint Town Planning Authorities and the County District Councils had been placed as a result of the Act. Following a questionnaire sent to officers in various authorities, a memorandum was prepared and finally submitted to the Minister of Transport in November 1937.

Towards the end of the 1930s, the TPI grasped the nettle of national planning, setting up, in May 1936, a National Survey and National Planning Committee. Lord Justice Scott, a Legal Member and Honorary Vice-President became Chairman, and PEP and Max Nicholson took a leading part in collecting information and drafting. TPI voted an unprecedented amount of £75 towards expenses. A report was prepared by mid-1938; it recommended the establishment of a National Planning Commission compiling a National Survey, co-ordinating government planning agencies and statutory authorities, and itself responsible to Parliament and able to publish reports and provide guidance for planning authorities[45]. This was submitted to the Barlow Commission, thus forming the second evidence from the TPI. The first submission was an unambitious statement of present shortcomings; this second represented a much more definite policy line.

As the professional body developed so did the need for an improved status for the planner, especially the local government officer. Consider this observation from a pseudonym, Jeremiah Barebones in 1936: 'It seems to me that in some ways the town planner is one of the most pathetic figures in public life today.' He referred to the 'altogether miserable fellow' who 'labours unhonoured and unsung, anonymous almost as a dead dog, under the title of Temporary Town Planning Assistant to the Borough Engineer of This or the County Surveyor of That'[46]. There had been long subordination to other local authority officers, particularly the engineer and surveyor, and the situation moved T. F. Thomson, then Planning Officer for North Oxfordshire, to consider that the town planner should enjoy 'at least a comparable status to that enjoyed by the medical officer of health'[47]. Thomson was, in fact, a leading proponent of the interests of the planning officer, and in 1935, he was successful in securing approval to the establishment of a Town Planning Officers' Section of the Institute, with the constitution of a Branch, like that of the North of England Division and the Scottish Branch, which had already been established.

The Section grew out of an earlier Town Planning Informal Dining Club, with which Thomson was also concerned. The purpose of the new Section was 'to provide facilities for the holding of regular meetings for those members having full time appointments as town planning officers or assistants to local authorities or Joint Committees and engaged wholly or principally upon preparation and administration of planning schemes.'[48] Not all its members were members of TPI and for several years a non-corporate class of Licentiate was introduced. The Section published its own Journal, the *Planning Officer*, edited by Thomas Sharp. It was dedicated to safeguarding and enhancing the status of the local authority planner.

A General Picture 1919–39

The TPI in its early years was without any of the physical attributes that the word 'Institute' implies. Its library was housed from 1916 at the SI in Great George Street, while Council met at a large number of locations, chiefly but not exclusively at IMCE, then at 92 Victoria Street. The TPI's address for correspondence was 4 Arundel Street, which was the headquarters of Potter's employer, E. G. Allen. This practice was in many ways the administrative centre for the developing TPI. Until 1933, the Secretary was paid only a nominal salary for his part-time work; his first salary, voted in December 1914, was £20 p.a., though at this stage in TPI's life, the amount of work involved was very small. Potter spent most of his time working in Allen's private practice, though increasingly he devoted more time to TPI's work, and his salary was increased in recognition. This duality, was not without its problems, however, and in 1920 he tendered his resignation. Nevertheless, he was prevailed upon to remain Secretary, and gradually the TPI were able to pay a more adequate recompense for his work. In 1933 he was voted £500 p.a. and Whitfield was appointed to the staff of Allen and Potter, as the latter's assistant. Potter did not become official full-time Secretary of the TPI until the partnership was dissolved during the Second World War.

In 1923 the practice obtained a suite of rooms in Maxwell House, 11 Arundel Street, and one room was to be for the sole use of TPI, who voted £70 p.a. for the room, the use of telephone and the services of Potter. Nevertheless, Council continued to meet elsewhere. The Ministry of Health became a favourite venue, though in 1926 a new regular location, Caxton Hall in Westminster, was fixed. This venue remained, with occasional exceptions, until June 1939, when the Institute was successful in getting the lease for a suite of offices at 11 Arundel Street and in October Council began meeting there. In the new and, indeed, the first permanent home, one of the first acts of Council was to recognize with unstinting praise, Potter's 25 years service with TPI.

Much of the day to day running and operation of the Institute was due to the work of Potter and the Honorary Secretary, Pepler. Apart from war service from 1916 to 1918, Potter attended every Council meeting after his appointment; Pepler attended every single meeting. They directed and guided the running of the TPI more than anyone else. Pepler, in particular, and to a lesser extent, Potter, acted with initiative and took part in many informal discussions with members and officers of other bodies, with groups within the Institute, and within the Ministry of Health. This informal influence, particularly of Pepler, in his capacity as Chief Town Planner at the Ministry, was important in making the influence of the TPI felt in Whitehall and in local authorities throughout the country.

Within the TPI policies were increasingly formulated by Committee. Many were set up for specific purposes, such as the National Survey and National Planning Committee of 1936. Standing Committees were, from 1915, the Education Committee: from 1922 the Competitions and Professional Practices Committee, and from 1935, the Parliamentary Committee. Often, however, matters were referred either to Sub-committee or to individuals or groups of individuals to formulate draft proposals which were then put to full Committee where appropriate, or Council. Thus, Unwin was responsible for many of the proposals for the Joint Examinations Board and the TPI Intermediate Examination, and the Sub-committee for the report of the National Survey and National Planning Committee. By 1939 it seems that the Recognized Schools Sub-committee, under Professor R. A. Cordingley's chairmanship, was taking an important part in formulating education policy, then being considered by full Committee, and later by Council.

However, the TPI was still run on fairly informal lines, and there was a strong element of a social club about meetings. The annual county meetings, held from 1919 onwards, included a programme of entertainments and social activities. The presentation to Pepler to mark his 21 years' service to the Institute in April 1935 had a warm, intimate flavour[49]. It was, perhaps, an attempt to foster this collective feeling as well as to provide more adequately for members in the provinces that the Branches had been formed. The issue had been considered from time to time by Council, but it was not until 1922 that a Sub-committee, under Pepler's chairmanship, was set up to look at the whole question. The principle of regional Branches was approved with a constitution modelled on the SI, with direct representation of Branch members on the Council. This part of the Institute's history is traced in chapter 10.

We can now turn to look at the planners themselves in this inter-war period. The town planner in the early years was, above all else, an enthusiast, reflecting the specialist interest of a handful of professions, social reformers and local councillors. On the local government front, planning fell to the engineer or surveyor and his assistants, aided perhaps by forceful, enthusiastic or knowledgeable local councillors and usually with the passive support of the town clerk. Elsewhere, however, it was often the practice to employ consultants to prepare schemes and plans, leaving the actual administration of the scheme to the local (often overworked) Engineer/Surveyor's Department. Future Presidents had these humble origins. Thus, F. Longstreth Thompson, as a young man, worked on schemes for the Borough of Middleton, and Tadcaster and Hunslet RDCs; Thomas Sharp was a Planning Assistant in Margate and Canterbury in the early 1920s; and Bernard Collins was Planning Officer to Winchester RDC before the Second World War.

It is difficult to piece together any kind of coherent picture about private planning practice in the early years. What seems evident is that no practice could survive just on planning; often town planning was 'latched on' to an architectural or mixed professional practice. The practice of Allen and Potter was an exceptional one in that it provided an administrative caucus for the TPI. Partners or Associates, at one time or another, included Pepler, Longstreth Thompson and also Thomas Adams. The practice of Thomas Adams, Longstreth Thompson and Maxwell Fry was notable for employing two young assistants in the early 1930s on their regional schemes in Essex: Collins and Buchanan, both later to become distinguished planners. Another notable practice was that of

Planners in Cardiff, 1933, for the Annual Country Meeting. *Left to right:* G.H. Whitaker (City Engineer), Francis Longstreth Thompson, G.L. Pepler, T. Alwyn Lloyd, A.R. Potter and F.M. Elgood.

Presidential Badge, designed by Mrs K. Winny Austin, and the figure medalled by Charles Wheeler. It was presented by the President, Past Presidents and Vice Presidents of the Institute in 1924.

Loyal Address, 23 April 1937, to King George VI on his Accession to the Throne.

To the King's Most Excellent Majesty.

The Humble Loyal and Dutiful Address of the Town Planning Institute.

Most Gracious Sovereign,

We the Council of the Town Planning Institute on our own behalf and that of the members of the Institute desire respectfully to tender our most sincere and hearty congratulations on the Accession of Your Majesty to the Throne and on Your Majesty's approaching Coronation.

We recognise with gratitude Your Majesty's many services to the State and Empire prior to Your Majesty's Accession to the Throne. We recognise in particular Your Majesty's unfailing sympathy with and interest in the work and objects of our Institute in connection with town and country planning as a means of securing healthy and pleasant surroundings for the homes of Your Subjects and of facilitating the conduct of industry and commerce and of preserving the beauties of the countryside.

We also recognise with profound gratitude Your Majesty's active interest in the provision of the means of recreation for the younger generation and in the promotion of the social welfare of the industrial portion of the Community.

We desire hereby to assure Your Majesty of our sincere loyalty and our deep affection and attachment to the Throne.

And we will ever pray that the blessing of Almighty God may rest upon Your Majesty and on Your Majesty's Gracious Consort and that Your Majesties may long be spared in health and happiness to reign over a grateful loyal and contented People.

Given under the Common Seal of the Town Planning Institute this 23rd day of April 1937.

President:

Honorary Secretary:

Secretary:

Sir Raymond Unwin, died in America in 1940 at the age of 76. He had contributed immensely to British town planning. Barry Parker wrote an analysis of his life's work in the *Journal TPI*, **XXVI**, No. 5, 1940. (*Courtesy of* Town and Country Planning Association)

Thomas Mawson and Sons. Primarily a landscape architect, Thomas Mawson had been responsible for a number of park layouts in the Potteries during the 1890s, and moved towards the developing town planning from this standpoint. His practice was based on Lancaster, though, always alive to developments in North America, he had offices in Vancouver. The private consultants who continued to be most involved with planning were, however, those who moved into University posts. Abercrombie, in particular, was well known for his development of regional planning while he was Professor at Liverpool (1914–35), and subsequently at London.

The main stream of TPI membership became that created by the new planning staffs. During the 1930s there was an increasing number of posts in local government for full-time town planners. Advertisements began appearing in the Journal in connection with such positions, and the formation of the Town Planning Officers' Section in 1935 was an important reflection of this shifting emphasis. Welcoming the new Section, Major Leslie Roseveare, in his Presidential Address of November 1935, spoke of the lack of fully-trained administrative officers and the need for positive planning by officers who were full-time officials. Basically the work of the planning officer/assistant was to prepare schemes and control development, either interim or statutory. Monitoring estate development plans was a common means of exercising control, whereby the town planner made improvements and tidied up the layouts by agreement with the developer, rather than by any statutory order. Very frequently the administration of the Restriction of Ribbon Development Act fell to the town planner; at the very least his work was intimately involved with the operation of this Act. Work in some counties concerned the problem of sporadic buildings and the preparation of positive policies for their grouping. The town planner therefore became part of the apparatus of local government, and the role of the consultant lost ground. The public through development schemes and development control became a little more aware of the existence of town planning. A symptom perhaps was the broadcasting in June 1937 on Northern Radio of a play 'Replanning Burbleton' by F. Leslie Halliday. It dealt in a humorous manner with 'the trials of the Surveyor, Planning Officer, and of the heroic Councillor who sponsors the scheme, and the reactions of the local public in the local pub.'[50]

Town planners gradually established themselves within a technical and professional niche largely concerned with design, at the expense of others involved with planning. The TPI bye-laws specifically mentioned the eligibility of medical officers of health to become Associates, and during the early twenties, there were moves to create classes of membership, especially for medical officers and valuers. But these suggestions came to nothing and by the end of the thirties, the situation was different. Associates, originally just over 11% of total membership, were, by 1939, only about 2%. In 1914 the label 'town planner' could be applied equally well to idealistic visionaries such as Howard, housing reformers and level-headed propagandists and councillors such as Aldridge, Shawcross and Nettlefold, academics, notably Geddes, and a mixed bag of professionals in both private practice and municipal employment, but by 1939 the label could not comfortably cover such a wide range. The significant change was the growth of a technical–professional membership willing and able to consider planning as their primary responsibility.

This is not to deny that there were leading TPI members with strong non-technical interests. Montagu-Harris was concerned with the County Councils Association; during the early thirties Alwyn Lloyd was Chairman of the National Housing and Town Planning Council as well as being President of TPI in 1933–34; and E. G. Culpin, President in 1937–38, successfully combined an active non-technical political life with high status within TPI. Though trained as an architect, he moved towards propagandist work in the Garden Cities and Town Planning Association, being its second permanent secretary. Later he became a member, first of Ilford Town Council and of the LCC, later becoming an Alderman and finally Chairman of the latter.

Though numerically always one of the smallest groups within TPI, the Associates included some significant names. Potentially at least, the class was a balance to the predominance of the design professions, but it never developed as such, and by 1939 was in absolute decline. Aldridge (and perhaps also Gaunt) were virtually the last Associate Members who took an active part in the Institute, without obviously conflicting with the main stream of a developing professionalism. Aldridge's readiness to put town planning into the political arena tended, as we have seen, to meet with some opposition amongst the more placid professionals, but nevertheless, until he left the town planning scene in the middle twenties, he was a forceful and respected TPI member. F. J. Osborn was an Associate Member for eight years from 1930 to 1938. In 1935 he was appointed Honorary Editor (which involved more influence than the name might imply), taking over from Culpin who had replaced Bruce at the time of his death in 1930. In 1937 a Sub-committee considering the Journal reported that it was desirable that the Journal of a technical Institute should be edited by a technical man, and, expressing warm remarks to Osborn, replaced him with T. F. Thomson. Osborn, intimated his strong dissatisfaction with the way in which the matter was handled; attempts at pacification failed and the following year he resigned from TPI. (He later became an Honorary Member.)

In conclusion, by 1939 the town planner had become less of a dedicated reformer and more an officer of local government, either in a permanent or temporary capacity. Increasingly he was a professional, though the meaning of professionalism was altering; a changing ethic allowed the safeguarding of a collective rather than an individual interest. However, he still had no great influence on shaping the physical environment; the scope of his work was limited and the powers which he exercised were heavily circumscribed. Nonetheless, there had been considerable progress. In 1914 the TPI was virtually unnoticed by other professional bodies, but by 1939 a developing professional status had been secured. Few had worked more for this than Sir Raymond Unwin and Dr Thomas Adams. Within a year both were dead. Their contributions had been outstanding, in town planning and as public servants. Unwin's energy kept him on committees and he never retired from practice; Adams was President of the Institute of Landscape Architects in 1937. As Britain entered into war, it was in more ways than one the end of an era.

REFERENCES

1. See also Cherry, Gordon E., *Urban Change and Planning*. G. T. Foulis, Henley-on-Thames, 1972.
2. Quoted in Graves, R. and Hodge, A., *The Long Weekend*. Penguin, 1971.
3. *Annual Report, Ministry of Health*, 1919–20, Cmd. 917.

4. Pepler, G. L., Progressive Town Planning, in *Proceedings of Conference*. The Manchester and District Joint Town Planning Advisory Committee, 1922.

5. Elgood, F. M., Town Planning Schemes, in *Proceedings of Conference*. The Manchester and District Joint Town Planning Advisory Committee, 1922.

6. *Annual Report, Ministry of Health*, 1920–21, Cmd. 1446.

7. *Annual Report, Ministry of Health*, 1930–31, Cmd. 3937.

8. *Annual Report, Scottish Board of Health*, 1928, Cmd. 3304.

9. *Annual Report, Department of Health for Scotland*, 1932, Cmd. 4338.

10. Abercrombie, P. L., Regional Town Planning, in *Proceedings of Conference*. The Manchester and District Joint Town Planning Advisory Committee, 1922.

11. *Annual Report, Ministry of Health*, 1931–32, Cmd. 4113.

12. *Interim Report of Departmental Committee on Regional Development*, 1931, Cmd. 3915.

13. Johnson, Paul Barton, *Land Fit For Heroes: the Planning of British Reconstruction, 1916–1919*. University of Chicago Press, 1968.

14. Addison, Christopher, *The Betrayal of the Slums*. Herbert Jenkins, 1922.

15. Howkins, F., *An Introduction to the Development of Private Building Estates and Town Planning*. Estates Gazette, 1926.

16. *Report of the National Park Committee*, 1931, Cmd. 3851.

17. Abercrombie, Patrick, The Extension of the Town Planning Spirit. *Journal of the Town Planning Institute*, **XII**, No. 1, 1925.

18. Townroe, B. S., Town Planning and the Man in the Street. *Journal of the Town Planning Institute*, **XVI**, No. 6, 1930.

19. Adshead, S. D., The Effect of the Act of 1919 on Uncompleted Schemes Commenced Before the War. *Town Planning Institute Papers and Discussions*, **VII**, No. 1, 1920.

20. Pepler, G. L., Twenty-one Years of Town Planning in England and Wales. *Journal of the Town Planning Institute*, **XVII**, No. 3, 1931.

21. *Journal of the Town Planning Institute*, **XII**, No. 7, 163, 1926.

22. *Journal of the Town Planning Institute*, **XII**, No. 6, 147–8, 1926.

23. Adams, Thomas and Lloyd, T. Alwyn, Professional Practice, *Journal of the Town Planning Institute*, **XII**, No. 9, 1026.

24. *Annual Report, Ministry of Health*, 1937–38, Cmd. 5801.

25. *Town and Country Planning, 1943–1951*, Ministry of Local Government and Planning, 1951, Cmd. 8204.

26. *Annual Report, Department of Health for Scotland*, 1938, Cmd. 5969.

27. Sinclair, Robert, *Metropolitan Man*. Allen and Unwin, 1938.

28. Vernon, R. V. and Mansergh, N. (Eds.), *Advisory Bodies: A Study of Their Uses in Relation to Central Government 1919–1939*. Allen and Unwin, 1940.

29. Edwards, A. Trystan, *Good and Bad Manners in Architecture*. A. Tiranti, 1924.

30. Stapledon, Sir R. G., *The Land Now and Tomorrow*. Faber, 1935.

31. Osborn, F. J., London: an Awful Warning to Glasgow, *Journal of the Town Planning Institute*, **XXIV**, No. 11, 1938.

32. Sharp, Thomas, *Town and Countryside: Some Aspects of Urban and Rural Development*. Oxford University Press, 1932.

33. *Garden Cities and Satellite Towns*. Report of Departmental Committee, Ministry of Health, HMSO, 1935.

34. Quoted in Skidelsky, R., *Politicians and the Slump*. Penguin, 1970.

35. Marwick, Arthur, *Britain in the Century of Total War*. Penguin Books, 1970.

36. Maxwell, R. C., Presidential Address, *Journal of the Town Planning Institute*, **XVIII**, No. 2, 1931.

37. *Geography*, **XIX**, 63, 1934.

38. *Geography*, **XXIII**, 1, 1938.

39. Town Planning Institute Council Minutes, Vol. II, 151.

40. Simon, Sir Ernest, Town Planning: Moscow or Manchester. *Journal of the Town Planning Institute*, **XXIII**, No. 12, 1937.
41. Abercrombie, Patrick, *Town and Country Planning*. Butterworth, 1933.
42. Simon, Sir Ernest, Town Planning: Moscow or Manchester. *Journal of the Town Planning Institute*, **XXIII**, No. 12, 1937.
43. *Journal of the Town Planning Institute*, **XX**, No. 12, 325, 1934.
44. *Journal of the Town Planning Institute*, **XX**, No. 10, 271, 1934.
45. *Report of the National Survey and National Planning Committee*, Town Planning Institute, 1938.
46. Barebones, Jeremiah, Pity the Poor Planner. *The Planning Officer*, **1**, No. 1, 1936.
47. Thomson, T. F., Some Practical Planning Problems. *Journal of the Town Planning Institute*, **XXII**, No. 7, 1936.
48. Town Planning Institute Council Minutes, Vol. II, p. 70.
49. *Journal of the Town Planning Institute*, **XXI**, No. 7, 169, 1935.
50. *Journal of the Town Planning Institute*, **XXIII**, No. 9, 243, 1937.

6 Wartime Affairs

The period 1940–45 saw substantial changes in planning. A number of Government reports contributed markedly to the development of national planning policies: these were on the distribution of the industrial population, on land values, and on rural questions. Considerable changes took place with regard to machinery of government; a Ministry of Town and Country Planning was established. Important new legislation entered the Statute Book. The trauma of war damage led to an enormous upsurge of plan making activity, as evidenced in the reconstruction plans for blitzed cities. National moods hardened significantly in favour of central planning and there was a deep determination to create a new social order and put an end to the urban and community problems of the past.

The first section of this chapter briefly reviews this background. Second, we look at developments within the TPI and the new professional self-confidence that emerged.

DEVELOPMENTS IN PLANNING

Between 1940 and 1942 there was a remarkable trilogy of State Papers, the Barlow, Uthwatt and Scott Reports. It is unnecessary to give a full review of these but mention must be made of the important aspects.

The Royal Commission on the Distribution of the Industrial Population was constituted in July 1937, under the Chairmanship of Sir Montague Barlow. The terms of reference were: 'To inquire into the causes which have influenced the present geographical distribution of the industrial population of Great Britain, and the probable direction of any change in that distribution in the future; to consider what social, economic or strategical disadvantages arise from the concentration of industries or of the industrial population in large towns or in particular areas of the country; and, to report what remedial measures, if any, should be taken in the national interest.' The Commission unleashed a spate of technical evidence and views about the national and urban situation of the inter-war years, both from the point of view of regional economic development and the state of Britain's congested, overcrowded cities. The evidence itself, and the way the Commission responded to it, is worthy of detailed analysis for a full understanding of the history of twentieth century planning: it encapsulates the full cross section of opinion as to the nature of the problem and what the remedies might be.

The importance of the report has been that many of its policy recommendations were accepted by all post-war governments, up to the present time. It was a milestone and a turning point in the development of planning. The report was completed in August 1939, but owing to the outbreak of war, it was not presented to Parliament until January 1940[1]. In essence, the main recommendations of the Commission were threefold. First, a Central Planning Authority 'national in scope and character' should be created; this Authority should take the form of a Board. Second, congested urban areas should be redeveloped and industries and industrial population dispersed from them. Third, a reasonable balance of industrial development should be encouraged throughout the regions of the country; the continued drift of the industrial population to London and the Home Counties was held to constitute 'a social, economic and strategical problem which demands immediate attention'. Two decades of analysis and prescription, from Chamberlain's Unhealthy Areas Committee to the Marley Report had borne full fruit.

Three members of the Commission, though signing the majority report, prepared a Note of Reservations. They wished to go further in operating controls of industrial development, not only in London, as the Commission had suggested, but over the whole country; they also wanted the powers of the Commissioners for the Special Areas to be transferred to the new Board. A further three members, including Abercrombie, felt unable to sign the main recommendations and argued that the situation demanded, not just a Board, but a new Ministry exercising full executive powers. In spite of the minority Notes, there was unanimity in condemning the existing situation and the inadequacy of government machinery or national policy to deal with it.

The Expert Committee on Compensation and Betterment, appointed in January 1941, under the Chairmanship of Mr Justice Uthwatt, was asked 'to make an objective analysis of the subject of the payment of compensation and recovery of betterment in respect of public control of the use of land'. In so doing, it was tackling a planning problem which previous legislation had not resolved, and which practical experience had shown, particularly during the 1930s, was gravely prejudicial to the interests of good planning. Land values had tended to rise for many years, especially in urban areas where demand gave land a building value far higher than the value for its existing use. Bomb damage was a new factor and the Committee was asked 'to advise, as a matter of urgency, what steps should be taken now or before the end of the war, to prevent the work of reconstruction thereafter being prejudiced'. The blitz in fact occupies an important place in the history of planning at this time: quite apart from the psychology of determination to rebuild, the fact of blitzed land necessitated new planning powers.

An Interim Report presented in July 1941[2] included two particularly important recommendations for planning. First, interim control of development should be extended throughout the country in order to prevent work being done which might prejudice reconstruction. Second, special reconstruction areas should be defined so that they might be replanned as a whole. The Final Report[3] followed in September 1942, and gave the Committee's solution to the compensation and betterment problem: it suggested the immediate vesting in the State of the rights of development in all land *outside built-up areas*

121

on payment of fair compensation, and a periodic levy on increases in annual site value. For *developed land*, compulsory purchase of the whole of war-damaged or other reconstruction areas was recommended, as well as land elsewhere to provide accommodation for persons displaced. These proposals marked a considerable extension of central planning powers over what had been regarded previously as possible and legitimate; and as with Barlow, it is remarkable the extent to which they formed the basis for new wartime and post-war planning legislation.

The Committee on Land Utilization in Rural Areas was appointed in October 1941 under the Chairmanship of Lord Justice Scott, an old campaigner in planning circles. The terms of reference were 'To consider the conditions which should govern building and other constructional development in country areas, consistently with the maintenance of agriculture and, in particular, the factors affecting the location of industry, having regard to economic operation, part-time and seasonal employment, the well being of rural communities, and the preservation of rural amenities.' L. Dudley Stamp was Vice-Chairman, and Thomas Sharp was Joint Secretary. Their report, presented in August 1942, contained recommendations quite as wide as the terms of reference might imply[4]. Its extensive coverage and lack of focus reduced the importance of the document, but its recommendations relating to the preservation of rural amenities, such as the establishment of national parks and improved access to countryside, were helpful to planning in that direction. An extension of central planning control over many aspects of rural development was implied.

While these reports were being considered, or were under preparation, important changes took place in the central machinery of government. In September 1940, the old Office of Works, enlivened since the rearmament programme started, became the Ministry of Works and Buildings. The important aspect of this was that Sir John Reith became the first Minister and he became a considerable influence on subsequent developments related to planning. He unleashed a new dynamism and enthusiasm for planning, and became a pivotal force in new developments. He gathered round him a nucleus of enthusiastic planners under Pepler and John Dower. The Ministry of Health retained its normal town and country planning functions, but Reith was responsible for long-term planning through the Reconstruction Group in his Department. The setting up of the Uthwatt and Scott Committees was also at his behest.

The next step was to transfer all town and country planning functions to a reorganized Ministry of Works and Planning. Reith was shortly dismissed by Churchill, seemingly on the grounds that he was going too far, too fast, and was replaced by Lord Portal. But the logic behind the establishment of a Central Planning Authority could not be denied, and effect was given to this by the Minister of Town and Country Planning Act, 1943. The new Minister was W. S. Morrison, a person with no conspicuous background in planning matters, but a train of events had been set in motion which could not now be stopped. The Ministry had responsibilities only for England and Wales; north of the Border central responsibility remained with the Department of Health for Scotland. The Board of Trade was responsible for industrial location in England, Wales and Scotland. In England and Wales the Ministry of Health was responsible for housing.

Important new legislation and Government proposals, in the form of White Papers in

Above: Sir Montague Barlow, Chairman of the Royal Commission on the Distribution of the Industrial Population, set up in 1937.

Above right: Lord Justice Scott, Chairman of the Committee on Land Utilisation in Rural Areas, appointed in 1941.

Right: Sir John (later Lord) Reith, a considerable influence on the development of planning particularly in the period 1940–46.

Together with Mr Justice Uthwatt, these three did much to affect the course of British planning during the war years. (*Courtesy of* Town and Country Planning Association) respect of planning, followed in the period 1943–45. The Town and Country Planning (Interim Development) Act, 1943, and the Town and Country Planning (Interim Development) (Scotland) Act, 1943, which received the Royal Assents in July and November respectively, extended planning control to all land in the country not already covered by a scheme or a resolution to prepare one. This had the effect that all planning authorities, irrespective of whether they were preparing schemes or not, could take immediate enforcement action against development which prejudiced their proposals. This was the recommendation of the Interim Report of the Uthwatt Committee, and the slow process of extending planning control that had gone on during the 1930s was completed to its full extent overnight. The extension of planning control powers was timely, because, at this time of the war, Government factory location was an important issue and the amenity-conscious were quick to point out the dangers to good planning.

Further implementation of Uthwatt came with the Town and Country Planning Act, 1944. Whereas the 1943 Act had been a stop-gap measure in planning control, the 1944 Act had more positive objectives, aiming to provide new powers for local authorities in reconstruction and redevelopment. They were enabled, for the first time, to buy land simply and expeditiously for certain planning purposes, namely to deal with 'areas of extensive war damage' and 'areas of bad layout and obsolete development'—blitzed and blighted land. There were other provisions which made this quite a complex piece of legislation: for example, provision was made for the designation and preservation of buildings of special architectural or historic interest, and the Act was also the first to make provision for relating planning control to land owned by statutory undertakers. The Act, which received the Royal Assent in November, applied only to England and Wales; a corresponding Scottish Act followed later.

It was, however, the 'blitz and blight' provisions which made this the important Act that it was. Until now there was no General Act which permitted planned redevelopment on an extensive, central area scale. The 1944 Act was a fundamental breakthrough in planning. The present generation of planners is accustomed to possessing planning powers that enable a local authority to undertake almost any development project; it is hard for them to imagine when this situation did not exist. In the early forties, the problem was of staggering proportions in the large cities. The complex situation in an area of 300 acres in Birmingham was described by Manzoni, the City Engineer, to a conference in 1941: nearly 11 miles of existing streets, mostly narrow and badly planned; 6 800 individual dwellings, the density varying locally up to 80 to the acre; 5 400 of these dwellings classified as slums to be condemned; 15 major industrial premises or factories, several of them comparatively recent in date; 105 minor factories, storage buildings, workshops, industrial yards, laundries, etc; 778 shops, many of them hucksters' premises; 7 schools; 18 churches and chapels; 51 licensed premises, and many miles of public service mains. 'Add to these a railway viaduct, a canal, a railway goods yard and a gas works, and you have a beautiful problem in redevelopment.'[5] A beautiful problem indeed, which demanded sweeping powers if effective planning were to be realized; the 1944 Act was a vital step in this direction. The beginnings of comprehensive urban planning date from this time.

It is impossible to exaggerate the progress these various steps represented for planning. The wartime situation had the effect of placing planning measures on the Statute Book that would have been almost unheard of five years earlier. Local authority powers were strengthened and extended to a considerable degree. An important White Paper completed the picture of Government's intention for the immediate future: this was *Control of Land Use* published in June, 1944, a paper which related to England, Scotland and Wales. It was largely concerned with proposals for the solution of the problem of compensation and betterment. The scheme now put forward was based on the principle that right development could only be secured and wrong development prevented, if there was complete control of changes in the use to which land may be put. The requirement to obtain consent to develop land was essential. With the granting of permission to develop, there would be a betterment charge at the rate of 80% of the increase in the value of the land; on the other hand, there was to be compensation on refusal of permission to develop. Payment of compensation and collection of betterment would cease to be the responsibility of local authorities, and would be centralized in a Land Commission. The bare bones of post-war planning had been laid.

This White Paper had another importance too. As the war drew to a close, it was a fundamental statement of intent about the direction of national planning. Three years is a short period in the history of planning, but the years between 1941–1944 had marked a Governmental acceptance as to what needed to be done after the war. One logical step led to another, and the coherent structure of a central planning system emerged. The Coalition Government grasped the nettle, and if we are looking for watersheds in planning thought *The Control of Land Use* probably represents one of the best examples. The first paragraph stated the position. 'Provision for the right use of land, in accordance with a considered policy, is an essential requirement of the Government's programme of post-war reconstruction. New houses, whether of permanent or emergency construction; the new layout of areas devastated by enemy action or blighted by reason of age or bad living conditions; the new schools which will be required under the Education Bill, now before Parliament and under the Scottish Education Bill which it is hoped to introduce later this Session; the balanced distribution of industry which the Government's recently published proposals for maintaining active employment envisage; the requirements of sound nutrition and of a healthy and well-balanced agriculture; the preservation of land for national parks and forests, and the assurance to the people of enjoyment of the sea and countryside in times of leisure; a new and safer highway system, better adapted to modern industrial and other needs; the proper provision of air fields—all these related parts of a single reconstruction programme involve the use of land, and it is essential that their various claims on land should be so harmonized as to ensure, for the people of this country, the greatest possible measure of individual well-being and national prosperity. The achievement of this aim is an interest of all sections of the community, both in this and succeeding generations. The Government desire to make that achievement possible.'[6] Never before (and never since) had a statement of national planning objectives been quite so clearly stated; it was indeed a remarkable affirmation.

We can now turn to other developments in planning. By 1944, 1 021 out of the 1 441 local authorities in England and Wales had become members of Joint Planning Committees, and the number of these Committees totalled 179. Regional planning received great impetus and ten Regional Planning Officers were appointed by the new Minister of

Town and Country Planning. Early in 1944 the Merseyside Joint Advisory Planning Committee was formed at the Minister's suggestion. In Scotland, three Regional Committees were set up, one for the Clyde Valley, one for Central and South East Scotland and the other for East Central Scotland; these embraced 75% of the Scottish population, and 38 out of the 57 Scottish planning authorities were represented on them. The Clyde Valley Committee dated from 1927, being set up in connection with road planning, but it was now reconstituted on a much wider basis; Abercrombie was appointed consultant. A great upsurge of interest in planning resulted from The Town and Country Planning (Interim Development) (Scotland) Act, 1943, which brought under planning control all land in Scotland. It meant that 27 Scottish planning authorities exercised planning control for the first time. In Northern Ireland the situation was quite different. The Planning and Housing Act (Northern Ireland), 1931, made provision for the preparation of planning schemes by local authorities, but not one was ever made. The Planning (Interim Development) Act (Northern Ireland), 1944, deemed all land to be subject to a resolution to prepare a planning scheme. A start to planning was made, and W. R. Davidge became adviser to the Northern Ireland Government.

An immediate problem concerned the blitzed cities. Reith decided to make a detailed study of a small number of them in order to establish points which could later be used in drawing up national legislation. The local situation often turned out to be very delicate from the point of view of who was to do the job of reconstruction, as well as the planning principles to follow. Coventry was a case in point, as described by Kenneth Richardson[7]. In 1938 Coventry had set up an Architectural Department under Donald Gibson. The City Engineer, E. H. Ford, remained responsible for town planning matters. A joint team between the two departments was set up in 1939 to work on a plan for the civic centre, but different concepts emerged: Gibson envisaged broad vistas and grand spaciousness, and Ford wanted a more intimate central area with a number of squares in the civic area. After the blitz the same two officers were requested to prepare a city centre plan, but after a clash of ideas the Council decided that primary responsibility in town planning should rest with the City Architect. The City Engineer became Joint Town Planning Officer (and President of the Institute in 1951–52). Until the end of the war there were strained relations with the Ministry, soothed by Ernest Doubleday, then the Regional Officer of the Ministry stationed in Birmingham. No town planning history can be free from conflicts of this kind; indeed there are times when it seems that history is structured round them.

With regard to London, Abercrombie was appointed in 1942 to prepare an outline plan and report for the area surrounding London, so as to form, with the plans of the City and County of London which were also being prepared, a comprehensive plan for the whole region. The City of London Plan, *Reconstruction in the City of London*, a Report of the Improvements and Town Planning Committee was published in July 1944; it was an unambitious affair, and in due time was rejected by the Minister. The *County of London Plan*, which was published in 1943, the product of J. H. Forshaw, the LCC Architect, and Abercrombie as consultant was much more important. The Town and Country Planning Association (recently renamed from the Garden Cities and Town Planning Association) were critical observers at this event, and F. J. Osborn called it a 'profound disappointment'. In a letter to Lewis Mumford he explained that: 'Abercrombie had the chance of a century. Great pressure was put on him by the LCC but he was in a position to stand out. Early on in the preparation I had an evening with him and Forshaw, and many times I pointed out to him that the cities of the whole world would be influenced by this Plan, if it were really sound and logical.' But 'the LCC is led by middle-class Labour Councillors, right out of touch with popular opinion but very close to the transport and public service interests, and terrified of a drop in rateable value or of a loss of their slum electorate. The plan, which contemplates 75% of London families rehoused in flats, and a merely "token" decentralization of people, and a brake on, rather than an encouragement of, decentralization of industry and business, is impracticable'[8].

But one should not necessarily rely on Osborne's assessment. It can in fact be seen as a major landmark in planning literature which had a profound effect on London and elsewhere. Lord Reith called for the report not only for the post-war reconstruction of London but also to assist him in framing legislation. Its effect on the LCC was pronounced and did much to put pre-war departmentalism aside (see p. 101). For the first time London's political leaders saw the picture as a whole with a co-ordinated plan embracing statutory planning, highways, housing, parks and education. This revolutionalized the structure of London's Government in the post-war era. Beside this, Osborne's criticism is rather trivial. The report did in fact recommend drastically lower housing densities than those prevailing pre-war; it did propose decentralization and it also inaugurated comprehensive reconstruction proposals for the East End and for the South Bank.

Abercrombie's *Greater London Plan* was circulated to authorities and reviewed in the press in December 1944, although not actually published until August 1945. It received a much more favourable reaction. From the ranks of the Town and Country Planning Association, Osborn supported it, although he maintained his criticism of the proposed redevelopment density. 'It is so great an advance on any other big regional plan that one must be enthusiastic about its general pattern', he wrote to Mumford[9]. Osborn was right in recognizing its importance, because it provided a strategic planning model for large cities and conurbations which served for at least 20 years. The principle objective was decentralization, and the locational distribution of people and jobs was explained against the setting of four concentric zones. The first, an inner ring, required an out-movement of industry and a reduction in population densities. The second, the inter-war suburban belt, needed no planning intervention. A green belt was the third ring which extended up to ten miles beyond the outer edge of the built-up area, far more extensive than Unwin's green girdle had been. The fourth was the outer country district which contained a number of settlements in a predominantly countryside area. Here the proposal was to preserve the general character of the area, but eight new towns were proposed for overspill population with accompanying industry. Altogether, the reduction of densities and the relocation to peripheral and outlying areas, meant a transfer of about one million persons. Suburban sprawl had had its day; creative town design and planned control took its place. The idea of decentralization through satellite development gained widespread acceptance, although it was not everywhere that New Towns were seen as the machinery for dispersal. The plan for the West Midland conurbation, for example, prepared by Abercrombie and Jackson in 1948, proposed no New Towns in its regional strategy.

The *Greater London Plan* was a remarkable testament to the planner's belief in his

GREATER LONDON PLAN

MILES 0   5   10   15   20

THE FOUR RINGS

☐ OUTER COUNTRY

▤ GREEN BELT

▥ SUBURBAN

▦ INNER URBAN.

■ THE ADMINISTRATIVE COUNTY OF LONDON.

ROYSTON

LUTON

BISHOP'S STORTFORD

HERTFORD

HEMEL HEMPSTEAD

ST. ALBANS

CHESHAM

CHESHUNT

WATFORD

HIGH WYCOMBE

BRENTWOOD

ROMFORD

SLOUGH — UXBRIDGE

TILBURY

WINDSOR

DARTFORD

CROYDON

WOKING

EPSOM

SEVENOAKS

GUILDFORD

REDHILL

HORLEY

HASLEMERE

N
W — E
S

The Greater London Plan, prepared by Abercrombie on behalf of the Standing Conference on London Regional Planning at the request of the Minister of Town and Country Planning, was published in 1944. It made an important step forward in the idea of planned location for industry and housing; the advocacy for planned decentralisation became the post-war model for all urban areas.

GREATER LONDON PLAN

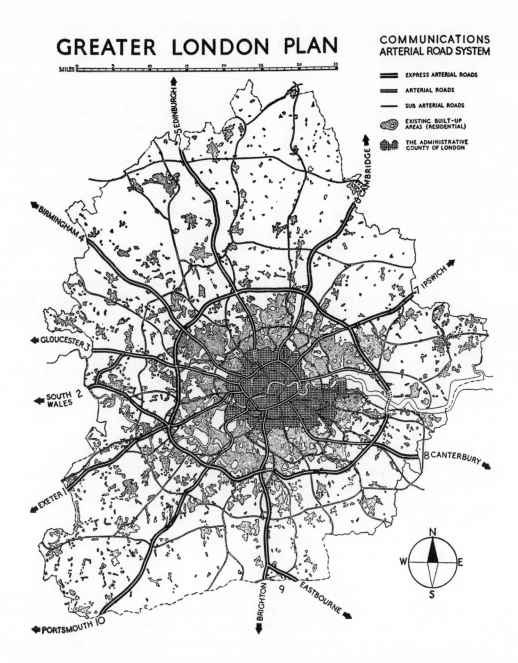

COMMUNICATIONS
ARTERIAL ROAD SYSTEM

EXPRESS ARTERIAL ROADS
ARTERIAL ROADS
SUB ARTERIAL ROADS
EXISTING BUILT-UP AREAS (RESIDENTIAL)
THE ADMINISTRATIVE COUNTY OF LONDON

The Greater London Plan (1944) also contained important road proposals. There were to be ten express arterial highways, linking up with those proposed in the County of London Plan. A sub-arterial road system would carry all the normal main traffic, but five new ring routes would connect the arterial roads and serve as bypasses around the congested centre. The geometric grand design to London was emphasized.

ability to control a complex system. But it would be wrong to dismiss Abercrombie as naïve or unduly arrogant. His approach to planning was shaped by the circumstances and assumptions of the time. The pace of future change was firmly expected to be slow, and therefore a plan for a 'once-and-for-all' change was perfectly permissable, the belief being that when change had been effected, the new system would continue in a steady state. (We know now that post-war London, and indeed post-war urban Britain has experienced change at a rapid rate—population increase, sustained prosperity, sharply rising standards, the car boom, and so on—but wartime Britain, obsessed by the issues of the thirties could not have foreseen this.) Furthermore, Abercrombie could assume a new machinery of government which would attend to the location of industry and to the problems connected with private speculation in land. Given this background the Abercrombie plan was justifiable. But this plan for a set of static conditions had, in the event, to cater for quite different circumstances: a period marked by change on an unprecedented scale.

There was a boom in planning literature which reflected the great popular interest in post-war reconstruction. Thomas Sharp's *Town Planning*, commissioned by Penguin, was published in 1940 and sold $\frac{1}{4}$ million copies, making it perhaps the planning bestseller of our time. The political parties and lobbies produced pamphlets; PEP published its frequent broadsheets; so too did the Association for Planning and Regional Reconstruction (APRR). From the Bournville Village Trust came *When We Build Again* (1941), a study based on research into conditions of living and working in Birmingham. The Town and Country Planning Association produced a series of booklets entitled *Rebuilding Britain*; it also reported on its wartime conferences. The Royal Academy held an exhibition on the replanning of London in 1942. Plans for the blitzed cities were produced. *The Plan for Plymouth* was a report published in 1943, prepared by J. Paton Watson (City Engineer) and Abercrombie; *The Replanning of Southampton* was a report of Adshead and H. T. Cook (Town Planning and Development Officer), published in 1942, and there were many others during these years. *How Should We Rebuild London* (1945) gave C. B. Purdom's garden city approach to the capital's problem, and by this time the model of decentralization was widely adopted. Abercrombie's *Plan for Kingston upon Hull* (1945), for example, continued his grand strategy of renewal, decongestion and satellite expansion.

The unprecedented public interest was encouraged by a number of organizations, the most important of which was the Town and Country Planning Association, with a programme of conferences and output of pamphlets. The Association's wartime conferences had been influential. The Oxford conference in 1941 supported the main recommendations of Barlow. The Cambridge conference in 1942 considered the needs of agriculture and rural life. Later conferences in London dealt with the future of the country towns and the relation of planning and housing to full employment. The leading figure was F. J. Osborn, prominent in political circles as a member of the Labour Party Post-War Reconstruction Committee and informal adviser to other parties. When Reith was establishing his embryo Planning Ministry, Osborn was given a room and acted as an unpaid, part-time under-secretary. The pressure of this propagandist body was widely recognized; a later quip had it that the notice on its door 'Town and Country Planning Association—Push' was almost a motto.

Professional bodies (quite apart from TPI) took a substantial interest in planning and reconstruction, many setting up special post-war committees and organizing planning exhibitions. The RIBA, in particular, took important initiatives. A number of new bodies began to take a greater interest in planning. The Co-operative Building Society issued booklets on housing and planning, some written by leading TPI members like Lanchester and Davidge. The Society of Friends established an Industrial and Social Order Council; and the Housing Centre concerned itself more with general planning issues. In addition, new bodies were set up during the war which contributed materially to the planning debate. The most important of these was the 1940 Council, set up to promote the planning of the social environment, working particularly through research groups. It worked closely with the TPI and, in fact, its Planning Committee was merged in 1940 with the TPI Research and Planning Group. Another Group was the West Midland Group on Post-war Reconstruction, a body which was to prove a great stimulus to regional planning.

The wartime years formed a period therefore when dramatic changes took place in the context of which planning operated. The idea of planning swept through virtually every aspect of Government activity; there was the determination to make plans for post-war years, to set our national house in order, to grapple with the problems we had shelved. These were the years when the structure of what we can now describe as the 'centralist planning system' was founded. The Minister of War Transport appointed a Committee of experts in 1943 to consider the design and layout of roads in built-up areas. There was a new look at the gas and electricity supply industries and inland transport. *A National Water Policy* was a Government White Paper of 1944. Government intervention in economic affairs was implicit in the *Employment Policy* White Paper of the same year. Government policy directed to bringing about conditions favourable to the maintenance of a high level of employment was foreshadowed. Influence on location of industry and its balance in particular areas was promised. A policy for agriculture took shape, as well as for fishing and forestry. In social matters, the Education Act, 1944, reconstructed the public system of education. In the Social Services, Sir William Beveridge presented his Report on *Social Insurance and Allied Services* in 1942; the Government's proposals followed in 1944 in White Papers on *Social Insurance*, *A National Health Service* and *Employment Policy*. The Ministry of National Insurance Act was passed in November 1944.

In housing, building programmes were drawn up and a host of technical studies gave advice to local authorities. Two in particular made an important planning contribution. *The Design of Dwellings* was a report of a Sub-committee of the Central Housing Advisory Committee, chaired by the Earl of Dudley; it was published in July 1944. It made new recommendations regarding design, planning and layout of dwellings, the first important ones since the Tudor Walters Report of 1918. Its proposals were incorporated in the *Housing Manual*, prepared jointly by the Ministry of Health and Ministry of Works, and published as a technical guide to local authorities in 1944.

An important supplement to the Dudley Report was the Report of a Study Group of the Ministry of Town and Country Planning on *Site Planning and Layout in Relation to Housing*. Among other things, it dealt with community aspects of neighbourhoods, of rapidly growing importance in town planning. There were two features. One was the idea of the neighbourhood as a device in orderly layout, based on adequate provision of facilities within walking distance and deflection of through vehicular traffic. The other was the wartime discovery of 'community' as a social basis for post-war planning. Literature in the 1930s pointed to a growing awareness of the importance of community life, but this was fanned in the war years by an enhanced sense of 'togetherness' in face of danger, emphasis on family life in social and moral reconstruction, and the idea of 'civic pride' in small units; for some, the idea of communistic living was explicit. The Becontree development of the twenties and thirties may have been a considerable technical achievement, but considerable social problems had arisen, as Terence Young for the Becontree Social Survey Committee described[10]. Later, Ruth Durant reported on social life at Watling, a LCC housing estate at Hendon and looked at the role of the Community Centre in local affairs[11]. The new concern for 'community' entered into planning. An extreme form was suggested by C. H. Reilly in a plan for Birkenhead with a physical setting based on small village greens which, it was believed, would create neighbourly contacts and eliminate family isolation[12]. There were quite outrageous claims at this time that physical plans could determine social patterns. With this rather wild context, the neighbourhood idea was incorporated in most of the urban plans produced at the time.

One final aspect of the wartime situation that affected planning was the new emphasis given to research, or at least the search for information. Geddes' idea of 'survey, analysis and plan' was rediscovered as fundamental in the planning process. Great attention was placed on the idea of the civic survey that preceded any plan making, and many of the plans that were prepared at this time were notable more for their survey introductions than the quality or realism of their proposals. There was considerable emphasis on collecting data and building up comprehensive knowledge, the implicit belief being that the full range of facts revealed about a particular town would point out the solutions to the problems. It was a manifestation of the consensus, a common-sense, a-political interpretation of planning that took shape in the 1930s.

PLANNERS AND THE PROFESSION

Members of the Institute thought and acted in harmony with the nation as a whole. They were readily able to identify their personal cause with the common fight. In his Presidential Address in November 1939 (never personally delivered because of the blackout and absence of Members), W. Harding Thompson declared that: 'We are fighting ... for the right of the community, whether national or local, to shape its own destiny in sympathetic co-operation with its neighbours.' There was a shared determination too, for he went on to express the hope that 'out of the anguish and tumult of war may be born ideas and ideals for a new order in the evolution of our country'[13]. The war soon cast its personal shadows, with the Journal reporting of Members who had joined the Armed Services, and before very long of internment and casualties. Short, poignant obituaries recounted the losses.

The first act of the Council, after the declaration of war, was to set up an Emergency Executive Committee with full powers to act on urgent matters if it was impracticable for the full Council to meet, consisting of the President, Vice-President and Honorary Secretary. It later became a Policy Committee, which developed as one of the most important in Council affairs. For some time official action was naturally interrupted, but

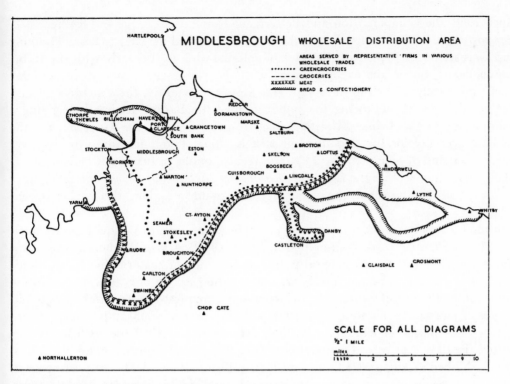

Middlesbrough Survey, 1944–45. This is an example of Max Lock's approach to analysing the geographic and economic background to urban planning, typical of the emphasis on research and data collection at this time. (Taken from his paper 'Survey and its Practical Application to Planning', *Journal TPI*, **XXXII**, No. 3, 1946)

Notice to Members, September 1939. The outbreak of war cast its shadows on professional life, and the September *Journal* carried this special note. It seemed appropriate that the first few pages of that *Journal* also reproduced the Institute's Report on 'Planning for Air Raid Protection.'

TOWN PLANNING INSTITUTE

NOTICE TO MEMBERS

Owing to the outbreak of war it has been found necessary to cancel the Annual Country Meeting, which was to have been held at Taunton, early in October.

For the same reason it may not be possible to carry out the usual programme of ordinary meetings. When any can be arranged a notice will be issued.

It is hoped to continue publication of the Journal, probably in an abbreviated form.

Never was planning so vital a necessity as it is to-day. In the present Crisis, members will be called to services of many kinds and may be out of touch with each other, but the fellowship which is the Institute will be united in thought and in the desire to plan for a better future.

Members are asked to keep the Secretary informed of any change of permanent address.

W. HARDING THOMPSON.
President.

September, 1939.

in April 1940, the Compensation and Betterment Committee, set up in October 1938, duly reported to Council. A new Research Group, later called the Research and Planning Group, was set up in 1940, with the idea of collaborating particularly with the RIBA Research Board, but in the event, it fused with the Planning Committee of the 1940 Council; the Group folded up in April 1942. More importantly, the Emergency Committee acted decisively following the publication of the Barlow Report by sending a Memorandum to the Prime Minister which impressed upon the Government 'the immediate necessity for the appointment of a National Planning Authority to direct reconstruction and development by whatever agency, public or private, it may be supervised or carried out.'[14] With the Institute's *Report of the National Survey and National Planning Committee* (1938) behind them, they were on safe ground in making this further recommendation.

Fighting for a better tomorrow had repercussions that were dramatic in professional circles. As the *Planning Officer* commented in April, 1941: 'A brief 18 months ago, town planning was regarded by the general public as a branch of rhetoric and by the landowner as a pestiferous nuisance. Today we find it rating second only to war news in the headlines of the Press, and forming the principal topic amongst "Letters to the Editor" in all classes of journals.'[15] Planning was given a totally new national importance. There were more candidates for examinations than ever before; in 1942 the 1939 figure was surpassed; in 1944 that record was doubled. The Town and Country Planning School was re-established in August 1943, this time held at Birmingham. As the war years passed, building and reconstruction plans were prepared and, in his Presidential Address in November 1943, W. Dobson Chapman spoke of 'the first trickles of the flood of planning work which threatens to engulf the war-depleted ranks of our profession'[16].

The importance of the years 1940–43 was that dramatically, almost overnight, there was a general acceptance of what planners, either through the Institute or through propagandist bodies, had been saying for decades. In consequence, there developed, within the TPI, a mood of professional self-confidence. It was a tremendous boost to morale for the planner to find his skills, hitherto largely ignored, suddenly accepted and sought after.

The White Paper, *The Control of Land Use* (1944), was eloquent testimony to the new realization. The inadequacy of the past was described: 'wrong use of land (resulted) in much loss, both to individuals and to the nation, of well-being, of time and of money. Good agricultural land was unnecessarily wasted, and the appearance of the country spoiled, by sporadic and unsightly building; public authorities were put to undue expense by the need of supplying water and other services to households strung out along the principal highways; road accidents (especially among children) were multiplied; valuable hours were lost each working day, and the traffic of great cities congested, because of the distance at which workers lived from their work; the standard of health was affected, and decency of living impaired, by overcrowding.'[17] What more could be said? This is what the TPI and the propagandist bodies had been proclaiming for a decade and more; now a Government White Paper declared it an evident truth. The psychological consequences of recognition were profound.

The result was a new attitude. The open seas of planning were vigorously defended against the piratical incursions of other professions, and efforts were made to ensure that the TPI planner was adequately equipped in training and status to survive the voyage. Whereas before 1939 there had always been the tendency to welcome those with first allegiance to other professions, during the war the Institute began to see itself much more as a professional body in its own right.

The more traditional line which stressed the position of the parent professions within planning, was put forward particularly by the engineers within the Institute. In his Presidential Address in 1942, Colonel W. S. Cameron, City Engineer of Leeds, laid emphasis on the part of the engineer in local government planning[18]. During the war years it was still the case that Presidents had often achieved distinction in other professions before assuming the highest office of the Institute. Sir Peirson Frank, a leading local government engineer, President in 1944–45, was among the last of such men. But a different opinion was gaining ground, one which looked on physical planning as a distinct body of knowledge and professional expertise. Naturally, its vigorous advocates were among the ranks of the 'up and coming' within the membership.

Relations with other professional bodies continued to be cordial, but there was no disguising the nature of the conflict. In October 1942, for example, Pepler reported to Council that IMCE had circulated local authority clerks to suggest that their members were the obvious persons to prepare planning schemes. TPI disapproved, but proposed not to engage in open controversy. When the professionalism versus propaganda question came to the surface again, the TPI instinctively adopted its old position. In April 1940, the Garden Cities and Town Planning Association asked for TPI endorsement of their national planning proposals, but Council decided that 'it does not feel that it would be appropriate for them to join with non-professional bodies in putting forward statements of a general kind.'[19] Sensitivity came to the surface later when some objection was raised in the Scottish Branch of the Institute, about the newly adopted name of the Town and Country Planning Association.

The question of the status of the planner, particularly in local government, was important. A Joint Council/Town Planning Officers' Section Committee, was set up in 1941 to consider the professional status of the planning officer. Lord Reith had appointed a Consultative Committee on Planning, and Lord Burleigh, as a member of the Panel (and Chairman of the 1940 Council), wrote to the TPI to ask about post-war professional needs. TPI forwarded an interim memorandum recommending that the Planning Department of any authority should be a separate one and that the planning officer of that authority should be a chief officer[20]. This concealed an uneasy compromise between TPI and IMCE interests because Cameron, in particular, saw planning in large cities bound up with the work of the city engineer.

The Town Planning Officers' Section continued to be a vigorous advocate of the status of the planning officer, submitting a number of resolutions to Council. Yet another Committee was set up in November 1944. Their report, published in 1945, contained the proposal that planning officers should have a salary scale of £750–£1 500 p.a.; chief planning assistants £500–£750; planning assistants (qualified) £400, (Intermediate qualifications £300)[21]. But the days of the Section were coming to an end. The circumstances which attended its birth were now different; TPI members employed by local government now outnumbered membership of other practising categories, and in the interests of presenting a unified front in the TPI, the Society was wound up in 1949–50.

The new self-awareness of the professional planner had its reflection in education matters. These are reported more fully in chapter 9 but we should note the significance of the new 5-year degree course set up at King's College, Newcastle, which provided a means of planning qualification that did not depend on previous professional qualifications.

It remains for us to note internal changes in the Institute. Early in the war disruption had affected most things. Even the Institute library was moved for safe keeping—by Potter and Doubleday in 1940 to the old dungeons of Warwick County Hall, formerly the Old Gaol. Normality was restored, but changes of a different kind occurred. In May 1944, new premises were obtained at 18 Ashley Place, on a 7-year lease at £750 p.a. Part of the suite was sublet to the Institute of Public Administration. Almost simultaneously, Potter's long-standing partnership with E. G. Allen (then Honorary Librarian) was dissolved and he became formally a full-time TPI Officer, at a salary of £1 000 per annum. The increasing work of the Institute demanded extra staff, and during 1945 serious difficulty was experienced with shortages, though there was some improvement by the end of the year when an Assistant Secretary and a Librarian–Editor had been appointed, and Mr Whitfield demobilized.

In June 1944, there were important reorganizations of Committees and Council representation on them. Five Standing Committees were formalized, with Policy and Finance (as it was henceforth to be known) and a Parliamentary Committee (which never met between 1939 and 1945). No Council member could be a member of more than three, but had to be a member of at least one. The Policy and Finance Committee consisted of the President, Vice-President, Immediate Past President and Honorary Secretary and Treasurer. In October 1945, another Research Committee was appointed.

During the war years, however, there were also changes in the Branches. Before, there had been just the Town Planning Officers' Section and the North of England Division and the Scottish Branch. An Irish Branch was formed in October 1941, and in December 1943, a Midlands Branch was finally set up, the idea having been mooted several times previously. The first overseas Branch, in South Africa, was approved in March 1944. The last Branch to be constituted in wartime was the South-West of England Branch, approved in May, 1945. A South Wales Group set up early in the war was not constituted as a Branch for some years.

The general picture is, therefore, of the TPI formalizing its organization and administration in order to cope with the increased work brought about by an extraordinary wartime situation, and the real emergence of planning as a profession for the first time. Potter and Pepler remained the major helmsmen of the Institute; continuity was assured through Pepler's permanent place on Policy and Finance Committee, as Honorary Secretary and Treasurer. All others as elected members could only normally influence events at these close quarters over a four-year period.

Enormous changes took place in town planning during this wartime period. These we have reviewed, but in conclusion we can also mention Holford's story that in Hyde Park in December 1944, one morning at 2 o'clock, he had heard 'anti-aircraft gunners discussing whether the compensation proposals in the White Paper were, in fact, improvements on those in the Uthwatt Report'[22]. The war years had raised physical planning to a new level of public acceptance; national statements of intent were far-reaching and, in 1945, the country was poised on the brink of further new planning developments. There could be no going back; society expected public control and direction of land use, anticipated (if scarcely understood) a new social order and looked forward to a new deal for town and country. The planner was among those charged with a profound purpose in building the physical conditions of a lasting peace and a better way of life. B. J. Collins, a future President and Planning Officer for London, visited Pompeii in the aftermath of the Cassino battle and had been moved to poetry; later verse, *Swords into Ploughshares*, captured his mood in 1945[23].

> Returned, returned the soldier from campaigning,
> Anon as planner to the task he chose,
> To think and draw and build a heritage
> More worthy of a race where glory knows
> Not conquest only but all the arts of peace—
> ...
>
> For all about his resurrected comrades
> He feels the bond that suffering has bound;
> He senses all the new determination
> Which degradation of their lives has found.
> Each man, he says, shall have a fairer living,
> A country focussed in a finer town,
> And he that understands the art of planning
> Shall now substantiate their true renown;
> ...
>
> Amid such thoughts the soldier while waiting
> A readoption of his former guise—
> Administrator, prophet, draughtsman, Planner—
> can hardly fail to sentimentalise.

This was the tide in human affairs that swept planning and its profession on into the second half of the 1940s.

REFERENCES

1. *Report of the Royal Commission on the Distribution of the Industrial Population*, Cmd. 6153, 1940.
2. *Interim Report*, Expert Committee on Compensation and Betterment, Cmd. 6291, 1941.
3. *Final Report*, Expert Committee on Compensation and Betterment, Cmd. 6386, 1942.
4. *Report of the Committee on Land Utilisation in Rural Areas*, Cmd. 6378, 1942.
5. Quoted in *Final Report*, Expert Committee on Compensation and Betterment, Cmd. 6386, para 11.
6. *The Control of Land Use*, Cmd. 6537, 1944.
7. Richardson, Kenneth, *Twentieth Century Coventry*. Macmillan, 1972.

8. Hughes, Michael (Ed.), *The Letters of Lewis Mumford and Frederick J. Osborn*. Adams and Dart, Bath, 1971.
9. Hughes, Michael (Ed.), *The Letters of Lewis Mumford and Frederick J. Osborn*. Adams and Dart, Bath, 1971.
10. Young, Terence, *Becontree and Dagenham*. Becontree Social Survey Committee, 1934.
11. Durant, Ruth, *Watling: a Survey of Social Life on a New Housing Estate*. P. S. King, 1939.
12. Wolfe, Lawrence, *The Reilly Plan*. Nicholson and Watson, 1945.
13. Thompson, W. Harding, Presidential Address. *Journal of the Town Planning Institute*, **XXVI**, No. 1, 1939.
14. *Journal of the Town Planning Institute*, **XXVII**, No. 1, 6–7, 1940.
15. *The Planning Officer*, **3**, 127.
16. Chapman, W. Dobson, Presidential Address. *Journal of the Town Planning Institute*, **XXX**, No. 1, 1943.
17. *The Control of Land Use*, Cmd. 6537,1944.
18. Cameron, Colonel W. S., Presidential Address. *Journal of the Town Planning Institute*, **XXIX**, No. 1, 1942.
19. Town Planning Institute Council Minutes, vol. II, p. 240.
20. *Journal of the Town Planning Institute*, **XXVIII**, No. 6, 243–5, 1942.
21. *Journal of the Town Planning Institute*, **XXXI**, No. 5, 180, 1945.
22. *Journal of the Town Planning Institute*, **XXXI**, No. 2, 46, 1945.
23. *Journal of the Town Planning Institute*, **XXXI**, No. 5, 183, 1945.

7 Planning and Planners 1945–60

The 29 years since the end of the Second World War represent almost half the total lifespan of the Institute. Moreover the period is the longest single stretch in the Institute's history which is not broken by the effects of international strife and national emergency. The three decades since 1945 have a certain unity in the development of planning because they represent the operation, in practice, of the planning system conceived in the war years, and given form in the later 1940s. Nonetheless, the span of years is at least divisible into two and the most helpful way of describing the events is to break at 1960. This date, in itself, is not particularly significant, but at the end of the fifties and the beginning of the sixties, there are clear points of change, not only in planning matters generally, but also in affairs of the Institute.

This chapter deals with the events of the first half of the post-war period. They began on a note of professional confidence and planning was swept along in a vigorous stream of new-found importance. In his Presidential Address of November 1946, Heck commented that 'whilst many of my distinguished predecessors doubtless felt that their term of office coincided with an important advancement of the scope and acceptance of planning, none ... have had the opportunity to take the helm at such an important juncture in the history and development of town and country planning.'[1] He was right. In the first four years of the new Labour Administration, three important pieces of legislation added to another passed in the last days of the Caretaker Government: new towns, a new planning Act and national parks supplemented distribution of industry as fundamental planks in post-war planning. The 1950s gave us the first experiences of the new system. Planners changed from prophets to bureaucrats as they became the new servants of the state machine. Euphoria soon became tempered with realism, and frustrations and a change in social and political attitudes blunted expectations; from a position of favoured son, the planner soon knew what it was like to be kept in place and ignored. Towards the end of the 1950s, there was considerable disillusionment about planning, although by the close of the decade a number of pointers suggested better things for the future.

Correspondingly, the Institute ebbed and flowed, with the tide turning in its favour at the end; in fact it was in a much stronger position professionally in 1960 than in 1945. It met with an early rebuff in its search for a Royal Charter, but internal reforms, and the helpful recommendations of a Government Committee, meant that a second application was successful, in 1959. The professional future was now much more assured. But the same year was marked, within a month, by the death of Pepler and the intimation of the retirement of Potter. Fifty years had elapsed since the passing of the first Act; 45 since the founding of the Institute, during which time these two had held together the affairs of the TPI.

This chapter has three main sections. First, we review briefly the planning background: legislation, the development of the new planning machine, and the way it operated in the 1950s. This allows us to look, secondly, at the new influences on planners as professional people, and, thirdly, at the changes which took place in Institute affairs.

The Planning Machine: Legislation

The Distribution of Industry Act, 1945, was rushed through Parliament before the Dissolution, and suffered some emasculation in the process. Nonetheless, it proved to be the foundation of British regional policy until 1960. The pre-war Special Areas were re-defined and renamed Development Areas: South Wales, the North East, West Cumberland and West Central Scotland. With a redrawing of boundaries to include important towns, previously omitted, the total population included in these areas rose from 4 millions (pre-war) to 6½ millions. Steps were taken to give effect to the dispersal proposals of the Barlow Commission, though the purists of the Town and Country Planning Association were disappointed not to see power which would have aided the removal of the industries from the large cities. Barlow had proposed a new Board to take over the work of the Special Area Commissioners, but the main responsibility was given to the existing Board of Trade. It was empowered to build factories, give grants or loans, make provision for basic public services and reclaim derelict land. An important new power, replacing the building licence system, introduced as a wartime control, was the Industrial Development Certificate, compulsory for new industrial development of more than 5 000 square feet. This was introduced in the Town and Country Planning Act, 1947.

Another plank in national location policy was to be through the building of new towns. The New Towns Act, 1946, was the first jewel in the Labour Government's crown. It was by then a matter of conventional wisdom, that cities could grow too big and that some measure of public control had to be exercised over them. Urban sprawl had become (to quote a book of the time for Christian laymen), 'a social cancer, destroying health, leisure and family life'[2] and the demand for new towns in post-war reconstruction was overwhelming. Their promise encapsulated all that post-war Britain sought to achieve in terms of physical rebuilding and a new social or moral order. The assumption was that 'community' as a social phenomenon could be created through the operation of physical planning. Typical was Mumford's advice on a rare visit to Britain, 'to plan for man as a human animal, to give him houses, neighbourhoods and towns which will teach him lessons of integrity and continuity, so that as he grows and matures, he will eventually go forth into and govern the world as a whole.'[3] Abercrombie's widely regarded *Greater London Plan* had suggested ten possible sites in the Outer Country Ring around London to receive the capital's surplus population, eight of which should be chosen for new satellite

Development Areas, 1945–60. The Distribution of Industry Act 1945 replaced the pre-war legislation for the Special Areas; they were redefined and renamed Development Areas. (*Courtesy of* Allen and Unwin. Taken from Gavin McCrone, *Regional Policy in Britain*, 1969)

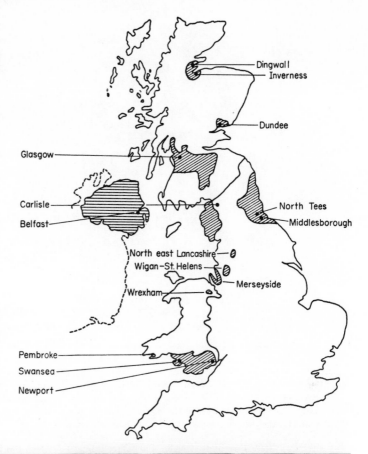

Lord Harmsworth and Lewis Silkin at the Hemel Hempstead New Town Exhibition 1948. Lord Harmsworth (left) was chairman of the Town and Country Planning Association; Lewis Silkin was Minister of Town and Country Planning. Hemel Hempstead was the first of the New Town Development Corporations to prepare an exhibition of its plans. (*Courtesy of* Town and Country Planning Association)

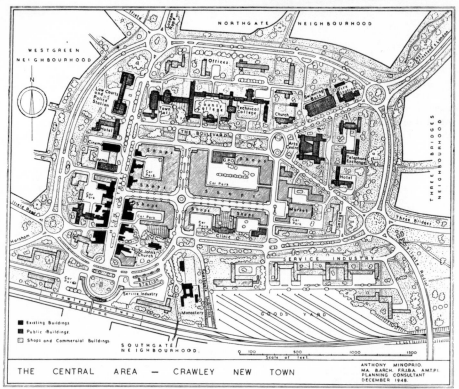

Central Area, Crawley New Town, Anthony Minoprio's plan, 1948. This incorporated the existing High Street, but the rest of the 95 acre scheme was entirely new development. It was planned on 'civic centre' lines with a 400yds long boulevard running east-west; public buildings were to the north, and shops to the south.

Central Area Proposals, Leeds. The Development Plan, 1951, proposed a new Inner Ring Road circumscribing the central area; a Civic Centre and new public buildings were proposed, but the shopping, office and business areas were regarded as static.

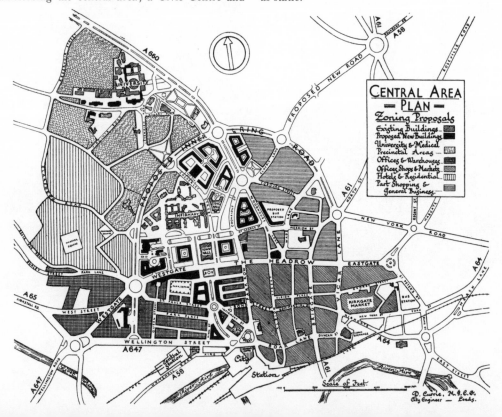

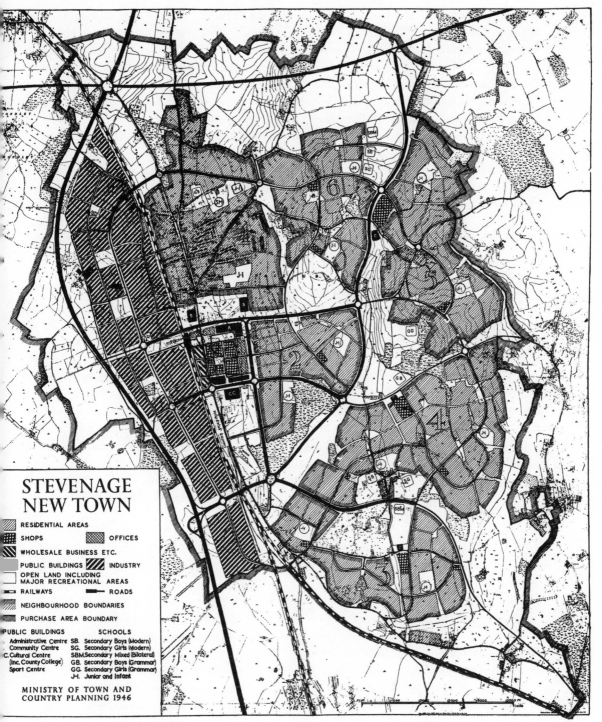

STEVENAGE NEW TOWN

- RESIDENTIAL AREAS
- SHOPS
- OFFICES
- WHOLESALE BUSINESS ETC.
- PUBLIC BUILDINGS
- INDUSTRY
- OPEN LAND INCLUDING MAJOR RECREATIONAL AREAS
- RAILWAYS
- ROADS
- NEIGHBOURHOOD BOUNDARIES
- PURCHASE AREA BOUNDARY

PUBLIC BUILDINGS
Administrative Centre
Community Centre
C. Cultural Centre (Inc. County College)
Sport Centre

SCHOOLS
SB. Secondary Boys (Modern)
SG. Secondary Girls (Modern)
SBM. Secondary Mixed (Bilateral)
GB. Secondary Boys (Grammar)
GG. Secondary Girls (Grammar)
J-I. Junior and Infant

MINISTRY OF TOWN AND
COUNTRY PLANNING 1946

Stevenage New Town, layout, 1946. The cellular structure emphasized the internal neighbourhood pattern. The segregation of land uses was carried to extreme lengths, with industry concentrated to the west of the railway line. A generous open space provision was made.

towns. The chance was not allowed to slip. In October 1945, Lewis Silkin, the new Minister of Town and Country Planning, set up a New Towns Committee under the Chairmanship of Lord Reith. The terms of reference reflected the new determination: whereas the Marley Committee of 1935 had been asked to examine experience gained in the establishment of garden cities and to make recommendations as to the steps which Government should now take, Reith worked in the certain knowledge that a New Towns policy was to be promoted. They were asked 'to consider the general questions of the establishment, development, organization and administration that will arise in the promotion of New Towns in furtherance of a policy of planned decentralization from congested urban areas; and in accordance therewith to suggest guiding principles on which such Towns should be established and development as self-contained and balanced communities for work and living.'

The TPI's pride was dented when none of its senior members were on the Reith Committee, especially when the RIBA President, Percy Thomas, was. Osborn, on the other hand, was a member and there was no shortage of town planning sympathies. But if there was reserve at the onset of the deliberations of the Committee, there was no need for caution at the outcome. A combination of Reith's dynamism, the wartime pressure that had built up about the way to tackle post-war problems, and the near consensus that existed about urban policy, all ensured speedy and far reaching recommendations. By the end of July 1946, two Interim Reports and one Final Report had been submitted, the sum being a comprehensive distillation of advice on which the Minister could act. In their own words the Committee had conducted 'an essay in civilization, by seizing an opportunity to design, solve and carry into execution for the benefit of coming generations, the means for a happy and gracious way of life.'[4] That was how the task was seen, and the determination and the high purpose of the words conjure up the spirit of the time; another age would simply not have expressed itself in that way. Even before the Final Report was presented, a New Towns Bill had been introduced in April 1946. A relatively short measure, it received the Royal Assent in December that year. It provided for the designation of sites for New Towns, the setting up of Development Corporations for their development and the range of powers which they would use.

The next year saw the Town and Country Planning Act, 1947. It received the Royal Assent in August and came into general operation on 1st July 1948. It began as a Bill to deal primarily with the recommendations of the Uthwatt Report, but ended as a comprehensive measure providing the basis for post-war, land use control. Its solution to the problem of compensation and betterment was radical. Where land was developed, the increase in its value resulting from the grant of planning permission was secured for the community by the imposition of a development charge, to be assessed and collected by a Central Land Board. This was recoupment of betterment. For compensation, a sum of £300 millions was set aside from which payments were to be made to owners whose land was depreciated by restrictions imposed by the Act. This meant that a person who was refused permission to develop land was not normally entitled to compensation, because the development value of that land had been vested in the State. This gave a situation very different to that obtaining in the 1930s and previously, when, as we have seen, the problem of payment of compensation by local authorities was a great obstacle to effective land use planning.

The 1947 Act achieved substantial effect through a new Development Plan system as successor to that based on planning schemes. A more flexible instrument, the Development Plan was intended to outline a basic framework of future land use against which development proposals might be considered. This was related to two other important aspects. First, all development was brought under control; with certain exceptions, it was made subject to the permission of the local planning authority. Secondly, only the larger authorities—counties and county boroughs—were entrusted with planning powers and at Herbert Morrison's insistence the LCC was the planning authority for London; hence the fragmentation of the past was substantially altered, 1441 planning authorities being reduced to 145. Another feature of the Act was the extension of provisions relating to amenity; previous legislation relating to the preservation of trees and woodlands, and buildings of special architectural and historic interest were, broadly speaking, re-enacted, but provisions for the control of outdoor advertisements were new.

The Act removed obstacles and provided a new legislative framework. It was an enormous step forward and provided great opportunities. The reception accorded to the Bill was very different from that of 1932. The TPI Parliamentary Committee met (for the first time since 1937) and its Memorandum, forwarded to the Ministry, expressed 'warm thanks' for the introduction of the Bill[5]. Town planners were clearly aware in the summer of 1947, that substantial changes were afoot. The Minister's Parliamentary Secretary, Fred Marshall, at the Annual General Meeting of the Institute that year confirmed that 'The Bill provides a great opportunity and at the same time it is a challenge to our national genius. It confronts local authorities and the Government with the greatest creative task of their existence and if its provisions are used wisely and well, it may well be that the passing of the 1947 Town and Country Planning Act will mark the date when we all enlarged our family souls and suited them to the bigger compass of a nation.'[6] This was fair comment. The promise of halcyon days was tempered with the realization of the enormity of the challenge.

The subject of National Parks constituted the third element in national planning taken up by the Labour Administration. During the war years, public pressure and various lobbies, particularly of the Standing Conference on National Parks (of the Councils for the Preservation of England and Wales) moved the Government irrevocably, albeit cautiously through Ministerial statements, to a position of accepting the principle of National Parks. There followed a private Memorandum by John Dower to the Minister in 1945, *National Parks in England and Wales*, a compactly written and impressive report. He delineated ten National Park areas, which drew up for the first time a kind of national 'shopping list', and recommended a National Parks Authority for their establishment. The logic of the centralist planning system was inescapable: if National Parks were to be provided *for* the nation, they should be provided *by* the nation. For Scotland, the report of the Ramsay Committee, also submitted in 1945, was on similar lines. Armed with these reports, the Minister invited Sir Arthur Hobhouse to chair a committee to consider Dower's report further, and in Scotland, Sir Douglas Ramsay agreed to chair a newly appointed National Parks Committee to make similar further progress. Hobhouse's *Report of the National Parks Committee (England & Wales)*, 1947, recommended the selection and delimitation of twelve National Parks and 52 additional 'conservation areas'; a

National Parks Commission was proposed with, at the local level, Park Committees. In Scotland, Ramsay proposed five National Parks, a Commission and Park Committees.

In 1949 the subsequent National Parks and Access to the Countryside Act did not give all that had been hoped for. A National Parks Commission was established and provision was made for the designation of Parks. The Act conferred on the Nature Conservancy and local authorities powers for the establishment and maintenance of Nature Reserves. There were new powers relating to public footpaths and access to open country and for the preservation of natural beauty. But the legislation related only to England and Wales; prevarication north of the Border meant that there was no National Parks Act for Scotland. However, eighteen years after the Addison Report of 1931, the Government could now claim some fulfilment of a long-standing idea. Lewis Silkin, introducing his Bill at the Second Reading, described it as 'a people's charter for the open air, for the hikers and the ramblers, for everyone who lives to get out into the open air and enjoy the countryside. Without it they are fettered, deprived of their powers of access and facilities needed to make holidays enjoyable. With it the countryside is theirs to preserve, to cherish, to enjoy and to make their own.'[7]

These were brave words, and the Minister could bask briefly in public approbation. His measures clearly reflected national demands, and had implications for land use control, but the TPI curiously adopted no overriding interest in matters of countryside recreation at this time. This was to come rather later. When invited to give evidence to the Hobhouse Committee the Institute preferred to rely on the judgement of their own John Dower, and Pepler replied to the effect that the Institute's views were already well expressed by him and it would be 'supererogant' to comment further[8].

The legislative framework provided a setting for the machinery of Government. A new Ministry accommodated a small galaxy of brilliant planners, including Holford, Stephenson, Shepheard, Casson and Wells. Within a few years they had dispersed to private practice, but in the middle forties they combined to lay down technical standards for the new planning system. The new Minister, Lewis Silkin, had a long apprenticeship in planning matters, having been Chairman of the LCC's Housing and Town Planning Committees and, between 1941 and 1943, of the Housing and Planning Sub-committee of the Labour Party's Post-war Reconstruction Committee. His influences on the course of planning in the later forties was considerable, as Minister piloting three major pieces of legislation through the House in three years. Having been raised to the peerage in 1950 as Baron Silkin of Dulwich, he was later quietly effective behind the scenes. Over the question of New Towns, Osborn acknowledged him to be a 20th century Edward I; his 1947 proposals for land use planning became the envy of many other countries; and over National Parks he steered the enthusiasm of the rabid protectors of national amenity into a practical, pragmatic plan for countryside recreation. Planning owes him a good deal. So too does the Institute, for he had a closer association with the TPI than any other Minister, before or since, and this was reflected in his visits to the Summer Schools.

With the appointment of Hugh Dalton as Minister, town and country planning became, for the first time, the responsibility of a Cabinet Minister. In January 1951, he took over certain of the environmental and local government functions of the Ministry of Health and became the Minister of Local Government and Planning. The purpose of this amalgamation was explained by Dalton as 'to inject more realism into planning and more planning into local government to the benefit of both.'[9] Evelyn Sharp has since confirmed that 'it was a Minister of Planning that he generally thought of himself, and Minister of Planning he was.'[10]

After the general election of October 1951, Harold Macmillan became head of the newly renamed Ministry of Housing and Local Government. The Institute maintained a discreet silence at the change of name, but disappointment and fear of a 'sell out' of planning was acute. In the event, the machinery of planning remained substantially intact and one is left to evaluate the contribution of particular Ministers. Macmillan's great success was in housing matters, achieving his promised target of 300 000 new houses annually. Later, Duncan Sandys achieved fame with his Green Belt circular. With Henry Brooke, however, the Ministry acquired a reputation of dullness and obsession with day-to-day local government matters to the relative exclusion of longer-term issues.

PLANNING IN OPERATION

During the 1950s the new planning system was made operative and there followed years of evidence as to its value and aptness. A progressive failure to attain the high expectations of planning soon became clear, and this was accompanied by a rapid change from enthusiasm to disillusionment by planners themselves in respect of their own immediate work. Pepler put his finger on the disenchantment in 1949: 'Here we are once more carrying out surveys and making plans. We seem to have done this before and no doubt we shall do it again and again before we are through. Perhaps some of us on our more irritable days, discerning the millennium as far off as ever, feel even a touch of the chill hand of despair as we struggle on.'[11] A year later, J. R. Atkinson was urging more work to be done on Development Plans: 'if this is not done then it may be that some of these early hopes will not be properly fulfilled; that the present vague feelings of frustration and lack of direction which is evident in so many quarters, may result in the ship of planning veering from its intended course'[12]. But the planners still had a sense of humour, and Longstreth-Thompson's 'Lines to a Development Plan' made light of the new difficulties as he traced in comic verse, in the Journal, the course of a County Development Plan[13].

The flexible operation of the distribution of industry policy was of high priority in the early post-war years. In 1946, Wrexham and Wigan–St Helens were added to the previous four Development Areas; in 1948, North East Lancashire, Merseyside and the Highlands of Scotland were also added, and the total of nine remained unchanged until 1958. Northern Ireland, which showed the acutest forms of economic difficulties, was not a Development Area but received its own inducements administered by the Provincial Government. The policy of aid to these districts was particularly vigorous between 1945 and 1947 when munition factories were converted and 'advance' factories built. But in the financial crisis of 1947, the building of these factories was stopped (and, in fact, did not restart until 1959) and the pressure on industrialists to locate them in Development Areas proved difficult to sustain.

In the early fifties unemployment remained low as the traditional industries of coal mining, shipbuilding and textiles experienced a post-war boom. In other words, Government failure to pursue a rigorous location policy was made possible by the fact that the situation of the 1930s had changed. But in the second half of the 1950s, the economic boom slowed down; retrenchment followed and the deflationary policies once again severely affected the underprivileged regions. Some measure of priority was then restored to regional policy. The issue of IDC's was more carefully controlled, and through the Distribution of Industry (Industrial Finance) Act, 1958, the number of Development Areas was increased when the existence of a high rate of unemployment was considered likely to persist. Short-term pragmatism was added to long-term policy. But, after fifteen years the regional problem still existed. Although the situation was undoubtedly better than would have been the case without legislation, the basic economic structures of the regions, with their inherent imbalance and dependence on 'problem' industries, had scarcely been affected. By comparison, the favoured regions of London, the South East and the Midlands, maintained their economic vigour.

The striking aspect of this regional concern was the emphasis on economic matters and job distribution, with a consequent virtual demise of regional planning as the 1920s and 1930s had known it. The 1947 Act permitted Joint Boards, but the full involvement of counties in planning and the disappearance of the District Councils as planning authorities, put an end to the need for the type of regional teams that had flourished before the war. Moreover, with the tight rein on numbers of civil servants, Regional Offices were curtailed and much of the initiative was lost from regional groupings. It was not until later that the regional planning idea re-emerged through the development of land use transportation plans.

The New Towns story follows a somewhat similar course to regional economic policy, although the timing is rather different. High endeavour was followed by eclipse. We began with an enormous flurry of activity, and this was sustained throughout the forties, although the results on the ground in terms of dwellings built, were disappointing. A substantial modification of the New Towns policy was introduced by the Conservative administration and as a permanent national strategy, it spluttered incoherently. By the end of the 1950s, it was clear that substantial population pressures in the big cities had built up to crisis proportions; a consistent and effective population distribution policy was required, and the New Town idea was not allowed to die.

Even before the Royal Assent had been given to the New Towns Bill, Silkin had designated Stevenage as a New Town, under provisions of the 1932 Act. Following opposition from local residents, the Designation Order was quashed in the High Court, but this judgement was later reversed in the Court of Appeal, and this decision subsequently affirmed by the House of Lords. This stormy beginning bode ill for the New Towns movement, but the determination of the Government won the day. Abercrombie's recommendation for eight New Towns was followed exactly, although the sites differed; designations were made for Stevenage, Crawley, Hemel Hempstead, Harlow, Welwyn Garden City, Hatfield, Basildon and Bracknell, between November 1946 and June 1949. Stevenage and Harlow alone remained from Abercrombie's list. There were a further four elsewhere in the country: Aycliffe (1947) to house workers on the adjoining Trading Estate, Peterlee (1948) to provide a central point among the East Durham mining villages,

Cwmbran (1949) to serve industry north of Newport, and Corby (1950) in association with the expansion of its steel works. In Scotland, East Kilbride (1947) provided for the planned decentralization of Glasgow and followed a recommendation in the Abercrombie–Matthew Clyde Valley Regional Plan; and Glenrothes (1948) served the East Fife coalfield.

The immediate evaluation of the contribution of New Towns had to be seen in the context of other housing priorities and the economic crises of 1947. The Government's housing programme constantly failed to meet targets and financial retrenchment severely hit the New Towns. By the end of 1950, just 451 houses had been completed in the London New Towns (with 2 109 under construction); Aycliffe in the Provinces boasted 141 completions. Belief in New Towns as the panacea of the propagandists needed the eye of faith; meanwhile, London squatters sought accommodation at any price and contributed to a mood of disillusionment that progress was not being made faster. Moreover, the actual undertaking of New Town development was associated with all sorts of difficulties, many of them undignified. Harold Orlans in his study of Stevenage asked 'Must utopia, realized, always disappoint?' as he described the struggle for power between different groups—the house versus flat addicts, the Development Corporation, the Stevenage Council, and the Ministry[14].

The Conservative administration added a further measure to policies designed to secure population redistribution, taking over a draft Bill produced by the previous Government. This was the Town Development Act, 1952, which sought to encourage the expansion of smaller towns at a distance from big cities. The idea was that through mutual agreement and co-operation, decentralization could be achieved without the need to set up a special agency in the form of Development Corporations; the local authorities themselves would accommodate the overspill of the 'exporting' authorities. The advantage of the arrangement was its flexibility, but experience showed that the problem of dealing effectively with what were, in fact, regional or subregional problems through voluntary schemes relating to the location and relocation of people and jobs, were insuperable. Rates of house construction improved and ultimately some major schemes were entered into, but there is no escaping the fact that in the vast majority of cases, regional development happened rather than was achieved. In any case, for many years only modest progress was made under this Act. Apart from the pioneer Worsley scheme involving Salford and Lancashire the potential of town development schemes was neglected for a number of years.

The Town Development Act did not apply to Scotland, and the focus there remained on New Towns. Scotland in fact claims the only additional New Town in the 1950s. This was Cumbernauld, another satellite for Glasgow. It achieved prominence through breaking away from the design characteristics of the so-called Mark I New Towns by going for higher densities and, through its pedestrianized layout, it dealt more effectively (if somewhat uncompromisingly) with the motor car. But in response to pleas for legislation on the lines of the English 1952 Act, particularly bearing in mind the problems of Clydeside, there followed the Housing and Town Development (Scotland) Act, 1957. Glasgow proceeded to conduct overspill agreements with a number of local authorities, beginning with Grangemouth, Haddington, Hamilton and Kirkintilloch.

149

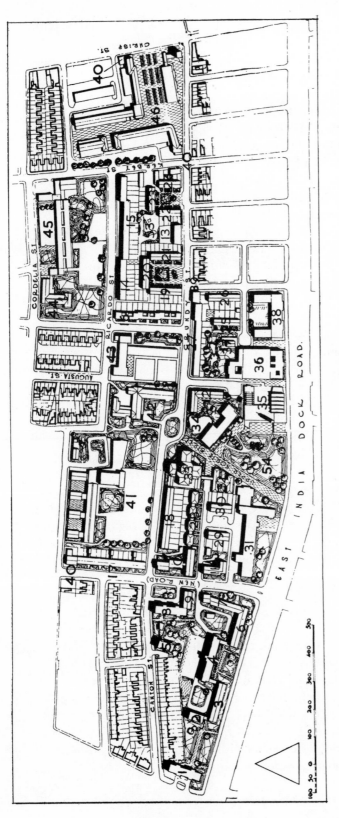

1–2	Six storey flats.
3	Three storey flats.
4–5	Six storey flats.
6–7	Three storey flats.
8	Six storey flats.
9–11	Three storey flats.
12	Two storey flats for old people.
13	Three storey flats (existing).
14–15	Four storey maisonettes.
16–17	Three storey (two storey maisonettes with flats over).
18	Two storey terraced houses.
19–24	Three storey terraced houses with a few single room flats for old people.
25–27	Two storey terraced houses.
28	Two storey linked houses.
29–30	Two storey terraced houses.
31	Health Centre.
32	Roman Catholic Presbytery.
33	Roman Catholic Church.
34	Upper North Street School (existing) will be used for future Community Centre.
35	Trinity Church and Hall.
36	Seamen's Mission and further extensions.
37	Trinity Church Manse.
38	Board of Trade Offices (existing).
39	Public House (existing).
40	New Public Houses.
41	Roman Catholic Secondary School.
42	Old People's Home.
43	Roman Catholic Primary School (existing school and future extensions).
44	Ricardo Street Nursery School.
45	Ricardo Street Primary School.
46	Shopping Centre and Market Place.
53	Children's Playgrounds.
54	Park.

The Lansbury Neighbourhood, part of the LCC scheme for the redevelopment of Stepney and Poplar, selected for the 'Live Architecture' exhibition of the Festival of Britain, 1951. Planners in the Architect's Department responsible for this development included Arthur Ling, Percy Johnson-Marshall and Leslie Lane. (See 'The Lansbury Neighbourhood', *Journal TPI*, **XXXVII**, No. 1, 1950)

Mount Skip Neighbourhood, Worsley, layout, 1952. Worsley was the first overspill reception area for Salford, begun in 1948. Four neighbourhoods were planned around a centre capable of expansion. The principles of early post-war neighbourhood design are well illustrated in this plan. (See G. Sutton Brown, 'Population Movement from South Lancashire in Theory and Practice', *Journal TPI*, **XXXVIII**, No. 8, 1952)

But trouble was brewing. What had been seen in the middle 1940s as a 'once and for all' solution, the location of overspill became an urban problem that just would not go away. An increasing population confounded the static forecasts of the war years and there were high inward migration rates to the big cities, especially in the favoured regions. Social dictates favouring dispersal and suburban living added to the continuous pressure for residential land on the peripheries of the larger towns. A Green Belt policy launched by Duncan Sandys as Minister of Housing and Local Government in 1955 further restricted the selection of building land, although it had other benefits. A slum clearance programme fuelled housing pressure in the public sector. The machinery for effective action was clearly creaking and the propagandist bodies redoubled their efforts to recapture the force of their earlier message. In the Midlands, the newly founded Midlands New Town Society drew attention to the gravity of the situation in that region. By the end of the decade Manchester and Cheshire were at loggerheads over development at Lymm, and Birmingham and Worcestershire were opposed at Wythall. By this time, of course, the New Towns that had been created were proving a success, albeit limited. Elsewhere the galloping rate of suburban and peripheral development, added to the virtual collapse of effective neighbourhood planning, laid planning open again to charges of 'formless sprawl'. There was a feeling of *déjà vu* about the situation: the old timers had seen it all before, and the young were restless in their disappointment.

One aspect of this was when the *Architectural Review* published its famous 'Outrage' issue in 1955, edited by Ian Nairn. A sharp attack on the current course of urban development, it was a prophesy 'that if what is called development is allowed to multiply at the present rate, then by the end of the century, Great Britain will consist of isolated cases of preserved monuments in a desert of wire, concrete roads, cosy plots and bungalows.'[15] The new word subtopia was coined to describe the suburbanization of town and country. Although the argument became lost in general issues of flats versus houses, low-density development and the utility or otherwise of gardens in residential land use, the article was wounding to planners on two counts. First, professional competence was at stake in planners' ability and aesthetic judgement in controlling development. Second, it was alleged that the horrors of subtopia were positively facilitated by the very planning machine which had been set up to thwart them; as Nairn concluded, 'the Brave New World has been twisted to become the decanting of overspills evenly throughout the countryside.'

Criticism of planning in the field of housing also came on another front, and perhaps of the two has remained the more insistent and damaging. Young and Willmott in *Family and Kinship in East London* (1957) questioned an important sociological aspect of urban redevelopment, namely the wholesale disruption of communities for the questionable benefits of living in an outlying estate. Social groups in Bethnal Green and 'Greenleigh' were studied. The authors suggested that the majority of the people wished to stay in the East End; they recommended building new houses around the local communities to which the people already belonged. They put their finger on an issue which the protagonists of dispersal had failed to appreciate: 'The question for the authorities is whether they should do more than they are at present doing to meet the preference of people who would not willingly forego these advantages, rather than insisting that more thousands should migrate beyond the city.'[16]

From housing and New Towns we turn to the new planning system based on the 1947 Act. The financial provisions were soon dismantled. Silkin's nationalization of development rights had proved unpopular with the interests of private property. As the Ministry confessed, 'Many people failed to understand what the Act of 1947 had done, and, whether or not, few landowners were willing to sell land which had development value at anywhere near its value for existing use. Whatever price they paid for land, developers saw the charge as a hindrance to development and a tax on enterprise; and, of course, where they paid more than existing use value for land without any assignment of the claim, and then had to pay development charge as well, the cost of development was increased.'[17] The Town and Country Planning Act, 1953, abolished the development charge and denationalized development rights; the Town and Country Planning Act, 1954, introduced new financial provisions. These were exceptionally complicated, but basically compensation was restricted to loss of that development value which accrued up to 1947, but not in the future. There was no substitute for the development charge.

Henry Wells satirized this latest measure at the St Andrew's Summer School in 1954 as 'the strange tragedy of Miss Bett (who had disappeared, apparently seduced by the wicked landowner) and Mr Comp (a consumptive who had for forty years been chasing Miss Bett but to no avail.' ... 'In 1947 they were nearly brought together by that distinguished matchmaker, Lord Silkin. In 1954, Mr Macmillan, the well known magician, while producing 300 000 houses in one year out of a hat with one hand has spirited Miss Bett away with the other. Do not miss our thrilling next instalment. Will Miss Bett be found? Will Mr Comp survive?'[18]

The situation produced by the 1954 Act was complex and anomolous. There was now, in fact, a dual market in land. While private sales were at current market prices, compensation for certain planning restrictions and for compulsory purchase was to be paid on the basis of existing use plus any admitted 1947 development value. The situation lasted five years: the Town and Country Planning Act, 1959, restored fair market price as the basis of compensation for compulsory acquisition. We had almost come full circle, and as the deep problems of compensation and betterment remained unsolved, the costly burdens of redevelopment fell heavily on the local authorities.

In other ways, however, the 1947 planning system was successful. One of the keys to the Act was the requirement of local planning authorities to prepare Development Plans—a set of proposals for future land use prepared in the light of a thorough survey of the area concerned. These were required by July 1951. Tynemouth was the first plan to be submitted for a whole area, in 1950. The first plan to be approved was that for Shoreham and Lancing Beaches as part of the Development Plan for West Sussex. Most were late in submission, but the majority were completed without too great delay. In Scotland, chronic shortages of staff delayed the submission of plans longer than in England, and there was little progress until into the sixties in some Border and Highland counties. Nevertheless, overall this was a record of success not achieved under previous legislation which had similarly required schemes to be submitted by a set date. Another key feature of the Act was the implicit requirement of a developer to seek permission before carrying out his project. The planning system became centred round 'development control', as well as the forward plan-making operation.

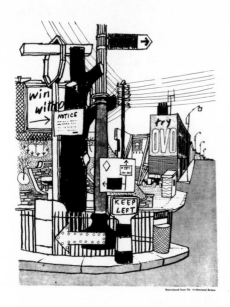

Subtopia. Gordon Cullen's drawing of visual shock in the post war environment, described by Ian Nairn in *Outrage*, The Architectural Press, 1955.

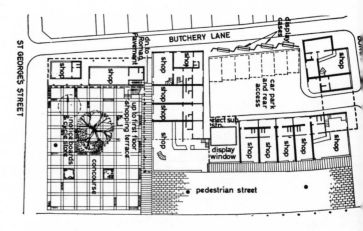

Longmarket, Canterbury, perspective and plan. J. L. Berbiers described his sensitive proposals in the *Journal TPI*, **XLIV**, No. 9, 1958. The Longmarket site in St George's Street was of great importance, with the Old City to the north and the new part of the Central Area to the south east. The vast south elevation of the Cathedral was in the background.

VIEW OF PEDESTRIAN STREET

A heavy administrative burden accrued for the local authorities and Central Government. The number of appeals rose from 2 318 during 1947 to 4 559 in 1949, but there was a drop in 1950 when the Minister in the General Development Order, 1950, offered relaxations in the procedure of development control, partly by removing relatively minor operations from the need to obtain permission, and partly by providing that 'outline' applications could be made without detailed plans. The number of appeals made in subsequent years rose, and this constituted a major grumble by the public. The actual working of the central planning machine became overloaded. Delays in approving development plans and in hearing appeals lengthened. The Franks Report (1957)[19], criticized the volume of minor and local work on which the department was engaged, and the scene was set for an important revision of this aspect of the planning process in the 1960s.

The 1947 Act gave new powers for reconstruction and redevelopment. The 1944 Act had provided for orders to be made 'declaring' an area of extensive war damage, whereupon the land was subject to compulsory purchase by the local authority. Sixty-two declaratory orders were made in England and Wales, totalling over 4 700 acres, but there were defects in the declaratory order procedure. The 1947 Act provided for areas to be 'designated' for comprehensive redevelopment and much more generous Exchequer assistance was given. But there was still a slow start to reconstructing war damaged city centres, due to a restricted capital investment programme. British cities showed their war scars for much longer than had been anticipated. By the middle 1950s, however, important starts had been made in Coventry, Plymouth, Hull and Sheffield, and London, and in the later 1950s the planning problem shifted from restoration of war damage to central area redevelopment on a comprehensive basis. The shop and office boom began, based on proposals by private developers, and aided by new investment sources. The device of the Comprehensive Development Area (CDA) was no longer adequate, and in the 1960s a non-statutory Town Centre Map was advocated as a new backcloth for local authority proposals, against which the commercial property projects could be seen.

The National Parks movement got off to high hopes. The Commission was charged under the Act to consider 'as soon as may be after the commencement of the Act' what areas should be selected as National Parks. Hugh Dalton wrote in his foreword to the First Report of the National Parks Commission that in the first nine months they had made a good start. But 'I do not pretend that I am wholly satisfied, since I had hoped to see three Parks actually designated before the end of 1950, and we have not quite achieved that.'[20] If this was disappointment, more was to follow. The Pennine Way, selected in 1950 as the first long distance route, was not finally completed until 1964.

In fact, the operation of the 1949 Act was not without its operational difficulties. Local authorities were not as enthusiastic as the Commission would have wished in implementing the intentions of the Act. The cost of local administration raised the spectre of increases in county rates. There was open conflict between Local and Central Government over the administration of National Parks. The idea of the Joint Board was taken up in the Peak District and the Lakes, but in subsequent Parks, Joint Advisory Committees became the *modus operandi* favoured by the counties. Where National Parks fell entirely within one county, administration was in the hands of a separate County Council Committee.

But by 1957 ten National Parks had been designated: Peak District, Lake District, Snowdonia, Dartmoor, Pembrokeshire Coast, North Yorkshire Moors, Yorkshire Dales, Exmoor, Northumberland and Brecon Beacons. The Hobhouse idea of 'conservation areas' had been dropped, but Areas of Outstanding Natural Beauty (AONB) took their place. The first was designated in 1956 and by 1960 others followed: Quantock Hills, Lleyn Peninsula, Surrey Hills, Cornwall, North Devon and South Devon, Northumberland Coast, Cannock Chase, Dorset, Shropshire Hills, and Malvern Hills. Progress on long-distance footpaths was slower, and even after approval of the route the actual completion of the footpath could take many years. In the 1950s the Pennine Way, Pembrokeshire Coast Path, Offa's Dyke Path and parts of the South West Peninsula Coast Path were approved routes.

It will be seen that these instances are all drawn from England and Wales. A National Parks Act for Scotland never entered the Statute Book. There were many other weaknesses and the combined operation of recreation planning and countryside preservation spluttered fitfully. The Commission proved a relatively weak organization, and local authorities were, themselves, poor spenders.

But wider issues were developing. The pressure of demand on land and resources increased. Growing numbers of cars and caravans had to be accommodated. Requirements changed as a more mobile population sought new facilities. Greater affluence and the growing incidence of a five-day week stimulated new demands. Holiday habits were changing, and the tourist industry expanded. There were other demands on land: service and military requirements, the demand for water, mineral workings, sites for nuclear and conventional power stations, and overhead transmission lines. The coastline in particular was severely at risk. The 1950s represented a running battle between the amenity conscious who, as purists, represented the nucleus of the National Parks movement, and various Government Departments or public bodies who made development proposals in the Park areas.

There were some minor successes for the Commission but two issues in the late 1950s showed the erosions that pragmatism could make on basic principles. One of these was the nuclear power station at Trawsfynydd, Snowdonia. The Commission commented that: 'The proposed power station ... must, however well designed, remain a large and incongruous feature, and must be entirely out of place in a National Park. Not only so, but the overhead super-grid transmission lines required for connecting the station with the areas of consumption and with the grid ..., would necessarily pass over many miles of hill country and moorland of high quality.'[21] Two inspectors heard a public local inquiry in February 1958. The Inspector of the Ministry of Power concluded that 'the presence of the nuclear power station would not irredeemably impair the amenities of the Snowdonia National Park.' The Inspector for the Minister of Housing and Local Government was Colin Buchanan. He thought that: 'The question to be decided was whether the urgency of the power programme and the difficulty of finding sites for nuclear power stations were so great as to justify what he regarded as grievous damage to the National Park; his judgement leant strongly to the preservation of the National Park from such development, but in view of the important questions of national policy which arise in this case, he did not feel able to make a formal resolution.'[22]

156

ake District National Park, Ullswater from Silver How,
he very epitome of those areas of fine landscape which
he National Parks enthusiasts have been so keen to
reserve. (*Courtesy of* Countryside Commission)

The Pennine Way. The provision of long distance foot-
paths was an important element in post-war proposals for
access to the countryside. Hugh Dalton as Minister of
Local Government and Planning was a keen advocate.
He is seen here walking the Pennine Way (3rd from left)
with Barbara Castle MP (4th) and Arthur Blenkinsop
MP (6th). (*Courtesy of* Town and Country Planning
Association)

Another proposal, in respect of Milford Haven where jetties, oil refineries and an iron-ore stocking ground were proposed on the edge of the Pembrokeshire National Park, conjured up visions of a future sprawling industrial complex. Other problems followed in 1960: a proposal for a second nuclear power station in North Wales, this time at Wylfra, Anglesey, and a proposal for a Ballistic Missile Early Warning Station at Fylingdales in the North Yorkshire Moors National Park. Consistency with National Park purposes came second to national economic or defence objectives, but for the amenity conscious among the planners (and they were still very much preservation minded) the worst fears of a weak 1949 Act were being realized.

By the end of the 1950s, or at least by the beginning of the 1960s, it was increasingly clear that the umbrella of planning powers, with which the centralist planning system had been invested, was deficient in certain ways. New problems or situations were emerging which the legislation of the late 1940s, itself so much designed to meet the problems of the 1930s, failed to tackle effectively. There was a new conflict between private affluence and public interests, nowhere better symbolized in the growing planning problem of the motor car; Buchanan's *Mixed Blessing* (1957) indicated this conflict. In other instances it was a case of failure to drive home a concerted policy for a sufficient length of time: here the the question of compensation and betterment was the prime example. The psychological importance of this was that the self-confidence of the planner began to erode in a welter of disappointment and frustration. Years of economic retrenchment in the public sector led to relatively little ever being accomplished. Slum clearance only began to get under way from the middle 1950s onwards. Derelict land remained an eyesore. Comprehensive redevelopment was slow. Even where new powers existed, the planning process was rarely quite as decisive as had been hoped. Advertisement control needed voluntary action by the advertisers themselves to remove unsightly displays. The heritage of old buildings of architectural significance was inadequately preserved by the process of the Ministry's List of Buildings, and the local authorities' powers of Preservation Orders. The foundation of the Civic Trust by Duncan Sandys proved that public confidence no longer necessarily reposed in the Local or Central Government planner and his ability to protect the environment. To achieve the vision of the future was no easy task; planning quickly lost its fire and relapsed uncomfortably into a short-term defensive regulation of development.

- THE PLANNER

The course of events within the Institute during this period took place against the developments in planning which we have just traced. The mood of the planning profession was influenced by that of the country as a whole. It was a reaction to successes and failures in post-war development, to satisfactions and disappointments, and to the growing, unmet needs that threatened the future.

The prospects for planning looked bright in 1945. An overwhelming Labour victory in the July General Election, ensured a national planning programme. The position of the planner in society reached a new high level. Planners were widely regarded as technical guardians of the public interest. Planners knew what was best and by virtue of their training and expertise, they knew what were society's best interests. We have seen that this professional attribute had been taking shape during the 1930s and that during the war it had assumed a reality. War had stressed the wholeness and common interests of all sections of British society; one of those interests was the need for physical planning to deal with the shaping of town and country. Professional planners found themselves called upon; their day had come. Thomas Sharp, in his Presidential Address in November 1945, suggested that their usefulness to the community 'comes from our having learned a particular specialist job of work and from having developed our judgement through experience in it'[23]. It was this specialism that was now in demand. Planners had something to offer which society wanted; it was an outlook on life and a set of values which offered a new lead in community affairs. Twenty years later, society was critical of the idea of any one body of interests representing society's common values—for professionals to claim it was regarded as arrogance and misplaced idealism—but in the aftermath of the war this was not at all a ridiculous view.

This place of the planner in society did not last long. The relationship between 'technical' opinions and political decisions and political processes, was a close one. Planning could not lie outside politics and the old propagandist issue came to the fore again when it was clear that planning could not rely on the certainty of advancement without securing public support for the ideas it claimed. Osborn expressed the position exactly at the 1951 Oxford Summer School: 'I certainly wish we would have pressures for the social purposes of planning from many more business men, manual workers, clerical workers, housewives, parsons, teachers, doctors, writers and others. But at the moment there is more mental and moral support for these purposes inside the planning profession and planning committees than outside. It's a topsy-turvy situation, but it is to their credit, and especially to the credit of the planning profession. As officials you have muzzles on your lips and chains on your ankles. But they are not a tight fit; you can still mumble common sense and shuffle towards the light and planning committee members do not have these impediments. If there are not padlocks on your hearts as well, it may be that the immediate hope for a re-emphasis of the social purposes of planning lies largely with you, if you can contrive to have all the issues put clearly to the public in the publicity of your draft plans. That might arouse enthusiasm and leadership in some of the tens of thousands who will assimilate the plans; and they, in turn, might organize the expression of the interest of the millions.'[24] Osborn recognized that, as a democratic process, the planning situation was all the wrong way round. Guardianship of the public good in one professional body was dangerous. But planners had not sought it; by and large they had had this role thrust upon them in the spirit of the 1940s when consensus values in society were proclaimed. Twenty years later they were heavily involved in attempts to ensure that energy came from below, from the ranks of the people, rather than from a technical hierarchy above.

The favourable image did not take long to tarnish. In the 1950s planners came to be regarded negatively, as bumbling bureaucrats who stalked the corridors of power as in an Ealing Studio film comedy or as anonymous public servants prescribing individual rights in an attempt to secure the faceless, planned state. George Orwell's *Nineteen Eighty Four*, published in 1949, reflected the lurking fear of what might be. The irony of public

159

attention *and* a negative image was a real one, because this was the first time the planner had virtually secured any public recognition at all. As Bernard Collins commented some years later in his Presidential Address, the planner in this situation 'may find himself unable to withhold the exclamation which escaped the lips of the middle-Western preacher when he was praying aloud for rain in his chapel and it was struck by a cloudburst'[25].

But it was unfortunately true that at this time two cases involving state interference with individual rights received a good deal of adverse public comment. One was the Crichel Down affair, where officials of the Ministry of Agriculture had behaved in a high handed way in the treatment of a private individual interested in purchasing the area concerned. The other was the Pilgrim case where a man had committed suicide over a compulsory purchase order. Sir Sydney Littlewood, a Legal Member, addressing the Annual Spring Meeting of the Institute in May 1957, reminded his audience that: 'John Citizen hates and distrusts the planners and we have about as good a press as burglars. The term "the planners" has become one of opprobrium and we have reached the stage where anything that is unpopular is blamed on to the planners even though the planners have no voice in it.'[26] Collins, in his Presidential Address in November that year, recognized the state of affairs too, in similar terms. They were in a situation where 'the planner is accused of bearing responsiblities he does not bear, possessing authority he does not possess, failing in duties which, in fact, are not his, and in which he is saddled with vague political opprobrium, a sort of darkly hinted totalitarianism which is so wide of the mark that he has found it difficult to combat'[27].

This led planners throughout the 1950s to pay attention to their public image. Holford's Presidential Address, in 1953, stressed the importance of good public relations. A programme of meetings on the theme of 'the Planner and the Planned' was organized, and in 1954 Council set up a Public Relations Committee. But the question of unfavourable public attitudes was still disconcerting. Desmond Heap, President in 1955, explained that 'there are no votes in town and country planning because nobody understands the thing— at least, not sufficiently.'[28] Thomas Sharp went deeper and found that 'to most people, planning has now become just a colossal bore and that to many others it is something actually to dislike with an active hostility. The hostility is, I think, something new. We used to be so respected—even if it was with the rather indulgent respect that idealists and do-gooders are generally given! And now we are not respected.'[29]

Planners were the victim of the age. In the 1940s common threads had pulled British society together. In the 1950s, society was hedonistic, issues of individual well-being replacing those of communal goals. J. K. Galbraith's *The Affluent Society*, published in 1958, symbolizes the decade: the idolization of a consumer-oriented society and the reviling of public service. This had an American setting but we can also see in Britain that the pursuit of private affluence replaced that of public programmes. The planner's worth was assessed accordingly.

There was another political characteristic to the fifties which had a considerable bearing on planning and all those associated with it, whether technical, professional or propagandist. One observer has noted that 'the mass of the electorate was more directly concerned with the standard of living than with the abstract causes championed by small

160

fringe groups at either end of the political spectrum.'[30] There was no serious debate about dismantling or extending the welfare state or about public ownership, and this reflected the broad satisfaction with the compromise between private freedom and public responsibility. In this context the fires which had provided the planning speculation of the thirties died down, and it became difficult to mobilize and sustain the power of lobbies and pressure groups to fight on planning issues. The same commentator observed that 'the generation which came to maturity in the 1950s, had been born in the Great War, schooled during the slums, conscripted in the Second World War and rationed for years afterwards.' Its inclination was to pursue security and comfort and short-run materialist objectives. When the planner failed to provide it he was criticized; when he did provide it, it was taken for granted.

Planning soon entered the doldrums. The planner himself became unpopular and his main work was unspectacular—the painstaking completion of Development Plans and day-to-day administration. The inspiration of the 1940s had gone and an outstanding impression is of a watering down of planning precepts. Planning was tainted with the austerity of the forties and the excessive bureaucracy of the centralist planning system. Disillusionment replaced heady optimism as society expressed private rather than public goals. Only gradually was the value of planning again recognized, this time as a national device to harness new technologies and provide settings for the exercise of private demands, and it took until the late fifties for this to become in any way apparent.

Another factor in the lowly image of the planner was the unprecedented State involvement in the planning profession from the mid-1940s onwards. This was in notable contrast with other professions where the focus was still on private practice and the interests of an individual client. State interference in the affairs of the British Medical Association met with howls of discontent, and RICS objected vociferously to the financial provisions of the 1947 Act. The TPI on the other hand quickly embraced a 20th century professionalism which accepted public control. Private practice lost ground to salaried employees, for a time almost completely. A substantial proportion of the planners' bread was now to be buttered directly or indirectly by the State, and at a time when public service had a poor image, the planner suffered accordingly.

All was not on the debit side however. Disillusionment never led to lack of security among planners. They were now armed with a set of rules, regulations and procedures and powerful measures in a legislative framework that would have been unthinkable some years earlier. Planning was a universal practice in local authorities and some departments were big and powerful. The planning officer had an established position of sorts, and there was promise of greater things to come. Great publicity attended New Towns as well as some of the early reconstruction work, such as Lansbury in East London, which was a show piece for the Festival of Britain in 1951. His own subject matter was advancing and he equipped himself with skills and techniques which made him more and more different from the other professions. The completion of Development Plans and starts on 5-year Reviews before the 1950s were out, marked solid achievement. Britain had never had such comprehensive planning activity before. (Only in Northern Ireland were there serious omissions.) The completion of the LCC Plan was particularly notable; years of activity before the war had now come to fruition. Consequently, although planning suffered reverses, there was no complete demoralization among professional ranks.

The relationship between societal moods and attitudes, and professional vigour (or lack of it) is a close one. We have seen that the 1950s were a period of professional aridity and anticlimax after the 1940s; the evangelistic fire was spent; public opinion lost interest; Conservative politicians accepted planning but accorded it a less positive role. Planning is a matter of social creativity and the source of inspiration wells from society as a whole; the mood of the time simply did not provide this. But this explanation did not make the circumstances for the planner any easier. They had to endure bitter criticisms when things went wrong. The famous 'Outrage' issue of the *Architectural Review* was a case in point. The inadequacy of development control in creating fine landscape was accepted, but as Collins remarked, 'to blame the town planners for the country's development not being of better appearance, is rather like blaming the plastic surgeon for the face not being better-looking.'[31]

THE TOWN PLANNING INSTITUTE

The actual work of the Institute can now be outlined. We shall see how its internal organization was adapted to meet new needs, how its sphere of interest and activities widened to new areas, how changes in its educational policy were made, and how, in 1959, after an earlier rebuff, it obtained its Charter.

At the end of the war, Britain was not alone in its urban planning problems. There was the common task of restoring war damaged areas in Europe and elsewhere: as Max Lock remarked: 'No architectural revolution has been more international and more swift than destruction.'[32] This stimulated a number of European links and renewed an international outlook. In 1946 fifteen members of Council visited Holland at the invitation of the Dutch Government and the Netherlands Institute of Housing and Town Planning. A reciprocal visit was arranged the following year. J. R. Howard Roberts, President in 1947, visited Poland with Lewis Silkin. The Journal considered a number of overseas planning problems and in February 1950, a complete issue was devoted to American planning. There were also articles on physical planning in relation to India, West Africa and South Africa.

During the later 1940s, however, probably the major impact on the Institute was the results of the shift away from private practice to publicly employed salary staff. One consequence was that the Town Planning Officers' Section terminated its affairs in February 1950. The membership of the Institute as a whole was now very largely local authority staff, and duplication of meetings and organizations was unnecessary. The Society had been a beneficial influence since the 1930s and it continued as a Standing Committee of Council. A County Planning Officers' Society was also founded, although not formally connected with the Institute. Compared with the rise of the salaried local authority planner was the decline in importance of the planning consultant. Before the war the small scale of planning work did not often justify the engagement of a permanent planning officer. Now, every planning authority was engaged in statutory planning and employed their own full-time officials. The Development Plan process, continuous because of its periodic revisions, replaced the *ad hoc* preparation of large schemes, and the private consultant lost ground.

The transition from an individual client-centred relationship to public professionalism raised difficulties regarding the planner's conduct at public inquiries. This matter was referred to the Committee for Competititions and Professional Practice in June 1949, and their recommendation was a fine example of pragmatism and adaptability in the new professional situation: 'a technical expert must give evidence as an expert and if pressed in cross-examination, give his own views, and of course explain that he is doing so'. He 'should, however, continue to give the Authority, by whom he is employed, every assistance in preparing the case'.[33]

The problem of the changing type of professional planner was accompanied by that of the supply of planners as a whole. Silkin made it clear that he was concerned that not only should there be no shortage of planners for his new machinery of planning, but also that there should be no lack of skills. At an April 1947 meeting of the County Councils Association, he suggested the important place administrators might play in planning, no doubt bearing in mind the men who would be occupying key technical and administrative positions in the new system. TPI Council took exception to this statement, and Pepler took up the matter at the Ministry. But at the Reading Summer School later the same year, Silkin continued to ask searching questions: 'Ought we to open the door today to the training of persons as planners for the planning team much more widely than we have done hitherto? Hitherto, as you know, we have selected our planners exclusively from three or four professions. Ought we to go much wider?' Later, he returned to his earlier theme: 'I should like to see distinction between the technician and the administrator very much blurred. I am putting this forward as a serious proposition; that the leader of the technical team should be chosen on account of his administrative ability, capable of leading a team and getting the best out of them.'[34] This thinking came to fruition when in May 1948, he appointed a Departmental Committee, 'to take account of the present and prospective scope of Town and Country Planning and to consider and report what qualifications are necessary or desirable for persons engaged in it, and to make any recommendations affecting those persons which appear to the Committee to be relevant.' The Chairman was Sir George Schuster.

Meanwhile, the TPI itself had been considering the question of widening the professional intake, although the outcome was minimal and not a little confused. In July 1946, Policy and Finance Committee authorized Pepler to discuss, with L. Dudley Stamp, the question of exemption of geographers from the Institute's Intermediate examination. Pepler's recommendation, after consultation, was that provided economic and social aspects were covered, exemption should be granted. This failed to secure Committee approval, however, and only partial exemption was forthcoming from certain papers in both Intermediate and Final examinations. The matter came up again when, in July 1947, the Special Committee on Recognition and Policy, presented a report on the whole question of the planner's qualifications and education, in part to provide a policy statement for use in connection with the Royal Charter application. Regarding the entry to geographers, economists and sociologists, the Committee decided that 'while they would warmly welcome them as part of the planning team, if they desired to become corporate members of the Institute they should take the normal course of examinations'.[35] No decision was reached on the matter of a Diploma in Planning Administration, to which Silkin had hinted in his Reading speech.

This attempted reform is traced in some detail to show the difficult position which the TPI was in. Though in principle it saw there was place for newer influences in planning, sudden changes in the composition of the professional body while the Royal Charter negotiations were going on would not have helped the Institute's case. On the other hand, they were aware that there were shortages of qualified planners: J. S. Allen drew attention to the fact that the newly-appointed assistants who were taking over planning from the consultants were still at the stage of studying for TPI examinations[36]. The Institute was also aware that Silkin was concerned, and as we have seen, he was not prepared to leave the matter in TPI's hands.

In the event, the setting up of the Schuster Committee provided a new opportunity for the TPI to prepare a memorandum with a concise statement on TPI aims. This was prepared by Pepler in July 1948, and the following four paragraphs set out the position in unequivocal terms.

'(a) The Government, Local Authorities, etc should unhesitatingly accept the Institute as the machinery for upholding and raising the qualifications of the Planner.

(b) That planning is a profession in its own right and not an appendage to another profession. The Institute has set itself to train a body of technicians and the work of the Planner cannot be carried out by an Administrator, however able, who is not technically trained.

(c) It follows that the person to prepare plans and be responsible for advising a Planning Authority should be a qualified practitioner in its broadest sense. The training of that man was for the Institute which is the only body wholly concerned.

(d) The Institute does not presume to suggest those past standards are unalterable and would welcome discussion to meet the increased scope of planning is developing.'[37]

Schuster reported, in September 1950, after sitting for rather more than two years[38]. They had received evidence from 70 persons and organizations and taken oral evidence from 20; they had visited local authorities. The Committee was composed of non-professionals in an obvious attempt at objectivity; Dame Evelyn Sharp of the Ministry was a member. Their report was of far-reaching significance. Their starting point was that planning was the regulation of the use and development of land in such a way as to take account of the social, economic and strategic objectives and to ensure that conflicting demands were reconciled in the best way possible in the national interest. This allowed them to regard planning as a social and economic activity limited but not determined by the technical possibilities of design. They recognized that the new planning system was only just getting under way so the time was not appropriate to attempt standardization in matters either of organization, or of education, or of the criteria for professional qualifications. In short, they advocated evolution by experience and a wide range of experiment. A number of recommendations followed.

For the organization of planning within a local authority the Committee saw that there were two main requirements. First, planning should not be treated as a detached activity to be left to experts, but as an integral part of the work of the authority; second, there should be unity in the handling of planning policy. This was a powerful confirmation of the new place and role of the local authority planner.

With regard to the chief planning officer, he needed to see the various stages of planning as one whole and continuous process with far-reaching social and economic objectives. This demanded creativity, imagination, a power of synthesis and a broad human understanding; a University education would develop these abilities. The officer need not possess technical skill in design, but he needed an expert qualification and an ability to understand and co-ordinate the work of other technically qualified staff. This sort of person and his qualifications was seen quite differently from the planner of the 1930s with his concentration on scheme preparation in a limited technical sense.

Concerning education for planners, the Committee thought that the Institute should not narrow the basis of membership. Their broad conclusion was that in order to produce the best potential planners, it was not necessary to devise a new basic discipline but to ensure that the students of recognized disciplines appreciated the planning significance of their own subjects. We shall trace the full importance of Committee's recommendation on education in chapter 9, but at this stage we should note that the TPI was given considerable impetus as the centre of an independent planning profession. The Joint Examination Board lost force and ultimately collapsed and the older professions were denied primacy in planning. The social sciences gained a new entree, and in particular, the geography element gained strength. Additionally, extra emphasis was given to University Planning Schools.

The Committee confirmed the TPI as the obvious foundation for the 'authoritative national institution' in planning that was required. But the basis of membership should be widened. In particular, the Council of the Institute should change. The old provision that nine out of the fifteen members of Council must be architects, engineers or surveyors should be rescinded, and a widening to represent the economic and social sciences was advocated.

The Institute gave qualified approval to the report. Ultimately, however, it was to have the effect of a considerable moral prop for the Institute. It enabled them to throw off the shackles of the other three professions. It was instrumental in widening the basis of membership. It encouraged higher education in planning. It stressed the importance of innovation and experiment, making it clear that the subject matter was evolutionary and not of fixed dimensions. It cemented and enhanced the place of the planner in local planning authorities.

Overlapping the period of the Schuster deliberations was the question of the Royal Charter. As an official endorsement and seal of approval on the aims, methods and achievements of a developing profession, it was eagerly sought after. The matter had been raised periodically in the past, but no steps were definitely taken until 1946, during the year of Thomas Sharp's Presidency. After consideration for some months by Policy and Finance Committee, Council resolved in April 1946: 'That the Town Planning Institute do present a humble petition to the King's Most Excellent Majesty in Council that His Majesty may be graciously pleased in the exercise of His Royal Prerogative to grant a Charter of Incorporation of the Members of the Town Planning Institute and of all said persons as may thereafter in pursuance of the said Charter become members of the body corporate or corporation thereby constituted; and that the common seal of the Institute be affixed to the said petition or to any supplementary petition or other document necessary or desirable for the purpose of the said petition or any proceeding before the King's Most Excellent Majesty in Council in connection therewith.'[39]

Before the petition could be lodged, preparations were necessary. Pepler prepared a draft case for the granting of a Charter, J. R. Howard Roberts dealt with the legal side, and there was some discussion as to the possible title of the Chartered Body and how its members were to be styled. The petition was not formally lodged until June 1947, when by coincidence, on the same day, the petition of the Institute of Municipal Engineers was also lodged.

Problems arose almost immediately. The other professional bodies felt offended that they had only learned of the application through *The London Gazette* and had not received the courtesy of notification prior to the lodging of the petition. At a meeting of TPI, RIBA, and RICS representatives held at the beginning of July, Howard Roberts took a conciliatory line, undertaking to hold up the petition to allow a discussion of their objections. Potter wrote to all the Institutions involved inviting discussion on the matter. RIBA and RICS remained willing to engage in discussions, ICE was now reluctant to negotiate and IMunE was entirely pre-occupied with its own Royal Charter petition.

Meanwhile, apparently, discussions were taking place between the three opposing bodies, and IMunE joined these. In December 1947, TPI attended a meeting at ICE represented by members of all five bodies, and it is clear that joint action had been decided upon. Sir Robert Hetherington, President of ICE, stated his Institution's terms of support of TPI's petition. If implemented, these would have consolidated the position of architect, engineer and surveyor in planning, to the extent of abolishing the TPI Intermediate Examination, and admitting only corporate members of the four Institutions to TPI. There were some concessions to newer interests, such as geographers, but not to the extent of allowing entry on the same level or with the same status as prior professions, who were to be actual chartered town and country planners. The Presidents of the other Institutions agreed with Hetherington's terms.

In retrospect, this was the parting of the ways. TPI wanted the support of the sister professions; they were old friends and there were many cross loyalties. But the cost was too high; as Howard Roberts pointed out, the other Institutions were 'asking a great deal of the Town Planning Institute, to jettison a fundamental part of its policy merely to obtain their support'[40]. In any case the Institutions' terms were regressive; all recent developments had indicated that planning could not be shared by the existing professional bodies. No such fixity was possible in the sharing of technical skills. Moreover, TPI claimed its own primacy and did not see itself as the chattel of the other bodies. But the die was cast and confrontation was joined. Sir Roger indicated 'no latitude and no prospect whatsoever'[41] of the ICE withdrawing from its stated position, and the other bodies concurred. A considered reply was necessary and there were some differences within the TPI as to just how the reaction should be phrased. The terms could not be accepted, but it was debatable as to how forthright the rejection should be. After drafting and redrafting, Howard Roberts' letter was in terms that had the effect of entrenching the other institutions in their opposition.

166

Consequently, RIBA, RICS and ICE lodged formal counter-petitions to the TPI's application in February and March 1948. The wording of each was almost identical. To quote from the ICE petition, the core of the matter was that: 'Town planning is not a separate professional activity. It requires the bringing together of the art of the architect with the skill of the civil engineer and the knowledge of the surveyor, as well as a knowledge of public administration, a judgement of economic trends and population distributions and other matters of a social character.' The Policy and Finance Committee engaged itself on answering these counter-petitions. In May 1948, its observations were forwarded to the Privy Council. These stressed the planner's independence: 'a plan for town or country is neither an architect's plan, nor an engineer's plan, nor a surveyor's plan, it requires a technique of its own and is, therefore, clearly a separate professional activity'.

At this point, the Schuster Committee was appointed and Privy Council suspended its consideration of the petition pending the Committee's report. As we have seen, when this was published two years later, it reflected better on TPI's standpoint than on that of the other professional bodies. It found no justification for the existing privileged positions of the architect, engineer or surveyor in town and country planning, and still less did it call for a strengthening of their position. New steps could now be taken regarding the Charter.

An important move was for the TPI to enlist official support; Beaufoy, Vice-President of the Institute, was in the Ministry of Housing and Local Government, and obviously a useful link. In April 1952, he wrote to Potter that Dame Evelyn Sharp 'appreciates the steps which the Institute had made towards widening its basis of membership. I think you will find a considerable measure of support.' Pepler later met Dame Evelyn who cautiously indicated that the Ministry could not express views on the petition unless invited to do so by the Privy Council. In May, Pepler had an informal discussion with Brigadier Killick, RICS Secretary, on relations between the two bodies. RICS had recently instituted a Town and Country Planning examination for surveyors and Killick wanted TPI membership, subject to practical experience, for holders of the RICS Diploma. It later appeared that if the TPI supported this examination, RICS would support TPI's Charter position. In June, Pepler had an informal talk with Spragg, RIBA Secretary, who felt that the RIBA's Town Planning Committee, whose composition had changed, might now be more amenable to limited change in the TPI.

During the following months of 1952, the TPI's petition was updated and forwarded to the Privy Council in October. In spite of recently expressed views, it soon became clear that TPI could expect no support from the sister Institutions. RICS remained the more willing to negotiate but in the event all the bodies registered formal counter-petitions. The RIBA and ICE stood by their 1948 objections, though with some amplification. This time the IMunE also registered its objections; basically it claimed to be an alternative town planning professional body, and it was pointed out that many engineers who were engaged on planning were not TPI members. RICS objected, though, for a time, it had seemed that they might not do so; in the event their counter-petition was not as opposed to the TPI position as the other bodies.

Lord Silkin, enlisted by Potter to provide help with the TPI's case, discussed the matter with Lord Salisbury, Lord President of the Privy Council. In a subsequent letter to Potter he wrote that he found Salisbury's 'real difficulty was in convincing himself as to the position of the Town Planner, i.e. whether Town Planning was itself a profession.' Further representations by the TPI on the objections of the other bodies were forwarded in June 1953, but the opposition from these quarters was weighty. In the end, the Privy Council concluded that the time had not yet come for TPI independence. On October 28th their verdict was despatched: 'the Lords of the Council have found themselves unable to recommend Her Majesty to grant the Charter prayed for'.

The refusal was a great disappointment, compounded by the fact that on many fronts planning was stagnating or in retreat. The Institute adopted a 'stiff upper lip'. In November, at a special meeting of Policy and Finance Committee, it was resolved that the Institute should remain a professional body rather than move towards the speculation contained in the Schuster Report concerning a 'national institution' which might or might not be coterminous with the professional Institute. A statement was prepared informing the membership of the refusal of the Charter, indicating that membership would be broadened and that a renewed petition would be submitted in due course.

But there was little progress for nearly three years. The matter was not taken forward until 1956 when Desmond Heap, then President, sounded out the attitude of the Ministry through a meeting with Dame Evelyn Sharp. Next year, following an Extraordinary General Meeting of the Institute, Article 24 of the Institute's Bye-laws (which gave the parent professions a privileged position on TPI Council) was amended; a Charter application was lodged with the Privy Council in November. Howard Roberts as Honorary Solicitor was responsible for its preparation, continuity thereby being preserved from the last submission. Letters were sent to the other Institutions informing them of the new situation, so rectifying the omission of ten years earlier. An interest this time was shown by the Law Society and, in addition to the other Institutions, they too requested copies of the relevant documents. Through the Law Society, the General Council of the Bar of England and Wales came to be involved and so by February there were six professional Institutions considering TPI's submission.

The case for a Charter for TPI was much stronger than when first submitted, and indeed when rejected only five years earlier. The Institute had continued to maintain its tradition of scrupulous professionalism. It could now claim to represent the great majority of those engaged in planning; in the counties all but a handful of county planning officers were TPI members, and only in the boroughs were other professions well entrenched. With regard to professional independence about a quarter of the Institute's membership had no other professional qualifications. Finally, it was clear that as a national activity town and country planning since the 1947 Act was now well established and that the actual operation demanded more than simply an amalgam of the land-based professions. In the new circumstances, RICS indicated that they would not oppose the new petition and RIBA went further, actually deciding to support. It was believed that the Ministry supported the TPI case.

But there was no acceptance from the others. ICE, I MunE, the Law Society and the General Council submitted three counter-petitions (the two legal bodies producing a joint memorandum). The engineers' objections followed their earlier pattern. The interesting new position was that of the lawyers. They had not objected earlier and during the previous year there had been friendly links between the Law Society and the TPI, when there was agreement that there was a place for both solicitors and town planners in the planning system. In July 1958, the TPI submitted its observations on the counter-petitions to the Privy Council.

In the deliberations which followed, the Law Society/General Council petition carried weight because of the suggestion that the legal profession might be threatened by the granting of a Charter. Given the fact that circumstances now made TPI's case much stronger, that the engineers' objections were consequently of less significance, and that the professional bodies' united front of objection had been dented by the defection of RICS and RIBA, it was now clear that the argument was going to be conducted according to different criteria, and indeed in different circles. In the event it seems that discussions between Lord Hailsham and Lord Silkin settled the terms on which the TPI this time got its Charter.

Hailsham, Lord President of the Privy Council, was a leading advocate and sensitive to the lawyers' angle. He accepted Silkin's claim as to inconsistency of the objections and agreed the measure of the support that existed. But he was concerned that TPI qualifications should not be used to facilitate entry to practicing as an architect, engineer, surveyor or lawyer. The position of the planning officer at public inquiries (whether he was an expert witness or an advocate) was an issue at the time, and it was felt that the TPI should deny the advocacy element of the planner's job at inquiries. If the Charter specifically excluded these possibilities, the indications were, after a meeting between Hailsham and Silkin at the end of the year, that TPI could have its Charter.

The provisions stipulated by Hailsham met with some concern. The President, Aylmer Coates, met Dame Evelyn Sharp in December 1958 and assured her that he would prefer not to have to make any concessions. In March 1959 he was invited to meet Hailsham, and Council considered its policy at two meetings that month. The general feeling was that TPI should not put itself in a position where borderline and ancillary work would be specifically excluded from the field of the town planner by the Royal Charter; much professional work could not be so rigidly demarcated. In April the Privy Council forwarded suggested amendments to Sir Howard Roberts, which formed the basis for an acceptable Clause 6:

(1) By virtue of his membership of the Chartered Institute a member may carry out such work, and only such work, as is directly referable to Town Planning or is, of its nature, ancillary thereto.

(2) No member shall engage in work recognized as being exclusively that of another profession unless he is also a member of that profession.

(3) In particular, no member shall carry out the work of an advocate unless he is a solicitor or barrister.

Having surmounted this hurdle, the course was clear. On June 15th 1959, Potter received a letter from the Privy Council indicating that the Charter was to be granted. Because of a delay by a printing strike, the Letters Patent under the Great Seal which contained the Charter of Incorporation were not forwarded until September 21st. It was a successful end to a long campaign.

THE HOUSE THAT NEVER WAS

A Building Society Spokesman has said "We want a house to look like a house." So do
planning committees, architects and eventual inhabitants. Each in their own way.

Site for dream house chosen by design-conscious John
Denizen, inheritor of £15,000 and seeker of gracious living. Has rejected
notion of buying ready-made House of Character after twelve months'
painful translation of estate agents' blurbs (e.g. For *"bold main-road position"*

read *"suicidal front entrance"*, for *"small but sheltered garden"* read *"adjoining
glue factory"* etc.), finally decides to build on site of bomb-damaged, and
subsequently demolished, Georgian residence in Stockbroker Lane,
Surrey.

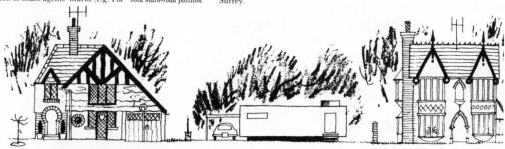

"Anti-Social Building," says local planning committee to
application for house planned round central courtyard. Architect has
satisfied client's requirements for single-floor living with maximum
privacy, but design obviously suffers from his lack of experience. Unlike
senile grocer on lay planning committee, has not lived in houses for eighty

years; is naturally less aware—as mere professional man—of what houses
should look like. Application to build rejected because single-storey house
with windowless front elevation would be "detrimental to local amenities
in road of superior two-storey development".

"Doesn't keep in keeping," says planning committee to
architect's alternative—single-floor, outward-looking, concrete house raised
to two-storey level on stilts. Client begins to regret employing reputable,
intelligent architect with inherent good taste. Rejection of plan—on ground
that house fails to match adjoining properties in style and choice of materials

—arrives by same post as letter from building society reporting inability to
make loans for "eccentric" property. ("Eccentric" subsequently defined as
property without hipped roofs, gables or site for random rubble and
gnomerie.)

"Mon Riposte," says embittered architect, "is timber-
framed, single-floor Tudorbethan structure with Contemporary car port,
pitched roof and East-Sheen-farmhouse-style chimney." Client innocently

submits drawing to planning committee. Accepted with enthusiasm in
principle, but rejected because fire regulations forbid timber-framed
houses abutting on to neighbouring buildings.

"Turn it sideways," says hysterical architect—with heavy irony—to unshaven rapidly-aging client. Client obediently submits to planning committee who admire it and comment on ingenuity of adapting chimney as podium and front steps as vertical feature. Scheme rejected on ground of fire dangers (timber-framed towers not permitted), infringement of ancient lights and "visual clash with dominant historical landmark" (i.e., verger of St Ethelred's would see house when shinning up belfry).

Some years later—or does it only seem so?—desperate client calls in Sir Portland Placey, famous as advisor on dignified classical façades. Sir Portland's modifications—incorporating completion of building's somersault—are under discussion just as demolition begins on expired-lease neighbours. Simultaneously local amenity association begins fight for reconstruction of original Georgian house on site. Public inquiry results in decision in favour of reconstruction.

Uncompleted neo-Georgian elevation is soon one of few assets of John Denizen, inheritor of £15,000 and seeker of gracious living. Consoles himself, while contemplating inflated overdraft, greying hair and fear of bankruptcy, with thought that £15,000 has bought him greater understanding of way top people's housing is planned—more in Harrow than in Ongar.

Site for dream house still undeveloped after months of bickering between amenity societies, council committees, etc. Eventually private developer of adjacent sites allowed to proceed with offer of purchase. His flat-roofed, nondescript housing which waits—with keyed brickwork—to pounce across gap has sailed past planning committee under title of "Desirable Georgian-style Maisonettes" (current OK word for flats). John Denizen accepts large sum to move. Buys House of Character in bold main road position with small but sheltered garden. Suffers alternately from glue-poisoning and pantechnicons in small of back. Is happy.

The conflict between private choice, architects and Planning Committees is brilliantly captured in this cartoon. (*Courtesy of Punch*, 20th April 1960)

These affairs which affected the Institute so markedly—the Schuster deliberations and the petition for a Charter—have been dealt with in some detail. Their importance can hardly be minimized, for after a difficult decade the professional body emerged strengthened for the testing 1960s ahead. But they are not only of a private concern, of relevance only to the Institute. They reflected on planning as a whole—its multi-faceted dimensions and its capacity for change.

Compared with these matters the rest of the work of the Institute during this period and of the changes that took place within the profession, seem of limited importance. But to present a balanced record it is necessary to sketch the main events.

Consequent upon the 1947 Act in particular, there was a strong emphasis in consolidating planning practice. Two widely read books reflected this: F. Gibberd's *Town Design* (1953) and Lewis Keeble's *Principle and Practice of Town and Country Planning* (1952). The Journal contributed by giving reviews of all Development Plans in a series of articles between December 1951 and October 1955. But a range of new issues impinged on planning and the planner was increasingly introduced to new subject areas. The growth of interest in the motor car was typical and Journal articles appeared on car parking, parking meters and aspects of traffic congestion. Beaufoy spoke to the 1957 Summer School on modern industrial developments including nuclear power, oil refineries and petrochemicals and this provided a new introduction to regional issues. The implementation of planning schemes increasingly absorbed planners' attention, particularly the management problem of comprehensive redevelopment (or to give the new American terminology, urban renewal), and the rebuilding of commercial city centres. Then there were the beginnings of a new emphasis on planning method, and the enlarging scientific apparatus of planning. One has the impression of a quickening rush of issues with which the planner became involved, or had involvement thrust upon him, at the end of the fifties.

This widening and expanding field of planning contained seeds of inter-professional conflict. The wonder is that they did not germinate more quickly. Perhaps it was a case of the TPI having to tread softly in view of the Royal Charter negotiations. In the forties the main conflict had come from the engineers over the issue of who should do local planning work. In the fifties difficulties emanated from the architects, because of the blurred lines of demarcation over questions of redevelopment, layout and design, and visual amenity. In the aftermath of the 'Outrage' publication a RIBA statement claimed that architects should have sole responsibility for architectural control under the Planning Acts. There was TPI objection to this and meetings between the two Institutes continued sporadically for some years before the matter died a natural death, although not before Basil Spence, President of the RIBA, had fanned the embers of the controversy by suggesting in a public address that planning committees be abolished for a trial period. Strangely enough, as we have seen, the RIBA positively supported TPI's petition for a Royal Charter, precisely at this time.

Another example of the expansion of planning was in its overseas interests. In 1957 the Journal started a series called 'Planning in the Commonwealth'. Holford introduced the series, noting the growing importance of the work being done overseas and the greater opportunities presented. 'In the Old Country it is fairly true to say that development lags behind planning... By comparison in Singapore or the Rhodesias development is rapid.

And extreme cases such as Kuwait, it is so continuous that planning cannot even catch up with it.'[42] The series continued until May 1959. Out of a TPI membership of about 2 600, 450 were now based overseas. To foster Institute ties, the Overseas section of the Summer School was started in 1957; the attendance of 76, compared with 530 at the main school, indicates the not inconsiderable interest right at the outset.

The widening base of planning was reflected in a widening membership policy as we shall see in chapter 9, but there was one particular difficulty which remained. The Institute's regulations allowed entry to Associate Membership by examination, or entry direct to Membership provided the candidates were at least 50 years of age and had achieved special eminence in town planning. The main problem was in attracting non-TPI professionals of mature standing to the ranks of the Institute. In 1952 it was proposed to lower the minimum age to 45 and to invite prospective candidates to selection by a special examination by Council (including submission of published and other relevant work) but the proposal was not acted upon. This was some embarassment because there were difficult cases to resolve: Myles Wright of Liverpool University was not elected to membership until 1959 and J. R. James, Chief Planner at the Ministry, not until 1962.

To conclude this chapter with a brief note on residual matters concerning the work of the Institute might be thought an anti-climax, but perhaps it is appropriate, for the unspectacular, routine work of a professional body is the basis of its strength. The Institute continued to be very active in its committees and working parties. In the 1950s the Institute through its Parliamentary Committee submitted evidence to the Franks Committee on Administrative Tribunals and Inquiries, set up in 1955; its memorandum was supported orally by Pepler in June 1956. The Institute submitted evidence to the Royal Commission on Common Land and to the Royal Commission on Local Government in Greater London. In this latter connection the TPI could point to notable earlier work of its own, having set up a London Regional Planning Committee, usually chaired by Heap, and which produced its own report in 1956. The Institute also gave evidence to the Local Government Commissions (England and Wales) though it did not comment on the particular areas in question. The Technical Committee on Traffic Engineering, set up by the Minister of Transport in 1958 received evidence from TPI via the Research Committee.

These many activities inevitably led to administrative changes at Headquarters. The Committee system introduced in 1944 had only been slightly amended and by the fifties the structure of eight Standing Committees was cumbersome. In 1957 major reforms were instituted. The number of Standing Committees was reduced to four: Policy and Finance, Education, Practice, and Research.

In November 1958, Potter advised Collins, then President, that he would soon be retiring from the Secretaryship. He continued on the understanding that he could resign on a year's notice. In April 1959, Sir George Pepler died and at the May Council it was learned that Potter had given his notice. It was a fitting moment that as the Institute in May 1960 held its last meeting as a limited company, so too ended the tenure of Potter, Secretary from the earliest days. Considering the difficult conflicts that arose in the 1960s, we might wonder how much the Institute missed the wise guidance of old. On the other hand it is possible to argue that both Potter and Pepler clung on too long so that after 45 years it was

Above: Sir Patrick Abercrombie, photographed in 1955. When he died in 1957 a link was broken with the earliest years of the planning movement. President and Gold Medallist.

Above left: Dame Evelyn Sharp, Ministry of Town and Country Planning, photographed in 1948. (*Courtesy of* Town and Country Planning Association)

Left: Sir George Pepler died in 1959. Twice President, Gold Medallist and Hon. Sec. and Treasurer of the TPI from its inception. Quietly monumental in his contribution to planning.

Below left: Alfred R. Potter, Secretary of the TPI, 1914–1960

Below: Lewis Mumford, a prolific writer on urban and planning affairs, and Gold Medallist of the TPI. (*Courtesy of* Town and Country Planning Association)

almost impossible to think of the TPI without them. In the circumstances, one relies on valedictories or obituries to reflect the real feeling of the time. Potter himself paid tribute to Pepler's involvement in Institute affairs: 'It was typical of him to take on the working part of the job, a characteristic which he has manifested throughout the whole history of the Institute. Always ready for new ventures and developments, I have never known him to refuse a task likely to benefit the Institute or further its objects.'[43] He was clearly held in respect and with affection and he rendered incalculable service. Of Potter, Professor J. S. Allen commented in his Presidential Address in 1960 on 'his organizing ability, his grasp of Institute affairs, and his friendliness to all members'[44]. Clearly, administrative soundness had been at the base of all the Institute's work during this long period.

And so this period came to an end marked by death and retirement of two old stalwarts. Other links with the past were broken: Abercrombie too had died in 1957. But the Institute's future had been affirmed by Government Committee and Royal Charter. Planning practice had entered into a new phase and was rapidly developing. If immediate post-war enthusiasm had been eroded by the acid of disillusionment, the promise of things to come was stirring new expectations. The new self-confidence was symbolized in the Institute's Gold Medal for outstanding achievement, already conferred on Pepler (1953), Abercrombie (1955), and Mumford (1957). But above all, the profession was now independent with its own seal of approval.

References

1. H. W. J. Heck, Presidential Address. *Journal of the Town Planning Institute*, **XXXIII**, No. 1, 1946.
2. Keable, Gladys, *Towns of Tomorrow*. SCM Press, 1946.
3. *Journal of the Town Planning Institute*, **XXXII**, No. 5, 178, 1946.
4. *Final Report of the New Towns Committee*, Cmd. 6876, 1946.
5. *Journal of the Town Planning Institute*, **XXXIII**, No. 3, 81, 1947.
6. *Journal of the Town Planning Institute*, **XXXIII**, No. 5, 135, 1947.
7. *Hansard*, col. 1493, 31st March 1949.
8. Town Planning Institute Council Minutes, vol. III, p. 82.
9. *Town and Country Planning 1943–1951*, Cmd. 8204, 1951.
10. Sharp, Evelyn, *Ministry of Housing and Local Government*. Allen and Unwin, 1969.
11. *Journal of the Town Planning Institute*, **XXXV**, No. 8, 232, 1949.
12. Atkinson, James R., Economic Policy and the Planner. *Journal of the Town Planning Institute*, **XXXVI**, No. 8, 1950.
13. *Journal of the Town Planning Institute*, **XXXVII**, No. 9, 227, 1950.
14. Orlans, Harold, *Stevenage: a Sociological Study of a New Town*. Routledge and Kegan Paul, 1952.
15. *Architectural Review*, **117**, No. 702, 1955.
16. Young, Michael and Willmott, Peter, *Family and Kinship in East London*. Routledge and Kegan Paul, 1957.
17. *Report of the Ministry of Housing and Local Government 1951–4*, Cmd. 9559, 1955.
18. *Proceedings*, Town and Country Planning Summer School, 1954, p. 94.
19. *Report of the Committee on Administrative Tribunals and Enquiries*, Cmd. 218, 1957.
20. *First Report of the National Parks Commission*, HMSO, 1950.
21. *Eighth Report of the National Parks Commission*, HMSO, 1958.
22. *Ninth Report of the National Parks Commission*, HMSO, 1959.
23. Sharp, Thomas, Presidential Address. *Journal of the Town Planning Institute*, **XXXII**, No. 1, 1945.
24. *Proceedings*, Town and Country Planning Summer School, 1951, p. 82.
25. Collins, B. J., Presidential Address. *Journal of the Town Planning Institute*, **XLIV**, No. 1, 1957.

26. Littlewood, Sir Sydney, John Citizen and the Planners. *Journal of the Town Planning Institute*, **XLIII**, No. 7, 1957.
27. Collins, B. J., Presidential Address. *Journal of the Town Planning Institute*, **XLIV**, No. 1, 1957.
28. Heap, Desmond, Presidential Address. *Journal of the Town Planning Institute*, **XLII**, No. 1, 1955.
29. Sharp, Thomas, Planning Now. *Journal of the Town Planning Institute*, **XLIII**, No. 6, 1957.
30. Pinto-Duschinsky, Michael, Bread and Circuses? The Conservatives in Office 1951–64, in Bogdanor, Vernon and Skidelsky, Robert (Eds.), *The Age of Affluence*. Macmillan, 1970.
31. Collins, B. J., Presidential Address. *Journal of the Town Planning Institute*, **XLIV**, No. 1, 1957.
32. Lock, Max, Reconstruction in the Netherlands. *Journal of the Town Planning Institute*, **XXXIII**, No. 2, 1947.
33. Town Planning Institute Committee Minutes, vol. III, 219.
34. Report of the Town and Country Planning Summer School, 1947, pp. 81 and 83.
35. Town Planning Institute Committee Minutes, vol. III, p. 34.
36. Allen, J. S., The Education of the Planner. *Journal of the Town Planning Institute*, **XXXIV**, No. 2, 1948.
37. Town Planning Institute Committee Minutes, vol. III, p. 119.
38. *Report of the Committee on the Qualifications of Planners*, Cmd. 8059, 1950.
39. Town Planning Institute Council Minutes, vol. III, p. 94.
40. Report of Meeting at Institute of Civil Engineers, 8th December 1947.
41. Report of Meeting at the Institute of Civil Engineers, 8th December 1947.
42. *Journal of the Town Planning Institute*, **XLIII**, No. 8, 1957.
43. *Journal of the Town Planning Institute*, **XLV**, No. 7, 1959.
44. Allen, J. S., Presidential Address. *Journal of the Town Planning Institute*, **XLVI**, No. 1, 1959.

8 The Period of Readjustment 1960–74

The year 1960 is an arbitrary mid-point in the post-war period. The year itself was of little significance for planning; for the Institute it simply represented the beginning of a new chartered era under a new Secretary. But nonetheless it is possible to discern a watershed in planning affairs about this time. A combination of circumstances conspired to a reawakening and quickening of planning activities, with the result that the 1960s were significantly different from the 1950s. Problems and issues changed and new ones emerged. Planning was called upon to be concerned with new tasks; it shed an old image and moved into new areas of involvement. This had enormous implications for the Institute with regard to membership and education: what was planning? who were planners and how should they be trained? For the profession, the sixties were a period of readjustment from one set of assumptions to another, and the progression was not made without great inner tensions.

As in previous chapters, this one begins with a review of the changing national planning situation, giving the backcloth against which developments within Institute affairs might be seen.

Planning 1960–74

The years immediately following 1945 saw the creation of the centralist planning machine: new units of planning administration at local and central levels, new powers of land use control, and a great extension of statutory planning. We have seen in the previous chapter that in spite of certain erosions during the fifties, many of the essentials of the central machine and its operation remained relatively intact. During this time the main focus of town and country planning was the development process, and planning was thought of as the harmonization or control of 'physical' forces which shaped land use and design. After this period the approach to centralist planning was modified; a rather different statutory planning process evolved; and the land and development orientation of town planning widened to embrace a range of other issues.

The changes have been complex, but perhaps a clearer understanding is given if we look at the developments from four points of view. First, the central planning machine has

177

continued to operate as the key to land planning, though with some variations ensuing from legislative changes. Hence industrial location, population distribution through New Towns and Town Development Schemes, National Parks and countryside matters, and housing issues have all continued to form major fields in national policy. Furthermore, the institutional framework of Central Government and local planning authorities has remained largely unaltered up to the present day.

Second, in some respects the central planning umbrella has even been extended. The problem of land values was tackled again in the sixties, and the Land Commission came and went; additions in the field of amenity preservation and environmental protection have been more lasting. Third, central planning has been considerably modified through devolution of responsibility to the local level, as evidenced through new approaches to plan preparation and the desire to enagage the public more in the planning process.

Fourth, we might observe that alongside the statutory planning process, either continuing enlarged or modified as above, there emerged new areas with which planning became very much concerned. For example, the huge problem of urban traffic led to developments in land use transportation planning. Regional economic problems bred a new look at regional development and regional planning. More recently, physical planning and land use control has mushroomed into a wider scale, that of the environment as a whole. For some years there have been emergent ideas about social planning, and this has focused attention on the needs of deprived areas and community development. In the late sixties the idea of corporate management took hold in local government circles and considerably affected the place of planning in administrative affairs. Finally, new quantitative methods in analytical work gave a new technical orientation to the planning process.

In these ways, planning developed rapidly during this period, and planners were exposed to the influence of a wide range of different disciplines and viewpoints. It was almost an age of confusion as old certainties were questioned and new fashions came into prominence. Above all, the rapidity of change was quite unparalleled; in just one decade or less planning was transformed from an exercise essentially of plan making and implementation on a prescriptive basis, to a wider and much more complex process which was pragmatic and adaptive. The only other comparable period was that of the forties, but then the events were evolutionary rather than revolutionary. Now the whole basis of plan preparation altered sharply. There could be no reliance on traditional skills, and in the drawing up of plans or schemes the planner entered into new relationships with other professionals and the public. Moreover the boundaries of the planners' expertise expanded into fields previously regarded as the concern of others, so that it became increasingly difficult to identify just where the planner's role began and ended.

There were a number of different reasons for these changes. Some were a direct result of the experiences of post-war planning, others stemmed from influences which were broadly societal in nature and which affected other professions in a similar way, while others were part of a reorientation of subject matter by academic disciplines and professions generally. In the first place it was recognized that the comprehensive, central planning process had serious deficiencies: some existing problems (particularly social) were not being tackled particularly well, and new problems were not being tackled at all.

178

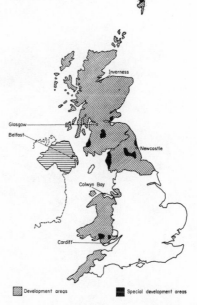

Development areas Special development areas

evelopment Districts, 1966. The Local Employment
ct, 1960, rescheduled the areas qualifying for assistance.
aken from Gavin McCrone, *Regional Policy in Britain*,
969. (*Courtesy of* Allen and Unwin)

Development Areas and Special Development Areas. The
1966 Industrial Development Act abolished the Development Districts. (Taken from Gavin McCrone, *Regional
Policy in Britain*, 1969. *Courtesy of* Allen and Unwin)

Wealdstone, Middlesex. A typical slice of suburban
London exhibiting the post-war package of low density
development, private gardens, detached and semi-
detached housing, within a framework of estate roads.
(*Courtesy of* Aerofilms)

Telford New Town, a quite different pattern from Weald stone. An interlocking form of medium density development, with vehicle/pedestrian segregation, characterize this neighbourhood in the setting of the Shropshire countryside. (*Courtesy of The Birmingham Post*)

Sir Frederic J. Osborn at his home in Welwyn Garden City. Born in 1885, he has been an indefatigable propagandist for the garden city movement ever since going to work in Letchworth in 1912. A fascinating insight into his ideals and activities is given in *The Letters of Lewis Mumford and Frederic J. Osborn*, ed. Michael Hughes, Adams and Dart, 1971.

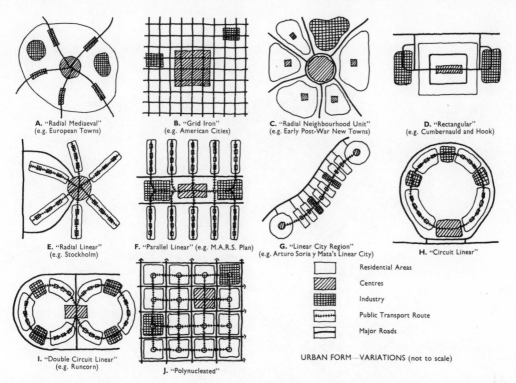

A. "Radial Mediaeval"
(e.g. European Towns)

B. "Grid Iron"
(e.g. American Cities)

C. "Radial Neighbourhood Unit"
(e.g. Early Post-War New Towns)

D. "Rectangular"
(e.g. Cumbernauld and Hook)

E. "Radial Linear"
(e.g. Stockholm)

F. "Parallel Linear" (e.g. M.A.R.S. Plan)

G. "Linear City Region"
(e.g. Arturo Soria y Mata's Linear City)

H. "Circuit Linear"

I. "Double Circuit Linear"
(e.g. Runcorn)

J. "Polynucleated"

Residential Areas

Centres

Industry

Public Transport Route

Major Roads

URBAN FORM—VARIATIONS (not to scale)

Variations in Urban Form. The 1960s saw new possibilities examined for ideal patterns of urban growth. There was a readiness to consider many alternatives and planners were keen to experiment with new systems. (See Arthur Ling, 'Urban Form or Chaos', *Journal TPI*, **53**, No. 3, 1967)

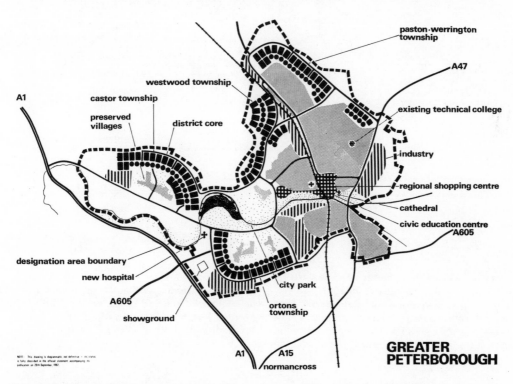

paston·werrington township

A47

westwood township

A1

castor township

existing technical college

preserved villages

district core

industry

regional shopping centre

cathedral

civic education centre

A605

designation area boundary

new hospital

city park

A605

ortons township

showground

A1   A15
normancross

GREATER PETERBOROUGH

Greater Peterborough, proposed scheme by Tom Hancock in 1967. A number of townships were envisaged as linked settlements in an expansion programme designed to increase the size of Peterborough to 185 000 people by the mid-1980s.

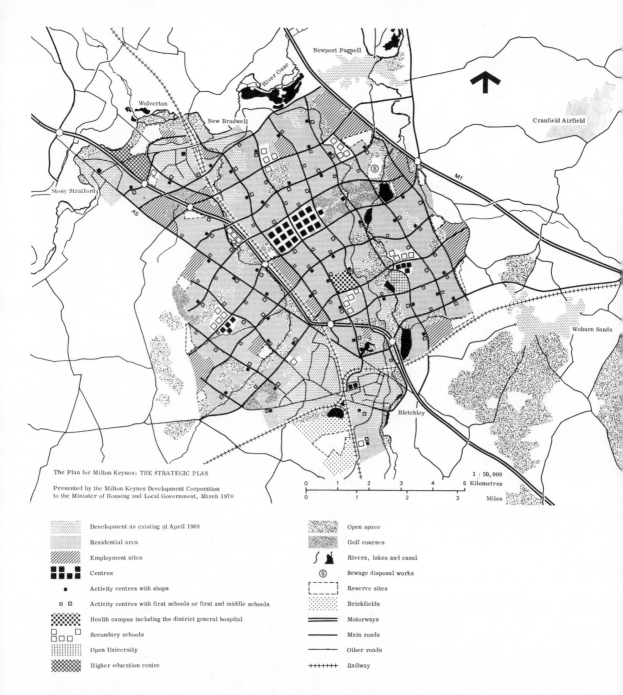

Development as existing at April 1969		Open space	
Residential area		Golf courses	
Employment sites		Rivers, lakes and canal	
Centres		Sewage disposal works	
Activity centres with shops		Reserve sites	
Activity centres with first schools or first and middle schools		Brickfields	
Health campus including the district general hospital		Motorways	
Secondary schools		Main roads	
Open University		Other roads	
Higher education centre		Railway	

Plan for Milton Keynes by Llewelyn-Davies, Weeks, Forestier-Walker and Bor. Designated in 1967 this New Town in north Buckinghamshire is perhaps the most interesting and controversial of recent proposals. The basic concept is a grid pattern of roads one kilometre apart, which forms a network of squares for residential development, ideal for the preservation of a strong sense of local community. Within the city boundaries (250 000 population by the end of the century) are the existing towns of Bletchley, Stony Stratford, Wolverton and New Bradwell and 13 other villages.

The operation of land use planning was proving insensitive to a range of social problems; reliance on the 'end-state' plans as typified by the Development Plan and other planning schemes could be quite misplaced.

Secondly, planners began to learn a good deal from political and social science, whereby planning as an element of social policy was seen to have both origins and consequences in the community. Planning was not just a land operation justified by technical considerations; it was also very much a matter of gains and losses to various groups, and the politics of planning took on a new significance. Bound up with this was the erosion of the wartime consensus in values: it became recognized that there was not just one course of action for the future but a number, each differently promoted by sections of the community according to their varying interests and relative power. This application had a marked influence on the way plans were prepared, and the confidence one expressed about alternatives. Above all there was no one certainty of the correctness or otherwise of a particular solution or line of policy. And in any case, the possibilities of ever achieving a particular long-term objective became more doubtful as the inter-relationships of cause and effect between various aspects of the developmental and social processes became more widely appreciated. Hence planning lost its positive, prescriptive, long-term image and relapsed into adaptive, short-term incrementalism.

As these factors became clearer, planning lost its old identity. There was a core of knowledge and of practice, but the boundaries of what constituted planning lost their former definition. Certain disciplines made inroads into planning as new specialisms were created, and at the same time planning expanded into other fields of practice. The planner's work overlapped with that of others, and the idea of planning as a team exercise gained ground.

We can now briefly sketch developments in planning during this period; first the continued operation of central planning; second, additions to it; third, modifications; and fourth the new fields which emerged.

The centralist planning objectives continued to embrace industrial location policies. Indeed, they were enlarged to include the question of office location. The Local Employment Act, 1960, replaced the provisions of the Distribution of Industry Acts. The old Development Areas were abolished and the areas qualifying for assistance were re-scheduled. Development Districts, based on Local Employment Exchange areas, were not scheduled on criteria of unemployment figures, and this had the effect of extending considerably those areas which could be grant-aided. At their peak, in 1966, the areas included nearly 17% of the country's total population. The same disadvantages remained, however, particularly the frequent changes in scheduling or descheduling areas, and this hardly gave confidence to industrialists or local planning authorities in long-term planning.

In 1966 the Industrial Development Act abolished the Development Districts, replacing them with new Development Areas on an even larger scale; almost the whole of Scotland, the Northern Region, Merseyside and most of Wales were now designated—a coverage of 40% of the land area and 20% of the population. The scheduling was not based on a strict employment criterion. A subsequent modification was the designation of 'Special Development Areas' as priority districts within. The inflexibility of the

Development District approach was considered by the Hunt Committee, and although many of the recommendations of their report *The Intermediate Areas* (1969) were not followed by Government, nonetheless the sharpness of demarcation between areas which were financially supported and those which were not has been eased through the concept of 'grey' areas.

The system of grants, loans and financial inducements continued with modifications and innovations from time to time, as, for example, the introduction of the Regional Employment Premium. An increase in advance factory building was particularly noticeable in the mid-1960s. In the meantime, control by Industrial Development Certificate remained, though with variations in the permitted floor space. A variation on this control device was adopted for the control of offices when Office Development Permits (ODPs) were required for office development.

During the 1960s the New Town's programme was revived. There were no further New Towns adjoining London, but Scotland and the provincial conurbations, in particular, benefited. The problem of finding sites for residential land led to difficulties between the conurbation authorities and the surrounding counties; voluntary agreements on Town Expansion Schemes were slow to be achieved, and in any case made for unconvincing strategic solutions. In the West Midlands, Dawley, later Telford, was designated a New Town in 1963 and Redditch in 1964. Skelmersdale (1961), Runcorn (1964) and Warrington (1968) were designated New Towns for Merseyside, and Washington (1964) for Tyneside. In Scotland, Irvine (1966) and Stonehouse (1972) were designated for Clydeside while Livingston (1962), south of Edinburgh, was an earlier addition for Central Scotland. In Central Wales, Newtown (1967) was designated in the hope of arresting rural depopulation. In 1965 the New Towns Act (Northern Ireland) permitted the designation of Craigavon (1965), Antrim (1966), Ballymena (1967) and Londonderry (1969). A new scale of New Town development came with the designation of Milton Keynes and Peterborough in 1967 and Northampton in 1968, the last two expanding existing towns of medium size; the intention in the case of all three was to develop to a size of approximately 250 000 population. A proposal for the development of Ipswich was not proceeded with. Central Lancashire New Town (1971) is an amalgamation of existing development with planned expansion to a size of half a million people. By 1971 the 28 New Towns in Great Britain (21 in England, 2 in Wales and 5 in Scotland) accommodated rather more than 1 400 000 people. This was double the population living in the towns when they were first designated, but it still represented an achievement much less than could have been hoped for by the framers of the 1946 Act.

With regard to Town Development, for a long time London was the only authority to pursue energetically the opportunities offered by the provisions of the 1952 Act. In this way certain towns in the outer London area developed rapidly: Swindon and Basingstoke to the west, and a variety of smaller towns elsewhere, including a number in East Anglia. By 1970 Greater London had agreed 31 schemes, with 90 000 dwellings proposed to be provided by the local authorities concerned. In other cases progress was slow. In the provincial conurbations the problem was less severe and therefore the need to secure voluntary agreements was that much less urgent; consequently the necessary degree of effective organization in both the exporting and receiving authorities was rarely secured.

184

There was a high mortality rate in terms of failure to agree schemes and the whole process was time consuming and not a little frustrating. Birmingham, for example, has negotiated with over 100 authorities, but has only 15 agreed schemes with 22 000 dwellings to be provided; Tamworth and Daventry are the main towns. In Scotland, the problem of Glasgow remained dominant; by 1964, 57 overspill agreements had been concluded between the city and receiving authorities, as far afield as Wick.

With population distribution, therefore, central planning has kept in operation the two measures which underpin regional and indeed national strategies. But the results of the policies have been obscured by massive private development on a scale which has considerably extended the peripheries of all large cities. During the middle 1960s revised population forecasts inflated the long-term housing problem (although progressively reduced in the 1970s) and the whole question of planned population distribution once again came to the fore.

In matters of countryside and recreation, the growing pressures of car ownership, mobility, affluence and greater leisure time which had been increasing in the 1950s came to a head in the 1960s. Michael Dower, son of John Dower, wrote of the 'Fourth Wave' as an explosion of demand equal in force and significance to the industrial and transport revolutions in our past history[1]. The designation of Areas of Outstanding Natural Beauty continued, and indeed gathered pace, 17 areas being designated between 1960 and 1970 ranging in size from Dedham Vale (22 square miles) to the Cotswolds (582 square miles). The long-distance footpath programme also continued, with approvals given to the Somerset and North Devon and Dorset Paths, Cleveland Way and the North Downs Way. On the other hand no new National Parks were designated.

The 1949 Act and the work of the National Parks Commission soon proved inadequate for the set of complex problems and challenges posed by the 1960s. The coast was subject to heavy pressures for development, and 'Enterprise Neptune', initiated by the National Trust, sought to achieve a more effective control. Additionally, regional conferences and reports on coastal preservations and development led to proposals in 1970 for the designation of 'Heritage Coasts' for special recognition within local planning authorities. But much more than this, the emphasis on National Parks and the related countryside measures of the 1949 Act needed fundamental review. The focus on recreation planning shifted from preservation of fine landscape and provision for walking and rambling to one of catering for the needs of car-borne population on the outskirts of large urban areas. There were new leisure interests: planning for water-based recreation, for new users of the countryside and for specific interests such as caravans, now became urgent. Under the stimulus of the Countryside in 1970 Conferences, the Countryside Act, 1968, became the new provider. It set up the Countryside Commission, replacing the National Parks Commission, and made provision for new developments, amongst which the most distinctive was the country park. In this way the familiar package of Central Government finance and initiative through a central Commission, harnessed to the executive action of local authorities, continued to be the basis of countryside recreation planning.

On matters of housing there continued to be extensive involvement in slum clearance, the improvement of older houses and the provision of new dwellings either in redevelopment areas or in new suburbs. The problems of Greater London were examined in the

The Gorbals, Glasgow. Redevelopment in 1962, showing the demolition of old tenements with new dwellings beyond. Glasgow's housing problems are exceptionally severe and their solution poses enormous planning questions affecting the Clyde Valley and much of West Central Scotland. (*Courtesy of* Central Office of Information)

Yateley Common Country Park, Hampshire. Three miles from Camberley and 6 miles from Farnborough, this area of heath land with ponds makes an ideal picnic/recreation area with facilities for riding, nature study and fishing. The Countryside Act, 1968, made provision for country parks, so introducing a new element in the range of facilities concerned with outdoor recreation. (*Courtesy of* Countryside Commission)

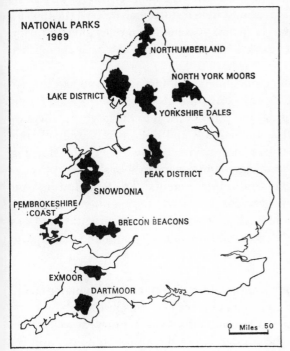

NATIONAL PARKS
1969

NORTHUMBERLAND
NORTH YORK MOORS
LAKE DISTRICT
YORKSHIRE DALES
PEAK DISTRICT
PEMBROKESHIRE COAST
SNOWDONIA
BRECON BEACONS
EXMOOR
DARTMOOR

0 Miles 50

AREAS OF OUTSTANDING
NATURAL BEAUTY
1969

Solway Coast
Forest of Bowland
Anglesey
Lleyn
Shropshire Hills
Norfolk Coast
Malvern Hills
Cotswolds
Suffolk Coast and Heaths
Chilterns
Gower
Surrey Hills
Kent Downs
Quantock Hills
East Hampshire
North Devon
Dorset
Sussex Downs
Chichester Harbour
East Devon
South Hampshire Coast
Isle of Wight
Cornwall
South Devon

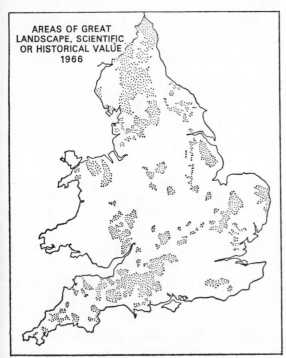

AREAS OF GREAT
LANDSCAPE, SCIENTIFIC
OR HISTORICAL VALUE
1966

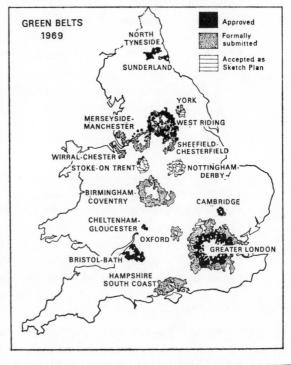

GREEN BELTS
1969

Approved
Formally submitted
Accepted as Sketch Plan

NORTH TYNESIDE
SUNDERLAND
YORK
MERSEYSIDE-MANCHESTER
WEST RIDING
SHEFFIELD-CHESTERFIELD
WIRRAL-CHESTER
STOKE-ON TRENT
NOTTINGHAM-DERBY
BIRMINGHAM-COVENTRY
CAMBRIDGE
CHELTENHAM-GLOUCESTER
OXFORD
GREATER LONDON
BRISTOL-BATH
HAMPSHIRE SOUTH COAST

Landscape Protection, late 1960s. Taken from J. Allan Patmore, *Land and Leisure*, 1970, these four maps show the extent of land in England and Wales protected for various purposes: National Parks, Areas of Outstanding Natural Beauty, Areas of Great Landscape, Scientific or Historic Value, and Green Belts. (*Courtesy of* David and Charles)

Milner Holland Report (1965) and a succession of Government Committee Reports advised on housing issues. The extent of slums almost defied statistical analysis. In 1965 an official estimate of 919 000 unfit houses in Great Britain was made ten years after an earlier estimate of 966 000, in spite of the fact that nearly $\frac{2}{3}$ million dwellings had been demolished in that period.

The figures obscured other estimates which may have been far higher, and an estimate in 1967 by the Ministry of Housing and Local Government suggested 1 800 000 unfit dwellings in England and Wales alone. Rising standards pointed to the large and increasing housing stock which could be classed as inadequate and due for replacement. But demolition began to be matched by the need for improvement of dwellings. The Housing Act, 1964, gave local authorities powers to declare 'improvement areas' thereby recognizing the environmental significance of housing improvement. The 1969 Housing Act gave wider powers to declare 'general improvement areas' and the number of improvement grants increased dramatically from 115–130 000 annually in the middle sixties to 180 000 in 1970, and 232 000 in 1971. But the intractable problems of unfit and inadequate housing remain, and further local authority powers in respect of priority housing areas are currently envisaged.

Public intervention in the housing market has therefore continued to be a major factor in the planning of urban renewal. In Scotland a coincidence of events in 1967 showed for the country as a whole the progress achieved in housing affairs this century, as well as the nature of the residual problem. 1967 saw the completion of the millionth house built by public and private agencies since 1919. In the same year, a report of a Sub-committee of the Scottish Housing Advisory Committee, *Scotland's Older Houses*, noted that the stock of housing was deteriorating more quicly than remedial action. The Committee estimated that there were about 273 000 houses in Scotland which needed to be demolished as soon as possible.

In all these aspects, a feature of national planning has been the close working link between central and local government. There have been important changes in both bodies. As planning shook off the lethargy of the fifties Whitehall found a stronger planning voice though not without years of departmental confusion. The Department of Economic Affairs lasted 5 years, the Ministry of Land and Natural Resources less than 2 years. In 1969, in an attempt to co-ordinate related activities, a new Secretary of State for Local Government and Regional Planning was given federal powers in relation to the Ministry of Housing and Local Government and the Ministry of Transport. In 1970 under the new Conservative administration the rational of this co-ordination was carried forward in the creation of the Department of the Environment. In 1968 a new Chief Planner, Wilfred Burns, was appointed from the ranks of local government where he was City Planning Officer of Newcastle. He was in his Presidential year of the Institute and this had to be cut short because of conflicting loyalties, though not without TPI Council disappointment.

In local government, the strengthening of planning was reflected in the creation of new Planning Departments in many of the major cities and larger towns where the planning function had previously been combined with that of (usually) the engineer and surveyor. By 1973, of the big authorities, Birmingham was notable for its retention of the dual role, but there were many others also without planning officers with their own departments.

In London, the old County Council was swept away in favour of an enlarged Greater London Council and new London Boroughs were created, which in due time had their own planning officers. Against the trend, GLC combined its Departments of Planning and of Highways and Transportation. Local government reorganization in 1974 (in England and Wales) was an added spur to the creation of separate departments. In short therefore substantial professional gains were recorded over the last decade, especially during the last year in terms of local authority position and status.

So much for aspects of how the central and local government planning machine continued its post-1947 operation. There were also certain additions. In the first place there was a fresh attack on the problem of compensation and betterment, this time by way of a capital gains tax introduced by the 1967 Finance Act, and a betterment levy introduced by the Land Commission Act of the same year. A Land Commission was established with the two objectives of securing land either by agreement or compulsory purchase so that it was available at the right time for the implementation of regional and local plans; and to ensure that a substantial part of the development value returned to the community. The betterment levy was in fact set at 40%. In 1971, like the Central Land Board 15 years earlier, the Land Commission was abolished because it was politically unacceptable. There had been a completed purchase of 2 800 acres of land, and £46 million of betterment levy had been collected. It would seem that it was a premature demise; there remain unresolved the problems of land assembly and release in a co-ordinated way, and the issues of compensation, betterment and rising prices of land.

The preservation and enhancement of amenity has been a central feature of planning from the earliest days both in the statutory planning process and in the ideas which surrounded the origins of the planning movement. We have seen how planning legislation gradually gave wider powers over the control of advertisements, preservation of trees and the protection of special buildings and of areas of architectural or historic significance. One extension of this element of planning came with the new powers to control caravan sites (through a system of licensing) contained in the Caravan Sites and Control of Development Act, 1960. In a different sphere there was the Civic Amenities Act, 1967. This was a private member's Bill, promoted by Duncan Sandys, President of the Civic Trust, which secured Government backing. Just as with housing legislation at this time, statutory recognition of environmental quality passed from the individual building to the area. It became obligatory for local planning authorities to designate conservation areas, 'areas of special architectural or historic interest, the character of which it is desirable to preserve or enhance'. Government-sponsored studies of historic cities formed another impetus.

This feature of statutory planning is very much linked to the wider attention that had been paid to the protection of the environment from the middle sixties onwards. The Clean Air Act of 1956 utilized the device of smoke control areas in which to eliminate smoke emission from chimneys. The Act of 1968 provided powers for directing a local authority to proceed with a clean air programme. The overall result, aided and abetted by a turn to gas and electricity for home heating, has been that British cities now have cleaner air and higher winter sunshine records than at any time since the early 1800s, thus meeting an early objective of environmental reformers.

Reclamation of derelict land represents the other dimension of environmental improvement with which planning has been concerned. Powers to deal with reclamation have been available for many years, but it was during the 1960s that finance became available rather more generously, through the Industrial Development Act, 1966, the Local Government Act of the same year and the Local Employment Act, 1970. On average, 2 000 acres or more per year have been reclaimed and landscaped, but recently there has been a gross annual increase in derelict land. Perhaps about 100 000 acres remain.

But the whole question of protection of the environment is moving into a higher gear. The event of European Conservation Year (1970) and the establishment of a Royal Commission on Environmental Pollution with very wide terms of reference are indications of this. The seventies will undoubtedly see an extension and redefinition of planning in environmental terms.

Attention to urban sport and recreation represents another addition to national planning. The Report of the Wolfenden Committee on Sport, *Sport and the Community* (1960), recommended the setting up of a Sports Development Council. This idea was not lost and in 1964 the Sports Council was created, followed by Regional Sports Councils in 1966; they have stimulated considerable interest in local planning authorities regarding the issues of leisure and recreation. The Regional Councils set up Technical Panels, and planning officers have frequently played significant roles in their work. Recreation research was promoted with studies of regional demand and case studies of particular facilities such as swimming, golf and sports centres.

Compared with these additions to the statutory planning process there have been some important modifications during the last ten years. The Development Plan procedure continued well into the sixties without serious amendment, with quinquennial reviews giving the opportunity of presenting plans in more attractive ways: colour was now available in contrast to the 'battledress notation' of the early fifties, and there was much less detail shown in favour of broad zonings. But a fundamental review of plan making and Development Plan preparation came with the Planning Advisory Group set up by the Minister of Housing and Local Government, Richard Crossman, in 1964; it was chaired by I. V. Pugh, a civil servant, and had members drawn from Planning and other local government Departments. The Group contained two future Presidents of the Institute, Walter Bor and Wilfred Burns. Their report, *The Future of Development Plans*, was published in 1965. They recommended changes which took into account the need for flexibility in plan making, to make them more than land-use maps and to make them more responsive to changes in economic and social trends, population forecasts and traffic growth. It was felt that a number of different types of plans should replace the system of Development Plans and Comprehensive Development Area Plans.

The recommendations were largely followed in the Town and Country Planning Act, 1968, itself foreshadowed in the White Paper, *Town and Country Planning*, of June 1967. The new system was now centred on Structure Plans, Local Plans and Action Area Plans. Structure Plans which many local authorities are currently preparing, are statements of general policy concerning development in the context of social and economic forces, rather than maps showing spatial allocations, as were the old Development Plans. Their content relates to broad land-use proposals (as opposed to detailed zonings) and policies concerning traffic and aspects of the physical environment. The emphasis is laid on broad

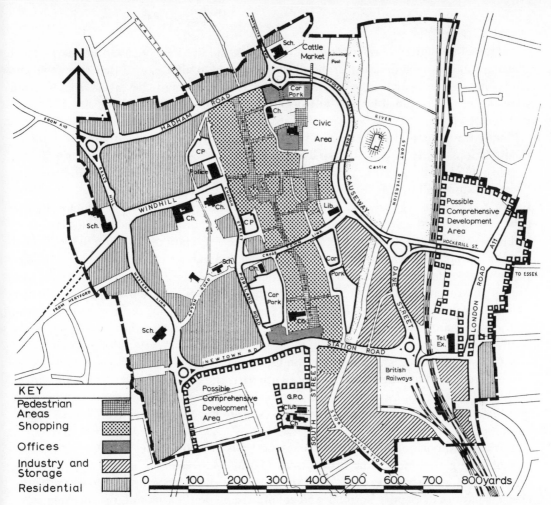

Central Area Draft Plan, Bishop's Stortford, Herts, 1962. This is an interesting example of how new ideas in town centre development were entering into the planning process: revised traffic proposals, pedestrianization, and a three dimensional appraisal of design. (See E. H. Doubleday, 'Bishop's Stortford. A Small Town Centre', *Journal TPI*, **XLVIII**, No. 9, 1962)

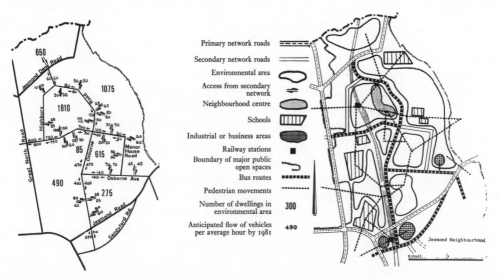

Proposals for Jesmond, Newcastle upon Tyne, 1966. This was an early experiment in improved plan presentation. On the left, information on traffic flows pointed to the possibility of planning the Jesmond Neighbourhood on the basis of 'environmental areas' (following Buchanan). On the right, a cartoon approach analyses the structure of the area.

strategies in the setting of relevant economic and social matters. On the other hand, local plans are to show the detailed proposals in respect of small areas, so that they form the backcloth against which development control decisions might be taken. Action Area Plans are rather similar but they relate specifically to areas where major changes are to be expected by reason of development, redevelopment or improvement.

There are at least two major aspects of this new procedure which constitute major modifications of the 1947 system. The first is that the 1968 Act permitted a significant degree of decentralization of decision-making away from Central Government. Structure Plans are approved by the Secretary of State but Local Plans and Action Area Plans are, subject to certain safeguards, the responsibility of the local authority; they do not require to be approved by the Secretary of State, but instead are adopted by the local authority.

The second is even more fundamental in that the Secretary of State has to be satisfied that the public have been fully drawn in to the plan making process. Adequate publicity has to be given to proposals before they are included in plans: a consequence of this is that draft plans are circulated for public comment before final plans are prepared, so avoiding a 'take it or leave it' situation. Further, adequate opportunity for making representation on the plans has to be given. In this way the 1968 Act incorporated those aspects of public participation discussed by the Skeffington Report, *People and Planning* (1969). A considerable change in outlook has taken place about the nature of planning since the mid-sixties in the context of changing attitudes about authority, the nature of government, the values of the individual against those of public decision makers, and how far the values of a pluralist society can be accommodated in a system of government which relies essentially on consensus.

The other important modifications to the post-1947 machine have concerned the structure of local government. The first post-war Labour Government declined to grasp the nettle of local government reform, and the anachronisms of geography, shown up by the obsolete pattern of County Borough and county areas and their boundaries, became more and more obvious. The urban spread of the fifties and sixties exacerbated the situation. London's outer boundaries and internal administrative divisions were redefined with the creation of the Greater London Council. Elsewhere there were a number of *ad hoc* modifications: some large Municipal Boroughs became County Boroughs, such as Luton and Solihull. The hotch potch of counties, County Districts and County Boroughs in the West Midlands was simplified into six County Boroughs covering the conurbation, surrounded by the counties. Elsewhere, as at Torbay and Teesside, new County Boroughs were created. A Royal Commission on Local Government in England and Wales under the chairmanship of Sir John Redcliffe-Maud was the occasion for a fundamental inquiry. In Wales proposals for reorganization had been made by the Local Government Commission for Wales and taken up in a Government White Paper *Local Government in Wales* (1967); in Scotland the Wheatley Commission investigated the situation. The Maud Report, *Report of the Royal Commission on Local Government in England* (1969), recommended the unitary principal of local government reform, namely the creation of a relatively small number of all purpose, single-tier authorities. The special needs of conurbations were recognized and in those areas top-tier Metropolitan Councils with second-tier District Councils were proposed. A contrary view was put forward by Derek Senior in a Memorandum of Dissent; his recommendations favoured a hierarchy of city regions with a large number of second-tier authorities. The *Report of the Royal Commission on Local Government in Scotland* (1969) proposed a two-tier structure with regional and district authorities.

The Labour Government accepted the broad outline of the Maud proposals but the incoming Conservative administration did not. A fundamentally different solution was favoured based on the division of England and Wales into two-tier authorities: Counties and District Councils, with Metropolitan Councils covering the major conurbations. The local government map of the country was redrawn in 1973 and against considerable opposition from professional planners and other interest groups England and Wales has (from 1974) a pattern of new authorities with different planning functions as between County and District Council. Scotland's new local government pattern takes effect from 1975. The new system has considerable significance for planners, and the full implications for the planning process can scarcely yet be foreseen. In years to come, the Local Government Act, 1972, may well be regarded as an important watershed in town planning affairs.

Reform of local government took place against a background of increasing planning work and a great concern for the quality of planning that was achieved. In 1971 more than 463 000 planning applications were submitted to local planning authorities in England and Wales; 83.3% were permitted, a proportion which has been roughly constant for a number of years. The administrative machine has been overloaded by planning appeals for some time. The current average duration between the lodging of a planning appeal and its decision by an inspector is 36 weeks; where it is decided by the Secretary of State it is 51 weeks[2].

The relatively self-contained idea of land-use planning, inherited from the forties, has been considerably widened since 1960. Perhaps the most obvious is in the field of transport and communications. The boom in vehicle numbers continued unremittingly[3]; in 1961 29% of households in Great Britain had regular use of one car, while in 1971 the proportion had risen to 44%. More than 8% of households now have the regular use of two or more cars. The consequential changes in mode of transport have enormous consequences for our urban environment. In the period between 1953 and 1971 the proportion of rail-way-passenger mileage fell from 20.6% to 8.2%, and public service vehicle-passenger mileage from 43.3% to 12.7%. On the other hand, private transport rose from 36.0% to 78.7%.

The scale and nature of the problem began to be clear in the early sixties. The conventional design solutions dated from the forties or even earlier; the last advisory manual of the Ministry of War Transport had been published in 1945. A new approach was needed. Vehicle–pedestrian segregation was admired in Cumbernauld and Coventry, both in the central area and its residential neighbourhoods, and Rotterdam and Vallingby as familiar European examples were praised, but an authoritative voice for British practice was lacking. The time was ripe for advances in concept and method.

A growing number of urban renewal schemes threw up increasing possibilities for re-shaping urban road patterns. Also, American work was showing the relationship between land use and traffic generation, forshadowing the new science of land-use transportation planning. Furthermore, a national motorway building programme began with the

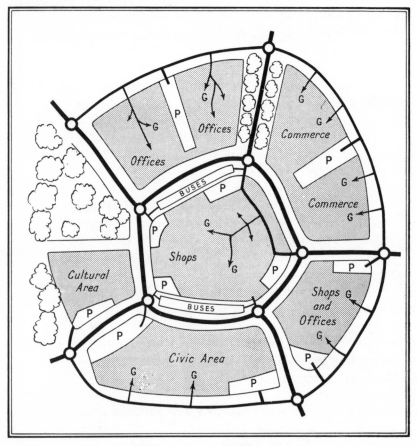

The Precinct Theory. An early illustration by C.D. Buchanan in *Mixed Blessing*, Leonard Hill Books, 1958. The main roads enclosed and divided the various zones, and gave access to bus stops, car parks (P) and goods and service entries (G). The concept was developed in *Traffic for Towns*, 1963.

L. laundry
P. public houses.
▨ children's play area
NS. nursery school
P.S. primary school
▢ meeting hall } over shops
▼ clinic

PARK HILL . SHEFFIELD .

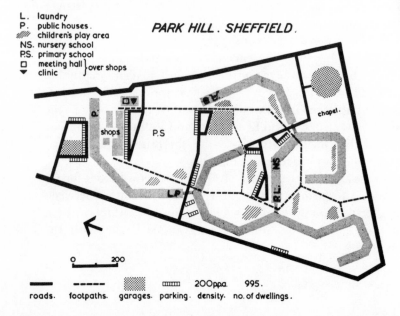

━━━ roads. ┄┄┄ footpaths. ▨ garages. ▥ parking. 200ppa. density. 995. no. of dwellings.

Colin Douglas Buchanan, I then Professor of Transpo Imperial College, London, President of TPI in its Ju Year. He emerged as a figure in planning in the 19 he received a knighthood was awarded the Gold Med the TPI.

Park Hill, Sheffield. A sch by J.L. Womersley, City Ar tect, for high density reside development incorporating fic segregation. (See Womersley, 'Housing the M Car', *Journal TPI*, **XLVII**, 8, 1961)

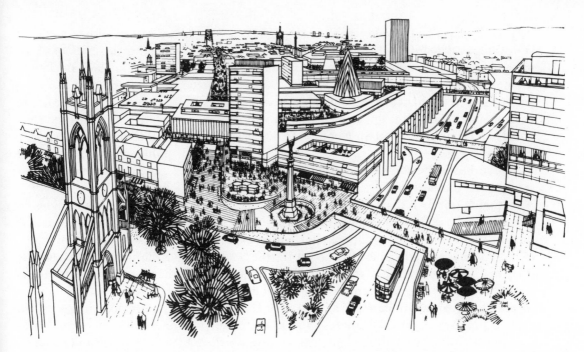

Central Area, Newcastle upon Tyne, artist's impression of redevelopment proposals designed to secure segregation of pedestrians and vehicles. The view looks down Northumberland Street from the north towards Tyne Bridge. (See Wilfred Burns, *Newcastle: A Study in Replanning at Newcastle upon Tyne*, Leonard Hill, 1967)

Western Avenue, London. A good example of a motorway superimposed on the urban scene. From a fine technical achievement and liberator of traffic congestion, it soon came to be regarded as an environmental menace and a detraction from, rather than an enhancement of amenity. (*Courtesy of* John Sani)

Preston By-pass, and professional road engineers were given a new lease of life as Government spending in this field increased. The turning point was the work of C. D. Buchanan which culminated in his report *Traffic in Towns*, published in 1963. Buchanan led a Study Group in the Ministry of Transport with the terms of reference 'to study the long-term development of roads and traffic in urban areas and their influence on the urban environment'. The Minister, Ernest Marples, appointed a Steering Group in June 1961 under the Chairmanship of Sir Geoffrey Crowther to work with Buchanan and to advise the Minister of the work being done and its implications for public policy. The Report was published in 1963 in a blaze of publicity and public debate, and proved to be a document of great importance.

Its timing was such that there could be ready agreement with both the assumptions on which it was based as well as the principles for future action which were put forward. The starting point was that 'conditions that now prevail in towns make it clear that traffic congestion has already placed in jeopardy the well-being of the inhabitants and the efficiency of many of the activities. The potential increase in the number of vehicles is so great that unless something is done the conditions are bound to become extremely serious within a comparatively short period of years. Either the utility of vehicles in towns will decline rapidly, or the pleasantness and safety of surroundings will deteriorate catastrophically—in all probability both will happen together.'[4] It was the form and management of urban areas that was at stake. Town planning took on a new dimension: transport planning was not just a matter for highway engineers, and conversely, urban design was not something from which highway engineers could be excluded.

Much of this had been said before, but never had the argument been pursued so relentlessly in a Government document, lavishly illustrated, compelling in its message. The approach to solutions, however, was novel and offered new scope. Whereas previously the traffic problem had been seen primarily as one of keeping vehicles on the move, resulting in an emphasis on the by-pass principle, Buchanan put first attention on the environment. Areas were delineated within which life was led and activities conducted, and this gave a cellular structure to a town's design. A new comprehensive concept of town planning was presented, with traffic as an integral part.

There were wider implications for transport planning as a whole and some of these were given effect later in the sixties. The basic ideas and proposals of the Buchanan Report were endorsed in the Government White Paper, *Transport Today* (1966). The White Paper *Public Transport and Traffic* (1967) contained a number of proposals taken up by the Transport Act, 1968. The Secretary of State was given powers to set up Passenger Transport Authorities to integrate public transport systems, and four conurbations have so far been selected. In London a similar objective was pursued in the Transport (London) Act, 1969, itself preceded by the White Paper *Transport in London* (1968).

The 1960s was the decade for traffic planning, and at local and subregional level the land-use transportation plan was widely adopted in the major conurbation areas as a basis for new plan preparation. Based on American experience in the fifties, a number of costly studies were set up based on extensive data collection as to traffic movement and forecasts for the future. Computers enabled this data to be handled and, by means of simulation techniques, allowed alternative models of land use to be prepared.

196

Important progress was also made in the field of regional planning. After the disappointments in the fifties two significant developments encouraged this. First, there was the onset of renewed economic difficulties in some of the underprivileged regions; second, there was the stimulus of transportation planning in most of the conurbations, as we have seen. Regional planning took on a new lease of life both as regional economic planning and then as subregional strategic planning.

Two White Papers in 1963, both programmes 'for Development and Growth' set the scene, for Central Scotland and the North East, the latter the so-called Hailsham Report, after its authorship. In the same year Robert Matthew's *Belfast Regional Survey and Plan* set out a strategy for Northern Ireland. There then followed a number of regional studies as Government Reports covering the South East, the West Midlands and the North West. In Scotland there were examinations of certain subregions: the Borders, Tayside and Highlands and Islands, while the setting up of the Highlands and Islands Development Board in 1965 was a practical exercise in regional, economic and social development. New ideas for regional strategies became current, in particular, the idea of linear growth corridors. The Plan for South Hampshire prepared by Buchanan and Partners took up this principle. A new institutional framework provided a fresh regional initiative. The creation of the Department of Economic Affairs was accompanied by the setting up of ten Regional Economic Planning Councils and regional co-ordination of a kind began to emerge. Reports of Economic Planning Councils primed the regional pump. The best work was done where the regional civil servants worked in concert with local planning authorities in the form of 'Standing Conferences'. The North Regional Planning Committee was the first to make strides in this direction and produced a number of research studies. A further encouragement was afforded by the setting up of Regional Sports Councils in 1966; they also conducted a number of regional studies. Lastly we should note the influence of a new body within Government, the Central Unit for Environmental Planning, charged with preparing feasibility studies for Humberside and Severnside; their reports were published in 1969 and 1971 respectively. But perhaps the most noteworthy step forward was in the South East where the *South East Study*, 1970, produced the first fruits of collaboration between Central Government and Standing Conferences. An assessment of the technical advances made in this field of planning over the last decade has been made by T. M. Cowling and G. C. Steeley in *Subregional Planning Studies: an Evaluation* (1973).

A number of subregional planning studies were promoted by Richard Crossman when Minister of Housing and Local Government and others have followed. The Leicester and Leicestershire study published in 1969 was the first to utilize the Garin–Lowry model of spatial allocations (see p. 200). This and those that followed made contributions to the research and analysis aspects of planning studies. A comparison of these documents with the regional planning exercises of the inter-war period and the late 1940s is an eloquent testimony to the very different approaches to planning that were being made. The basis of plan preparation was different, so too were the contents of the plan, and its presentation.

These developments in regional planning were accompanied by increasing attention given to national strategic planning. Quite apart from the rediscovered need for co-ordination of investment decisions and the obligation to reduce the imbalance between favoured and unfavoured regions, the *bête noire* of the sixties was the spectre of population growth. An additional 20 million people by the end of the century was forecast and variations on the dispersal of that population were popular exercises. Since then, population forecasts have been substantially reduced and the fervour for this basis of national planning has waned.

Other aspects of planning developed considerably during the last ten years. They have scarcely entered into the process of statutory planning, but they are examples of the developing frontiers of the subject matter. First, the idea of social planning. The changing scene was described by G. E. Cherry's *Town Planning in its Social Context* (1970), in which it was shown that the planning emphasis was shifting from the built environment and land use to that of the social environment. A whole new set of objectives and assumptions about planning was replacing the mechanistic and deterministic principles on which planning was previously based. One origin of this change of emphasis was a critical evaluation of the actual performance of the statutory planning process. It was seen that the problems of the community were not necessarily met by plans that had been prepared, or the operation of the process that had been set in motion. There was a gap between policy and achievement, first because the precise objectives underlying the plan were not made specific, second, because social policy objectives could not be met by physical/spatial policies alone, and third, because there was an inadequate understanding of the interlinked processes which affect planned change. This led to much less reliance being placed on physical plan preparation; the days of the grand manner plan in the form of Abercrombie's London of 1944 were numbered. Another consequence was the new attention paid to clarification of objectives, and evaluation of results: in short, what should be done, for whom, and why, and who benefited from the activity? Then there was the focus on process: what were the factors which affected a particular course of action, institutional as well as 'physical'?

This led to the view that it was increasingly difficult to identify town planning as an individual independent process. Crises of confidence followed as to just what was town planning. Between extreme viewpoints, the middle of the road conclusion has been to continue to emphasize land management and the development process as the kernel of the subject matter, though in the implicit context of an economic and social setting.

Within the field of social planning, an important influence has been the radical view which holds that town planning has been a conservative agent, failing to be the reallocative process that it pretended to be. It has been argued that in our structured society, in which resources are distributed unequally, town planning has actually been part of the reinforcing institutions that preclude disturbance of that status quo. A new focus in planning has therefore fallen on the roots of urban deprivation and the factors inherent in our social structure which promote it. Previously, it was argued that planners were more concerned with tackling the apparent manifestations of the problem through housing reform and land-use control. As a result, there is increasing attention, particularly by younger generation planners, to community planning at the local level and the help given to local communities to articulate their own problems and aspirations. The developments of advocacy planning and 'planning aid centres' are part of these trends.

Contemporaneous with the development of social planning was the work done on 'systems'. The extraordinary network of links and interconnections have been laid bare by

198

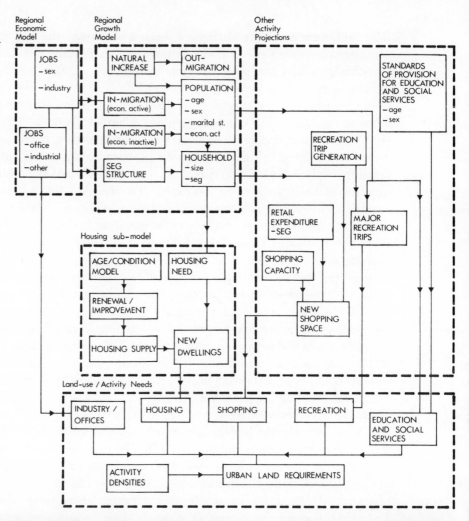

...uantitative framework of ...ructure Plan Area Forecasts. ...ee Tim Rhodes, 'Research ...echniques in Structure Plan-ning', *Journal TPI*, **55**, No. 6, ...970. This illustrates the new ...mplexity of planning method; ...outlines a computer-oriented, ...odel-based approach to the ...mulation of the main activity ...stems in a South Hampshire ...udy.

...esidential Installation, 1965. *...om the left:* Dr N. Lichfield ...enior Vice President), L.W. ...ane (Past President), L.B. ...eeble (President) and P.R. ...athbone (Secretary).

J. B. McLoughlin and G. Chadwick, both professional planners in this field. They have stimulated not only new methods in planning, but a totally new understanding of process and change within planning. McLoughlin's *Urban and Regional Planning* (1969) outlined the application of the general principles of systems analysis and control to the planning task. Planning as a cyclic process was emphasized, physical planning being described in terms of the 'control of complex systems'. Chadwick's book *A Systems View of Planning* (1972) outlined a theory of town and regional planning based on cybernetics, systems theory and related fields. For planning practice a major implication has been that the devising of plans for cities and regions should be centred on the fullest possible under-standing of the system to be managed. The development of models to stimulate the systems behaviour became a major preoccupation of many planners.

Another advance in practice was to see planning in relation to corporate management. From the Institute's ranks Tony Eddison in *Local Government Management and Corporate Planning* (1973) has examined the different types of plan making that goes on in local government and recommends the idea of management by objectives as an operational framework not only for town planning but all local government departments. He defined planning as 'the process of preparing a set of decisions for action in the future directed at achieving goals by optimal means and of learning from the outcome about possible new sets of decisions and new goals to be achieved.'[5] Once again there is emphasis on thinking of planning as a process; Eddison's important contribution has been to follow other workers in this field in showing how a robust system might be devised to produce decisions and action on planning problems.

This section is concluded with a brief reference to new research dimensions in planning that have arisen in the last decade. Much has happened since J. N. Jackson's *Surveys for Town and Country Planning*, published in 1963. Planning has been drawn out of the relatively simple era of 'survey, analysis and plan', as advocated by Geddes, into the complexities of new research skills. Forerunners appeared in the late fifties when greater use was made of statistical techniques in articles and reports. There were advances in method: N. Lichfield's *Economics of Planned Development* (1956) was a pioneering work which stimu-lated work in studies of cost benefit analysis. Research in local authority departments was expanded, as the TPI's *Register of Planning Research* indicated. Developments in quantitative method and the broad application of social research techniques ensured a continuing momentum. An early concentration was on information systems and data banking. In a TPI publication, L. S. Jay contributed the *Development of an Integrated Data System* (1966). Since then research has embraced work on urban land-use models, partic-ularly residential location models, based on the American work of Ira S. Lowry and Robert A. Garin. E. L. Cripps has been a notable contributor in British work. Research has also encompassed the development of gravity models, particularly for shopping analyses, gaming simulation, threshold analysis and forecasting. Within a short space of time, planning took on a new technical armoury, absorbed from fringe disciplines and related fields of study.

This has been a brief and selective review of the changes which have taken place in planning since the beginning of the 1960s. The essential part of the planning process has remained: the concern of statutory town planning for land use, urban form, design and layout, control of development, provision of new facilities, and renewal and improvement of housing and environment. There have also been modifications and additions as we have seen. But above all, planning has become greatly extended in concept and practice, brought about by a wide involvement with other related fields of activity and encouraged by new approaches from the social sciences. New agencies in planning are now operating, and this has resulted in a very confused, though stimulating scene. We have not yet evaluated, for example, the contribution of the Civic Trust over the last 15 years: its role in street improvement schemes, derelict land, the Lea Valley proposals in East London, and the stimulation of civic societies. Neither have we yet fully assessed the significance of public participation in planning: episodes such as the redevelopment of Covent Garden, or the third London Airport and new public pressures impinging on environmental conservation are of great importance in recent planning history. Moreover, in due time we shall probably see that sagas such as the development of Piccadilly Circus, regional shopping centres in various parts of the country or the Greater London Development Plan Inquiry will affect our planning system in a very material way. So much has been in flux over the last decade: we can now turn to see how the Institute reacted to this changing situation.

THE INSTITUTE 1960–74

Against the significant changes in planning and related matters that have been described, above, there were two related developments in Institute matters that overshadowed almost everything else. These were the questions of membership policy and education. The latter is considered in chapter 9, and in this section we concentrate on the membership issue. In conclusion we will, for the sake of completeness, touch on administrative and other changes that took place in the Institute.

In December 1961, Council authorized the setting up of a Special Sub-committee 'to consider and make recommendations to the Policy and Finance Committee with particular reference to membership policy and recruitment to the profession'. The terms of reference were also to review the financial situation and to make recommendations as to suitable alternative premises. This important brief had a wide scope: no wonder that Policy and Finance Committee at first thought that the group should be called 'The Future of the Institute Committee'.

The pressures that had been building up in the fifties could not be contained much longer. Planning had been in the doldrums for some years and there was a restiveness with many aspects of the scene. The Institute might now have its Charter, but it could not rest on that. In urban planning authorities, one dissatisfaction began with the question of the continued lowly status of the planning officer. In 1961, out of 83 County Boroughs in England and Wales 76 had a planning officer who was also chief architect or engineer/surveyor, sometimes all three. In 42 cases the planning officer was not a member of the Institute. In Metropolitan Boroughs only 6 out of 29 planning officers were members, and in Scottish Boroughs 12 out of 24 were members of the Institute. G. E. Cherry argued, in 1962, that enhanced local authority status was overdue: 'Recent successes at Newcastle, Sunderland, Leicester and Newport should be regarded as Battle Honours in a war of attrition, designed to secure professional recognition.'[6] A year later the Journal carried an open letter to the President and Council of the TPI from J. C. Holliday and A. S. Travis, to the effect that they were glad to see the recent policy statement by the Institute regarding the establishment of separate City Planning Departments, but making a plea for policies to be outlined on a wide range of planning issues, including planning education[7]. These comments were from a critical rank and file, but official utterances still tended to be complacent. At the General Meeting of the Institute in November 1962, for example, J. G. Jefferson, the retiring President, perhaps alluding to the title of Keeble's book *Town Planning at the Crossroads*, published in 1961, said that a year ago some thought that the Institute stood at the crossroads; today it seemed to him that the road lay clear ahead[8]. D. W. Riley, the new President, spoke of change in the world, and therefore the need for planning, but hardly foresaw the traumas of the next decade[9].

The Committee set up eleven months previously was already working. L. W. Lane became Chairman; a well regarded member of the Institute, later to become President (1964), he was a past Planning Officer of London, and currently Advisor to the Civic Trust. In March 1963, his Committee issued an Interim Report, which was generally well received by Council. In May its Final Report, *Recruitment and Membership*, was issued and subsequently sent out to Branches for comments by October that year. It was a four page memorandum of short, succinct statements. It stated that a deep inquiry on the philosophy, theory and practice of town and country planning had been made and suggested what the future pattern of membership of the Institute should be. Paragraph 3 read simply that: 'By a majority we have concluded that changes of a radical nature are needed.' Therein contained all the seeds of years of debate: a majority verdict concealed an anxious minority; the radical changes were not to everyone's liking.

The problem was expressed in the memorandum in terms of what the changing demands of planning required; the solution was seen as a reconciliation between the generalist and the specialist. The following may be quoted at length because, in representing the opening shot in the war of the 1960s, it also became the point to which the argument frequently returned: 'The scope of planning today has widened to such an extent that it is no longer possible for any one person to become an expert in each of the varied subjects with which it is concerned. What is needed essentially is a team job requiring the bringing together under effective leadership, many different skills, all working to the same end. To meet this challenge, our fundamental proposition is that the profession should embrace, within its corporate membership, both generalists and specialists all of whom will be trained to be members of the planning team. Some of the members can have a general grasp of the planning field as a whole. Others will take their places making a specialist contribution. But all must have a basic knowledge of the essential elements of planning practice, theory and law, and it is this common purpose and interest which should be the distinctive characteristic of the planning profession.' It followed from this that the examination syllabus should be revised.

The memorandum went on to consider classes of membership, the contribution of the Planning Schools, trainee schemes and the place of practical experience. Returning to the need to broaden the Institute's membership, two proposals were made which were to receive some later prominence. The first was that direct membership of the Institute, previously applicable to persons of at least 50 years of age, who had attained special eminence in and made a special contribution to town planning, should now be extended to cover persons of 45 years of age. The second recommended that serious consideration be given to widening the range of degrees recognized by the Institute as giving exemption from the Institute's Intermediate Examination.

Branch comments provided wider opinion when Council considered the memorandum again in November. Discussion centred inevitably on the controversial proposals regarding membership and education, and these were referred back to the Special Committee. Lane relinquished the Chair and the immediate Past President, D. W. Riley, took over. More significantly, C. D. Buchanan by this time had become President; he was keen to make progress in liberalizing entry to the planning profession, and this reflected his recognition of the breadth and composite nature of planning activity as described in *Traffic in Towns*. In June 1964, towards the end of his Presidency, Council resolutions were passed which committed the Institute to major changes in matters of entry and examinations.

But the Annual General Meeting of the Institute that month revealed unease at the hint of reforms then being considered. Thomas Sharp felt that the views of the membership should be obtained by referendum and an Associate Member, Paul Kriesis, asked for clarification of the Council's intentions. Buchanan hinted at the possibility of further consultation with the Branches. A Special Meeting of Council, in October, served to bring matters to a head. On this occasion, Keeble was critical of Buchanan's haste in finalizing the matter, and Hellier, a Past President, proposed that the membership be consulted further. This line was adopted and two documents were dispatched to all corporate members in December, with a request for replies before the end of January 1965.

Council was taking decisive action, and there were insistent voices that it should. But it was not acting in isolation, there being a number of pressures influencing it in this direction. The wider context of planning became more and more obvious; important societal changes to which planning must respond, were now becoming apparent. J. R. James, for example, in a Journal paper called 'The Next Fifty Years' pointed comprehensively to the questions of economic trends and technological progress, population growth and its new distribution, growth of leisure and the need for research[10]. It was also significant that 1964 was Golden Jubilee Year. Meetings that year brought a lot of people together from a wide background; at the Golden Jubilee Dinner in March there were 520 members and their guests, and the Jubilee Conference was attended by 800. Planning was exposed briefly to national gaze, and thoughts were focused on its potential and limitation. Some took the chance of making important reflections. Dame Evelyn Sharp, for example, considered that 'Planning will not wait, and we, the clients cannot wait. What is going to happen in the planning field in the next five years is so tremendous that I think the people engaged in planning are going to take charge, unless you yourselves can take charge. The question in my mind is whether the Institute can find a way of adapting its policies to the facts.'[11] This observation was being made in other circles too, particularly in the light of the debate on *Traffic in Towns*. Planning had a good press from Buchanan's work, but it was the team work approach advocated by him that was seen increasingly as the basis for future planning, perhaps to the embarrassment of those in the profession who preferred a different role for the planner.

Although it was scarcely appreciated at the time, a fundamentally new recognition of planning was being made. So far, the design bias of planning had been unchallenged, inherited from the concepts and methods of engineering and architecture. Consequently, Abercrombie's plan for Greater London in 1944, the urban strategies throughout Britain which followed it, and the 1947 Development Plan system had all seen the urban problem in land-use, design terms. Town planning was an activity which prepared and implemented schemes for future spatial, physical forms. But it was now being dimly perceived that planning could be something very different: intervention in, or guidance of a sequence of events—in other words, *process*. This concept was a much wider planning method, one which encompassed explicit formulation of objectives, evaluation of alternatives and monitoring of results. It took a long time for this new recognition to take root (and in the event, articulation depended a good deal on contributions by American planners) but from the early sixties there developed an awareness that future notions of town planning might be rather different from those of the past. Doubts as to what planning was all about troubled many; some who recognized the force of the new insights saw the need for changing professional positions; those who preferred to rely on trusty concepts of the past were forced into defensive postures. The situation in the mid-sixties was tailor-made for deep conflict.

Leslie Lane's Presidential Address in 1964 underlined the matter of change in no uncertain manner. He said he was the fifth President in a row to hammer away at this topic, and quoted Nicholas in 1960, Jefferson in 1961, Riley in 1962 and Buchanan who, in 1963, had devoted the whole of his Address to these matters. He referred to one of the objectives set out in Clause 4 of the Royal Charter: 'The objects of the Chartered Institute shall be the securing of the association of those engaged or interested, professionally or otherwise, in town planning and the promotion of their general interests.' He went on: 'We have celebrated long enough the achievement of a Royal Charter. We can no longer duck the issue, that having achieved this status, it lays upon us an obligation of understanding of service to the country which is broader than some of us realize. The design and control of our physical environment has now turned out to be of such momentum and importance that it is a matter of national concern, involving approaches from widely differing attitudes. The dilemma which confronts us as a professional Institute is to uphold, on the one hand, progressive and austere professional, educational and creative standards in the field of our endeavour and, on the other hand, to so widen our membership, that we do quite genuinely constitute a more comprehensive professional forum on town planning, which will be respected, much more than it now is, by government; by people at large and by other professional bodies.'[12] The wind of change could not now be denied. All too quickly there were gale warnings.

Of the Council's documents sent to members in December 1964 one was a memorandum entitled *Membership Policy*, a short report explaining the basis of the Council's proposals. The second was essentially a voting card to record agreement or disagreement with three resolutions. These were as follows:

(1) 'that the policy for corporate membership shall extend ... the privilege of member-

ship to all persons making a professional contribution to planning of a general or specialist kind';

(2) that 'the examination requirements of the Institute be revised to make them appropriate to the new membership policy so as to provide for those who wish to qualify over the whole field of planning and for those who wish to specialize in some part of it ...';

(3) 'that for a period of two years only the Council may admit to corporate membership persons of 40 years of age or over, who are qualified in a related discipline, and are known to be contributing substantially to planning, subject to a professional interview and to such tests as the Council may require.'

As the explanatory document indicated, the modifications to membership policy were proposed so that membership could be broadened in order to admit qualified members of the planning team to corporate membership even though the nature of their individual contributions might vary. It was also seen necessary to facilitate entry to corporate membership of people of 'mature judgement and experience' who, although they had not sought membership through the existing channels, nevertheless had manifestly demonstrated their ability to contribute to planning. Assurances in the document were given that this was not a dilution of planning; the idea of the 'comprehensive planner' was still valid; the proposals did not involve 'backdoor' entry to membership; and the needs of the present membership were well safeguarded. Once again came the reminder about time: for three years this had been discussed and the prevarication and uncertainty which was now associated with the Institute had not gone unnoticed by other bodies. The time for action and decisions had come.

But the issues were professional dynamite, and the fuse had been lit. The significance of the pressures of change which had begun to crowd upon planning, and the role which the Institute should play in the new situation, were only dimly perceived: perhaps not at all by the majority of members, certainly only by a relative few. Those who were already engaged in planning where team operations had developed, or had seen the evidence in other countries, particularly America, needed little persuasion that the Council proposals were on the right lines. But many reacted quite differently: suspicion of the non-TPI chief officer who might be gaining admittance to membership through his status; reluctance to widen membership of a body to which they themselves had only just won hard earned admission (the products of the new Planning Schools with their singular qualification were amongst these); confusion as to what was happening; and, hostility against a Council (and certain members) who were felt to be steamrolling the proposal to a speedy, and probably wrong, conclusion.

In January, Thomas Sharp and 28 other corporate members requested the convening of an Extraordinary General Meeting to discuss the two documents. This was held on the 29th of the month in Church House, London. A full account of this meeting, published later in the Journal, revealed the fears and hopes that contributed to that charged occasion[13].

After an introduction by the President, Sharp spoke vigorously in colourful language. He thought the memorandum one-sided and tendentious, and as a method of obtaining support, he 'had never heard of such extraordinary procedures outside a totalitarian regime'. He thought the arguments advanced about town planning and team work 'damnable and pernicious nonsense'. The nub of his objection was that the Institute was a separate and distinct profession. It was beyond his understanding that the Council had 'allowed itself to become so bemused by these specious arguments about teamwork as actually itself to become the instrument of our destruction'. There was a further objection. Sharp thought the conduct of the Council over the Meeting to be incompetent. Resolutions could have been passed if three weeks' notice of the meeting had been given. The Secretary had received Sharp's request on 7 January, and, because of the need to arrange the Meeting before the date on which submissions were due (31 January, a Sunday), it meant that the EGM had to be held on 29 January. Three weeks' notice was not possible: regulations allowed the Secretary up to 14 days to obtain advice, issue notices, and take other necessary administrative steps. Therefore, this meeting was not one at which resolutions could be passed. There was some criticism of the Secretary and the Council in this, but the President soundly defended their actions.

A number of speakers followed, mainly against the Council's proposals. J. J. Brooks, past Chairman of Education Committee, thought that 'what is now proposed is simply easier entry with lowering of professional standards, a procedure which would not be tolerated by any other profession.' Sir William Holford thought the Institute should not debase their currency, and stressed the individuality of the planner: 'If they (the public) cannot tell the difference between a qualified and practised town planner on the one hand, and an architect, an engineer, a surveyor, an auctioneer, or an estate agent ... then our profession has no future.' Professor R. H. Kantorowich had severe misgivings about educational policy and thought the Institute's proposals clearly 'off course'. G. A. Atkinson asked 'what it is, precisely, that the Council are getting at', so echoing the bewilderment of many. E. A. Rose, on the other hand, spoke on the results of a meeting held in the City Planning Department, Manchester, which had given opinions in favour of resolutions one and two, but against number three. G. Grenfell Bains also spoke in favour; so too did T. F. W. Clarke, a Council member. T. Morton reflected another commonly held view that the plea to liberalize entry to membership was no more than a disgraceful attempt to raise numbers. L. B. Keeble, Senior Vice-President, left the Meeting in no doubt about his opposition and hinted at lack of loyalty by some members of the Council: he did 'not think the first allegiance of all members is to the Institute'. His criticism was just as severe as Sharp's had been; he reacted vehemently against the Council's views on team work, the idea of specialists in planning and the proposals of the Education Committee. The debate swung the other way again with L. B. Ginsburg who regretted a trade unionist attitude among members of the Institute. D. G. Robinson referred to the separate and special way of looking at things that characterized planners. R. W. Dale tried to take the heat out of the situation, but Buchanan found it necessary to stress once again the issues which Council had faced: the choice was to remain a small and uninfluential Institute, or to take a very much wider view. Finally Sharp persisted in putting his proposition (not a resolution because this was not constitutionally possible) that the Council should take no further action on the memorandum, that the questionnaire should be disregarded, and that any future questionnaire should be 'conducted on proper democratic lines'. The meeting supported this proposition by a 75 per cent majority.

Next month the results of the questionnaire became available. The replies from 1 718 forms returned were

	Agree	Disagree	Indefinite
Resolution 1	784	914	20
Resolution 2	880	812	24
Resolution 3	532	1 158	16

The views received from the Branches indicated many objections, although there was support in a number of cases for resolutions one and two.

This was a serious reverse for Council. They could claim that the issues on which the new proposals had been formulated were not understood, but there was no doubt that the proposals had raised a combination of suspicion and hostility. Moreover, the Council could be criticized for the way it had handled the situation. With hindsight, we can now say that this was a 'learning process'. The techniques of conducting an examination of membership issues and related matters of great sensitivity simply had to be learned the hard way. Assertions of what was required was not enough; there had to be a reasoned argument. Moreover, it could not be rushed; in the end it took 10 years for a consensus to be arrived at.

In March, 1965, an *ad hoc* Committee composed of the Chairman of the Standing Committees and Honorary Officers was appointed to consider further progress. It was left in no doubt as to the mood of the profession. The membership voted with their feet and at the Council elections of June 1965, there were some surprises: Sharp came back on to the Council, heading the poll, and some old stalwarts including J. S. Allen, M. J. Hellier, J. G. Jefferson and D. W. Riley, all Past Presidents, were not re-elected. Arthur Ling, Junior Vice-President, was not elected, and W. Burns took his place.

The arguments continued to be rehearsed. In a Journal paper at this time, J. B. McLoughlin from the University of Manchester considered directions which the planning profession should follow. He was in tune with those who had reacted so strongly against the Council's proposals. He put the options starkly: 'As long as planning is regarded primarily as physical design, construction and development writ large, people trained and skilled in such fields will feel justified in making claims to professional recognition as planners too. As long as the conception of planning remains flabbily eclectic it will be harried and prodded by sharper minds and in this form it may eventually die the death of a thousand cuts.' He went on: 'Planning is too important to be entrusted to a team of 57 varieties and must have a professional institute which is proud to represent a unique skill rather than to be a club for interested participants.'[14] This seemed to be just what the Institute wanted to hear. (With hindsight, it is a surprise to reflect how sharply McLoughlin's views on planning and the profession were to change over the next few years, see p. 254.)

On the other hand from Anthony Goss came a Report which kept alive a different viewpoint. In December 1962, he had been commissioned by the RIBA to examine the architect's contribution to and training for town planning. He was assisted by a Steering Committee chaired by Arthur Ling. A full-time research assistant was M. J. Croft, who supplemented data provided by a TPI survey of membership in April 1962. Goss's Report, *The Architect and Town Planning* (1965), drew attention to the inadequacies of the qualifications and experience of planning of many senior local government officers. As a general conclusion it was observed that 'all the professions traditionally engaged in planning, as well as newcomers to the field, must appreciate how much inter-professional jealousies inhibit the progress of planning, and must be prepared to sink their rivalries in a serious attempt to develop inter-professional training and inter-professional collaboration in mixed teams.'[15] The Report, published in May 1965, had a mixed reception, being a victim of its timing as much as anything else. Events in the TPI membership controversy almost guaranteed difficulties for it, and the Steering Committee's accompanying Report was interpreted by some as a take-over bid of planning by the RIBA. Furthermore, perhaps the RIBA had hoped for more so that they could use it to press for independent RIBA planning qualifications in Urban Design; in fact from this quarter the Report came to a quiet end.

1965 was Lewis Keeble's Presidential Year, and he took the opportunity in his Address of giving his version of the membership issue. He considered that 'It really started innocently enough with a suggestion that architects and engineers might be deterred from qualifying as town planners by having to take papers in the Institute's final examinations on subjects which they had already, at least partly, covered in the course of acquiring their entry qualifications ... It was next suggested that architects were further discouraged from embarking on a planning career because it already took them so long to acquire their architectural qualification that the additional time customarily spent in taking a planning qualification was likely to mean that they would be about 30 years old before they were qualified in both.' The next arguments were that there were really two different kinds of planner, the generalist and the specialist, and that planning was a team job. This was Keeble's version, and the extract has been quoted at length to show just how widely apart were the two sides in the argument; their perceptions of the issues and what was required was totally different. With powerful personalities in the battle, no wonder emotions were so roused. But one thing was certain: as Keeble remarked of the recent election, 'the result was a complete success for the candidates who before the election jointly declared their view that the Town Planning Institute should be an independent body representing an independent profession.'[16]

This was not to say that those who argued differently had given up. In the Journal in which Keeble's Address was published, Arthur Ling had a letter to the Editor on membership policy: 'We cannot ignore the reality of the planning situation today when a great many town planning projects are, in fact, being dealt with by teams which include specialists as well as generalists... The scope of town planning now is broadening and its complexities are increasing. If the Town Planning Institute allows only for a membership of one rigid pattern, then we may well see moves to establish new institutes of, say, transportation planning or regional planning.' He went on to propose a new class of Associate Members for specialist contributors to planning; to avoid ambiguities over titles, present Associate Members would become Members, and Members would become Fellows.

Early in 1966 a new document emerged from Policy and Finance Committee. Eventually this became a booklet entitled *Progress Report on Membership Policy*, circulated to members in May 1967. It explained the evolution of Council policy on membership and the beginnings of revising the examination syllabus, against a new statement of Council policy adopted in December 1965 and January 1966. The new policy stated:

(1) that membership be 'open only to those who, after a systematic training, have passed tests of examination and experience to demonstrate that they have adequate knowledge, skill and sense of professional responsibility to engage in Town Planning throughout its full range'.

(2) that Council consider the setting up of a new non-corporate class of membership to be called an 'affiliated' or 'subscriber' class, entry by nomination or invitation. This was for those engaged in a field contributory to town and country planning, but who did not represent themselves to be town and country planners.

It followed that the Education Committee now had to review its tests of membership and hold discussions with academic and professional bodies on the training of skills contributory to town planning.

The document, and indeed the proposals, had aims which were both internal and external to the Institute. Wounds had to be healed, and there had to be a coming to terms with a changing conception of planning. In the event, a discussion document written in measured tones and with reasoned argument, was a significantly different document from the short, assertive reports of previous years. It was nonetheless quite decisive and put forward views of singular confidence. The argument was that town planning was a process in which activity 'the chartered planner plays the central and crucial professional role'. His special skill qualified him to organize and co-ordinate all planning operations, and to design and control the implementation of the plan or policy. Other disciplines or professions participating in this process were contributors. Much hinged on the examination policy which sought to control the generalist philosophy, and this is described in chapter 9.

Action had already been taken on the question of contributory skills. Representatives of professional Institutes and learned societies responsible for the education of the various contributory skills in the planning process were invited to a conference at the Institute in April, opened by Frederick Willey, Minister of State at the Ministry of Housing and Local Government. This was Lichfield's particular contribution; appointed to the Chair of Economics of Town Planning at London in October 1966, he was a member of a number of professional bodies, and his breadth of interest extended to the newly founded Regional Studies Association. In his Presidential Address[17] he made it clear that he thought the Council was on the right lines in attempting to secure harmonious collaborations of the professions in land use planning, without entering into the difficulties of trying to bring into one Institute all the professions concerned with planning.

Events were now less dramatic. Lichfield's emphasis on contributory skills served to take the heat off the situation. Burns, too, in his Presidential Address in October 1967[18] praised the idea of greater co-operation with other professions and it was clearly politic not to inflame passions unnecessarily at this time. Work was going on concerning a revision of the education syllabus, embodying the generalist approach, but this was a lengthy process and could only have its effect in the long term. It was not until Professor R. H. Kantorowich's paper 'Education for Planning' given at a General Meeting of the Institute in April 1967[19] that the outline of the Education Committee's scheme became widely known (see p. 228).

Overall, the period 1966–68 was one of relative quiet after the happenings of 1964–65.

But although the difference in approach between various protagonists of planning thought were temporarily obscured, they flared into prominence on certain occasions. An example was the paper given by Thomas Sharp at the Hastings Conference in May 1966 in which his philosophy of planning was exposed as starkly different from many other professional members. He condemned out of hand the recent Report of the Planning Advisory Group, describing it as 'a hopelessly unbalanced and dangerous document'[20]. He was taken to task by two members of the Group. In discussion, Burns commented that 'even the greatest minds once in a while lapse into absurdities or go astray. I fear that this is what has happened to our notable speaker today'; Bor remarked that 'Dr Sharp is now fighting the wrong battle'. This exchange served to highlight the very different way planning was regarded between those of dissimilar backgrounds, experience and intellectual persuasions. The new style of planning, the assumptions on which it was based, and the implications which it raised, were anathema to some.

In June 1967 the Journal gave some interesting statistics on membership during the previous 30 years. Election to Associate Member over that period was summarized as follows:

	1936–46	1946–56	1956–66	
Direct entry planner	7.6	22.2	39.8	
Architects	51.2	45.4	27.5	
Engineers	24.2	14.3	4.5	per cent
Surveyors	8.45	9.1	6.9	
Other degrees (e.g. geography)	8.45	9.0	22.5	
	447	1 126	1 239	number

There were striking differences to record, particularly over the last decade. The direct entry planner now formed the majority annual intake; architects, engineers and surveyors were not entering the profession in their previous proportions, while those from a different academic background were increasing rapidly—particularly from the social sciences, especially geography. The data could be interpreted variously but there could be no dispute that membership structure had changed. Perhaps the realities of the situation were becoming more widely appreciated. Certainly there were indications of changing attitudes, and there was a good deal of adverse comment from the Branch meetings on the proposed affiliate/subscriber class when the Institute's document of May 1967 was circulated.

Another factor we should note in the period of the mid and late 1960s was the emergence of the student voice in shaping Institute opinion. The Association of Student Planners (ASP) was formed in May 1964 at a meeting held in the Department of Civic Design, University of Liverpool, attended by representatives from six recognized Planning Schools. A consolidating conference was held shortly afterwards in Newcastle. An early achievement of the Association was its publication of *Planning Education* in October 1966. It pointed to several disturbing features in the state of planning education and to the wide gap of understanding that existed between students in Planning Schools and the Institute. The Association used its available space well in the Journal with notes of a distinctive radical view. Its searchlight on planning and Institute affairs helped to sharpen a critical approach amongst younger members. ASP eventually became the Junior Members' Forum, and student representation on Council and its Committees was obtained.

By 1968 there were signs that the membership/education policy was again bursting into life as an Institute issue. There were many signs of a changing situation. Outside the Institute there was increasing adverse criticism against the avowed claim of the TPI for primacy amongst the many bodies engaged in the planning process. Within the Institute Sharp was now no longer a member of Council and Keeble left to take up a Readership at the University of Queensland—important departures because these were people with personal followings in the affair of 1965. Within the membership as a whole there continued to be expressions of belief, as under Lane and Buchanan, that the Institute must change to adequately encompass and reflect the 'new planning'. Arthur Ling, Head of the Department of Civic Architecture and Planning at Nottingham, was now President and in his Presidential Address of October 1968 the issue was once again exposed: 'One thing we can be sure of is that the scope of planning will need to be even wider and more comprehensive during the next ten years and it should draw in even more disciplines into its theory and practice ... The full range of planning is already beyond the scope of a planning syllabus or a practice except on a very general basis, and it is becoming necessary for planners to concentrate at least some of their efforts into spheres of activity within the full range ... The Institute's title has long been out of date as a description of its now wider interests and perhaps the time has come for us to decide on a change to a new title "The Planning Institute".'[21]

Events now quickened, and the Institute came under pressure, internally and externally. The wheel of fortune had changed with a vengeance. In the early 1960s a majority of the Council of the Institute, in the face of no great interest to those outside the profession, attempted to lead opinion by advocating a widening of planning practice and a liberalizing of its membership and education policy. It was defeated in this. But the issues on which the debate was based remained unresolved, and increasingly it was found that the Institute was not in a position to determine its own future. The issues lay outside as well as inside the Institute and the Sharp–Keeble line looked less and less likely to hold support. Severe criticism of the Council's policy was now encountered and the arguments became sharper as doubts were expressed about the role of professions in contemporary society and about the very idea of professionalism. Within the Institute new voices advocated wider approaches to planning. F. J. C. Amos and J. S. Millar resurrected the generalist/specialist debate at the January 1969 Council. Amos' paper to a General Meeting in February left no doubts as to his view about the breadth of planning[22]. Whereas earlier in the sixties the case for widening planning had very much a transportation base, now the case extended to social planning, the broad social and economic context of planning and the new field of corporate planning. Above all, the new structure plan process implied a wider operation of planning.

Other difficulties concerned education. In October 1968 it had been learned that the RIBA was considering the establishment of an Urban Design Diploma. This raised important implications, and Education Committee came under some pressure from the President's Advisory Committee to give greater recognition to specialist interests in the syllabus. In 1970, the TPI agreed to consider the RIBA's Urban Design Diploma for recognition if satisfactions could be given on other requirements. This was the tip of an iceberg. The late sixties had seen the emergence in Universities of a number of planning oriented courses of study, which could not be recognized by the Institute under its education policy. Academic needs seemed out of step with Council policy on membership and education.

The questions of who was a planner and what was planning were raised more insistently. One example was when D. E. C. Eversley was appointed Chief Strategic Planner to the GLC in 1969; with no TPI qualifications he was the subject of raised professional eyebrows. More importantly, Lady Sharp's report *Transport Planning: The Men For The Job* (1970) made little reference to the TPI and its contribution to this field. Once again, the issue was what sort of Institute was needed to meet the needs of planning then and in the future. The long haul of restructuring the Council's policies began all over again. A change in personalities was again significant. On the education front, an important figure to leave the scene was Professor Kantorowich, who was not re-elected in the Council elections of June 1970.

The early meetings of the 1971 Council were devoted to a new approach on the membership question, and a Discussion Paper drawn up under the direction of Sylvia Law, *Town Planners and Their Future*, was circulated to members in December. Comments from Branches and individuals were requested by March 1972. This Paper which proposed and discussed options for the Institute to follow, was very different from its predecessors. The early ones had contained relatively little by way of explanation; they had been assertive and asked for early decisions. In 1967, there had been more reasoned argument, but the conclusions were remarkably self-confident in tone, claiming a role for the Chartered Planner which later judgement found to be exaggerated. Now, in the light of contemporary change, a range of seven options was postulated for the Institute to follow:

(1) The Planning Society, a learned society, covering the field of corporate/economic/social and environmental planning, with membership open to all engaged or interested in planning as a process.

(2) Institute of Planning, relating to the field of corporate/economic/social and environmental planning.

(3) Institute of Community Planning, concerned with economic, social and environmental planning.

(4) Institute of Environmental Planning, adapting the profession to one which included all those concerned with planning the physical environment.

(5) Institute of Environmental Planning, maintaining and reinforcing the preoccupation with the total physical environment of town and country, but adapting the profession to include all those directly involved in the physical planning process; also to relate the process of physical planning to corporate planning.

(6) Town Planning Institute, with the present boundaries of concern, but with the objective of securing the association to those engaged or interested in town planning.

(7) Town Planning Institute, with the present boundaries, with no change being made to its membership or education policies.

At Council in April 1972 it was learned that there was a clear preference for (5) above, option 4A in the Institute's Paper, although the idea of the Institute of Planning appealed

26 Portland Place, London, the Institute's latest premises. It is one of a terrace of distinguished brick and stucco houses designed by the Adam brothers about 1770, and facing west over Portland Place. The lower part is occupied by the Royal Society of Tropical Medicine and Hygiene, but over 4 000 sq ft of accommodation is still left for R.T.P.I. purposes.

Knights Bachelor, Birthday Honours, 1967. (R) Sir Frederick Gibberd, architect planner for Harlow New Town, planning and landscape consultant with a large range of commissioned work. (L) Sir Hugh Wilson, Planning Officer for Canterbury and later Cumbernauld; subsequently in private practice, joined by J. Lewis Womersley.

to many. Accordingly the 1972/73 Council charged itself to amend its membership and education policies, and in August 1973 a further Discussion Paper was circulated to all members: *Town Planners and Their Future: Implications of Changes in Education and Membership Policy.*

With regard to membership, the system of membership application based on evidence of practical experience in more than one aspect of planning was abandoned in 1973 and a new method of application drawn up. The generalist obligations for practical experience 'in the full range' were withdrawn. The nature of experience now 'may be generalist or specialist; it may be broad-based or contributory to one field; it may be gained in team work or in an individual capacity; it may relate to research, teaching, public service or private practice.' Concerning education, more opportunities for innovation or experiment are proposed. Less standardization in planning syllabi is suggested, and specialist concentrations in subject matter recommended. Overall, a basic objective enshrined in the Discussion Paper is a more flexible approach in both membership and education policy compared with the Council document of May 1967.

A ten-year story seems to be coming full circle. The membership in 1972 accepted a viewpoint which was very similar to that suggested in the proposals of Lane and Buchanan, put forward (though not quite for the same reasons) in 1963–65. The Keeble–Sharp position has not been sustained; neither has the Kantorowich education policy. The 1973 proposals represent a more assured, flexible datum line from which further evolutionary changes no doubt will develop.

Three other items concerned with membership remain to be considered: legal membership, planning technicians, and status of membership.

In the early years of the Institute's history lawyers occupied a near equal position to architects, engineers and surveyors. 'Lex' formed a central part of the crest of the Institute. But the importance of the Legal Member faded, and after 1945 only two, Howard Roberts and Desmond Heap, became Presidents. In 1964 their position was considerably affected by the general aim of the Privy Council, to discourage the use of designatory letters for partially qualified persons. Although there was a view within the Institute that the legal classes caused no confusion with planners proper, the Council in that year proposed to discontinue designatory letters for Legal Members. Although there continued to be regret about this demise, the fundamental objection of the Privy Council remained and in 1967 it was agreed that the Legal Associate Member class should be phased out. In October 1970 it was resolved that the whole corporate class of legal membership should be discontinued after 1st January 1975. This arrangement was incorporated in the revised Charter of 1971.

The question of planning technicians assumed importance with the technical developments of planning during the sixties. Under TPI sponsorship various ONC and HNC courses were started for the training of town planning technicians. The Institute, both centrally and through the Branches, took the initial steps, prepared draft syllabuses and gave encouragement to the development of the courses. In 1971 a Society of Town Planning Technicians was formed following joint meetings of Institute representatives and technicians.

Under the revised Charter classes of membership of the Institute were changed to bring designations more in line with other professions. Members became Fellows, and Associate Members became Members. This seemed a small point, but it served to draw attention to the distinction between classes of membership. Anomalies had crept in over the years and one result was that Fellows had proportionately much more representation on Council than was justified numerically. In fact progression from Member to Fellow had long since ceased to be a normal event for a mature person aged 30 or over; there were suggestions that the Fellowship class had been devalued through neglect and that the system of a two-tier membership structure had fallen into default. The anomaly of numerical proportion and Council representation remains a discussion point.

This chapter concludes by considering a number of administrative and internal matters with which the Institute was concerned during this period. These related to premises, staff and finance, and committee structure.

In June 1960 Philip Rathbone succeeded Alfred Potter as Secretary of the Institute. He was no stranger to the planning world, having been Secretary of the Housing Centre in London before the war, and afterwards (successively) a member of the Ministry of Town and Country Planning, the National Parks Commission and latterly Secretary of the Scottish Branch of RICS. The Institute is remarkable for the fact that it has only had two Secretaries in its 60 years: both have been dedicated servants contributing much to stability and continuity. The long service of L. Whitfield and C. E. J. Herd, stalwart administrators at Headquarters, was recognized by Council in 1972. Robert Williams has been a valuable new recruit as Senior Administrative Assistant to share an ever-increasing work load of Institute business. Successive Editors of the Journal (latterly Michael Wright, Harold Lewis, Mark Pritchard, and currently Margaret Cox) have transformed the appearance of the Journal in a number of different layouts and designs.

In 1964 the Institute left 18 Ashley Place and moved to its present premises, 26 Portland Place. Ashley Place was included in a major redevelopment scheme and no long-term renewal of the lease could be expected. The premises were demolished in 1971. The new premises, part of the original Adams terrace houses situated north of Oxford Circus, gave a total floor area of over 4 000 square feet compared with the 2 500 square feet in Ashley Place.

The new premises were, of course, an added financial strain, but extra burdens were being carried anyway as the total scale of the Institute's work increased markedly in the sixties. It is not surprising that there has been a recurrent theme of financial problems. At the AGM of 1964 membership subscriptions were raised considerably: from 9 to 15 gns for 'home' Members and from 7 to 12 gns for Associate Members and from 2 to 3 gns for students. Overseas subscriptions were less. A combination of inflation and the increase in Institute work necessitated a further rise in subscriptions, taking effect from 1971: 'home' Members to £21, Associate Members to £17. 10. 0 (£17.50) and students to £4. 10. 0 (£4.50).

The enforced shortage of staff, from which the Institute has long suffered, threw extra weight on the system of Institute Committees. A number of modifications were made during the sixties to make their work more effective. Functions which for a long time had been the prerogative of individuals, particularly Pepler and Potter, now had to be formalized, and new mechanisms were evolved. The last Committee restructuring had been in 1957.

One particular weakness was the burden of work that was falling on the Education Committee as membership applications were increasing.

In 1964 membership was split from education, and Practice Committee became Public Relations and Practice Committee. A President's Special Committee was created; its work soon ranged from general matters to important policy. In 1967 it was decided to reduce the number of Council meetings in a normal session from ten to seven and to give greater responsibility to Standing Committees. Policy and Finance became known as Finance and General Purposes, and the President's Advisory Group was instituted, so returning in a sense to the informal shaping of policy that took place in the Pepler–Potter era. In 1969, Research Committee ceased to become a Standing Committee and was re-constituted as an Advisory Group, allowing membership to be extended to non-TPI members. Public Relations and Practice Committee was renamed Professional Activities. In 1973 a more fundamental restructuring took place with a reduction of Standing Committees to two, one dealing with Internal Affairs and the other with External Affairs. Each is composed of Council members and Branch representatives on Council, and two students nominated by Junior Members' Forum. Each is concerned with policy, and matters of detail are the responsibility of Boards with a wider membership. Lastly, we should note changes in the election procedure of Council, specified in the Supplemental Charter of 1971: only half the members retire each year, election therefore being for a two year service.

This last period of the Institute's history has been one of great change. Stalwart figures in the life of the Institute have now passed, and increasingly the Institute is composed of and governed by people who have not shared in the corporate traditions and outlooks of the past. Louis de Soissons, designer of Welwyn, died in 1962; Lord Samuel, an Honorary Member of the Institute since 1915, who succeeded John Burns at the Local Government Board, died in 1963. Lieutenant Colonel Henry Philip Cart de la Fontaine, an Associate Member as early as 1917, President in 1950–51, died the same year. E. G. Allen, in practice as an architect and town planning consultant since 1905, and President in 1936–37, died in 1964. The next year there followed the death of William Dobson Chapman, President in 1943. In 1968, A. R. Potter, secretary of the Institute from 1914 to 1960 died at the age of 76. J. W. R. Adams, son of Thomas Adams died in 1969, M. J. Hellier in 1970, Lord Silkin in 1972 and F. Longstreth Thompson, stepbrother to George Pepler in 1973. With these men there passed a whole generation for whom planning had represented much in their lives. From now on the Institute was served increasingly by those who were not tied to the shackles of the past.

These losses served to compound the difficulties which the Institute experienced during this period: adjustment to the great changes in town planning affairs and the traumas within the profession. Nonetheless, the Institute ended the period stronger than it began it. Foremost local government planners in city and county occupy the Presidential Chair, bringing prestige to their authorities and power to the Institute. In earlier years it is true to say that not all Presidents were nationally known figures; more recently they invariably have been. In recent years Presidents have represented some powerful and well known authorities: Burns (Newcastle), Bor and Amos (Liverpool), Turnbull (Devon), Double-day (Hertfordshire), Millar and Nicholas (Manchester), Coates (Lancashire), Riley (Staffordshire) and so on. Membership has increased almost to the 10 000 mark, and its growth shows no signs of slackening. More and more members attained prominence in professional life, and national honours, including life Peers and Knights Bachelor, came their way. Professional influence has extended throughout government circles, both central and local. Its institutional status has been further enhanced: following application in 1970 through the Home Office, permission was granted in 1971 to use the prefix Royal in the Institute's title.

No profession stands still, and the issues of the later seventies are now being forged. Perhaps they relate to the role of professions in society: what is important in professional life, and what has professionalism to offer in the last decades of the twentieth century? How can professional people be best educated to cope with issues in a rapidly changing world? The next two chapters on education and other professional matters refer to these and related questions.

References

1. Dower, Michael, *Fourth Wave, The Challenge of Leisure*. Civic Trust, 1965. (*Architects' Journal*, 20 January 1965.)
2. Heap, Sir Desmond, Professions and Professionalism: What Next? *Chartered Surveyor*, **106**, No. 1, 1973.
3. *Passenger Transport in Great Britain 1971*, Department of the Environment. HMSO, 1973.
4. *Traffic in Towns*. HMSO, 1963.
5. Eddison, Tony, *Local Government: Management and Corporate Planning*. Leonard Hill Books, Aylesbury, 1973.
6. Cherry, Gordon E., The Town Planner and His Profession. *Journal of the Town Planning Institute*, **XLVIII**, No. 5, 1962.
7. *Journal of the Town Planning Institute*, **LVIII**, No. 5, 151, 1963.
8. *Journal of the Town Planning Institute*, **XLVIII**, No. 10, 306, 1962.
9. Riley, D. W., Presidential Address. *Journal of the Town Planning Institute*, **XLVIII**, No. 10, 1962.
10. James, John R., The Next Fifty Years. *Journal of the Town Planning Institute*, **50**, No. 1, 1964.
11. Sharp, Dame Evelyn, Reflections on Planning. *Journal of the Town Planning Institute*, **50**, No. 6, 1964.
12. Lane, Leslie W., Presidential Address. *Journal of the Town Planning Institute*, **50**, No. 10, 1964.
13. Special Supplement, *Journal of the Town Planning Institute*, **51**, No. 3, 1965.
14. McLoughlin, J. Brian, The Planning Profession: New Directions. *Journal of the Town Planning Institute*, **51**, No. 6, 1965.
15. Goss, Anthony, *The Architect and Town Planning*. Royal Institute of British Architects, 1965.
16. Keeble, Lewis B., Presidential Address. *Journal of the Town Planning Institute*, **51**, No. 9, 1965.
17. Lichfield, Nathaniel, Objectives for Planners. *Journal of the Town Planning Institute*, **52**, No. 8, 1966.
18. Burns, Wilfred, Presidential Address. *Journal of the Town Planning Institute*, **53**, No. 8, 1967.
19. Kantorowich, R. H., Education for Planning. *Journal of the Town Planning Institute*, **53**, No. 5, 1967.
20. Sharp, Thomas, Planning Planning. *Journal of the Town Planning Institute*, **52**, No. 6, 1966.
21. Ling, Arthur, Planning and the Institute. *Journal of the Town Planning Institute*, **54**, No. 9, 1968.
22. Amos, Francis J. C., Approach to Planning. *Journal of the Town Planning Institute*, **55**, No. 4, 1969.

9 Education

An important feature of professional bodies is the great regard they have for the training of their members. The RTPI is no exception. We have seen in chapter 3 that shortly after the founding of the Institute one of the first steps taken was to make provision for town planning education, and this high priority in the Institute's work has been maintained throughout the 60 years of its existence. The ways in which education policy has been pursued are interwoven throughout the Institute's story, reflecting the drive for higher standards, as well as forming part of the struggle for self-identification amongst the interests of competing bodies. Objectives in education reflect changing attitudes towards planning. Educational syllabi mirror phases and subject fashions in the development of planning. Education policy is firmly keyed in with the membership policy of the Institute the way planners are trained is linked with membership requirements. Professions differ in the weight they place on control over the education of their members; the RTPI differs strongly from the RICS for example. At the present time, ideas are changing as to the extent to which professions can and should determine their own educational requirements: the RTPI is now considering this very issue. The Institute's education story can be illustrated from all these points of view.

As described earlier (see p. 54) the first Town Planning School was at Liverpool University, where W. H. Lever contributed to the founding of the Department of Civic Design in 1909, with money from a successful libel action against a newspaper. Courses were provided for graduates in architecture. The Lever Chair was endowed in 1912, the first occupant being S. D. Adshead. His staff included Liverpool Corporation Officials, Brodie and Dowdall, together with Abercrombie and Mawson. The second initiative came shortly afterwards, with financial support from Cadbury, when Raymond Unwin was appointed part-time lecturer in town planning at the University of Birmingham. He gave two undergraduate courses in the Department of Civil Engineering from 1912 to 1915, after which the sessions were discontinued until 1920; these were 'Civic Design and Town Planning' and 'Social Origins and Economic Bases of Towns'. A third centre emerged in 1914 when a Department of Town Planning was created in the Bartlett School of Architecture at University College, London. Adshead became the first Head, occupying the Chair until 1935. Postgraduate courses were for architects, surveyors and engineers.

Within the professions the IMCE had shown interest in planning education before 1914, but there was clearly a good deal which the newly founded Institute could do. In fact the TPI rapidly came to occupy the central place in the pioneering of town planning education, both by developing initiative itself and through its relationships with the University Departments. During the 1920s a single set of standards for judging town planning expertise was developed and the Institute played a primary role in that achievement.

The first TPI examination syllabus was drawn up in December 1916. Qualifications for entry were as significant as the actual syllabus itself. Those taking the examination were members of RIBA, SI, IMCE and ICE; alternatively they were architects, engineers or surveyors, possessing intermediate qualifications in their professional examinations, or Matriculation Certificate, or Oxford or Cambridge Senior Local Examination Certificate, or other standard approved by Council. In short, entry was determined by prior qualification by the three land professions at Final, Intermediate or other level. Furthermore, practical experience was required in the form of at least one year in an office where practical experience in town planning was obtained. Five subject areas were defined for the examination: history of town planning, town planning practice, and town planning in relation to three particular aspects, architecture and amenities, engineering and surveying, and the law. Candidates were also required to make a sketch plan and write a short report on a subject set in a day's examination. Additionally, candidates had to submit a design for a set piece of town planning with a report, the subject being communicated two months before the date of the examinations. This examination structure remained unaltered until the early thirties.

The first examinations were held in 1920, having been delayed by the war. Only a handful of candidates came forward, however; the number reached double figures for the first time in 1926 when there were 16 candidates, and the highest number for any one year before 1932 (when a new system was introduced) was 35, in 1929. A total of 146 candidates were examined in this way from 1920 to 1931, and even this figure included 'resits'. One landmark was in 1928 when the first woman applicant entered the examination.

Before 1920, election to the Institute had been on merit. But with the introduction of examinations as standards of planning expertise, they increasingly became the accepted means of entry to the profession. Direct election to the Institute remained, for example by those who had passed town planning examinations at Universities and who possessed suitable practical qualifications. The question of recognizing the Schools for exemption from the Institute's examinations was considered intermittently, but no definite action was taken until the early 1930s. By that time the TPI had taken the initiative, and soon the newly established schools were applying for recognition.

The constitution of the Town Planning Joint Examination Board in 1930 proved an event of long-standing significance. The background to this was that the IMCE and the RIBA had Certificate or Diploma examinations in town planning, but neither was recognized in any formal way by the TPI. The SI had a special paper in their examination which related to town planning. This was an unsatisfactory situation for all parties and as early as 1925 the IMCE had suggested a joint discussion with the RIBA and the TPI. A meeting took place in April that year, though with little in the way of tangible results. In 1927 Education Committee was again discussing the lines on which co-operation with other bodies might be made. Unwin prepared a memorandum and in 1928 it was decided that the SI should be included in any scheme so that the valuation and estate development aspects of town planning could be adequately dealt with. Pepler discussed this with Goddard, the secretary of SI, and an informal conference was held in January 1929.

This meeting was successful in that a common aim was agreed, namely 'establishing a common requisite standard of attainment for any person desiring to qualify as a practitioner or specialist in any branch of town planning, and the avoidance of overlapping'[1]. The final details were settled in December 1929. A Joint Examination Board was proposed, to consist of eleven representatives, five from the TPI (including at least one joint member from each of the three other bodies), and two each from the RIBA, SI and IMCE. Having received formal approval by all the bodies concerned, the Board began its operations in 1932.

It is not clear who gained most advantage from the new arrangement. For the Institute, it could be shown that uncertainty was ended by virtue of the fact that common standards of expertise had at last been laid down. Also it represented a final coming to terms with town planning as a subject matter over which the other three bodies held no individual primacy. On the other hand, the parent professions obtained the position of collectively dominating education in town planning, thereby consolidating an earlier influence. In the event, the TPI had the majority of candidates during the thirties under the Joint Board arrangement, the qualifications of the other professional bodies attracting relatively few candidates, and it seems that as things transpired the TPI benefitted considerably from the arrangement.

An important adjunct to the setting up of the Joint Board was the introduction of an Intermediate Town Planning examination. Previously entry for TPI examinations was confined to those who had passed the examinations of the parent bodies, wholly or in part; now entry was further extended to those who had passed an Intermediate examination in Town Planning. The implication of this was that it allowed direct entry to the profession by examination, irrespective of membership of other professional bodies. This was the first practical step of loosening the ties with the parent profession—18 years after the founding of the Institute. In the evolution of the TPI as an independent professional body, this diminished stipulation of prior membership of another professional body was clearly of great significance.

Unwin had prepared a memorandum outlining a possible syllabus for an Intermediate examination. Progress was deferred until the details of the Joint Board had been finalized, but in April 1931 a draft syllabus was ready and the first Intermediate examinations were held in 1932. There were seven candidates. It was the prelude to a successful venture, for the number of candidates rose steadily each year during the thirties so that in 1939 71 sat the Intermediate examination, compared with 111 candidates for the Final.

In 1937 consideration was given to whether Intermediate qualifications of the other professional bodies were sufficient justification for direct entry to TPI Final examinations. In 1938 the Education Committee resolved that they were not, and in future only Final examinations carried exeption from TPI Intermediate. Council approved this measure in 1939, to take effect from the 1940 examinations. This was a further undermining of the supremacy of the older professions in entry to TPI examinations, and the independence of the Institute grew accordingly.

During the thirties the approved Town Planning Schools began seeking exemption from the Institute's examinations. The first initiative in planning education had been taken outside the Institute, indeed before the Institute was founded, but the University sector did not pursue its new enthusiasm very far in the early years and it was not until the 1930s that really significant developments took place. At first it was through the Institute that subsequent progress was made at all, and it was a case of the Schools following the Institute rather than taking much of a lead themselves. Initially the Institute's view was to encourage the existing Schools to model their courses on TPI courses, but after 1932 the procedure was to grant exemptions from TPI examinations. By the outbreak of the Second World War the TPI was firmly established as the primary qualifying body for town planning.

Of the early Schools, Liverpool continued to flourish, albeit on a small scale. By the end of the thirties an annual intake of six to eight full-time Diploma students were registered, with 40 to 60 part-time Certificate students. W. G. Holford succeeded Abercrombie in 1935 as Head of the School and in 1939 the staff consisted also of Wesley Dougill, Research Fellow, R. H. Mattocks, lecturer in Landscape Design, Reginald Poole, lecturer in Civil Engineering and Surveying, Mortimer Ward (Civic Hygiene), J. J. Clarke (Civic Law) and W. A. Eden (Rural Studies). Among the students who had passed through the School were future Presidents of the Institute, T. Alwyn Lloyd, J. S. Allen and Holford himself; architects Trystan Edwards, R. H. Mattocks (also a future President) and G. Maxwell Fry; a future Manchester professor, A. C. Holliday; also Norah Dumphy who later had the distinction of being the first woman town planning officer (to Tynemouth and North Shields).

London was a smaller School. Its activities only really started after 1918 with a one year course designed to assist those returning from the war. Longstreth-Thompson was among those who took advantage of this intensive training. Originally Adshead was the only member of staff, but later was assisted by the Professor of Engineering at the University and a legal expert from the Ministry of Health. Later Longstreth-Thompson himself lectured on surveying in relation to town planning. The strength of the School seems to have been its ability to call on well-known figures in matters relating to planning, and its location in the capital was obviously an asset in this. A three-year Diploma course was established, recognized by the Institute in 1932.

At Birmingham, planning courses were resumed in 1920, the one lecturer being William Haywood, supplemented by local authority officers in the city, including Humphreys, later a TPI President. In spite of the support of the Bournville Village Trust the course did not develop into a separate Department, perhaps because the University lacked an Architectural School, frequently the most important stimulus in this direction. But there were movements elsewhere. At Armstrong College, Newcastle, the School of Architecture was reorganized in the early thirties under Professor R. A. Cordingly and a division of Town Planning was added. R. Neville Brown was the first lecturer, succeeded on his death in 1937 by Thomas Sharp. The Department grew rapidly just before the outbreak of war with lecturing assistance from the School of Architecture. At the Leeds College of Art the

School of Architecture set up a separate Department (unique in being a School of Town Planning and Housing) under J. S. Allen in 1934. Among the part-time lecturers were W. S. Cameron, later City Engineer, and Desmond Heap, Deputy Town Clerk of the City, both future Presidents. In the same year the Edinburgh College of Art set up a Department of Town Planning with a one-year Diploma course intended as an adjunct to other professional qualifications notably in architecture and engineering. Planning studies had started here as early as 1925, important contributions in the successful development being made by F. C. Mears, Chairman of the Scottish TPI Branch and local authority officers from Edinburgh and Midlothian. In 1935 a full town planning course was introduced at Manchester University under the influence of R. A. Cordingly, Professor of Architecture (late of Newcastle). Lectures had been instituted much earlier, but the full development did not come until the later thirties. A Certificate and Diploma, occupying three or four years' part-time study, was offered for those from parent professions; a course was later introduced which allowed direct entry into town planning. By the outbreak of war the department had about 30 students. Of the lecturing staff, W. Dobson Chapman was to be a future President of the Institute.

During the thirties TPI recognition was granted to these six Schools, Liverpool, London, Newcastle, Leeds, Edinburgh and Manchester, and also to the Architectural Association School in London. There were courses elsewhere which were not recognized: in addition to Birmingham they existed at Cambridge, the Cardiff School of Architecture, the College of Estate Management, Glasgow (Royal Technical College) and Aberdeen. There were also correspondence courses. Bearing in mind the small student demand the number of recognized Schools was probably adequate. In 1939 the Recognized Schools Sub-committee of the Council decided that recognition 'should not be extended very much further and that the institution of one further School would probably satisfy all requirements for some years to come'[2]. The policy of the Institute was to grant exemption to Schools within defined geographical areas, in an attempt to provide adequate national coverage. An application in 1939 for the development of a Planning School at Sheffield University was not approved: the view was that there were preferable locations elsewhere.

It was not until the late thirties that the basic structure and concepts behind planning education began to be in any way seriously questioned. Formal education still favoured architecture and engineering. Perhaps the inauguration of the Town and Country Planning Summer School in 1933 as an experiment for providing additional educational facilities for those engaged in planning, was a spur to new outlooks. But there were other influences. Unwin, for example, in a paper read to the Institute in 1935 spoke of the need to equip the right type of men for the activity of comprehensive regional and national planning; he doubted 'whether in our specialized courses for those who seek to become professional planners of town and country we are carrying the study and training of the wider problems involved far enough.'[3] A more positive broadening of the basis of education was also openly contemplated by Pepler in 1938; he cast doubts on the adequacy of the TPI Syllabus in its omissions regarding sociological and economic aspects of planning[4]. There was no great innovation and experiment in the Schools themselves in matters of planning education—perhaps as Cinderella Departments they had very limited room for manoeuvre—though we should record in Holford's School the valuable link with the Social Science Department. But initiative for change was not entirely lacking and the Recognized Schools Sub-committee, established by the Institute in 1936, composed of academics, took an increasingly important part in formulating TPI policy on educational matters.

As we have seen in chapter 6 the advent of war served to promote far-reaching changes both in planning and within the Institute. The education field did not escape the searchlight of scrutiny, nor was it protected from the pressing demands for new approaches. In the spirit of a new found confidence, self-identification was urged, and this had great implications for the education of planners. There were voices both within and outside the Institute which pressed for change.

A paragraph in the Scott Committee's *Report on Land Utilization in Rural Areas* (1942) stated bluntly that: 'We are not satisfied that the training of either planners or architects is adequate for the work they will be called upon to perform if our recommendations are adopted. We are of the opinion that many employed as town planners are inadequately trained in the broader aspects of their work'[5]. We should of course recall that Thomas Sharp was Secretary to the Scott Committee; as an academic he was no doubt keen to make this point. But he was not alone in commenting on the challenges which now faced planning.

The needs of reconstruction presented enormous tasks and it was doubted if educational and professional skills were being harnessed in an appropriate way. W. S. Morrison, for example, the new Minister of Town and Country Planning, addressing the TPI in June 1943 commented that: 'The researches upon which sound planning must in future be based will demand in an increasing degree the special knowledge of the statistician, the geographer, the agricultural economist, the transport expert, the social scientist and many other experts.' He went on to say that: 'We must now examine the sources from which the planners of the future are to be drawn and consider carefully how far the various skills upon which the planning of the present and the future will call can best be woven into that network.'[6]

This was a challenge to rethink educational objectives and methods, and during the next five years the Institute tried to respond. Its inability to do so effectively led to the deliberations of the Schuster Committee, which we have already noted in chapter 7. It is at this point that the question of education policy and the more general issues of member composition of the Institute become particularly intertwined.

In spite of the avowed willingness to accommodate change, which had been expressed in the late thirties and which continued to be expressed, there were in fact many constraints operating on the Institute which made it impossible for it to take the action which might have been desired. For one thing, there was the entrenched position of the parent professions. During the war years they also shared in the increased interest in planning, and in the circumstances they were even less likely to abandon their existing claim on education. For another, there was the formidable balancing act of the Joint Examination Board. In the interplay of relationships it was inevitably that the TPI's actions were delicate compromises between the interested parties rather than the pursuance of radical reform. Only modest changes therefore took place. An example was the attempt to relate social science to planning education. Geography and other subjects were incorporated in the TPI curriculum.

In the middle forties there were a number of skirmishes concerning the Joint Board, the results of which showed how difficult it was going to be to move in any decisive way. Dobson Chapman, for example, drew up a syllabus for a new Associate Membership examination, designed for those who wanted to become planners rather than those who wanted a planning qualification in addition to their main professional interests; the latter were to be examined only in certain parts of the main syllabus. But the implication of a dual standard of qualification was not to the liking of the Board. Another example concerned the introduction by the RIBA in 1944 of a town planning qualification. It was to be a diploma, to be obtained independently from the Board. The RIBA was prevailed upon to call the new qualification a Distinction in Town Planning, and not to put it forward as the normal method of qualifying. Finally, we might note that the ICE was admitted to the Joint Board in 1950 after some years of discussion over balance of interests. All this showed the extremely tentative state of planning education, TPI being anxious not to upset a delicate status quo.

In the meantime there had to be determined action on at least two fronts. First, it was necessary to cope with the sudden increase in the number of people who wanted to become planners. There was a rise in the number of candidates for annual examination, and a series of seven three-month Completion Courses was devised to facilitate the rapid qualification of those whose progress had been interrupted by war service. These were organized at the School of Planning and Research for National Development, which started as a postgraduate department of the Architectural Association in 1935; wound up in 1938 it had continued to exist independently as the Association for Planning and Regional Reconstruction. Second, another School was recognized by TPI; this was the Nottingham College of Arts and Crafts in 1943.

But there were longer-term issues. A five-year degree course in town and country planning was set up at King's College, Newcastle, in 1945, which did not depend on previous professional qualifications, and which set a new level in academic respectability. This inspired the Recognized Schools Sub-committee of TPI to set up a Special Committee on Recognition and Policy, essentially to examine methods and means of town planning education in this country and 'in Empire countries overseas', and to inquire into the policy and system of recognition of Schools. The Committee in 1947 recommended recognition of the new King's College course and considered that it should be regarded as a model for others. One consequence was that a very similar course was set up at Manchester in 1948. In the same year two more Schools were recognized, one on a temporary basis only, at the Royal Technical College, Glasgow, and the other, reflecting the growth of planning overseas, at the University of Witwatersrand. The association with Universities was noticeable: eagerness to embrace this sector of higher education was made clear in the decision not to grant recognition to Schools not associated with Universities. At the same time TPI control over education was made explicit, quite apart from School recognition, Education Committee deciding that 'no School of Planning should be recognized unless the effective head of the department has a qualification in planning satisfactory to the Institute'.[7]

224

But planning education was unlikely to change very much without intervention from parties outside the controlling bodies. The Schuster Report on *Qualifications of Planners* (1950) provided the new initiative. To appreciate the new recommendations which came from this source, we should first be reminded of the state of affairs then existing.

The TPI had recently revised its Intermediate and Final examinations so that they were now composed as follows. Each examination had two parts, testimonies of study and oral examination, and written examination. In the Intermediate examination five testimonies were required: measured drawings and sketches, a historical study of a particular piece of townscape, field surveying and levelling, a set subject for design, and working drawings. Seven 3-hour examination papers were obligatory: elementary construction of buildings, roads and bridges, surveying and levelling, historical development of planning, history of architectural and garden design, principles of design, central and local government, and outlines of planning law. There was also a 6-hour design examination ('drawn subject'), and a practical test in surveying and levelling. In the Final examination, candidates submitted four testimonies in Part I, three drawn exercises in design relating to problems set by the Examinations Board, and one relating to an area chosen by the candidate. In Part II there was a field day and the following 3-hour papers: historical development of planning, town planning practice (two papers), sketch plan and report (two parts), architectural design and amenities in relation to planning, civil engineering in relation to planning, surveying in relation to planning, law in relation to planning, outlines of social and economic organization, and elements of applied geology and economic geography (the last two being new papers recently introduced). The planning student of the early 1970s might well blanch at the structure of these examinations, particularly the close relationship to other professional subject matter, the heavy emphasis on design and land, the implied ability in draughtsmanship, and the slender recognition of geography and social science.

The recognized Schools in the country had various approaches within that framework. The School of Civic Design at Liverpool provided two courses, a 2-year, part-time Certificate and a 1-year, full-time Diploma, only the latter providing exemption from the TPI Final. (In 1951 the Certificate course was dropped and the Diploma was replaced by a 2-year, full-time, postgraduate course which gave much less emphasis on architectural design, and which could be taken by a graduate in almost any subject.) The Department of Town Planning, University College, London provided Certificate and Diploma courses similar to the unrevised Liverpool courses; entry was restricted to candidates qualified in architecture, engineering or surveying. The King's College, Durham (Newcastle) 5-year degree course was the first recognized course which did not require the preliminary qualification of the parent professions. It set a new model for integrating planning as one subject. At the Leeds College of Art, the Department of Town Planning and Housing offered a 1-year, full-time or 2-year, part-time Diploma, similar to the old Liverpool Diploma, for candidates qualified in architecture, engineering or surveying. The Edinburgh College of Art also provided a similar 1-year, full-time Diploma course but in 1948 the course was extended for more practical work and to encompass the revised TPI syllabus. The Division of Town and Country Planning at Manchester University established a 5-year degree course in 1949 similar to the Newcastle one and continued its

Certificate and Diploma courses. The School of Planning and Research for Regional Development provided a Diploma for 1-year, full-time and 1-year, part-time students mainly from the parent professions. The London Polytechnic (Regent Street) provided a 3-year, part-time evening course leading to a Diploma, again from qualified architects, engineers or surveyors. For similar entry the Nottingham College of Arts and Crafts provided a 2-year, part-time course, shortly to be altered to a 1-year, full-time and 1-year, part-time, and a 3-year, part-time course; the School of Architecture at the Royal Technical College, Glasgow was devising its post-graduate Diploma course also on a full-time and part-time basis. Other courses were provided, but not recognized by TPI, as follows: Department of Estate Management, Cambridge, College of Estate Management, London, Technical College, Cardiff, the Northern Polytechnic, Holloway, Leicester College of Arts and Crafts, and the South West Essex Technical College and School of Art. This review of the situation in 1950 shows the heavy influence on entry to courses which the parent professions exercised, only Newcastle and Manchester offering entrance unrelated to this background, though Liverpool quickly followed suit.

The Schuster Report was important in its implicit and explicit recommendations about planning education. We have already made mention of this Report (see p. 164); but we might recall the emphasis placed on widening the membership of the Institute, the store placed on a University education, and the suggestion that the chief planning officer need not possess technical skill in design. The Committee thought that the 'right preparation' for planning was a degree course in one of the established subjects, followed by a post-graduate course in planning. As to the nature of the post-graduate part there should be variety and experiment; entry by arts graduates should be allowed. Post-experience training was thought desirable. Above all it was thought necessary to avoid the creation of a 'specialist in blinkers', and it was suggested that the best potential planners would be produced not through devising a new basic discipline, but by ensuring that students of recognized disciplines appreciated the planning significance of their subjects.

Perhaps it was not appreciated fully at the time, but Schuster sounded the death knell of the primacy of the parent professions in town planning. Throughout the report there was a constant theme that expressed the view that planning was something different from the product of engineering, architecture and surveying. Nonetheless developments in town planning education did not follow the pattern Schuster laid down. In fact it was the undergraduate courses that developed first, with an insistence on the unique basic core of the subject matter. Postgraduate courses came later, and the development of specialisms later still.

Change took place gradually. The fifties was a period of anti-climax after the high expectations of the forties, and planning was in the doldrums. No new British Schools were recognized during this time. Perhaps if planning had been in an expansionist phase, innovation in planning education on Schuster lines might have a feature, but it was not, and a cautious evolutionary course of development occurred. In 1951 the Master of Civic Design course at Liverpool permitted entry by graduates outside architecture, engineering and surveying. In 1953 Council adopted the policy that holders of approved degrees in geography and economics be exempted from the Intermediate TPI examination. Subsequently the actual examinations themselves were revised to take fuller account of the changed emphasis of planning in the light of the Schuster recommendations. Greater stress was placed on the social, economic and geological aspects of planning and it was hoped that the Recognized Schools would follow the syllabus alterations.

An increasing proportion of TPI members now qualified in the Schools. The peak year for TPI examinations was 1949 and from the fifties onwards the Schools became the main influence in education rather than the professional body. The Town Planning Joint Examination Board continued to exist but was of declining relevance. The majority of candidates for its examinations had always entered under the auspices of the TPI; of the other contenders the IMunE was the most important. In 1949 there were 316 TPI candidates, 95 from the IMunE and 6 each from the RICS and the RIBA. In 1959 only 5 candidates were from the IMunE, and the remainder were from the TPI. The Schuster Report recommended that the Board be dissolved, and a number of attempts to act on this was made, though with no great determination. Perhaps it was kept going while the delicate discussions over the Charter were being held; certainly the granting of the Charter ensured the end of the Board. The death of its Chairman, Pepler, brought Beaufoy to the chair, and the Board was dissolved in January 1961.

At the end of the fifties the syllabus for the Institute's Intermediate and Final examinations differed little from the beginning of the decade. One difference was that in Part I of the Final a 5 000-word essay was an alternative to three drawn subjects—a slight easing of the design bias of the examination. In November 1959 Education Committee felt that there was 'nothing vitally wrong with the present syllabus'[8]. The 1960s produced very different evidence.

Two new issues brought about a flurry of activity. One was the expansion of higher education and the upsurge in the number of recognized Schools. The other concerned renewed speculation about the purpose and content of planning education, and this was very much linked with the wider membership question, which we have considered in chapter 8.

Both the Robbins Report (1963) and the Heyworth Report (1966) were significant for planning. The former, on Higher Education, set the scene for the expansion of the sixties, and the latter, on Social Studies, was instrumental in the setting up of the Social Science Research Council, with its own consequences for postgraduate work in planning and related disciplines. But before the recommendations of either Committee could be acted upon, the problems of planning staff shortages and recruitment difficulties were being recognized. In May 1963 Council resolved to approach the Minister of Education and the Minister of Housing and Local Government to impress upon them the urgent need to expand training facilities for planners; four new Schools of Planning and the expansion of existing Schools were suggested. The anxiety continued, and the previous wisdom of recognizing only University Schools was questioned. At first the compromise policy was 'University Schools if possible', but in time, with the expansion of Polytechnics, this became untenable, and Polytechnic recognition ultimately came on an equal footing with that of Universities. Polytechnic degrees are conferred by the Council for National Academic Awards (CNAA). This Council established a Town Planning Panel to undertake the detailed evaluation of courses submitted for degree recognition, and the RTPI is represented on this Panel.

New Schools recognized after 1960 were as follows: City of Birmingham Polytechnic (1961), University of Edinburgh (1963), Universities of Adelaide and Natal (1964), Lanchester Polytechnic, Coventry (1965), Glasgow School of Art, Duncan of Jordanstone College of Art (Dundee), Oxford Polytechnic, and University of Sheffield (1968), Polytechnic of the South Bank (1969), University of Wales Institute of Science and Technology, Cardiff (1970), Liverpool Polytechnic and University of Nottingham (1971) and Queens University, Belfast (1972). A large number of courses was also established during the sixties relating to specialist aspects of planning, particularly regional planning and transportation studies. They had no wide, generalist foundation and were not recognized by the TPI. A good deal of confusion was caused by this proliferation and it provided a fertile field of discontent for those who saw the Institute's education policy restrictive and outmoded.

The TPI's own examinations were of ever decreasing significance as a means of qualification. But the syllabus formed the yardstick by which planning courses in the Schools were recognized, and it is therefore necessary to look in some detail at the changes which have been made over the last ten years. As part of the linked issue of education and membership policy, the Lane–Buchanan proposals in 1963–64 for realignment by the Institute had implied, rather than specified, changes in education policy. But the Council's proposals were rejected in favour of a policy which emphasized the unique nature of planning as an independent subject. A generalist syllabus was then devised which sought to cover the full range of planning, although providing some options. The Institute's *Progress Report on Membership* (1967) presented a revised scheme for the Final examination. The underlying approach was to test whether a candidate had 'adequate knowledge, skill and sense of professional responsibility to engage in town planning throughout its full range.' A four-part syllabus was devised covering the general background to planning, the central core of theory and technique, a practical study (with options) and supplementary studies, both practical and written. The practical study had to fall within one of four spatial scales (local, urban, metropolitan and regional, and rural and regional resource planning) the choice being determined by the candidate's selection among the options in the supplementary studies.

Professor R. H. Kantorowich, Chairman of Education Committee, outlined the basis of his approach to a General Meeting of the Institute in April 1967. In the very complicated activity of planning, he acknowledged that persons from a number of disciplines were involved, but considered that: 'The town planner is called upon to carry the central and crucial professional responsibility because his special skill is a command of the planning process as a whole. He has been trained to organize and co-ordinate all necessary planning operations as well as to design the plan, and, once it has been approved, to control its implementation and in due course to review it.'[9] As clear and logical expositions of a structure for town planning education, the Institute's *Progress Report* and Kantorowich's paper were without parallel in the history of the Institute. The proposals were warmly supported and the revised TPI syllabus came into operation in 1970.

But within a very short time the assumptions on which the logic of the Kantorowich syllabus had been based were being questioned. It was soon doubted whether it was possible or desirable to educate in order 'to engage in planning throughout its full range', and the claim of unique expertise commanding the planning process was the subject of increasing dispute as time wore on. The planning-oriented (but non-recognized) courses in various Universities were flourishing and there was clear student demand for the themes they offered. There were renewed doubts as to whether the generalist base of the new syllabus was the *only* approach to planning education, and whether all those who had not benefited from courses based on this syllabus could reasonably be excluded from professional membership. The issues were conveniently reviewed by a Working Group, which included members of the RTPI, set up in November 1970 under the chairmanship of F. J. C. Amos, then Senior Vice-President of the Institute; it was supported and accommodated by the Centre for Environmental Studies. The Group sat until March 1972, and its report *Education for Planning* was published in 1973[10].

The Group set its sights widely and attempted to dissociate planning from its institutional history; instead it set it in terms that might apply to any kind of organization—steersmanship, or 'governance' as they described it, and more or less co-extensive with management. They recognized multiplicity and variety in city and community and the involvement of many kinds of agency in urban governance; they therefore foresaw the existence of many different kinds of planner. Whereas some in the past had seen the professional education of the chartered town planner as the one permissable kind of planning education, the Group showed that it was possible to see urban and regional planning differently, recognizing that 'in reality many kinds of education have been serving the total field of urban administration'. It was a case of turning the issue upside down: instead of starting with the one umbrella of planning education and trying to make that cover all aspects, the Group considered the nature of the problem and began to conceive what educational system could be devised for adequately training and harnessing skills to deal with those issues. The Report went on to show where gaps existed in planning education and proposed a new system that had an intermeshing pattern. It was not the purpose of the Group to specify the scope of a town planning education; nonetheless for the first time a coherent new framework had been sketched as an alternative to the approach of the all embracing generalist syllabus which the RTPI had adopted.

The climate of opinion about educational matters was already changing within the Institute. Recommendations for fundamental changes in education policy flowed from the membership selection in 1972 of option 4A in the Discussion Paper *Town Planners and Their Future* (see p. 212). These have now been incorporated in another Discussion Paper considered by the membership during the autumn of 1973. Briefly, it is now proposed that the Institute should accept more flexible arrangements in the form and structure of planning education, including the development by the Schools of special interests in one or more aspects of planning. It further recommends variety in postgraduate planning education; two alternatives are suggested, two-year courses of either the present type or of a two-stage version beginning with a full-time year for 'basic' planning followed by 'applied planning' specialist components. The system of recognition is also being reconsidered, with the setting up of a 'Visitor Panel' with a wide range of experience. Basic requirements for recognition are also being revised in order that they might concentrate on the principles of the planning education rather than detailed context. Finally, it is suggested that the Institute's own examination will in due course be phased out.

Meanwhile, there had been developments concerning planning courses outside the United Kingdom. In 1973 there were five overseas Schools with recognized courses; the Universities of Sydney, Melbourne, Adelaide, Witwatersrand and Natal. In every case recognition had been given prior to 1966 when the Institute published its first Policy Statement on the question of School recognition; there had been no Visiting Boards and the courses were then out of line with current requirements. It was resolved in 1973 that partial recognition be substituted for full recognition. This meant that exemption could be given in respect of a substantial part of the Institute's Final examination, but applicants would be required to sit further papers for full exemption.

A 60-year saga in planning education has worked itself out with a sharp twist and reversal of policy over the last eight years. In itself, the history of planning education presents a nice case study of the buffeting pressures on the professional body as it has tried to meet one of its original objectives, subsequently enshrined in the Charter. It highlights the changing perceptions as to the nature of planning, particularly the identification of the core of knowledge, and the place of specialisms around it. It reveals starkly the gaps that can open up between education based on past assumptions and that required for new forms of planning practice.

As early as 1953 an American planner, Lloyd Rodwin, observed that in Britain, 'The planner was taught to think physically, visually, technically. He still does. He was only crudely familiar, if at all, with the nature and use of research and scientific method. He knew little of the thinking or the applicability of the social sciences, particularly economics and sociology.'[11] This was how it affected the performance of British planning in the post-war period. There was an emphasis on design rather than method; cities were thought of as physical artifacts rather than social systems; and there was no systematic understanding of the social and economic environments over which control was sought. In the sixties the imbalance of the planner's education was exposed. He had been trained to be a designer and a shaper of physical form, but he lacked an understanding of the workings of the community to which he was responsible. Increasingly, he took the blame, fairly or unfairly, for all that went wrong in the developmental process and much more besides.

This shortcoming in the post-war education system has prompted David Eversley[12] to observe that the planner now has a totally different role to perform in society compared with the past. His task is 'to arbitrate, to adjudge the claims of the various factions, to settle priorities'. In the planner's education therefore 'the ability to listen will be more important than the ability to write a plan. The willingness to explain and to discuss, will be preferred to apologetics. The propensity to adapt an existing plan to changing circumstances will be more in demand than the obstinacy required to carry through an approved project.' Eversley's claim is that the planner today is not adequately trained for the tasks which society has thrust upon him.

One does not have to accept the whole of Eversley's thesis to agree that the way the planner is trained and educated is bound up with perceived concepts of planning and the expected role of the planner in society. In recent years of change, the importance and significance of planning education has been seen as never before. It is vital to fit the man to the task he has to perform, and for this reason it is certain that in the future development of the Institute, educational issues will remain central in its affairs.

230

REFERENCES

1. Town Planning Institute Committee Minutes, vol. I, pp. 54–6.
2. Town Planning Institute Committee Minutes, vol. I, pp. 179–180.
3. Unwin, Sir Raymond, Urban Development. The Pattern and the Background. *Journal of the Town Planning Institute*, **XXI**, No. 10, 1935.
4. Pepler, G. L., Education for Planning. *Journal of the Town Planning Institute*, **XXV**, No. 1, 1938.
5. *Report of the Committee on Land Utilisation in Rural Areas*, Cmd. 6378, 1942, para 240.
6. *Journal of the Town Planning Institute*, **XXIX**, 73, 1943.
7. Town Planning Institute Committee Minutes, vol. III, p. 163.
8. Town Planning Institute Committee Minutes, vol. VI, p. 248.
9. Kantorowich, R. H., Education for Planning, *Journal of the Town Planning Institute*, **53**, No. 5, 1967.
10. *Education for Planning*. Report of a Working Group at the Centre for Environmental Studies. Pergamon, 1973.
11. Rodwin, Lloyd, The Achilles Heel of British Town Planning. *Town Planning Review*, **24**, 1953.
12. Eversley, David, *The Planner in Society: the Changing Role of a Profession*. Faber and Faber, 1973.

10 Branches and Professional Organization

Attention to education has been one aspect of the professional life of the Institute. Another has been the organization of the corporate life of the members through the device of Branches.

The formation of Branches, in order to provide more adequately for members outside the London area, was considered from time to time by Council during the early years of the Institute. But it was not until 1922 that a Sub-committee, chaired by Pepler, was set up to consider the matter. The committee approved the principle of regional Branches with a constitution modelled on that of the Surveyors' Institution (Pepler was also a Chartered Surveyor); this gave direct representation of Branch members on Council. Council approved the draft constitution and regulations of the proposed Branches, in July that year. The objectives were defined as follows:

(a) To bring the members into closer touch with the Council and to assist the Council in ascertaining their local wants and wishes.

(b) To give county members an extended influence over the admission of new members from their own districts and to provide them with additional means of furthering the object of the Institute.

(c) To give county members opportunities for holding meetings within their own region.

(d) To provide machinery for holding Local Examinations and occasional county meetings of the Institute and generally for increasing the interest of all classes of members in its welfare.

The Branches were to be constituent parts of the Institute, with money voted to them from Council.

The first Branch was the North of England Division, formed after an informal meeting held in Manchester, in 1922. The area concerned covered the whole of the four northern counties, the three Ridings of Yorkshire, Lancashire, Cheshire and Derbyshire, and, in spite of its title, the North Wales counties of Anglesey, Caernarvonshire, Denbighshire and Flintshire. The first meeting of the Branch was held in 1923. A second Branch was set up in 1930, to cover Scotland. A third Branch did not relate to a geographical area but extended to a section of the membership, the town planning officers; their section was set up in 1935, and, as we have seen, ran its own Journal and acted as a distinctive pressure group in Institute affairs. Indeed, in spite of its late start, by the outbreak of the Second World War it was the largest of the three Branches; in 1938 its budget was rather more than £80, compared with the North of England with £50 and the Scottish Branch with £20. These three developments were part of a conscious professional building of the Institute to secure reputation and status, and should be seen in conjunction with progress on other fronts, in particular, the question of examination syllabus, arrangements for education of planners and the code of professional practice with regard to fees and competitions.

The new situation provided by the war years acted as a great catalyst for change, and the later years of the 1940s saw a large expansion of the Branch network. Following an Irish Branch, approved in 1941, a South West of England Branch was created in 1945. A South Wales Branch was added in July 1946, institutionalizing an informal group that had existed for a number of years. In the same year the Town Planning Institute of New Zealand was wound up and a Branch established in December. In 1948 the East of England Branch was set up. In 1950 the Midlands Branch which had been created in 1943, was split into two, to cover North and West. In another split, by referendum, Derbyshire broke away from the North of England Division to join the North Midlands Branch; it changed its name to East Midlands in 1967. 1950 also saw the setting up of the South East of England Branch. Previously this area had been well served by London meetings and its planning officers had been members of the Town Planning Officers' Section of the TPI South Eastern Group. There was a heavy concentration of well-known names, and the first Executive Committee of the Branch contained four future Presidents: J. G. Jefferson, D. Heap, B. J. Collins and E. H. Doubleday. Two overseas Branches were approved, for South Africa in 1944 and Malaya in 1951. Meanwhile the Town Planning Officers' Section was wound up in 1950, the *raison d'être* for their existence having been overtaken by new events. With the disappearance of this group, the financial distribution changed: in 1951 the Scottish Branch, the South East of England Branch and the North of England Division (in that order) each had grants of over £100 for their annual budget. The basis of financial support was determined by Policy and Finance Committee in 1946 as 5 shillings per corporate member to be returned to the Branches. In the case of national Branches, it was to be 25 per cent of the subscription; this included the Scottish Branch which was also given an extra £50.

This rapid geographical extension of the Branches did not just encourage a wider coverage of professional activities. It implied a new 'grass-roots' element in the Institute's life and permitted healthy opportunities for comment on and ultimately participation in matters of TPI policy. In 1951, a conference brought all Branch Chairmen and Honorary Secretaries into direct contact with Policy and Finance Committee, and after 1954 this became a regular event. The Institute was still highly centralized, however; Policy and Finance Committee kept a firm hold on policy matters, deciding in 1951, for example, that the possibility of referring education decisions to Branches was quite out of the question. Nonetheless, from the fifties onwards Institute affairs increasingly became a matter for both Council and Branches. It was not a straightforward or necessarily predictable relationship; on some issues the Branches would exert pressure on Council to adopt a certain line, while on other matters, which Council wished to promote, they were a restraining influence.

The Branches soon acquired the tradition of being markedly practice-oriented; Branch members found their chief inspiration round matters relating to their day to day work. They held meetings largely addressed by chief officer colleagues on topics of immediate interest, or they conducted site visits of professional significance. For example, twenty years of Branch meetings in the South East have covered topics such as advertisement control, decentralization, the right use of land, caravans, post-war development of West Ham, water supply problems in the Thames Valley, control of the external appearance of buildings, town centre plans, rural surveys, procedure on planning inquiries, operation of Planning Acts, green belts, London traffic problems, enforcement control, car parking and development control in Central London. There have been visits to New Towns, the Road Research Laboratory and the Central Electricity Generating Board.

Branches did not develop a radical, questioning role which might have been the case if the Planning Schools had shown greater involvement; they were essentially down to earth, practical-minded, social units with an eye on stimulating corporate loyalties and giving assistance and encouragement to the younger generation in 'apprenticeship' style. In this way they have tended to be conservative, self-sufficient bodies, catering primarily for the direct needs of local members, particularly those engaged in planning practice. Only during the last five to ten years has this image changed, as a greater number of younger planners in or just out of full-time education have sought new requirements from Branch affairs.

At first the Branches were a little self-conscious and quick to be assertive of their professional position. This explains, for example, how, in May 1954, there were objections from the Branches to the representation of other professions as of right on the Council, to the continuance of the Joint Examinations Board, and to the widening of membership to include geographers and economists. On the other hand, the question of an examination for planning technicians was favourably considered. Branches expected the Council to be vigorous and to stand up for their professional rights; in this sense they were an important spur to action and a check against unnecessary caution. Typical was the East of England Branch which suggested in 1957, 'that on matters of national importance or policy the Institute, as the most important body on planning thought, did not express its opinion as forcibly as other professional bodies. The views of some other Institutions could generally be seen expressed in the national press but the Institute was too cautious or modest and opinion should be voiced.'[1]

The emergence of the Branches as a new potential force in Institute affairs soon made it necessary to forge links between them and the Council. In June 1957, when certain Committee reorganizations were made, Council agreed that there should be six Branch representatives on an enlarged Policy and Finance Committee. Under the 1973 reorganization, Branch representation was enlarged still further.

During the sixties the significance of the by now well established Branch structure was recognized. From 1963 onwards a number of policy documents were circulated to the membership and collective comments were organized through Branch meetings. Indeed, in its policy making the Institute became heavily dependent on the mobilization of Branch opinion. At first the Branches retained their tradition of conservative outlook. The relatively thin gruel of illustrated lectures on matters of current practice which had formed the staple diet for Branch meetings throughout the fifties and early sixties, proved to be insufficient intellectual food to withstand the first shocks of the Membership Policy debates. Membership at the grass roots was largely not ready to consider the new issues put before them. There were exceptions to this, as we shall see, but by and large the generalization holds true. An example is afforded by the Branch resolutions passed early in 1965 in respect of the previously circulated document on Membership Policy. For example, the West Midlands Branch viewed 'with grave disquiet' the Council's resolutions of October 1964, and 'was particularly concerned, and indeed shocked' at the statement in the Memorandum that the idea of planning as an entirely clear-cut activity had become untenable. The Branch went on to say that the Memorandum's views were 'mischievous' and 'could only do irreparable harm to the professional standing of the Chartered Institute'. The South Wales Branch expressed 'its grave concern and displeasure at the ill-considered and undignified manner in which the matter is being handled'. Other Branches objected, though in rather more cautious tones[2].

However, it is clear that the Branches allowed considerable variety of views to come forward: they were not monolithic expressions either within Branches or between them. Much depended on the interplay of personalities in the Branches at a particular time. Hence, while considerable opposition to Membership Policy in 1965 was being expressed nationally, the Scottish Branch accepted resolutions 1 and 2 without a division, and this, at a meeting attended by 57 people. Branch variety also resulted from the strength of the Junior voice and how it was organized. The West Midlands Branch was the first (in 1950) to set up a Junior section for student and junior members under 35, and this undoubtedly released initiative and enterprise and stimulated corporate loyalties; ultimately (in 1973) undue fragmentation of the sectional interests of the whole membership became apparent and the Junior section was consequently wound up. The changing circumstances of the late sixties and seventies brought junior members into Branch affairs much more, and opportunities for responsibility sharing were taken; student members now sit on Branch Executives.

Branches do not have constant boundaries, and flexibility in structure also gives variety of expression. New situations sometimes demand new arrangements for meeting needs and mobilizing local opinion, and an example of this can be seen in the fate of the North of England Division. In 1966 an unwieldly geographical area was divided when three Branches, Northern, North Western and Yorkshire took over existing non-executive groups. New large concentrations of planning staff in Lancashire and the North East in particular demanded local autonomy. In the South East Branch, geographical distance is similarly a problem, and a membership of about 2 600 is now split into four chapters as a three-year experiment: Weald, London, Southern and Chiltern. For all these reasons Branch characteristics have changed markedly over the last five to ten years; new questioning voices have found their way into Branch affairs and there has been an opening of Branch life to wider concerns through inter-professional meetings and speakers not drawn from established planning ranks.

The Branches have come to occupy a very special place in the life of the Institute. With slender financial resources they have struggled to provide a local point of contact for those with a common professional interest; without the tacit support of a very large number of local authorities in providing time and resources and accommodation this would often not have been possible. A handful of dedicated professional patriots have kept Executive Committees running and have undertaken business both referred to them from Council and emanating from their own ranks. Programmes of meetings have served to unite the fragile interests of adherents: a social night out, professional education and the occasional opportunity of challenge to those in higher authority has been the unlikely alchemy for a successful continuity of endeavour. Branch histories are full of the experiences which constitute the essence of a corporate professional life at local level. The Institute would be the poorer without the long service of many who have worked for their Branches for many years: S. H. Baker of the South of England Branch, and also Honorary Secretary of the Branches Liaison Committees; James Macauley, a Secretary of the Scottish Branch from 1922 for many years; K. Cox, Secretary of the South West of England Branch from 1948 to 1969; W. Bean, Secretary of the former North of England Division in the fifties and sixties; and many others so worthy of mention. There are also many local initiatives to record. For example, the Junior Weekend Summer School at Grantley Hall run by the North of England Division, and taken over by the Yorkshire Branch, has been highly regarded; so too has the Urchfont Design Course organized by Wiltshire County Council to help students taking TPI Examinations, especially the Testimonies. The Branches absorb a heavy responsibility when the Annual Spring Meetings are held in their areas; they take over social functions and a number of administrative arrangements.

After the Second World War the planning profession took on an international flavour through developments in the Commonwealth. But the overseas links were complicated by a number of factors. One was the fact that the formation of Branches directly dependent on Headquarters in London proved to be an unsatisfactory method of maintaining or fostering contact; after that of Malaya, only one new overseas Branch was formed in the fifties, that for Central Africa (Rhodesia and, at that time, Nyasaland) in June 1953. The other concerned the changes in world power that were taking place as colonies achieved independence and dominions adopted positions of much less reliance on the United Kingdom.

Within this broad framework the Institutional developments varied according to the particular circumstances in each country. In New Zealand a new national body was formed called the New Zealand Institute of Professional Town and Country Planners. It became the TPI New Zealand Branch, on the proviso that 60 per cent of its members were also members of the Town Planning Institute; it had much greater freedom than any other Branch. More typical was the form of affiliation with TPI by developing Commonwealth planning institutions: there were the affiliation of the Australian Planning Institute in 1955 and South African Institute of Town Planners in 1958, and the alliance of the Institute of Town Planners of India in the same year.

The Australian Planning Institute (API) replaced individual institutes in New South Wales, Victoria and South Australia. (The Town and Country Planning Institute of Australia was founded in Sydney in 1934; the Planning Institute of Australia in Melbourne in 1944; and the Town Planning Institute of South Australia in Adelaide in 1947.)

The new Institute was founded in August, 1951, at a Federal Conference attended by Pepler and Holford. It was recognized that Branch links with TPI were no longer appropriate and Pepler produced a memorandum on affiliation with overseas institutions; this was approved by Policy and Finance Committee in November 1952, and became Institute policy. Negotiations were conducted between Pepler, representing the Institute, and Professor Denis Winston of the University of Sydney, on behalf of the Australian body. Good relations were obviously forged during this time; Winston's course at Sydney was recognized in February 1952, and the School at Melbourne University in 1958. On Pepler's death, Winston wrote that in Australia 'he will always be remembered for his generous help and wise statesmanship' and paid tribute to 'his appreciation of the non-colonial status and temperament of Australia'[3]. The API has progressed strongly, publishing its Journal and holding Conferences. It was granted Royal status in 1969—before, in fact, the Institute achieved its own honour.

With regard to South Africa, the position was much more confused and it lacked the benefit of the warmth of personal relations. The new national institution was formed in 1952 but the Branch continued to exist. In November 1954, Policy and Finance Committee resolved that the Branch should continue as long as there were members who desired it. But by the next year it seems that the Branch had ceased to exist and as yet there was no affiliated body to replace it, though this matter had been under discussion for some time. In December 1956, it was reported that the actual position regarding the South Africa Branch and the national body was unknown, and the annual grants were not paid either that year or the next two. But in 1958 the South African Institute of Town Planners applied for affiliation and this was granted in October. Then followed a wrangle over unpaid grants; TPI refused to pay retrospective grants, though the assets of the Branch were handed over to the new body. New difficulties were ahead regarding reference to racial discrimination in the regulations of the affiliated body, this matter being raised in Policy and Finance Committee in March 1960. The question came to a head in 1973 and is considered on p. 238.

In India the outcome of developments was an alliance rather than an affiliation agreement. The Indian situation was different from that in Australia and South Africa in as much that education matters had never been an issue (and nor have they since as there have been no TPI-recognized Schools in India), and a greater independence from TPI seemed to be demanded and justified. The Indian Institute of Town Planners dated from 1951; it was inaugurated in January 1952 by Max Lock. Great strides have been taken since, curiously with little attention by the TPI. For example, the Indian Institute's first conference in 1952, in Delhi, on Town Planning and Housing, had an exhibition on Planning in the UK—but it was through the British Council that this was arranged. Subsequently the Institute began its Journal, annual All-India seminars have been held, a School of Town and Country Planning, established at Delhi in 1955, has been complemented by a number of planning courses at the Institute of Technology, Kharagpur, and the Institute's activities have received appreciation in official political circles. The first mention of an Indian body in Institute records, however, was not until October 1953. For some years an affiliation agreement was under discussion, but by 1957 it was referred to as an alliance. This agreement was concluded in May 1958.

In the sixties the overseas situation developed without any clear pattern. On the one hand, new Branches were formed; on the other, the tendency towards independence was marked. A small Hong Kong Branch was set up in 1963. Only 18 RTPI members are currently listed as resident in Hong Kong, and various relaxations in the Branch regulations have been made in view of its diminutive size. In 1966 the Malaysian Branch split to become the Malaysia and Singapore Branches. In 1973 the Singapore Branch was dissolved and funds were handed over to the new Malaysia Institute of Planners. Political developments in Central Africa occasioned some speculation as to geographical coverage, but currently Malawi appears to be part of the Central Africa Branch.

Elsewhere equality of status has been pursued. In Australia the affiliation agreement with the API was renegotiated as an alliance agreement in 1966. The next year it was decided to renegotiate the South African affiliation as an alliance. In 1969 the New Zealand Branch was dissolved to become the New Zealand Planning Institute as a consequence of another alliance agreement. It is a small body with only about 200 members (including students); it does not engage in the education of planners nor does it set examinations. This new form of agreement permitted a loose form of association with the Institute. All grades of overseas members visiting the UK were welcome to attend Institute and Branch meetings and to make use of the Institute Library; reciprocal courtesies were to be extended to TPI members visiting countries abroad. Each Institute undertook to consult each other on constitutional matters, examinations and Codes of Professional Conduct. Subject to certain safeguards, members of TPI were eligible for membership, and subscription rates were reduced.

At this point the question of attitudes towards issues in South Africa became more important, and during 1970 and 1971 a number of letters appeared in the Journal on the Institute's position. In November 1970 Rathbone wrote to the Secretary of the South African Institute for information on entry restrictions to that body and to recognized planning courses, and on eligibility of professional planners for posts in South Africa. The reply in January 1971 was to the effect that no restrictions were applied to membership of the SAI in regard to sex, race or colour. Any restriction on entry to a University planning course depended on the rules of the University and any government control. Vacant planning posts were filled according to conditions laid down by the employers. Information on these matters was subsequently gathered from the other affiliated or allied Societies. The next step was that the Institutes in Australia, New Zealand and India were asked if they would accept the insertion of a clause in their respective Agreements that 'Each Institute declares that it will exercise its membership policy without regard to race, colour or creed.' Australia and India agreed; New Zealand preferred the wording 'Each Institute will continue to ...'.

In 1972 Rathbone sent a copy of a draft Alliance Agreement to the SAI, based on the Alliance Agreements with the other three Institutes, amended by the inclusion of the new clause. The outcome was indeterminate. The matter came to a head at the Annual General Meeting of the RTPI in July 1973 when there was a motion from two members that the Institute should terminate its Affiliation Agreement with the SAI and should terminate recognition of the two listed Schools. During this meeting it was reported that in view of the many difficulties involved in assessing standards of overseas courses, Council

238

had already resolved that full recognition be withdrawn from *all* overseas courses previously recognized by RTPI, including courses both in Australia and South Africa. Letters from the Heads of the Planning Departments at Witwatersrand and Natal were read, affirming that in neither case did they exercise discriminatory practices. After lengthy discussion, a Resolution was passed, as an amendment to the original Motion to the effect that Council should proceed with the Alliance arrangements and partial recognition of courses provided that it regularly reviewed the situation. Council subsequently resolved to act on this Resolution.

The internationalization of planning has resulted in another form of linkage, namely the Commonwealth Association of Planners. The idea was proposed to Council by Ling in February 1969; he thought the Association a logical consolidation of the ad hoc organizational changes which had been taking place in the profession in various Commonwealth countries during the last decade. It was decided to give recognition to the new relationship and responsibilities which have been established. The matter took shape quickly, and an Interim Executive Committee of the Association (CAP) met in Ghana in October 1971. Rathbone served as Interim Secretary during the formative period of the Association and Ling became President. A successful conference was held in Delhi in March 1973 with representatives from 15 countries; Amos was the RTPI representative. The Association is financially supported by the Commonwealth Foundation, though on a decreasing annual grant; further support from Member Institutes is likely in the future.

Internationalism outside the Commonwealth has not been promoted with any energy or constancy. Doubleday led two TPI study tours to North America in 1959 and 1967, but there are no formal links with the American Institute of Planners or the Planning Institute of Canada. Instead, international relations have tended to depend on personal contacts; the Institute maintains a list of Corresponding Members from overseas. There has also been reliance on the efforts of the International Federation for Housing and Town Planning, while the Town and Country Planning Association has filled continental gaps with its frequent study tours. There is one major and important exception to this general situation: the Planning Summer School for Overseas Members, which in recent years has been attracting good numbers and papers of high quality.

A Commonwealth strengthening has been matched by quite a new challenge in Europe. There are no professional planning Institutes in Europe, planning being an activity for a number of different skills. The question of eligibility of practice in Britain and other countries is a crucial one and delicate negotiations are currently being conducted to safeguard the position of British town planners in this country and abroad. The International Society of City and Regional Planners (ISoCaRP) has established an EEC Liaison Committee on which there are representatives of the professional organizations from each member country. RTPI is the UK representative[4]. In the meantime the Institute appropriately held its Annual Meeting in April 1973 in Amsterdam. The expressions of reciprocal goodwill recorded there are likely to herald years of anxious developments during the seventies as the meaning and implications of British professionalism find a new framework in the new setting of Europe.

REFERENCES

1. Town Planning Institute Committee Minutes, vol. VI, p. 81.
2. Special Supplement. *Journal of the Town Planning Institute*, **51**, No. 3, 1965.
3. *Journal of the Town Planning Institute*, **XLV**, No. 8, 202, 1959.
4. *Journal of the Royal Town Planning Institute*, **58**, No. 10, 458,

11 An Overview: Planning and the Profession

This account of the evolution of British town planning has unfolded largely in chronological sequence. Only with regard to education and Branch affairs have topics been identified for separate analysis. Furthermore, the account has been essentially descriptive, although with passing commentary as to the significance of various developments. An attempt is now made to draw the many strands together and offer some broad observations on the nature of British planning this century, and the development of the planning profession. The account concludes with a look at the future.

By way of introduction, we might remark that if growth and extension of activities are relevant criteria, the sixty years of the Institute's history have been remarkably successful. In just two generations, from an early tight-knit circle of earnest reformers, there has developed a major profession. At the first meeting of the Institute in 1914 sixty-four persons were nominated for membership in various categories. By 1939 the membership had reached almost one thousand and is now in the region of ten thousand. Steady progress was maintained over the first two decades, after which a recognizable 'take off' occurred. In 1935 there were over 400 members of all categories. Activity quickened and by 1939 the total stood at more than 900. By 1946 this had almost doubled to 1 700. By 1960 it was just over 4 000 and by mid-1973 it was nearly 9 500. Expansion therefore is accelerating markedly. Moreover the increase in numbers is being achieved through entry by student members, thereby ensuring a high total membership figure for many, many years. In 1935 one in eight was a student member; in 1939 the proportion was one in six, in 1946 one in five; in 1960 one in four; and in 1973 less than one in three.

Success can be measured in other ways. For example, by any comparison, many of the Institute's members have made notable contributions to academic and professional life; they have been rewarded with the highest public honours. A new professional body has taken its place beside others of longer establishment. Admittedly it made a slow start, but perhaps the cautious grounding was beneficial. As late as 1933, a standard text on professional organizations, *The Professions* by Carr-Saunders and Wilson, failed to make mention of the TPI. In 1952 another book on professions though of a very different reputation, *Professional People* by Lewis and Maude, could refer to the planning officer as 'that lowest form of local government life'. Today no serious book on British professions could reasonably exclude full reference to the RTPI.

Over a lengthy period the Institute proved itself by capacity for responsibile conduct of its affairs; it consolidated its core of knowledge, extended its sphere of concern, and satisfactorily promoted the education of its members; ultimately it obtained a Royal Charter and fixed its reputation and importance in national affairs. Carved out of three land-oriented professions, and with only a slender base for self-identity, it gradually usurped many of the interests and skills of its sister bodies and took over and integrated a number of their former functions in a new umbrella of activity. Its professional members are now beginning to infiltrate and occupy senior positions in fields which have been previously the concern of others, particularly in social affairs and administration. The question of status for the town planner, particularly in local authorities, was for a long time a sensitive one for the Institute, but in recent years opportunities for planners both in local authorities and elsewhere have widened substantially.

In matters of government and administration, the development of planning has been equally spectacular. From a miniscule 1909 Act, planning and related legislation has crowded upon the statute book. Unprecedented powers of government control have been extended to the way our land and buildings are used and developed; our environment protected; community facilities enhanced; our roads planned; and the way in which our housing and social needs are met. The place of planning in both central and local government has mushroomed as part of the general growth of twentieth century bureaucracy, but its relative position has advanced out of all recognition. From a handful of people in the Ministry of Health before the First World War there emerged a Planning Ministry in the Second, subsequently to become a central part of a new gigantic Department at the present time. Within local authorities the first steps which saw the appointment of a town planning assistant in the borough engineer's office led to the creation of large departments in their own right in both counties and County Boroughs.

The successful rise of planning can also be seen in that as an activity and as an operation of local and central administration, the very word has now entered everyday vocabulary. Planning is an issue of public importance, impinging on the lives of people in myriad ways: housing, slum clearance, new towns, motorways, recreation in town and country, shopping, schools, factories and jobs, airports and national communications. From a relatively single-minded obsession of those dedicated to housing and land reform, planning has become a matter of the widest public interest and relevance.

Planning has successfully claimed the attention and support of people from a range of backgrounds: skilled technicians, professionals, reformers, idealists, propagandists and politicians. It has given key words and ideas which have helped to shape twentieth century history—garden cities, green belt, new towns, neighbourhoods, 'Radburn' and zoning are just a few examples. It has helped to shape our towns in ways which have overridden the facts of economics, geography and market forces. It has embraced objectives most of which, by and large, society as a whole has also valued; at times it has been a pace-setter, setting before the community ideals which have later become conventional wisdoms. It has had a wide appeal, taking sides neither for nor against one particular sector of society. The very fact that in 1974 planning occupies the position it does in public affairs,

242

and that the Institute has grown to the size it now has, clearly implies many successful qualities and characteristics.

Planning during this century has been one of the integral features of our social and economic history. It has underpinned a period during which the bulk of the country's population has become better housed and better provided with a range of community facilities; also during which our towns and cities have expanded and have been reshaped. In a period of great change in society it has dealt with problems connected with urban growth, redevelopment, traffic, usage of the countryside and regional disparities. The solutions it has adopted and actively pursued are part of the social history of our time.

These are broad statements, and a more critical assessment is necessary. It is not easy, however, to evaluate the broad achievements of planning because the original goals or intentions have rarely been specified. It is difficult to compare results which can be measured against objectives which were seldom made explicit. In any case this is a large question and it is impossible in these pages to assess the many efforts which have been made to intervene in the process of change in town and country during this century. One would be led into examinations of regional policy, location of employment, attempts to deal with road traffic, protection of amenity, land-use control, and so on. But to speculate, the conclusions would probably be that, at most, planning has had mixed success, with some failures, and more often than not, unforeseen (and perhaps unhappy) consequences. Especially where fundamental social trends have been at issue, it may be suspected that certain developments (good or bad) would have happened anyway, planning or no planning.

Peter Hall's study of *The Containment of Urban England* (1973) is a case in point. In comparing the chief results of the 1947 planning system with the original intentions, he observes that there are three unambiguous and certain impacts. One is the fact that urban growth has been contained, and this was an objective. The second is suburbanization, the reverse of what was intended. The third is the inflation of land and property prices since the late fifties, on an unprecedented scale, something which the finance provisions of the 1947 Act had set out to control. Moreover, consequent upon these results the fact is that there are some people who have benefited and some who have paid. Those who have benefited include rural inhabitants, gaining through inflation, those with a stake in the property market, inhabitants of new and expanding towns, and owner occupiers, especially the early ones. Those who have paid include many suburbanites who on average have less floor space and are housed at a higher density than their equivalents in the thirties, local authority tenants housed in high-density, high-rise developments, and low-income private rented families in the big cities. In this way, the 1947 system, aiming at urban containment, and the creation of self-contained and balanced communities has had the effect of giving the most benefits to the more advantaged members of society and the least to the less advantaged.

It is therefore with disappointment and humility that the planner might look back on some of his achievements. He now recognizes that any system of planned intervention in land use and social change is fraught with unknowns. He cannot afford to be arrogant about either his intentions or any certainty as to the outcome. Hall's masterly analysis of recent urban developments in England sharpens the discomfort of the planner when he (in respect of post-war change in Outer Metropolitan London) he is told that, 'something like it would have happened anyway, plan or no plan. The living patterns and to some extent the job patterns would have occurred without a 1947 planning system at all.'[1]

To revert to the place of planning in this present century: the social history of modern Britain contains a number of themes which are well illustrated in the evolution of planning. The rise of the qualifying profession, for example, is one feature of the century. A study of the RTPI affords a classic example of one of these: its formation, development, training of members, emphasis on standards and professional conduct, and its pursuance of status. The phenomenon of the explosion of knowledge has applied to planning as much as any other social science and landbased skill; again, a study of planning reveals the way in which this has affected a particular subject area, with results in terms of fragmentation and specialisms.

A further example is the question of social attitudes; their emergence and relative strength, and the effect they have on public policies. Within planning there are many examples available for analysis. Take, for instance, attitudes towards urban growth. Public awareness and concern increased sharply in the thirties, particularly in response to London's growth. A mixture of garden city propaganda, recommendations of the amenity conscious bodies, and the scientific advice of the technical planner brought to popular acceptance a complex and long-term solution which implied unprecedented controls over private development and the national planning of population distribution. Other examples are the discovery of the countryside for mass urban leisure in the thirties, the demand for planned reconstruction in the war years, the conservation movement of the sixties, and issues such as the concern for environmental protection, quality of life, the anti-motorway movement, the demand for public participation, and so on.

A study of twentieth century planning also sheds light on the development of political ideas in contemporary social history. The political attitudes and assumptions which attended the 1909 Act changed greatly by the time of the 1932 Act; the 1947 Act reflected considerable change and the 1968 Act showed further shifts of emphasis. The years of the two wars are watersheds; what was only just acceptable at the outset of each was outmoded by the end. The housing provisions of the 1919 Act were only possible because the 'homes for heroes' campaign was popularly supported. National parks, shelved during the thirties became inevitable during the forties; the demand for easy and further access to the countryside, refused during the thirties, was readily met in 1949. Compulsory planning powers, kept at arms' length in the inter-war years, suddenly became necessary during the war when churchmen, politicians, architectural visionaries and social idealists combined to popularize a mood of reconstruction and community regeneration. More recently, the logic of central control has been eroded in favour of the need to satisfy new forms of popular engagement in public policy and planning decisions.

The twentieth century has been a battleground between democracy and totalitarianism, and the events with which planning has been concerned have a bearing on this. In the thirties, the planning performances of Britain and other Western countries were compared unfavourably with those of Germany, Italy and Russia. The Moscow ten-year plan, the grandiose plans of Hitler for the reconstruction of Berlin and autobahn achievements attracted intellectual support for the dictator's way of government. The question

244

of effective planning in a democracy of British style assumed a serious urgency. The search for new machinery of Government, which allowed a centralist form of town planning to develop, operating through local authorities, was met quickly in the wartime emergency.

THE NATURE OF PLANNING

At the outset it is necessary to distinguish between the idea of planning as a graphical representation of a future physical form, and that of planning as an ongoing process. The distinction is fundamental. For most of this century town planning in this country saw its purpose in the preparation of unitary plans for a point of time in the future; they were maps showing an ideal future spatial form. Largely from American sources, another meaning of planning has been provided: this is the idea of process, a sequence of events from objectives to results. The development of systems analysis helped planners to see the inadequacy of relying on plans of the old type, but the transition from one style of planning to the other during the last ten years caused great professional difficulties.

There are a number of insights which a historical study can give to our understanding of town planning. First, we can confirm the very great importance of the contribution of ideas surrounding social purpose and creativity. They have both stimulated fervour for planning and sustained enthusiasm within the profession. We noted the importance of these ideas in the origins of planning and at no time have they been absent from the ideology of the planner. A combination of religious purpose, social justice, egalitarianism, political radicalism and aesthetic considerations of civic art and design has conspired to be a powerful inner drive which has harnessed technical skills in meeting planning objectives. Before the turn of the century the literary dreams of William Morris concerning the future of London in *News From Nowhere* created a style of imaginative thinking, and supported a restless drive to attain a perfect future. The idealistic schemes of many plans have fallen subsequently into that mainstream of thought and action. R. H. Mattocks in his Presidential Address in 1941 began by saying that: 'Today, the "young men" of our profession "are seeing visions and the old men are dreamin' dreams" of what may result if post-war reconstruction is properly directed.'[2] Out of the tumult of war was forged a stronger idealism, and appropriately Mattocks concluded with an extract from Jerome K. Jerome's *All Roads Lead to Calvary*, with its vision of London of the future: 'A city of peace, of restful spaces, of leisured men and women; a city of fine streets and pleasant houses, where each could live his own life, learning freedom, individuality; a city of noble schools; of workshops that should be worthy of labour, filled with light and air; smoke and filth driven from the land; science no longer bound to commercialism, having discovered cleaner forces; a city of gay playgrounds where children should learn laughter; of leafy walks where the creatures of the wood and field should be as welcome guests helping to teach sympathy and kindliness; a city of music, of colour, of gladness.' Town planning has fallen heir to utopianism of this kind.

This idealism has sustained a fundamental belief in the validity of basic planning objectives, a kind of certainty of pursuing the right course. Although this sense of conviction is not necessarily expressed these days, there have been occasions in the past when confidence in role and performance was strongly felt. At an Institute Meeting in Canterbury in 1925, the Dean's sermon during a service in the Cathedral was significant. First he echoed support for planning in East Kent (the Archbishop had been instrumental in setting up the East Kent Development Committee, and Abercrombie's Report had just been published). He went on to comment on Ezekiel's vision of the city and temple (his text), believing that town planning was the fruit of a vision. 'The eye is lifted up. The heart is touched and the imagination kindled by some dream of what might be, some reaching out beyond the present position and the present need to a farseen ideal. Without a vision the people perisheth. Without a vision public opinion is dead. Without a vision I will not say that the Town Planner's designs are empty and cold but the Town Planner himself cannot live.'[3] The Dean continued: 'To make your city a well-ordered beautiful and healthy place, where men, women and children may live and work and play, with sunshine and air and ample open spaces—certainly that is a high and sacred service. To remove the hindrances to pure and honest living, to set the soul of the pursuer free, ... to teach the citizens of today and tomorrow, by the things you set before their eyes and the standards you supply, the supreme value of the things of the Spirit, is a holy and religious calling.' Pepler thought that Cathedral service marked a new step in the history of the Institute; it had 'urged the dedication of our art to the service of mankind'[4]. No wonder a recent critic has spoken of planners being Evangelical Bureaucrats, driven by the belief that they are right when others consider them to be wrong[5].

Side by side with the visionary impulse has been the particular attraction of futurism. An element in the origins of planning was the scientific utopianism as expressed by H. G. Wells, and a subsequent recurrent theme in planning has been to positively embrace the future as an ideal worth striving for as part of man's perfectability. The implication was that the future must be 'good' and in this way the planner has tended to be on the side of 'development', on the assumption that this represented progress and human achievement. The recurrence of this was the speculation in the sixties of 'inventing the future', harnessing new technological aids to secure the perfect world.

Associated with this idea has been the reaction against the substandard and the shoddy. The early planning movement was given a particular impulse by the horror of the ugly and the degradation of human life that the Industrial Revolution had promoted. A complex of related social forces included anti-urban sentiments, guild socialism against industrialization, the belief that human identity could be accommodated not in large cities but in small units, and the support for civic art in the beautification of our towns. The stream of thought and activity can be traced from Morris and his Arts and Crafts movement to Unwin and garden suburb design, to the slum clearance drive of the 1930s, to the builders of the post-war new towns, to concern over environmental protection, and to contemporary speculation about quality of life. The visionary, the futurist and the perfectionist enter deep into the planner's makeup. In recent years these traces have been obscured, but they are there. Planning owes much to those intuitive leaps in the dark stimulated by ideas born of restlessness and a sense of dissatisfaction with what is compared with what might be. Graham Ashworth asked in a Journal paper 'Where have all the wild men gone?'[6] They are still around.

Planning soon claimed for itself a core of knowledge and concern, separate from but related to the three parent professions. Basically, it related to land and the development process, the way in which land was laid out and used, the visual amenities which could result and the relationship that development had to other matters. From the start, then, it drew heavily on the contributions of architecture, engineering, surveying and the law. There emerged a new field of expertise, straddling the boundaries of four existing participants. It was given a rationale and identity because of a number of factors. One was a synthesis, a co-ordination and an understanding of the related parts, so perceptively analysed by Geddes in the early years. Second, the parent professions were themselves unable to act in this integrated way. Third, the new field related to problems at the turn of the century which needed new insight, new approaches to solutions and new institutional arrangements. Those interested in planning at the turn of the century and who formed the early adherents of the movement saw in the new Institute a relevance to unmet problems and possibilities which the other existing bodies could or would not take up. The emergence of planning, therefore, was an institutional response to a set of problems which needed to be tackled in a certain way.

In the first instance there was no unique body of knowledge for planning. It absorbed overlapping fields and was given life through an approach to problems and a set of objectives relating to land and people. From the very start planning was a way of looking at things, rather than a question of skills to tackle a particular problem. It was given institutional terms of reference through successive legislation and the emergence of a statutory planning process. Throughout its history the identity of planning continued to depend heavily on a set of shared objectives rather than uniqueness of knowledge. For many years the work done by the planner could be, and very often was, done by people trained in other professions. It was only with specialization in education that planning offered a set of skills and insights which other professions and academic training did not. Sir Raymond Unwin well described the objectives of planning when, in November 1938, he was presented with the first Howard Memorial medal by the Garden City and Town Planning Association. 'The true purpose of planning ... is to afford greater and wider opportunities for securing the right location of human activities, and for creating in our pleasant land an environment more appropriate than any which could possibly result from haphazard development; and to foster a new and better order of life.'[7] Planning began, therefore, with a split personality; it received its driving force from a set of objectives which belonged to the British liberal, humanitarian tradition inspired by precepts of architectural and social ideals. These it harnessed to a set of technical skills which belonged to other fields of study or practice. Many people therefore felt they could share in the uniqueness which planning claims. This bedevilled the internal structure of the profession but yet it fed it new rich intellectual food for its preservation and growth. The dependence on shared skills and objectives still remain in large part. We must expect, therefore, that the boundaries of planning will never be constant or fixed; it will expand and contract, overlap or take over existing fields, just as it always has done.

An important characteristic of planning which we can detect throughout its history has been its ability and readiness to adopt and justify very different types of solution for the same problem. The broad principles as enunciated by Unwin (above) can be interpreted in design or implementation terms in a variety of ways. Environmental design is a question of cultural or societal preferences, and during the present century these have changed with bewildering rapidity. There are no fixed design or planning solutions. Schemes with a lengthy history bear testimony to this; what is acceptable in one decade of fashion may not be acceptable in another. Proposals for central area redevelopment in the 1930s were quite different from those adopted in the 1960s. Designs for accommodating the motor car in city centres have varied considerably—Birmingham has been redeveloped quite differently from Coventry only twenty miles away, due to a combination of professional and political dictates. Proposals for motorways may be thrilling one year, feared the next. Housing designs have ranged from twelve to the acre individual units, to integrated high-density blocks, to flats of thirty storeys: all have been praised and all have been derided. Satellite towns have been abandoned for finger development and then for corridors of growth, and so on: it all points to the advisability of not claiming the latest viewpoint as the greatest wisdom. Planning is not an exact science, it is an art, the periodic expression of values.

Another aspect of the changing nature of planning is the enormous explosion of knowledge which has taken place during this century, in keeping with all other subject areas. All professions have witnessed the mushrooming in the growth of technical expertise, and consequently there has been a fragmentation of most professional areas into constituent specialisms. In the face of this, planning has attempted to maintain one of its main important contributions, that of synthesis, which meant a generalist, integrating tradition. The importance of specialisms within has always been recognized, but their growing significance within the total process caused one of the dilemmas of the sixties. It is a moot point how far the explosion of town planning knowledge can still be contained within one professional ambit: the challenge for educationalists is to preserve that rare understanding of synthesis and outlook but yet give due scope for specialist insights.

Another aspect of change represents the nature of the planning process. We have seen two strands. One is the view that planning is a rational, a-political, common-sense view to solutions which meets the public good. This was prevalent, particularly up to the forties and it did not effectively collapse until the late fifties. Planning was seen as a matter for technical expertise, which in itself could not be wrong, and which could be harnessed to any political power block. In the thirties some people were attracted towards totalitarian regimes because they 'got things done'. Second, on the other hand, is the view that politics, far from abandoning planning, actually is part of it, because planning represents decision-taking on behalf of or by the public; alternatives are at stake, and planning is concerned with choices. This is the current viewpoint, and the change has resulted in considerable differences in the planning process. The first assumption encouraged the prescriptive plan—a package of proposals prepared by technical officers, adopted by the government or authority in power, which represented a programme of development which all should follow. It was an 'end-state' plan, a fixed view of things. The second political assumption, however, demanded more open-ended plans. There was no monopoly of wisdom by the technical officer and plans became adaptive, flexible and shaped by considerations which were 'non-technical'. Public opinion became the political dictate.

There are, therefore, a number of examples of change within planning. But there are also examples of constancy. One is that planning in this country has been essentially practice-based and client-centred. It has not been at ease when dealing with the abstract or with theory. It is significant that the very first two issues of the Institute's Journal (Papers and Discussions) were devoted to the Ruislip–Northwood scheme, and throughout, planners have made their contribution in practical situations: scheme preparation by private consultants, and engagement in the statutory planning process. Few academics have contributed outside the development process. This is by comparison with America where developments in planning thought rather than practice have been more characteristic, especially in recent years. This has meant that British planning has centred round land and development and related issues. The essence of British town planning is about the development process, and the synoptic context within which it is set. If it were to move very far from this it would be in danger of losing, perhaps, the one sure thing it does relate to. In recent years the land and design aspects of planning have been overshadowed by other interests, particularly social- and management-oriented. It might be expected that this fashion will not continue, and at the present time a renewed interest is being shown in environmental design: perhaps this is one of the keys to the immediate future.

With these characteristics planning has embraced a number of repetitive themes throughout the century. Fundamentally, they have two points of origin: first, the search for order, amenity and convenience in the physical environment, and second, belief in the ability to create a new social order.

The origins of planning owe much to a reaction to chaotic Victorian development, where adjoining uses were unharmonious in appearance and function and where the land-use pattern reflected myriad land ownerships. Local bye-laws and the Public Health Acts began the process of an ordered environment, and the Planning Acts after 1909 encouraged the trend towards clearly defined land-use patterns. Planning sought to achieve more open space, sunlight, and air in overcrowded cities; decentralization and the reduction of congestion helped in this. Land use rationalization (zoning) gave a new spatial order to our urban environment, a principle taken up in the Development Plans of the fifties. It was not until the sixties that a reaction against undue obsession with order set in. Jane Jacobs in *Death and Life of Great American Cities* (1961) argued that cultural and physical diversity was something important in the life of a city and she charged planners with deliberately eradicating it. Later, Richard Sennett in *Uses of Disorder* (1970) argued that disorder was a positive value and that we should positively plan for disorder.

With order went beauty, and this again has been a repetitive theme, particularly with regard to cities. The Industrial Revolution produced a century of ugliness which planning was charged with remedying. Both the Arts and Crafts movement and the phase of applied civic art provided an important line of activity which has run throughout planning. The obligation has been to plan beautiful cities through designing for the new and preserving that which is worthwhile from the old. Planning objectives have embraced city building as an art form and have never been indifferent to the ideas of good appearance and beauty.

Convenience has been a theme manifested in many ways—the convenience of planned distributions, and planned transport, of economic efficiency and so on. It provides an obvious framework for many planning activities.

The social basis of planning again shows a number of repetitive themes. At the turn of the century the European tradition in planning had been derived from a 'public works' background. But developments showed that it was the British garden city and the housing reform movement that provided the more imaginative, compelling and secure base for the future. The key target became not just fine civic architecture but the improvement of living conditions. In the twenty years before the First World War there was intense intellectual speculation about social progress and ideas concerning the dignity of man. Liberal politics embraced social reform, and developments in planning have to be seen in this context. Letchworth had a distinctly humanist interpretation, supported by earnest reformers with great optimism and confidence. There was the belief that what they were creating was a new way of life, a new social brotherhood, and a solution to the social problems which people recognized in Victorian England.

Another aspect of early planning was its flavour of environmental determinism. Better housing, lower residential densities, sunlight and fresh air were linked with improved health, the eradication of social discord, the promotion of happiness and the solution of moral issues like drunkenness and vice.

Since these early days there has never developed any coherent body of thought or practice about social planning. There have simply been periods of alternating fashions as interpretations of need varied. It has ranged from futurism and long-term idealism expressed in such terms as 'providing for the good life' to what we now regard as 'instant incrementalism' — tackling social problems through an effective programme of social welfare. But an underlying approach and outlook has permeated planning and given it an unmistakable ethos. For example, planners have usually asserted that neighbourliness, social mixing and human interaction are positive ideals. This holds good from Toynbee Hall in the 1880s to the Radburn superblock of 1929, from Reilly Greens to the villages of Washington New Town, from the ideals of Henrietta Barnett at Hampstead to those of Reith and his architectural translator, Gibberd, at Harlow, from the Reverend Charles Jenkinson and his Quarry Hill flats at Leeds in the late thirties to the post-war designers of Roehampton, and from Purdom's Letchworth to the philosophy behind Milton Keynes. Planners have expressed belief in the fostering of social relationships and this has affected physical design at the local level.

The planner in his work has tended to emphasize human values as opposed to technological values in his work. He has been motivated to believe in small groups and the value of human identity. In the need to give man a personal place and role in life, the planner has tended to decry the big city and its anonimity; instead he has been a willing advocate of small-scale development and 'civic pride'. Town planning in the sixties does not necessarily repeat this evidence, for the planner in this period succumbed to the attraction of the gigantic, and perhaps the inhuman, but the point still holds good.

In town development the provision of social facilities is an obvious way of meeting needs. Planners have always regarded this as an important part of their work. Planned development has implied a full range of facilities and this had led planning into a close relationship with social administration, social service co-ordination and recreation planning.

Ideas about the way in which social objectives are attained have changed in recent years. Early assumptions were based on precepts of social engineering, and a similarity of approach straddled the period from J. S. Buckingham to Lord Reith. But current favour is given to the concept of social evolution, the idea that planning is a catalyst whereby society itself makes certain moves of self-adjustment in its values, aspirations and objectives. Planning for satisfaction and for fulfilment thus becomes something built up from below rather than directed from above.

THE PROFESSION

We look finally at the RTPI as a profession. Its origins and subsequent development conform closely with the evolution undergone by other professional bodies. It has had a fairly typical history and the challenges which now face it are similar to those which face many others.

The planning profession in its formation grew directly from the Victorian proliferation of new forms of occupational associations. This was a time when public estimation for professions increased, and their social respectability and standing was enhanced. There were a number of earlier important changes. The older organizations, like law, medicine and the church were reformed. A number of study societies appeared like the Geological Society, founded in 1807, the Zoological Society (1824) and the Royal Geographical Society (1830). But then a new type of professional organization evolved, designed to improve status and working conditions of those engaged in a particular field. One of the early examples was the Provincial Medical and Surgical Association (1832) which in 1856 became the British Medical Association. Another was the National Union of Teachers, founded in 1870 as the National Union of Elementary Teachers. A characteristic of this type of organization was that they made no attempt to qualify anyone to practice; they were for fully trained people and no unqualified or non-practitioners were admitted. This was the difference from the qualifying professional associations which came to enjoy a spectacular development in the latter half of the nineteenth century. Forerunners came with the Institution of Civil Engineers (1818), the Institute of British Architects (1834), the Pharmaceutical Society (1841), the Royal College of Veterinary Surgeons (1844), the Institution of Mechanical Engineers (1847) and the Institute of Actuaries (1848). The number of qualifying associations multiplied, spreading to other types of engineers, surveyors, chemists, librarians, accountants, auctioneers, and company secretaries. In 1877 the Law Society had become fully responsible for all solicitors' examinations, and so, by this time, the parent professions to planning had become firmly established.

The period after the 1880s was particularly prolific, with a dozen new associations appearing each decade between 1880 and 1910. There were emphases on the organization of engineers, accountants and a number of related land professions involving surveyors, estate agents, valuers and auctioneers. After 1910 the decennial formation rate doubled, with engineering, accountancy and the land professions generating new organizations; management and administration became another occupational area subject to organization; later, anciliary medical services produced organizations. It was in this period that the TPI emerged—albeit haltingly with slow development, as we have seen. The context for its creation and evolution is one of great professional growth fostered by specialization, the need for new facilities for education and training and reaction to the scope of the work of existing bodies. The organization of a new subject field, planning, as a qualifying association was a typical event of this period.

Once established, the Institute had to withstand a number of obstacles. One must have been the onset of war in the very year of its foundation. An immediate consequence was the considerable contraction of planning practice, only offset later by the reconstruction fervour in favour of planning. The small number of practitioners must have made future stability problematical, although the fanaticism of the propagandists was a complementary support. A concentration of activity in London had to be overcome, and in this the development of the Branch network was important. Another obstacle was the feebly developed practical aspects of planning: in 1914 only a handful of planning schemes had been prepared and a small number of housing layouts on garden city lines undertaken. The development of new methods in the early 1920s like zoning and regional planning exercises were the first expansions to the core of practical expertise. A constant problematical hazard, rather than a hurdle, was the obvious presence of rival, parent organizations; it was not until 1932 and the inauguration of the TPI Intermediate examination that some measure of real independence was achieved. From the point of view of education, there was still a good deal of variation in training received by practitioners, both in formal training and in practical experience, and this again was a constraint on effective professional growth for perhaps twenty years.

The question of status was a sensitive one in this period. Without it, the Institute was not in a position to influence in ways traditionally open to professions; how it secured that status was a matter on which feelings ran high. Crude propaganda was something for other bodies; public honours and broad political influence was another matter. The importance of this comes through in the ecstatic congratulations of the Editorial of the Journal in 1935 when the President, Herbert Humphreys, was knighted in celebration of the Centenary of Local Government. 'This honour is the more flattering to us as in the official announcement Mr Humphreys was specifically designated as the President of the Institute.'[8] The Editorial went on: 'Mr Humphreys has done good solid work. He represents a side of Town Planning in which it was for some time perhaps lacking. It was always so easy for fools and wilful obstructionists to talk about the "long-haired brigade" when Town Planning was mentioned ... we are bound to realize that we have passed out of the stage of experiment into that of achievement, and that the edifice we dreamed of years ago is being built up solidly stone by stone out of experience gained in many parts of the world.' To achieve professional status in this inter-war period the Institute had to work very hard; every straw was clutched. The showering of responsibility upon it during the wartime years and afterwards, came with relative suddenness.

The profession survived and finally flourished. Two factors in its favour might be identified. One was the development of a statutory planning process consequent upon legislation. A new area of local authority work emerged, confined initially to just a few Councils, but to become, in theory at least, obligatory on all of a certain size during the twenties. This stimulated an activity which quickly demanded an independent organization for its development. Second was the existence of enterprising, enthusiastic people devoted to the idea of planning, and dedicated over many years to the success of a professional institute. Geoffrey Millerson has observed that: 'The history of every association is the record of one or more devoted individuals, whose spark ignited a movement, or revived a decaying structure.'[9] The RTPI is a good illustration of this. Potter and Pepler for forty-five and forty-four years respectively represented just the enterprise and continuity that was demanded. The Institute has never seemed to be without servants of outstanding dedication, loyalty and high endeavour. Richard Pepler has continued the family tradition, now occupying the position of Honorary Solicitor. The Adams family was also outstanding, father and son (Thomas and James) being Presidents and another brother, Fred, achieving high distinction in America.

After its establishment, the Institute proceeded on predictable lines designed to enhance its reputation. The amateur declined in influence and was replaced by technically qualified personnel. It devised ways of meeting the needs of its members through meetings in London (and later elsewhere), through its Journal, through opportunities for education, and through encouraging social activities and the development of an *esprit de corps*. Only with non-provision of welfare benefits through a benevolent fund has there been any obvious omission. It conducted a determined search for status. The obtaining of a Royal Charter was pursued from the mid-1940s to a successful end in 1959; entry to the profession has been carefully protected; educational standards have been kept high; professional codes of conduct rigidly adhered to. As a result of all these measures, a basis of knowledge and practice was defined and a professional self-consciousness developed. At the same time the profession was more and more widely recognized by other professions and by the public.

The RTPI has been very successful in its development, but in recent years there have been increasing signs that the factors which have promoted a steady growth and quiet progression are now changing. New kinds of occupations are developing and changes are occurring within old occupations. Stresses and strains are being felt within many organizations and the RTPI is no exception. The investigations of the Monopolies Commission are likely to keep the spotlight on professional services for some time. Contemporary change in occupational structure has had, and is having, a major impact on planning. Many new skills have emerged in fields related to planning and the difficulty has been to make flexible arrangements for accommodating new people within an already broad-based Institute. The scope of what might constitute planning has widened, so that the unique contribution of synthesis is made almost impossibly demanding. Furthermore, the question of salaried employment, particularly in the public services, has destroyed an old feature of professionalism, that of private practice and fee-paying clients. For these reasons, and others, doubts have been raised as to whether planning is best served by a professional body or whether some form of learned society is the better answer. The Membership Document in 1971 raised this as an option.

The arguments have been well rehearsed. On the one hand professionalism is claimed as a progressive force in society with qualities of expertness and objectivity. Moreover, the client relationship has served society well by an acceptable reconciliation of the welfare and rights of the client with public interest. Professional ethics and the maintenance of standards are proven safeguards for both the private individual and public domain. Furthermore, professions are flexible in their organization and have proved capable of responding to new needs in an evolutionary way. Therefore to reason that professions cannot meet the needs of contemporary change and the future is unthinkable. In short, as Kantorowich has remarked, 'to dismantle professionalism is to forego excellence and to license mediocrity'[10].

Professional organization is important in a number of respects: it implies high standards of competence; its members are subject to discipline and control, restriction and limitation. All these, it is argued, are in order to maintain integrity, elevate standards and protect society. Without a professional organization, these are at risk. As Carr-Saunders and Wilson observed 40 years ago of professions generally: they are stable elements in society. 'Their members are conscious of the past; they are aware of a long chain of endeavours towards the improvement and adaptation of their technique. The old formula presses upon them; they inherit, preserve and hand on a tradition.'[11] This holds good for the RTPI, and in a world of bewildering change many are thankful for just that. In the same vein, Barrington Kaye in his study of the development of the architectural profession asserts that the main function of professional associations was to guarantee 'competence and integrity, without which the market for professional services would quickly become chaotic'[12]. Again, at the present time this merit is seen to be particularly valuable.

The arguments against professions are that they are inherently inflexible and restrictive, inhibiting freedom and regressive to a set of new factors. With regard to planning, membership of RTPI is claimed to be unduly restrictive for posts in local government; senior planning posts should not be constrained by professional ticket. Moreover, the Institute has been restrictive in its education/membership policy, denying entry to many who would have a contribution to make. In short, what is needed for the best evolution of planning as it moves into broad fields of urban management is the withdrawal of professional boundaries which serve as a constraint on new occupational structures which might emerge. McLoughlin has argued that 'town planning is not really a unique skill but a context for the operation of many kinds of skills'[13]. He criticizes the Institute for an excessive concentration on questions of techniques and the employment market: 'What it has done in the past, and what it hopes to continue doing, is to qualify people with a set of skills most of which are possessed by others, and which lack any distinct and united theoretical underpinning or value system. At the same time it hopes that its corporate members will enjoy what are virtually monopoly rights in a particular part of the employment market', although these markets are being considerably reshaped.

The balance of these arguments is a matter of personal judgement. It seems to me that the benefits of professionalism are real and are not attainable to the same degree in other forms of voluntary organization. Professions have served society well and should not be discarded without very good reason. It is perfectly true that some inflexibility, restrictiveness and lack of capacity to respond to changing requirements are and have been characteristics—but they are features which apply equally well to any social organization. It is by no means proven that learned bodies would provide a more suitable mechanism for advancing planning or protecting society. In the meantime the sensible course of action would be to enhance the benefits of professions rather than to seek to limit them, or to transfer them to another framework of organization. All Institutions *are* flexible—remarkably so; they owe their existence to flexibility. McLoughlin's verdict above was written before the RTPI Discussion Paper 'Implications of Changes in Education and Membership Policy' in 1973, a document, the very existence of which illustrates the capacity for change.

As a result of sixty years' growth, the planning profession has now acquired a social identity. Many features are well known. For example, it is a matter of common observation that it is a male dominated profession: only 7% of all members were female in 1971, although 10% of student members were of that sex. An interesting student thesis by Susanna T. Marcus has quantified other evidence[14], admittedly with a small sample of 112. The social status of membership was described as 'undifferentiated middle class' with nearly half coming from professional or executive backgrounds; two-thirds had fathers who had attended public or grammar schools. Forty-five per cent of the membership qualified in another profession before entering planning; thirty-four per cent held a degree either in town planning or another discipline. The remaining twenty-one per cent were direct entry planners who had either taken a diploma in planning or the Institute's own examinations. One feature of the professional career of members was very great geographical mobility. Earnings were similar to architects, but less than solicitors or dentists. Political attitudes were more to the left of centre than average; religious affiliation similar to national patterns. Daily reading taste leaned to *The Guardian*, followed by *The Times* and *The Daily Telegraph*. A most interesting conclusion concerned the nature of the planners' professional commitment. There seemed to be basic satisfactions experienced by planners in two main fields. One concerned creativity in the craft of town planning, the intellectual stimulation received from problem solving and the possibility of seeing one's work implemented. The other related to the desire to improve the physical environment. The idealism and reforming spirit noted elsewhere contributes substantially to satisfactions in belonging to a profession concerned with shaping the future and dealing with social problems.

THE FUTURE

The planning historian is entitled to speculate on the future, though he does so with little more certainty than any other observer of the contemporary scene. The relevance of past developments to current trends and future possibilities is relatively slight, particularly as a new set of circumstances seems to be emerging. It seems appropriate to give a personal viewpoint, however, because at the present time there is much speculation at the course which planning appears to be taking. In brief, one argument is that the task of planning cities calls for new academic and professional alignments and that town planning as we have known it since the war is unsuited to the task. Is this interpretation correct, and if so, what is the likely outcome? What will the profession be like in 2014, what tasks will it be performing, and what technical skills will its members possess?

It is an inescapable observation that considerable changes are affecting planning. (This in itself is almost a trite remark because there has been virtually no time during the last sixty years when this was not so.) But not only do old problems change, new ones emerge, and the pace at which this is happening is undoubtedly quickening. Planning has long dealt with the question of land allocation; but now there are greater numbers of people to be considered and the problems of reconciling conflicting demands are more insistent. The housing problem shows no signs of going away, and indeed changes with every decade; public health now is not the issue, but opportunity to express personal preferences is. The question of physical mobility has long thrown an emphasis on public transport and roads; we now have to reconcile the need for personal transport and the necessity to re-model urban environments. The search for air, space and sunlight encouraged a whole new approach to residential design; that solution to environment has now slipped into another dimension, 'quality of life'. The smoke control lobby is now just part of a larger question of pollution. The simple solution of garden cities has now become blurred as cities have spread at low density into city regions. Regional planning, once the task for land-use allocations and road proposals, has moved into the sphere of socio-economic strategy and transportation planning. The leisure needs of society were once met by achieving standards of open space in cities and reserving beautiful tracts of countryside beyond; now the rural areas with their water, woods, hills and fields are exploited as a recreation resource for urban dwellers. City centre renewal was forced upon us by the Blitz; now greater ravages might be considered by the speculative developer or commercial enterprise. Planning for employment was formerly a case of factory location; it is now just as much a matter of offices, where the processing of data has replaced the processing of raw materials. Centrally directed planning is now weakening before experiments in popular forms of participation.

Town planning has managed to embrace all these aspects and more in its umbrella of activity, but it is now being asked to be concerned with other issues, particularly related to questions of social policy. For example, the threat of social polarization in our cities, long since in evidence in the USA, now throws up a whole range of new questions as urban areas expand with prosperous suburbs to leave behind a deprived inner middle. We have the paradox of rapidly rising living standards, but with opportunities for the good life relatively denied to an important minority. The questions of economic, social and environmental underprivilege are being refocused and redefined. Wider still, the issues of ecological equilibrium and sound management of the world's natural resources raise implications for the safeguarding of desirable human environments: there are town planning questions here which have scarcely begun to be formulated.

We have shown repeatedly in earlier sections that town planning has not for long kept to defined boundaries or areas of concern. We have observed a further recent broadening of planning activities. This was both a cause and consequence of the 'systems' phase in planning: when it is seen that everything affects and influences everything else, the relevance of old academic and professional boundaries is challenged. In particular, it has been demonstrated that physical plans have social implications; it is now appreciated that land-use allocation plans have considerable social consequences, some of them quite unintended and unforeseen. Planning is also broadening through the current concern for the environment, now described in the widest terms. Furthermore, the engagement of planning with the public has brought it into fields of political science and a new way of understanding and dealing with the community and its needs.

The whole operation of planning is now seen as enormously complex. A high-water mark of prescriptive planning on a grand scale was possibly Abercrombie's plan for Greater London in 1944. In one document he interpreted the needs of London, social, economic and physical. In one package of proposals he outlined what needed to be done. The issues had been narrowed down to black and white alternatives, and in a master sweep he sketched the solutions as one integrated physical and social design for the metropolis and its region. Today this would be unthinkable. The Greater London Development Plan of 1969 was quite a different planning exercise, finding the issues not clear cut but wide open for various interpretations; no finite solutions could be postulated. The difference over just a quarter of a century sums up all that has happened by way of change in planning.

It is argued, therefore, that town planning is really a question of policy planning; it is an on-going, problem-oriented activity, with no fixed end products, but with objectives set by perceived social goals, changing over time. A new task of planning cities is being recognized, where complexity and uncertainty are the keynotes. The Law of Requisite Variety has it that a complex system requires procedures of equivalent complexity to control it, and this is applicable to urban, rural, or regional systems. In the past, planning problems were tackled by a confused hotch-potch of disciplinary skills and a professional client-oriented service, in which the town planner has emerged as a central figure, though open to criticism as a Jack-of-all-trades. What is now required, the argument continues, is for the urban (or other) system to become the focus for a new form of public management. In this new process the disciplinary and professional skills would be regrouped under a new analytical and management-oriented framework. A new style of planning would emerge, designed for the complexities which are presented. The present process, with planning roughly at the centre because of its claims to at least understand if not control the many interdependencies of the system, would be replaced by a constantly shifting set of skills, unconstrained by institutional boundaries, assembled to respond to the issues which emerge.

In a set of essays in which these arguments are deployed, Peter Hall, comments that: 'A planner trained in 1930 would have been reasonably at home in the planning office of 1960. The same cannot be said for the planner trained in 1960 who finds himself in the planning office in 1970'[15]. If this is so, it dramatically highlights both the nature and rapidity of change which is currently affecting planning and the profession. But is this an accurate assessment? And if it is, or nearly so, are the implications necessarily those outlined in the paragraphs above?

One nub of the argument seems to lie in the capacity or otherwise of existing institutional arrangements to be sufficiently flexible to perform adequately in response to very different situations. It might be observed that there was as much difference between the Planning Acts of 1932 and 1947, as there was between 1947 and 1968, yet a fundamentally similar institutionally-supported government system proved sufficiently adaptive not only to avoid breakdown but to show a variety of response to new needs. New planning wine has been poured into old planning bottles—repeatedly—without the skins bursting. Of all the disciplinary and professional fields in urban and regional matters, planning has proved to be more flexible than most, and the limits of its flexibility do not yet appear to have been reached. As a personal preference, therefore, I would be cautious about the need to devise radically new institutional arrangements centred on public management, if the argument is that existing ones will clearly not suffice. This is not to reason in any way that town planning could or should seek to become dominant in new fields rather different from the one it presently covers, for example, social policy planning or natural resource management. It seems eminently clear that these, for example, cannot be the preserve of any single profession. But town planning is likely to continue for some time its existing role of integrator in the governmental system, if only for the reason that it is the only academic and professional discipline which seeks to offer the much needed basis of understanding the inter-relationships in our urban and regional system. Add to this its practice of design skills, and land use and developmental management, and one has a formidable pool of expertise, which it would be foolish to dismantle or disperse.

The arguments for new institutional arrangements in our urban and regional government are a counsel of perfection. The difficulty about devising complex control procedures to cope with complex systems is that complexity is a perceived phenomenon. Our cities are no more complex now than they were in 1900; it is our perception of the system that has changed. Our style of planning and urban management is essentially a political product. Society gets the sort of planning that it wants, and there is no certainty that any desired style will last for very long. It may even be that planning will revert to a former type in future years. It is, for example, by no means implausible to speculate that consensus values will be rediscovered in our pluralist society, or that public demands will be made for simple explanations rather than complex uncertainties. Too great a sophistication in the planning process is impossible. Prevarication about issues and answers will breed its own response; failure of government to act speedily will bring a certain political harvest. We have to accept that public attitudes are fickle and there can be no certainty as to what will be demanded of town planning and public management. In the meantime, I would prefer not to throw the baby out with the bath water. Those who recommend substantial change on the basis of contemporary analysis run the risk of putting too great a stress on factors which time might show to have less importance than might otherwise appear. It is reasonable still to argue that town planning is very likely to maintain a highly individual place in the field of urban and regional management and that its boundaries of concern and expertise might remain no less identifiable than at the present time. If they do change, they will change slowly, and certainly within ways which can be accommodated in any organizational structure. Town planning is not likely suddenly to become lost in a free interchange of skills relating to urban management.

But, whatever happens in the future, town planning is not likely to lose its sense of imagination and social purpose. This was well described by Holford in his Presidential Address of 1953: 'The planning process ... is a compound of three related activities in the adjacent territories of science, design and administration. We maintain that these activities are compatible with one another; that their co-ordination ... deserves professional recognition and special training, and that when this co-ordination is achieved it amounts to a social service of an important and civilized kind. One could not describe as anything less than that the preservation, creation and development of the environment in which we live.

'If we did not believe this, we should leave the task of research and inquiry to social scientists and economists, design to architects, engineers and landscape designers, administration to corps of central and local government servants working under political chiefs. And we should no longer contend that what we can do as planners is greater than the sum of what these other professions can do independently.'[16]

Holford went on to express his profound belief in the concept of planning as a social art.

258

That idea may be rediscovered yet. In the meantime, the fuse of purpose, creativity, imagination and social responsibility is still the one to distinguish planning from any other form of environmental management. Over the last sixty years it has added something very important to our national way of life. Let an Honorary Member have the last word, one who has been very close to the development of planning through Government eyes since the early 1930s. Dame Evelyn Sharp reflected in 1969: 'Sometimes in moments of despair one wonders in the Ministry, whether planning is possible at all, or at least whether it is worth the effort—and the abuse. But of course it is; if we didn't have it we should have to invent it.'[17]

REFERENCES

1. Hall, Peter, *The Containment of Urban England*, vols. 1 and 2. Allen and Unwin, 1973.
2. Mattocks, Robert H., Presidential Address. *Journal of the Town Planning Institute*, **XXVIII**, No. 1, 1941.
3. *Journal of the Town Planning Institute*, **XI**, No. 12, 311–313,1925.
4. *Journal of the Town Planning Institute*, **XI**, No. 12, 279, 1925.
5. Davies, Jon Gower, *The Evangelical Bureaucrat*. Tavistock Publications, 1972.
6. Ashworth, G. W., Where Have All The Wild Men Gone? *Journal of the Town Planning Institute*, **53**, No. 8, 1967.
7. *Journal of the Town Planning Institute*, **XXV**, No. 2, 60, 1938.
8. *Journal of the Town Planning Institute*, **XXI**, No. 8, 195, 1935.
9. Millerson, Geoffrey, *The Qualifying Associations*. Routledge and Kegan Paul, 1964.
10. Kantorowich, R. H., Education for Planning. *Journal of the Town Planning Institute*, **53**, No. 5, 1967.
11. Carr-Saunders, A. M. and Wilson, P. A., *The Professions*. Oxford University Press, 1933.
12. Kaye, Barrington, *The Development of the Architectural Profession in Britain*. George Allen and Unwin, 1960.
13. McLoughlin, J. B., The Future of the Planning Profession, in Cowan, Peter (Ed.), *The Future of Planning*. Heinemann, 1973.
14. Marcus,Susanna T., Planners—Who are You? *Journal of the Royal Town Planning Institute*, **57**, No. 2, 1971.
15. Hall, Peter, Manpower and Education, in Cowan, Peter (Ed.), *The Future of Planning*. Heinemann, 1973.
16. Holford, Sir William, Presidential Address. *Jourbal of the Town Planning Institute*, **XI**, No. 1, 1953.
17. Sharp, Evelyn, *The Ministry of Housing and Local Government*. George Allen and Unwin, 1969.

Appendix 1
Presidents of the Royal Town Planning Institute

1914–15 Thomas Adams DEng, FRIBA, FSI
1915–16 Sir Raymond Unwin Hon LLD, PPRIBA
1916–17 John William Cockrill MInstCE, ARIBA
1917–18 Edmund Rushworth Abbot OBE
1918–19 Professor Stanley Davenport Adshead MA, FRIBA
1919–20 George Lionel Pepler FSI, Hon ARIBA
1920–21 Henry Edward Stilgoe CBE, MInstCE
1921–22 Robert Armstrong Reay-Nadin JP
1922–23 Henry Vaughan Lanchester LittD, FRIBA
1923–24 Thomas Hayton Mawson
1924–25 William Thomas Lancashire MInstCE
1925–26 Professor Sir Patrick Abercrombie MA, DLit, FRIBA, FILA
1926–27 William Robert Davidge AMInstCE, FRIBA, FSI
1927–28 George Montagu Harris OBE, MA
1928–29 Edward Willis MInstCE, FSI
1929–30 Richard Barry Parker JP, FRIBA
1930–31 Frederick William Platt FSI
1931–32 Richard Cowdy Maxwell OBE, LLD
1932–33 Francis Longstreth Thompson OBE, BSc, AMInstCE, FSI
1933–34 Thomas Alwyn Lloyd OBE, JP, Hon LLD, FRIBA, FILA
1934–35 Sir Herbert Humphries CBE, MInstCE
1935–36 Major Leslie Roseveare OBE, MInstCE
1936–37 Ernest Gladstone Allen FRIBA
1937–38 Ewart Gladstone Culpin JP, FRIBA
1938–39 Joshua Edward Acfield AMInstCE
1939–40 William Harding Thompson MC, FRIBA
1940–41 Oswald Alfred Radley CBE, MC, LLB
1941–42 Robert Henry Mattocks
1942–43 Colonel William Spottiswoode Cameron TD, MInstCE
1943–44 William Dobson Chapman MA, LRIBA, FILA

1944–45	Sir Peirson Frank TD, MInstCE, FSI
1945–46	Thomas Sharp CBE, MA, DLitt, FRIBA, PPILA
1946–47	Henry William James Heck MIMunE
1947–48	Sir James Reginald Howard Roberts CBE, JP, DL
1948–49	James Whirter Renwick Adams OBE, PPILA
1949–50	Sir George Lionel Pepler CB, FRICS, Hon ARIBA, Hon MIMunE
1950–51	Lieut-Colonel Henry Philip Cart de Lafontaine OBE, TD, FRIBA
1951–52	Ernest Hone Ford OBE, MICE
1952–53	Samuel Leslie George Beaufoy CBE, FRIBA
1953–54	Professor Lord Holford MA, BArch, DCL, Hon LLD, ARA, PPRIBA, PPILA
1954–55	Ernest Harvey Doubleday OBE, FRICS, MIMunE
1955–56	Desmond Heap LLM
1956–57	Maurice James Hellier OBE, AMIMunE
1957–58	Bernard John Collins CBE, FRICS
1958–59	Udolphus Aylmer Coats BArch, FRIBA
1959–60	Professor Joseph Stanley Allen BArch, FRIBA
1960–61	Rowland Nicholas CBE, BSc, MICE
1961–62	John Geoffrey Jefferson MICE
1962–63	Denis Wearing Riley MIMunE
1963–64	Professor Sir Colin Douglas Buchanan CBE, BSc, AMICE, ARIBA
1964–65	Leslie William Lane FRICS
1965–66	Professor Lewis Bingham Keeble MC, BSc, MA, FRICS
1966–67	Professor Nathaniel Lichfield PhD, BSc, FRICS, AMIMunE
1967–68	Dr Wilfred Burns CB, CBE, HonDSc, Meng, MICE
1968–69	Professor Arthur George Ling BA, FRIBA
1969–70	Phipps Turnbull OBE, TD, ARIBA
1970–71	Walter George Bor FRIBA
1971–72	Francis John Clarke Amos CBE, BSc, ARIBA
1972–73	John Stanley Millar BArch, ARIBA
1973–74	Professor Graham William Ashworth BArch, MCD, ARIBA

Appendix 2
Gold Medal of the Royal Town Planning Institute

The Gold Medal is awarded at the discretion of the Council for outstanding achievement in the field of town and country planning and is international. Six awards have been made:

1953 Sir George Lionel Pepler CB, FRICS, Hon ARIBA, Hon MIMunE. Past President 1919–20, 1949–50

1955 Professor Sir Patrick Abercrombie MA, DLit, FRIBA, FILA. Past President 1925–26

1957 Lewis Mumford

1961 Professor Lord Holford MA, BArch, DCL, Hon LLD, ARA, PPRIBA, FILA. Past President 1953–54

1963 Sir Frederic James Osborn Hon MTPI

1967 Professor Sir Colin Douglas Buchanan CBE, BSc, AMICE, ARIBA. Past President 1963–64

1971 The Rt Hon Lord Silkin of Dulwich CH

Index

Page numbers in *italics* refer to illustrations.

267

Index of place names

Page numbers in *italic* refer to illustrations